AF471125

Kathleen Dayus was born in Hockley, Birmingham, in 1903. Her first book, *Her People* (1982), won the J. R. Ackerly Prize for auto-biography. This was followed by *Where There's Life*, *All My Days* and *The Best of Times*. In later life she spent much of her time visiting old people's homes where she read from her autobiography. In 1993 she published *The People of Lavender Court*, inspired by the stories told to her by Annie Green, a Birmingham woman whom she met in a community home. In recognition of her contribution to the writing of Birmingham's history, Kathleen Dayus was awarded an honorary Master of Arts degree by the University of Birmingham in December 1992. She died in 2003, just before her hundredth birthday.

The Girl from Hockley

KATHLEEN DAYUS

Edited by JOANNA GOLDSWORTHY

Virago

VIRAGO

First published in Great Britain in 2006 by Virago Press

Originally published in five individual editions as
*Her People, Where There's Life, All My Days, The Best of Times,
The Ghosts of Yesteryear*

Original books Copyright © Kathleen Dayus 1982, 1985, 1988, 1991, 2000

The moral right of the author has been asserted.

A CIP catalogue record for this book is available from
the British Library.

ISBN-13: 978-1-84408-302-2
ISBN-10: 1-84408-302-0

Typeset in Jenson by M Rules
Printed and bound in Great Britain by
Clays Ltd, St Ives plc

Virago Press
An imprint of
Little, Brown Book Group
Brettenham House
Lancaster Place
London WC2E 7EN

A member of the Hachette Livre Group of Companies

www.virago.co.uk

Contents

*To Christina Rainey,
my granddaughter*

Introduction

Our Yard

One day, a few years ago, I found myself walking through a part of Birmingham I hadn't seen for a long time, Hockley, where I was born in 1903. Then the whole district was so crammed with humanity it was more like a rabbits' warren. It was what people today would call a slum I suppose, and the people who lived there would be pitied as the 'have-nots', but then there was no pity and we were left to sink or swim, rise or fall, as best we could. Yes, this was where I was born and the poor people who struggled to live until that struggle killed them were my people.

So as I was walking by the George and Dragon where I had shivered on Christmas Eve singing carols for a few pence to buy a small treat that my mother and father couldn't afford, I thought, these people may have had nothing, but they don't deserve to be forgotten. My people: my parents and their friends and my brothers and sisters and the rest of us who fought for a crust here ought to be remembered now that the National Health Service, council houses and colour television have clouded our memory of where we came from and who we are.

People then were superstitious. They had no education and some couldn't even read and write: they never had the chance to learn like everyone has today. What we didn't have we had to do without, and what we didn't know we had to find out the hard way, although more often than not it was the wrong way. The menfolk were mostly out of work and the women had to earn a living by taking in washing, or carding linen buttons, or sewing on hooks and eyes by the light of a piece of candle. There was never much of a fire in the grate but plenty of ashes from old boots or anything else that could be found to burn to warm ourselves. When we were fortunate enough to have coal, every lump was counted. Us kids would run a mile for a farthing or a piece of bread and dripping which we'd have to share with the rest.

The grown-ups always tried to help each other the best way they could, but they found it very hard, for some had large families to feed and clothe; ten, twelve and even sixteen in one family was not uncommon. Sometimes their language was terrible but they had harsh conditions to put up with. Consumption was well known in our district and there were plenty of burials. The only people who did a good trade were the undertaker and the midwife. If you couldn't afford a midwife one of the neighbours would oblige, which resulted in many a baby dying before it had even opened its eyes and many a young mother as well. They were worn out and old women at forty, with children dragging at their dry breasts, a practice which was prolonged because they believed that if they kept a child to the breast until it was three years old they wouldn't become pregnant again. However, this rarely stopped them producing a large family despite the warnings they were given. I can recall many young children pulling at their mothers' skirts, crying to be picked up for a feed. You would hear the child cry out, 'I'm 'ungry, I want some titty.' Then the mother would lift her child up and pull out a breast while she walked along or sat on a step. There was often no milk there and the bosom there used to be was an empty, flat piece of flesh but this comforted the child and the mother, who hoped that the child would get something out of it even if it was only wind. Those children who did survive had to begin work at a very early age to help feed themselves and their parents, otherwise it was starvation or the workhouse.

Our street was called Camden Street. Along one side of this street facing the high school wall ran ten terraces or 'groves'. Ours was Camden Drive. There were five houses or hovels with five more back-to-backs to each terrace. They were all built the same: one large living-room, one bedroom, and an attic. There were also cellars that ran under each house, damp, dark and cold. Here was where they kept their coal, 'slack', or wood when they had any, which was never very often. Sometimes the shopkeeper down the next street would leave an orange-box with a few speckled oranges left in it outside the shop, or a soap-box or perhaps a wet-fish-box. Then there would be a mad rush of us kids and many a fight would ensue as we dragged the box home for our parents to put on the fire. We'd skin away the mould on the oranges and share them out with those not lucky enough to grab a box.

My mum and dad slept in the bedroom over the living-room and my brothers, Jonathan and Charlie, slept in another bed in the same room. My other brother, Francis or Frankie, and my sister, Liza, and I slept in the attic over the bedroom and my eldest sister, Mary, had her bed in the other corner of the attic facing ours. Mary was twenty and was going to be married soon, when she was twenty-one. She had to wait because Mum and Dad would not give their consent until she was of age. In 1911 my brother Jonathan (Jack) was nineteen and Charlie was eighteen, Liza was eleven, Frankie was ten and I was eight years old. Us younger ones slept three in a bed; Liza and I at the top and Frankie at the bottom.

We lived in the first house in the fifth 'grove' which we called 'our yard'. Next door lived Mr and Mrs Buckley and their six boys and one girl. In the third house lived Mr and Mrs Huggett with ten children: five boys and five girls. Next door to the Huggetts lived Maggie and Billy Bumpham. They had no children, or none that I knew of anyway. The neighbours used to say they weren't married and I could never understand this because I used to watch them undress and get into bed together – they never drew their blinds because they had none. What they did have that I loved was a little bull-terrier called Rags. Mrs Taylor lived in the last house in our yard. She had seven children and as many cats of both sexes who were continually producing offspring of their own. Mrs Taylor gave them to neighbours who needed them, to eat or clear away the mice. Everybody in our district had plenty of these. What she couldn't give away she drowned in the maiding-tub. No one knew what had become of Mr Taylor. Some people said she was so expert in drowning cats that she must have drowned him too.

At the end of the yard stood three ashcans and five lavatories, or closets as we called them. These consisted of a square box with a large round hole in the middle. Us children had to hold the sides of the seat otherwise we could have fallen in. You can imagine the stench in summer! Next to the closets were two wash-houses where every washday everybody did their weekly wash. Like all the outhouses they were shared between the five houses in our yard and the five that backed on to us.

There were always rows over whose turn it was to clean the closets so to save further quarrels Dad put a big padlock on one and gave Mrs Buckley next door a key to share. We kept our key on a cotton-reel tied with string behind our living-room door. The other closets were left open for anyone to use and they were filthy. We had to hold our noses as we passed by, but Mum and Mrs Buckley always saw to it that ours was kept clean: her girls and Liza and I had to do it in turns while the women looked on. Finally, there was a gas-lamp in the centre of the yard and also a tap where everybody got their water for all household uses.

No one had a garden, not a blade of grass. There were cobble-stones everywhere. If we wanted to see any flowers we went to the churchyard to play. We were often sent there, out of the way of our parents. We would take a bottle of tea and some milk for the younger ones who were transported in our go-cart. We nicknamed the churchyard 'Titty-Bottle Park', a name that stuck for years. We'd tie the go-cart to a tree or a tombstone and play at hide-and-seek or perhaps some of us would change the stale water in the jam jars and rearrange the flowers. We'd be happy for a while playing at our games until the vicar appeared with his stick to chase us away. But try as he might he could never get rid of us; we always returned the next day.

All our homes were in old buildings that were tumbling down. The rent was usually three shillings a week; that was when the landlord was lucky enough to be paid. I've seen him wait until his tenants came out of the pubs at eleven at night. If they couldn't pay their arrears he'd send along the bailiffs, but as often as not they'd already done a moonlight flit. Down the street someone would borrow a hand-cart, on the chattels would go and into another house they would move, for empty houses were common at that time. They were still the same old sort of hovel, though. The landlord rarely did any repairs so people did their own after their own fashion. When Christmas was drawing close they scraped together a few pence to buy some fresh wallpaper to brighten up the walls. I remember Dad used to paste ours with a mixture of flour and water and when Mum wasn't watching he'd mix in a bit of condensed milk. He swore it stuck the paper better but Jack said it only gave the bugs a good meal. Dad never stripped the old paper off. 'I daren't. It's only the bugs and the paper that's holding the walls up.'

They were dirty old houses; everyone had vermin or insects of some description. There were fleas, bugs, rats, mice and cock-roaches – you name it, we had it. But I'll still say this for our mum: although we were as poor as the rest, she always kept us clean. Many times we had to stay in bed while she took the clothes from us to wash and dry in front of the fire so that we could go to school the next day looking clean.

Our mum was also very cruel and spiteful towards us, especially to me. I can picture her now as I write. She was a large, handsome woman, except in her ugly moods. She weighed about sixteen stone and always wore a black alpaca frock, green with age, which reached down to her ankles, and a black apron on top. On her feet she wore button-up boots, size eight, which it was my job to clean and fasten with a steel buttonhook that hung by the fireplace. Mum always pretended she couldn't bend when she wanted her boots buttoned. She had long, black hair which she was always brushing and combing. She twisted it round her hand and swung it into a bun on top of her head. Then she'd look in the mirror and plunge a long hatpin through the bun. She called this hatpin her 'weapon'. Sometimes when she went out she'd put Dad's cap on top which made her look taller. She was always on the go, one way or another. I felt sorry for her at times and I tried my best to love her but we all lived in fear when she started to shout.

Many a time we felt the flat of her hand, Liza, Frankie and me. We never knew what for at times, but down would come the cane from its place on the wall. If we tried to run away then we really had it. Neither our parents nor the neighbours had any time to give us any love or affection and they didn't listen to our troubles. We were little drudges and always in the way. You may ask who was to blame for us growing up like this in squalor, poverty and ignorance. We were too young to understand why then, and I don't think I understand yet, but there it was, we had to make the best of it.

Chapter 1

Chickenpox, Mumps and My Friend Winnie

The day I was five years old my mother registered me at the local school. I remember my teacher, who was a small, dumpy person, very stern and forbidding, with a weather-worn, wrinkled skin which made her look older than her years. She was never seen without a bamboo cane carried at the ready.

We were taught our ABC sitting on bare wooden floors which always smelt strongly of disinfectant. Many of us kids didn't even have bloomers or knickers, and if teacher happened to notice us with our legs apart, she would rap our knees with the cane.

'Disgusting,' she'd yell out for all the other kids to hear. 'Showing all you've got! It's disgraceful the way some of you girls are sent to school! Tell your mothers, aunts, or sisters, or whoever's in charge of you, to find you some kind of bloomers! Otherwise I shall send you back home next time you come.'

The kids who were lucky enough to own a pair of bloomers would titter and call after us:

Maggie Brown's got no drawers
Will yer kindly lend her yowers

When I got home one Friday afternoon, I told my mum that the teacher had said she would send me home if I came again without bloomers.

'Yer'll afta buy 'er a pair, Polly,' I heard my dad say to Mum.

'Buy 'er a pair?' she yelled. 'Where do yer think the money comes from? It don't grow on trees, yer know.'

'Well, try an' mek 'er a pair out o' my old striped union shirt. It's beyond patchin', any'ow,' Dad replied.

'I was goin' ter cut that up fer towels,' she answered.

No more was said. Dad went out to fetch in the tin bath from off the outside wall, for Friday night was my bath night. As I sat splashing myself all over in the warm carbolic soapy water, I noticed Mum had already begun to cut up the shirt, and was trying to codge two legs together, as she sat by the fire facing me.

I remember wearing those monstrosities until they had gone too far to be patched any more. Some time later, one of our neighbours was lucky enough to buy an old second-hand sewing machine. Soon after that all the neighbours pooled their pennies and bought some brown calico and made all us unfortunates new bloomers. But I was only allowed to wear these when I went to church, or Sunday school. For everyday school I had to wear my codged-together ones.

When we were a bit older we moved up off the floor to long dark oak forms, which seated four. Raised above each form was a lean-to ledge, with a slot for our wooden pens, and four holes which held our crock ink-wells. Everything always smelt of disinfectant or paraffin.

One day at school I began to itch all over. My teacher noticed me scratching, and with a scowl on her face she called me out in front of the class. As I stood beside her, she said loudly, for all to hear, 'Have you got fleas? If you have, you had better sit in the back row.'

'No, Miss. I just itch,' I answered nervously.

'Turn around, and face the class!' she said sternly.

Keeping me at arm's length, she lifted my hair with a pencil; when she'd had a good look, she gave me a hard poke with her thumb in the middle of my back.

'Now get back to your seat. And don't let me see you scratching again, or I'll send you to the clinic.'

I knew all the other girls' eyes were on me as I held my head down and walked slowly back to my seat. I felt ready to cry. I was glad when I looked up at the clock that hung on the wall over the blackboard, and saw that it read a minute to twelve. That next minute seemed like an hour, until teacher took up the iron bell from her desk to let us know it was time to march in single file down the narrow dark corridor, and out into the street.

I was still tearful as I entered our house, hoping Mum was not at home. But she was standing black-leading the grate. As she had her back towards me I took the opportunity to give my back a good hard rub against the edge of the wooden sofa. Suddenly she turned round and saw me.

'What's up with yer now?' she yelled.

'I itch all over, Mum, an' now me back feels sore,' I whimpered.

When she had looked at my back, she grabbed my hand and hurried me along to see Dr Mackay, who lived in a bow-windowed shabby old house, just around the corner, with his wife and three children. He did all his consulting in his front room, and his back room was the dispensary, where his wife gave out bottles of medicine or whatever was needed. You didn't have a prescription to take to a chemist in those days. His visits were as low as sixpence, but even that was a lot for poor people to pay; you could get a couple of meals for sixpence then.

Mum and I sat on the long, hard form in the narrow corridor, which smelt strongly of disinfectant. There were several other women waiting their turn, with small children and babies in arms. When it was our turn, Mum stopped whispering to the woman next to her, and almost dragged me in. The doctor was a large, thickset man, with unruly red hair and a moustache. I began to tremble with fear, wondering what he was going to do or where he would send me. He frowned over the top of his spectacles, first at Mum, then at me, then, turning his gaze on Mum again, he snapped, 'Well?'

'I've brought me daughter fer yer ter see, doctor. Yer see, she keeps scratchin' 'erself.'

'Take her behind the screen and take her clothes off,' he snapped impatiently.

Quickly Mum undressed me, taking off all but my threadbare shift. As I stood there shivering with fear and cold, she went to tell him that I was ready. As soon as he saw me he told Mum to take off my shift, and there I stood, naked. I looked away and closed my eyes. When it was my bath night, I always felt dirty when I looked down at my nakedness. Now here I stood, as naked as I was born, with this man staring down and prodding me. I couldn't for the life of me open my eyes until he'd stopped. Then I heard him say to my mum, 'Get her dressed at once, and wait in the corridor until I bring you out some powder.'

'What's 'er got, then?' I heard Mum ask, as I hurriedly fumbled to get dressed.

'Chickenpox,' he snapped.

While we waited in the corridor again, one of the women asked Mum what was wrong with me. I expected her to say 'Mind yer own bloody business,' but she didn't for once. When she cried out 'Chickenpox' I saw everyone move away from us quickly.

When the doctor gave Mum the powder he told her to dab it on the chickenpox sores twice a day. For four weeks I stayed away from school, with Mum roughly dabbing my neck, back and chest. I was also kept isolated from the rest of the family. This meant I couldn't sleep in the same bed as my brother and sister, so I had a bed made up for me on the wooden sofa downstairs. During those four weeks my mum had a regular jaunt to the school clinic for bottles of disinfectant to wash our clothes with, and use around the rooms.

When I got well again I started back to school. But three weeks later I was sent home with a sore throat. I was too scared to tell my mum in case she took me to see the doctor again, but at school the next day I vomited all down my frock, and my teacher gave me the cane and sent me home.

As soon as Mum saw the state I was in, she cried out, 'What yer bin eatin' now?'

'Nothin', Mum, but me throat is sore. *Please*,' I pleaded, '*please* don't tek me ter that doctor again.'

'Open yer mouth an' let's look,' she shouted.

She blew some dry sulphur powder down my throat, then she dragged in the tin bath from off the wall outside. I had a bath, then I was sent straight to bed.

'An' yer can stay theea, until I can find time ter see ter yer!' she yelled impatiently.

Although I cried as I climbed the attic stairs, I was pleased she didn't take me to see the doctor again. But I was still feeling sick and restless. I couldn't even swallow my spittle without it hurting me. Later that afternoon, I plucked up my courage and, regardless of what my mum would say or do to me, I got out of bed and went downstairs.

'Mum,' I cried, as I sat on the stairs, 'I think I'm goin' ter die, I can't swaller, an' my throat feels on fire.'

She soaked one of my dad's old woollen socks in camphorated oil and pinned it around my throat, then sent me back upstairs again.

During the night I tossed and turned. My throat was so hot and dry, I felt I must have a drink. But I was scared to wake my mum and ask her: waking her at any time was the worst thing any of us could do. Barefoot and in my threadbare shift, I crept quietly down the stairs. When I reached the first-floor landing I didn't feel quite so nervous, for I could hear Mum and Dad 'sending the pigs home to market'. Downstairs I slipped Mum's black shawl over my head and shoulders and, picking up a mug from the table, I went out to get some water from the tap in the yard. It was a lovely moonlit night, and the gas-lamp in the yard lit up all the houses and the yard. I drank three mugs straight down of that delicious cold water. I had just filled the mug again to take indoors, and was about to cross the yard, when I heard the sound of cartwheels coming down our narrow cobbled street. Scared, I hid behind the wall that divided the back-to-back houses, but as I peeped over it, I could see quite clearly two ragged individuals, a man and a woman, pushing a flat hand-cart with their few chattels: two wooden chairs, a table, two straw mattresses, an iron bedstead, and other odd utensils. Following close behind were a small boy and girl.

' 'Urry yerselves, yow two kids,' I heard the man say. 'We ain't got all night.'

I realised that this family, like a good many more families in those days, were doing a moonlight flit. As I peeped from my hiding place, I saw the man and woman push the hand-cart into the next yard and enter the empty house at the back of ours. These people were to be our new neighbours.

Shivering with the cold night air, I hurried indoors and quietly crept back upstairs again. By now my throat had cooled down a little, and it didn't seem to be quite so painful. I looked down at my brother and sister, and, glad to see they were still asleep, I snuggled down on the warm mattress beside them. Soon I fell asleep too. The next thing I knew, Mum was yelling up the attic stairs.

'Yow betta 'urry yerselves, yow three, fer school, afower I come up theea an' tip yer out.'

Liza and Frankie leapt out of bed first. I would never dress or undress in front of them, so I waited. Then as soon as they went down the stairs I jumped out of bed and began to dress quickly.

When I was only half-dressed I happened to glance into the piece of looking-glass that hung over the small fireplace. I got the shock of my life. Staring at me I saw another face with narrow slits for eyes. Quickly I looked around the room expecting to see someone there, but there was no one. When I looked into the mirror again and put my hands up to feel if it was *my face* I could see, I got scared. My face and neck were twice their normal size, and my puffed eyes were just slits. Screaming, and half-naked, I ran down the stairs.

'Mum! Mum!' I screamed, aghast. 'Look at me face!'

'Oh, my God!' she yelled out. 'Yow've got mumps!'

I had to stay in bed for two whole weeks. But I was glad about one thing: I had the bed to myself. Liza and Frankie slept in Mum and Dad's room, on a makeshift bed on a straw mattress.

Kind neighbours sent whatever titbits they could spare, and, with Mum's home-made concoctions, my face soon came back to its normal size. Although I was very pale and thin, I wanted to go back to school, for I was missing my playmates. But when I asked my mum, she snapped at me, 'No! Yer can't go yet, yer can 'ave another few days 'elpin' me with the washin'.'

I followed her down the yard, where she handed me the bucket.

'Yer can start fillin' this, an' bring it in the brew'ouse.'

It was a heavy galvanised bucket, one my dad had brought home from somewhere. I'd got it half filled, and was about to carry it to the brewhouse when I dropped it quick, and ran behind the brew-house door for cover.

'What's the matter with yer now? An' where's the bucket o' water?'

'Ssh, Mum,' I whispered. 'The school board man's knockin' our door.'

'Well, yer betta stop theea till 'e's gone.'

We both watched as he knocked several times on our door. Getting no answer, he walked away. He came back the following afternoon just as Dad was soaking his feet in a bowl of hot water. As soon as I saw him, I hid on the stairs. When he knocked, Dad called out, 'Come in.'

'I've come about your daughter,' he said at once. 'She's not attended school for three weeks, so I've come to warn you, if you don't send that child to school you'll be having a summons.'

'The missus couldn't send 'er, she's 'ad mumps,' was Dad's reply.

'Well, you have to send in a doctor's note,' he answered.

Dad said he hadn't got coppers to spare for a doctor's note, but he would see that I went next day. Mum and Dad quarrelled. In the end she promised him I would go next day. But she still kept me to help in the house. A week later Dad received the summons. He was fined half a crown and given seven days to pay it. But the good, kind neighbours rallied round, and with their few pennies they were able to pay his fine.

After more quarrels I was happy to be back at school. But I found some of the girls kept their distance from me, afraid they would catch what I had lost. I snubbed them in return. Then, as I stood alone in the playground, a little red-haired girl came up to me.

'Yow 'ad mumps?' she asked at once.

'Yes,' I snapped, 'an' what's it ter do with yow? An' who are yow? I've never seen yer before.'

'Me name's Winnie Nash, I live in the next yard.'

'Ooh, I remember, yer the new people come ter live in number nine.'

'Yes. Want a piece o' toffee?' she asked as she handed me a piece of treacle toffee.

'Thank you, but yer betta not let teacher see yer suckin' it or yer'll get the cane.'

'I'd like ter see 'er or anybody else lay a finger on me, an' they'll get what for.'

She was quite a little spitfire, but I liked her, and from then on we became good friends. We went almost everywhere together, and shared whatever we had. She was just three months older than me, and the same height. But, apart from that, we were as different in looks as chalk is from cheese. I had long dark hair and was pale and thin. She was plump, with a round, rosy face covered with freckles. And she was very pretty.

I took her home one day to meet my mum. Mum usually didn't like the girls who called for me, but I was pleased to see she took to Winnie at once.

As we were walking up the hill, we met Winnie's twin brother, Willie. He was so much like Winnie, you couldn't tell them apart, only that he wore much too large ragged trousers, well below his knees.

When we left school the following day Winnie said she had to hurry home to help her mum. I didn't want her to. I said I wanted someone to talk to.

'Would yer like ter come 'ome an' meet my mum, then?' she asked.

'Will she mind?' I asked.

'Course she won't, I told 'er yesterday I'd bring yer some time, so come on, don't be shy,' she said, as she took my hand.

When we got to Winnie's I was surprised to see such an untidy house. Everything seemed to be cluttered about everywhere. There were old coats thrown over chairs, and strips of cloth strewn across the table. Squatting on the floor sat Winnie's mum and dad. They too had red hair. And when they both stood up they looked like Tweedle Dum and Tweedle Dee.

'Come an' sit down if you can find room, an' would you like a cuppa tea?' Winnie's mum asked.

'Yes, please,' I answered.

'Put the kettle on the fire then, Winnie, while I get the things in off the line.'

What I expected to see her bring in was a basket full of washing, but instead she had an armful of old grey, black and brown coats that she gave to her husband to cut into strips.

On the way home, I asked Winnie what her dad did for a living.

'Oh, 'e's in the rag trade,' she said.

'What yer mean, the rag trade?'

'Well, 'e's really a rag-and-bone man, but when anybody asks, we all say that, because it sounds better.'

'But what's yer mum and dad cut the coats into strips for?'

'Well, Mum makes peg rugs, and sells them fer a shillin'. Sometimes when she gets an order, I take one, or maybe two, and charge another tuppence, which I keep fer meself.' So that was why she always had plenty of sweets to share with me.

One day during the summer, I went with her to take two rugs to a woman who lived a few streets away. When Winnie knocked on the door she came out and said she was sorry, but she only wanted one.

'But me mum said yer wanted two.'

'I'm sorry, dear,' I heard her say, 'but my sister's changed her mind.'

'Yer can 'ave 'em both fer two an' tuppence,' Winnie said.

'I only want the one, or not at all,' she replied firmly.

'Very well,' Winnie replied, 'an' thank yer.'

She gave her the peg rug, and took the one and tuppence.

As she walked down the path Winnie dropped the two pennies down her stocking, and said she would try to sell the other one next door. She lifted the brass knocker. But the woman who came to the door shouted at us, 'Be off with yer or I'll set the bloody dog on yer.'

'Yer can 'ave it fer a shillin',' Winnie said.

'I don't want it!' she yelled again.

When she tried to shut the door Winnie pleaded, and pushed the door wider. But as soon as we saw the bull terrier growling at us in the hall, we ran for our lives. When we glanced back we saw the dog was gaining on us. Now, Winnie wasn't able to run as fast as me, for she was carrying the rug. But as soon as the dog got near enough, she turned around and flung the rug at him and fled. When we got some distance away, we looked back to see the rug going around in circles with the dog beneath, trying to free himself. Then we hurried to explain to her mum what had happened.

'Never mind, as long as he didn't bite you,' was all she said.

The next day, Winnie told me her dad had found the rug lying in the gutter, so he brought it home in the cart.

Chapter 2

The Pig's Pudding

Everyone in our district was more or less poor. They never knew from where or when the next meal was coming. Most of them had to have parish relief but what they received was insufficient to feed us growing children, let alone our parents as well. Each Friday morning or afternoon, according to their surname, they queued up for their rations. Each person had a card for coal, bread, margarine, a tin of condensed milk, tea and sugar. They received more and some less according to their circumstances and the size of their family. No one was given any money. The officers in charge decided this would be spent on beer, tobacco, snuff and other unsuitable commodities. Therefore those that didn't indulge in those habits had to suffer for those that did, but everyone did little odd jobs on the quiet to get some extra coppers. Some didn't care, as long they could manage to borrow or beg a cup of sugar, a piece of soap or half a loaf until they could collect their next ration card. They were artful: they never returned the same quantity. It was a smaller cupful or less than half a loaf and no soap. Thus they wore out their welcome. It only happened once to Mum – 'once bitten twice shy', she used to say. No one ever came to borrow at our house a second time.

She was independent-minded and, although we too had to

have parish relief sometimes, she wouldn't ask a neighbour for anything. She used to say, 'What we ain't got we'll goo without.' Nor would she have any neighbours in our house unless it was essential. She said they only came to see if you'd got more than them. If anybody did call and ask Mum to help them out, her reply would be blunt.

'I don't arsk yow fer anything so don't arsk me! I don't borra and I don't lend!'

With that they'd get the door slammed in their face for their pains. Mum was very hard, but then the neighbours said she could afford to be because they thought she had more coming in than they did. Perhaps they were right: Jack was at work as was Mary, but Jack didn't give Mum much and nor did Mary who was saving to get married. At this time Charlie had already left home and Dad was unemployed like the other men. So we can't have had it much better than other families in our yard.

We were forbidden to play with the kids who had dirty heads but how we were to know they had dirty heads I never understood. They were our friends, so we played with them despite what our mum said. I came indoors one day with one of my girlfriends and Mum pounced.

'Come over 'ere, yow! What yer doin' with yer fingers in yer 'air?'

I walked slowly towards her. I was afraid. She knew and I knew that I had disobeyed her. Suddenly she slapped me across the face and grabbed me by the hair.

'Kneel down 'ere and put yer 'ead between me legs!' she shouted.

I did as I was told and she combed my hair so hard with the steel comb that I began to scream.

'That'll teach yer ter defy me . . . And if I do find anything 'ere I'll cut the lot off!'

Later that evening I waited for Liza to go to bed first, then I lit my candle and crept up the stairs so as not to wake her. I checked to see that she was asleep then I blew out the candle and slipped into bed beside her, but as usual she was only catnapping and all of a sudden she kicked me out of bed. I fell with a bang on the floor.

'You ain't sleepin' with me! You've got ticks in yer hair!'

'No I ain't! You ask Mum!' I shouted back at her with tears in my eyes.

At that moment the attic door flew open and in came my brother Jack.

'What's all this bloody racket about?' he bawled. 'I carn't get any sleep!'

'Liza's kicked me out of bed,' I cried, hoping to get a few words of comfort from him, but all he said was, 'Shut yer cryin', yer big babby.'

He struck a match and gazed down at Liza who was pretending to be asleep again.

'She's not asleep. She's only pretending,' I cried.

'Don't you dare to answer me back!' he said sharply, and he pushed me into the corner between the bed and wall and left me there and returned downstairs.

During all this commotion Frankie had lain quietly at the bottom of the bed but, when Jack had gone, he jumped out of bed and pulled all the clothes off Liza.

'If you don't keep yer hands off Katie and give her more room in bed I'll pay you out when I get you on yer own.'

Liza was afraid of Frankie when he was in one of these moods so she moved over without saying a word and I climbed back into bed.

Next morning when we went downstairs Mum beckoned me over.

'Come 'ere, yow!'

I went slowly towards her, thinking to myself what have I done wrong now?

'What was all that bangin' I 'eard larst night?'

'It wasn't me, Mum, it was Liza. She kicked me out of bed again.'

'What do yer mean, "again"?' She shook my shoulders roughly.

'I never did, Mum,' Liza lied. 'Katie's telling lies.'

I was surprised when Mum turned to Liza and said, 'You speak when yer spoken to . . . I know who's telling lies.'

Then turning to me again she spoke angrily, 'I'll put the cane across yer backs if I 'ear any mower from either of yer!'

Frankie's job every day was to take the tin bowl to the tap in the yard and fetch our washing water. But on this morning the tap was frozen when he went out. The Jones and Buckley kids were already there waiting for the water to thaw. I took a burning piece of paper which I pushed up the spout. It started to trickle and eventually Frankie managed to half fill the bowl. We took it inside and stood it on the stool.

'Can I have a drop of hot water in here, Mum?' he asked. We were both shivering with the cold.

'No yer carn't! I ain't got none till the fire's lit, so hurry yerselves or yer'll be late agen fer school and miss yer breakfast.'

All the poor children in our school were provided with a breakfast, so when the bell rang out at five minutes to nine we had to be ready and waiting. The kids from our yard would rush up the street like a lot of ants because if you were not in line when the bell stopped you would be lucky to get any at all. The breakfast consisted of an enamel mug of cocoa and two thick slices of bread and jam. The bread was usually stale or soggy. Dad would get up very early some mornings and earn himself a few extra pennies fetching the big urn which contained the cocoa, and the bread and jam. He had to wheel it along to the school in a basket carriage and when he passed our yard Mum would be waiting with a quart jug hidden underneath her apron. When she could see no one about, Dad used to fill it with cocoa. She would have helped herself to the bread and jam too but Dad stopped her because they were all counted.

This morning we dashed up the lane to get there in time for

breakfast but the bell stopped ringing. Frankie grabbed my hand and dragged me along.

'Come on! We can still make it, Katie!'

But I started to cry. 'We're too late now and I'm hungry!'

We hadn't had anything to eat since tea-time the day before, and then only a piece of bread and dripping.

'Shut yer blarting!' Liza hissed as she pushed us inside the door. Our teacher was calling the last name from the register when she saw us come in.

'I see you three are late again. I'm afraid you are too late for your breakfasts.'

'But we're hungry, Miss!' pleaded Frankie.

'Well you can stand at the back of the line. You may be lucky,' she answered sharply.

We reached down a mug each from the ledge but when it came to our turn all we had was some warm cocoa, watered down, but no bread and jam. There was none left, and by the time our lessons were over at twelve o'clock we were very, very hungry.

On our way home from school we had to pass a home-made cook shop where we always paused to look through the window at all the nice things on show. This particular morning we stayed longer than usual, pressing our noses to the pane of glass, saliva dripping down our chins. There was pig's pudding, hot meat pies, hocks, tripe and cakes of every sort staring back at us. Worse than the sight of this potential feast was the smell. It was too much for Frankie who burst out: 'I'm so hungry I could smash the glass in and help myself.'

'And me!' I said.

'Don't you dare,' said Liza, who was afraid he would.

'Well, why should they be on show when we're so hungry?' asked Frankie.

Liza had no answer; she too was dribbling down her chin and she didn't stop Frankie who glanced quickly up and down the street to see who was about and hissed: 'If you two look out for me and as soon as "Skinny Legs" goes around the back of the shop I'll nip in quick and help myself to a few.'

Everyone called the shopkeeper this because he gave short measure and he never gave you a stale cake or a loaf like other shops did. Anyway, it seemed ages before Frankie did anything but at last he saw Skinny Legs go through to the back of the shop and he dived in whilst Liza and I watched the street to warn him if anyone came along. I saw his hand in the window as he grabbed hold of a roll of pig's pudding and several hot meat pies. He came out, stuffing them under his gansey, and the three of us ran off down the street as fast as we could but before we had gone many yards Frankie stopped.

'Catch hold of these pies, Liza, they're burning my belly!'

'No,' she replied, 'I don't want any part of 'em!'

'No? But you'll take your share to eat 'em, won't you!' he snapped.

I was sure someone would come along and overhear us so I put my hands up his gansey and pulled down the pies. He wasn't kidding, they were hot, but my hands were so cold I was glad of the warmth.

'Did anyone see me?' he asked anxiously.

'Yes. He did.' Liza was pointing at Jonesy, one of the lads from our yard. 'Hello, how long have you been there?' said Frankie.

'Long enough, and I seen what yer bin dooin' an' all, an' if yer don't give me some, I'll snitch on yer.'

We all knew he meant it, so reluctantly Frankie pulled down the roll of pudding from his gansey and handed it over to Jonesy who dashed off home after saying he wouldn't tell anyone. But I knew he'd snitch all right. Then the three of us ran down the yard to the wash-house to eat our pies. I don't think I ever tasted anything like that meat pie. It was delicious. Afterwards as we came from the wash-house we saw Mrs Jones walking towards our house. We knew we were in trouble but we didn't care now that our appetites were satisfied. Mrs Jones didn't like our mum, in fact I don't know who did, so I wasn't surprised by what happened next. Mrs Jones knocked loudly on our door and Mum lifted the corner of the curtain to see who was there. Seeing Mrs Jones she opened wide the door and shouted for all to hear, 'What do yow want?'

Mrs Jones stood on the step with her hands on her hips, grinning like a Cheshire cat. She always liked to get a dig at Mum, so she shouted louder so the neighbours could hear. 'I've got news for you, Polly. Your kids 'ave pinched some of Skinny Legs' pies.'

She didn't mention the pig's pudding though.

'I don't believe yer and get away from my dower, the lot on yer! Goo an' look after yer own kids.' And Mum slammed the door shut.

I thought, one day the door is going to fall off.

When Mrs Jones had gone away she came out again to call us in. Mrs Jones was still gossiping with the others.

'Come in, yow three. I want some explainin'.'

Liza quickly unburdened herself about how Frankie had stolen the pies and the pig's pudding.

'Pig's pudding? She never said anything about any pig's pudding!' Mum was furious.

'Frankie gave it to Jonesy,' said Liza.

'Well, we'll see about that!' said Mum.

She was fuming. She couldn't get out of the house quick enough. On went Dad's cap, off came the apron, and round the backyard she marched. When she got to Mrs Jones's door she banged twice, as hard as she could. All the neighbours lifted their windows and popped their heads out while some of them crowded round to watch developments more closely. They knew Mum was big enough to eat Mrs Jones.

Mum shouted, 'Yow can come out. I've seen yer be'ind the curtin.'

Slowly, Mrs Jones opened the door a little way to face Mum standing there, hands on hips, chest puffed out.

'Yer crafty old sod! Yow never told me that my Frankie giv' your lad a roll of pig's pudding. Now what about it? An' I ain't gooin' from 'ere till I get it.'

Mrs Jones was scared now, thinking what Mum might do, so she shut the door quickly and we all heard the bolt rammed home.

But Mum wasn't finished. 'Yer better 'and over that puddin' or else!' she demanded, her fist in the air.

Suddenly the window shot up and the pig's pudding came flying out. It caught Mum on the head and everyone began laughing, but Mum ignored them and grabbed hold of us and the pudding and marched us indoors. She never bothered about what the neighbours thought or said as long as she didn't hear them. Woe betide them if she did.

'Get yer clo's off and get up them stairs. I'll get yer dad ter deal with you two when 'e comes 'ome.'

We didn't go back to school that afternoon and all we had to eat that day was the meat pie each. It was late when we heard Dad come up the stairs so we pretended to be asleep. We knew he wouldn't wake us. Sure enough we soon heard his receding footsteps on the stairs. In the early hours of the morning Frankie crept downstairs and brought up a cup of water and a thick slice of bread and lard. We shared this between us while Liza slept on. Then we climbed back into bed and finally fell asleep.

Chapter 3

Saturday Nights

One afternoon Dad came home pleased and excited. This was pleasing for us as well because he wasn't often happy.

'Where's yer mum, Katie?' he asked.

'Down in the wash-house, filling the boiler,' I answered.

'Well, go down and tell her I've got a lovely surprise for her.'

I hadn't seen Dad so cheerful for a long time so I ran down the yard and, seeing Mum through the steam in the wash-house, I called out to her, 'Come quickly, Dad's got a surprise for you!'

'What's 'e want now? Mower money for beer I suppose,' she snapped.

'No, Mum. I don't think so. He's too excited.'

'Hm . . . we'll see,' she mumbled.

She stopped to put some more slack under the boiler, then, with me trailing behind, marched down the yard. She never walked like other women, she always seemed to stride along, taking big steps with her back straight and her head held high. When we were indoors she took Dad's flat cap and her hessian apron off, then staring at Dad she said, 'Now, what do yer want this time?'

'Give us a kiss first, then I'll tell yer,' he replied, putting his face forward close to hers.

'Don't be daft!' was her reply to this show of affection. 'I ain't got time any mower fer that sort of thing.' She turned her back on him.

I felt so sorry for Dad; he looked so dejected as he stood looking at her. I can never remember Mum and Dad kissing each other: they were always snapping or not on speaking terms. Dad flopped down in his chair and lit his pipe. Then Mum raised her voice and shouted at him, 'Well, come on, Sam! Let's know what it's all about.' She was getting impatient.

Dad turned around in his chair and told her he'd got a job. 'It's hard work, and it's only twenty-five bob a week. I don't mind the hard work, Polly, but it's long hours, six in the morning until six o'clock in the evening.'

'That ain't much money for all them hours,' was all she said.

Then she went out again to the wash-house with her apron over her arm. I stood there waiting for Dad to say something more, but he just got up from his chair and walked out.

'Can I come with you, Dad?' I asked.

He just nodded, so along I went, walking behind him. I knew he was going to the Golden Cup to have a drink. He met Mr Taylor inside, and thanked him for getting him the job. Mr Taylor bought Dad a pint and a pop for me. As I sat just inside the door, filling a Woodbine packet with sawdust from the floor, I noticed four navvies stroll in. I could see they were already well oiled. They called for a pint each and then began a song. I knew some of the songs they sang so I joined in.

'Come and give us a song, littl' 'un,' said one. But I was too shy, so Dad came over to me, picked me up and sat me on the counter.

'You want to hear my Katie sing?' Dad asked proudly.

'Yes, mate,' they replied.

When I sang someone always gave me a halfpenny and some-times a penny, so with this in mind I burst forth with my favourite, 'Mid Pleasures and Palaces'. Everyone in the pub joined in after I had sung a few lines, including the publican and his wife. When I had finished my song I heard one of the navvies say to Dad, 'That kid's got a sweet voice, yow ought to get her trained, mate.'

They each gave me a penny. I felt like a queen when they applauded me and asked me to sing some more, but Dad lifted me down from the counter.

'You better be off now before yer mum sees yer.'

He took threepence from me and left me with a penny and the excuse that I could have the rest when he came home. I never did, but I went home happy knowing that Dad had the threepence instead of Mum.

Monday morning came and Dad rose early to start his first day at the casting works. When he returned home that evening I thought he looked miserable, tired, dirty and wet through: it hadn't stopped raining all day.

'It's hard and dirty work in that casting shop, Polly,' he sighed as he flopped into his chair. Mum was preparing supper, but she appeared not to hear him.

'Shall I pull your boots off, Dad?' I asked.

He neither said yes or no, nor did Mum, so I bent down on the floor and untied the laces, pulled off his boots, stood them on the fender to dry and passed him a torn piece of towel to dry off his hair.

'I don't mind the hard work, Polly,' he continued at last. 'But last night I couldn't sleep.'

'Why? I dain't keep yer awake,' was her sharp answer.

'Oh no,' replied Dad. 'I was afraid to get to sleep in case I over-slept on my first day. Where's the alarm clock gone from off the mantelshelf?'

'Why ask? You know it's in pawn with the rest of the things. I'll get them out at the end of the week.'

'I carn't wait until then,' he pleaded.

Mum went on preparing supper which was bread and cheese, a pint of ale and a bit of Spanish onion.

'I know what I'll do,' he said, jumping up from his chair and reaching for his cap.

'Now where yer gooin'?' Mum shouted across the table.

'I'm going to ask Fred the lamplighter to tap his pole on the bedroom window when he comes in the mornings. Keep my supper till I get back.'

He swallowed three parts of his pint and dashed out. As usual I followed. Fred happened to be coming down the yard to light the gas-lamps when Dad bumped into him.

'Hello, Fred,' Dad said. 'You're just the chap I'm looking for. I've got a job for you. Will you tap my bedroom window every morning?'

'It'll cost you a tanner a week and a pint,' said Fred, scratching his head.

'Very well, you old fraud,' smiled Dad. He knew very well what the charge was.

'That's what all the others pay me,' said Fred, a bit indignant. 'But don't tell anyone, Sam. If the Gas Department find out I'll lose my job.'

So each morning at break of dawn Fred did his job as promised. Then on the following Saturday night Dad met him in the pub. I was an inquisitive child and always followed Dad or anyone else I knew to find out what was happening, but on this occasion they turned and noticed me drawing in the sawdust behind the door.

'You'd better be off before yer mum comes after yer,' the lamplighter said, pressing a halfpenny into my hand as I followed them out. Reluctantly I walked home with the coin safely hidden down my stocking.

When I arrived at our house I noticed Mum was standing on the step with her arms folded across her chest and looking like thunder. Now what have I done? I thought to myself. She was glaring all the while as I approached her, then she bellowed, 'Where 'ave them two gone?'

I acted as though I didn't know, hoping I would not be forced to tell her.

'Who do you mean?' I asked.

'Yer know who I mean! That Fred an' yer dad.'

'They went in the Cup, Mum, but they've left now and gone down the street,' I answered truthfully.

'I think I know where they are. If there's any treatin' to be done they can treat me.'

She mumbled to herself as she went inside, snatched down a flat cap from the back of the door and slapping it on top of her bun, she marched down the street. I trailed behind her as usual to watch developments. She arrived at the King's Head, flung wide the door and shouted, 'Anybody seen my Sam?'

Everybody looked round, but no one answered; they only shook their heads.

'I'll find 'im if it's the larst thing I do!' she fumed, as the door banged after her.

I looked up the street and saw Dad walking towards the Cup. He didn't see Mum, but she saw him just as he was going inside. Her strides grew bigger and when she reached the pub door she pushed it wide and entered. Kicking the sawdust out of her path she went up to the counter.

'Mine's a pint!' she called out to Dad.

Everyone stopped talking, and a hushed quiet descended. They all knew what Mum was like when she was in one of her moods. I watched her bosom heave up and down as she breathed heavily. Then she flopped down on one of the benches, all sixteen stone of her.

Dad came over to her and gave her a pint. Poor Dad, I thought. She tipped her head back and drank it down. Dad was always giving in to her when she was in a bad mood. He tried not to answer her because we all knew she would have the last word. It was the only time we got any peace when Dad took no notice of her. I often looked at the picture of Mum and Dad that hung on one of our walls. Mum had been quite a good-looker and Dad was handsome when he was young. Dad was still handsome, despite his years of worry and toil, but Mum looked older than her years. Today I realise why she was like she was. It must have been a terrible ordeal for her and the rest of the women who had to live in one room and two bedrooms and bring up thirteen and even more children. They had no bathrooms, no hot or cold water in the house and had to live on relief when they could get it. These women were tired and worn out when they reached the age of forty. Some never lived to that age; many were claimed by consumption, childbirth or plain hard work.

Now that Dad had started work we all had more to eat. He would bring in a joint of meat for Sunday, whereas before I used to fetch fourpenn'orth of pieces. Our clothes and knick-knacks started coming out of pawn, and life in general at our house seemed more pleasant for a time. However, Dad still collected the relief without telling them he was working. Then one day I remember Mum warning him, 'I think yer better sign off, Sam, before they find out.'

'I'll stay on a bit longer, Polly. I don't know how long me job's going to last.'

'Oh, well! Please yourself. If yer goo ter prison, don't say I didn't warn yer,' was her only answer.

No matter how bad our neighbours seemed, they always tried to help one another in their own kind of way. They would never 'snitch' on each other, because they were all doing odd jobs on the side without reporting them to the relief officers. They had to do this; it was the only way to make ends meet. But they had to be extra careful to hide things away when the visitor came to call because they were always poking around to find out what was happening. With that in mind, Dad signed off after having two free weeks.

Saturday dinner-time, Dad had his first wage packet and, after giving Mum hers, he went off down the pub to get his quota. Later, when he came back, he lined us up. There was Frankie, Liza, several of our school friends and me and he took us to the Saturday afternoon matineé. We used to make an awful clatter in our clogs and Dad in his heavy boots, and even the horses turned their heads to see where the noise was coming from. Along the cobbled street we marched in a line like little soldiers, so proud were we to be treated to the pictures. Up the stone steps to the top of the gallery we climbed, then rushed madly to get a good seat on one of the low forms. It was wonderful to watch the silent films and hear the pianist banging away at the piano. We were sad when it was all over because we never knew when we'd get another treat like this. As we went out, the 'chucker-out' who stood on the door gave each of us a bag of sweets.

'You've been behaving yourselves, haven't you?' he said.

We couldn't do anything but behave with Dad with us. When we got home it was growing dark and Mum was waiting for Dad to take her out for the usual Saturday-night drink. I can see her now, standing on the doorsteps in her white starched pinafore which she kept especially for these Saturday nights, with her arms folded across her huge bosom and Dad's flat cap stuck on top of her head.

'And about time too! I've bin waitin' for yer this last 'arf 'our, and I want these kids in bed!'

Dad didn't answer, so she turned to me. 'There's tea in the pot an' bread an' drippin' on the table and when you've 'ad it get up to bed. An', yow two . . .!' she called out to Frankie and Liza.

Dad had walked off while she was giving us our instructions but she didn't let him get far before she caught him up. Frankie and Liza didn't drink their tea. They said it tasted like old boots, and no wonder, the enamel teapot was chipped and cracked through being stewed on the fire so often. I was too thirsty to care what it tasted like; I even drank Frankie's and Liza's share. After feasting on the bread and dripping, we lit our piece of candle and went up to bed. However, we didn't get undressed that night: this was the Saturday night and we were going to be entertained.

We all looked forward to these Saturday nights when we saw Battling Billy, as he was universally known, who became a little peculiar when he'd had too much to drink. He would then offer to fight anyone in sight. Our parents never took any notice of him. They understood why he was like he was: Dad said he was more to be pitied than blamed. He'd fought alongside Dad in the Boer War and was shell-shocked.

None of the pubs would serve Battling Billy because of his antics, so his wife Maggie used to fetch drink in bottles from the outdoor for him and he always seemed to have plenty on a Saturday night. Downstairs we hurried and when we emerged into the yard we saw some of our neighbours already there. The children were sitting on old mats and coats on the wall, waiting for Battling Billy to appear. Our friend Jonesy and his mum kept our places. We hadn't waited long when Billy dashed out of his house, just like a bull at a gate. He was only a small man, but he had a lot of strength, the more so when he'd had too much to drink. He was swearing and performing worse than ever, and soon everyone was laughing at him. He looked very comical, running back and forth in bare feet and red flannelette combs or vests. He reminded me of one of the warriors out of our school history books. The cats flew in all directions to get out of his way. He stared to the right and left and with the yard broom in one hand and a dustbin lid in the other he yelled at the top of his voice, 'Charge!'

Using the lid for a shield, and thrusting the broom handle forward, he yelled again, 'Charge! . . . Let 'em all come!'

Suddenly, he shot a glance up at the wall and saw us sitting there. He put the shield up to his face and peeping round its edge he shouted at us, 'Come on down, all you bloody Boers!'

Then we all began to scream. We'd never seen Billy in such a fierce mood before. But Maggie and his bull-terrier were used to him and they both stood on the step waiting for him to tire himself out so that he could be put to bed. To us he seemed worse than ever and we clung to our places on the wall for all we were worth. He was going strong. He ran down the yard, yelling, 'Charge!' again and this time thrust the broom handle through Mrs Taylor's only unbroken window. As the glass shattered, someone shouted down the yard that the cops were on their way. But Billy was too wrapped up in what he was doing.

All the police in the local lock-up knew Billy, and they never took him to the cells unless he became too dangerous.

'If you don't behave yourself we'll have to drag you there.'

We'd all heard this but he continued to kick and struggle so that the other two policemen had to help take him away. By this time Billy's dog Rags had seen what was happening and he too joined in. He grabbed hold of Billy's combs and tried to prevent him being carried off.

During all this performance Maggie still stood on her doorstep watching. However, when she saw that things were threatening to get out of hand she walked over to Billy and spoke to him.

'Go along quietly, Billy, and I'll bring the rent book in the morning to bail you out,' she said, soothingly. Then she gave him a kiss, picked up the dog and walked towards her door with the dog under her arm.

Mrs Taylor shouted from her attic, 'You ought to be ashamed of yourself, Maggie, letting the cops take your Billy away. And remember, I want me window mended.'

'Push your head back in and look after yer own! I'll look after mine,' she yelled back. 'Anyway, if you want ter know it's the only time I get a wink of sleep when the cops tek 'im in.'

Then she went off and we heard the door slam behind her. Tempers were always getting frayed because things never seemed to go right for these people. They skimped and saved to make ends meet, but they knew it was hopeless, so they gave up trying, or, worse, caring. Many's the time I've heard and seen them quarrelling with each other and coming to blows over the least little thing, but they didn't mean to say or do these things. They would be friends again the next day, and meet in the pub to discuss their troubles as usual.

Chapter 4

Rabbits and Hares

It was the middle of winter and our boots were letting in water. It was no wonder we had snotty noses, coughs and colds. Each winter all our parents put in applications for boots and clothing. Our teachers would inspect us, then, after giving us a form for our parents to fill in, she would warn us that everything must be written down correctly. If not, our parents would be in trouble. Some people tried to claim what they were not entitled to, but the teachers could tell who was in need just by looking at us all. In our street alone there were at least sixty or seventy poorly clad children and most of them were at our school. I always read our leaflet to Mum and Dad and explained what it was all about because Mum couldn't read or write, and although Dad could write, he only read the newspaper (when he could afford to buy or maybe borrow one).

The annual distribution was an exciting day. We went along to the supply office to be fitted out with clothes, boots or clogs, as well as being given a mug of hot soup which the Salvation Army supplied. The girls were fitted for woollen combs and bloomers, navy blue woollen slips or jerseys, and thick black woollen stockings. The boys had vests or combs, navy-blue woollen ganseys and trousers that hung over their knees. Most of these clothes were ill-fitting but we had to wear them or go without. I told my teacher once that I didn't like any of the clothes because they were so coarse and rough to wear and she shouted at me, 'You should be very grateful. Beggars can't be choosers.'

When we emerged from behind the screen in our clobber, Frankie and I had clogs, and Liza had boots. Mum asked us why we didn't get boots. Frankie lied and said there were no boots left to fit us, but really we preferred clogs. We loved dancing a clog dance on the cobbles down our street. These articles all had to have holes punched in them or be marked with an arrow so that our parents couldn't pledge them. If they had done, they could have been fined or sent to prison. Everything else of any value went into pawn, sometimes for food, but mostly for beer. There were pots, pans, clocks, kettles and umbrellas, if you were lucky enough to own one. Everything went to the pop-shop, or 'uncle's', as we called it. I used to hate the pawnshop as much as I did washdays, because there were always rows on these occasions.

Mum always did the washing on Monday morning, wet or fine, and when she was finished in the wash-house she left the hot suds in the boiler for the next woman. This went on day after day, each one leaving the soapy water for the next in order to save buying extra soda or Hudson's Powder, Lively Polly or Rickett's Blue. There was always plenty of blue in the water because it was thought things looked better blue than grey: they never managed to get clothes really clean or white. Some women would scrub their wash until nearly dark, sometimes by the light of a piece of candle or the glow of the boiler fire. On a rainy day this washing would be taken indoors to dry, ready for the pawnshop. I remember two lengths of rope nailed across our kitchen as a permanent fixture. We had many a back-hander off Mum if we didn't duck our heads low enough under the washing. The washing had the distinctive smell of carbolic soap. It took up every available space – hung over the fireplace, draped on the fireguard, on the pictures, in fact any-where where there was space to be found.

When it was fine Mum and Mrs Buckley from next door would be up very early before anyone was awake to get their washing done and hung out on the clothes line in the yard. Nobody got any extra sleep when it was Mum's washing-day. Bang! Bump! Bang! Bump! The maiding-tubs made a dreadful noise as they rolled them round to the wash-house. Then they would start agitating the washing with their dollies, singing at the tops of their voices in time to the rhythm. Mum had a powerful voice and she knew it. She always let rip for anyone to hear and Mrs Buckley tried to keep up with her. It was always the same song and Mrs Buckley always sang it off-key, but Mum's rendering of 'My Old Man Said Follow the Van' drowned Mrs Buckley out. Then when they'd eventually finished and the clothes were pegged out on the line, the next two neighbours would begin theirs. Mum used to fold and squeeze the washing through the mangle to remove the water and to press it if the iron was being used by one of the other women. The old mangle squeaked and groaned each time the handle turned. The cogs wanted oiling but we had no oil, so Dad poured paraffin over it.

'It helps,' he maintained. He also sewed rags round the rollers to stop the rotten wood getting into the clothes, making the mangle look as if it had come out of hospital. Then when everything was folded up and ready for the pawnshop, Mum would call out down the yard, 'Maggie! Nell! Liz! Are yer ready?'

'Yes, we're ready.'

Then down the street they'd go with their bundles under their arms to the three brass balls. I followed, as usual. They knew I was following behind but they took no notice of me. They never did, unless it was to run their errands for them. When they arrived at 'uncle's' Mum was the first, as usual.

'Can yer loan me fower and six? I've put in extra today.'

He gave the washing a good going over before he replied, 'I'm sorry, these are getting a bit worn but you can have three and six-pence.'

Mum gave him one of her dirty looks, but he wasn't afraid of her and just glared back.

'Take it or leave it! Next one.'

So Mum quickly grabbed what was offered, less a penny for the ticket, and went down the entry to wait for the others. Then off to the local they went to wet their whistles. This routine was repeated week after week. In, out, in, out, more often in than out, it was never any different.

It was on a washday like this when Mum gave me sixpence wrapped up in paper.

'Katie!' she called down the yard. 'I want yer to goo down ter Longman's and tell 'im I want a fresh rabbit. Tell 'im it must be fresh or else! And 'urry, I want to get it in the pot.'

I did as I was told, but when I got there he just glared down at me.

'Does she want it skinned?'

'I don't know,' I answered timidly.

He left the skin on, wrapped it up and I ran back with it clutched under my arm. It didn't smell very fresh to me, and when Mum took it from me she sniffed it, then threw it across the table and began raving.

'Now yer can tek it back right now! It stinks!'

I picked it up. Oh dear! It smelled awful but I wrapped the newspaper round it as best I could and took it back to the butcher's. When I arrived Mr Longman was still standing outside in his blue and white striped apron with his straw boater on the back of his head. I peered up into his huge, round face trying to appear confident as I timidly spoke to him.

'Mum says you've got to change this rabbit.'

'What's the matter with it?' he bawled at me.

'It stinks!' I bawled back, and pushed it under his nose.

'I'm not changing it. What's yer mum want for a tanner?'

But I was feeling courageous now, and I attacked him.

'I don't know. I know this though, Mum'll give you what for if you don't change it.'

'Be off with yer, yer cheeky little sod!'

Next thing I knew he hit me across the head with the rabbit and it fell to the floor. I picked the rabbit up off the floor and wrapped it up in the newspaper and off home I went.

'He won't change it,' I wailed, hardly before I had entered the door.

' 'E won't, won't 'e. Well I'll see about that!'

The neighbours heard Mum shouting, and came out on their doorsteps to see what it was all about. Mum went in and on went Dad's cap, off came the apron and, holding the rabbit at arm's length, she marched down the street. Some of the neighbours with their children followed. So did our cat, Pete, and some of his friends. Mum knew they were all behind her to see the fun but she didn't mind. She enjoyed having an audience and encouraged her followers.

'I'll show 'im.'

When she saw Mr Longman she flung the rabbit across the counter and shouted for all to hear, 'What yer mean by sayin' you ain't changin' this? I asked for a fresh one and I want a fresh one!'

'But I ain't got another one,' he replied nervously.

Mr Longman saw the size of Mum and how angry she was, and hurried back into his shop. Mum glanced up and saw a large rabbit hanging from his wall on a hook. She didn't need prompting, and stretched up on her toes and reached it down and called into the shop, 'Then I'll tek this one.'

This brought him running after Mum who was striding up the street with her prize.

'Come back here!' he shouted. 'I'll call a copper.'

Mum looked over her shoulder and, to the immense amusement of the crowd that had gathered, yelled back at him, 'Yow do! An' I'll 'ave yer pinched for sellin' rotten meat!'

With her head held high she marched home with the parcel under her arm, smiling all over her face.

'It's a woppa,' she kept saying to herself.

Dad was there to greet us. 'What's all the commotion about? You've had the bloody street in uproar again.'

Then she told him the story. 'But 'e dain't get the better of me. An' 'e 'ad the cheek to say 'e'd call a cop.'

She tossed the parcel on to the table for Dad to see and when he saw what it contained he was first surprised, then angry.

'It would've served you right if he *had* called a cop. This ain't a rabbit, it's a bloody hare!' He glared at her.

''Are or no 'are, it's goin' into the pot,' she replied, and began to skin it. Dad knew it was no use arguing, so he stamped out of the house leaving Mum to prepare our dinner.

I helped scrape the carrots and peel the onions and when everything was ready Mum put all the ingredients into the pot which was like a witch's cauldron hanging over the fire from a hook that swung out from the grate. This completed, she went out mumbling about the day's washing and how it would never be done.

'Come an' tell me when it starts to boil an' I'll be back to mek the dumplin's,' she called back to me.

Just then Frankie came in and I told him about the commotion. We both laughed uncontrollably about Mum's behaviour. I asked him if he thought Mum would be pleased if I made the dumplings. I'd often watched them made so I foresaw no problem. Frankie agreed and stood up on Dad's chair, reached up for the mixing bowl for me and fetched the flour from the cupboard over the sink. I rolled the flour up into balls after pouring the water on. They were big and looked good enough to eat before they saw the pot but I'd forgotten to mix in the suet. Anyway, it was too late and

Frankie thought they would not taste too rubbery. I felt proud of my handiwork and could hardly wait to call Mum. After moving Mum's bloomers and Dad's pants further along the fireguard we leaned over and dropped the dumplings into the pot. The pot was boiling merrily away over a fierce fire and Frankie and I stood back to admire our workmanship. The flames licked round the pot and before our eyes the dumplings seemed to rise. We looked at each other: the dumplings were growing too big for the pot and were continuing to swell! It was then that we realised what we'd done. We'd made them from self-raising flour and we hadn't allowed room for them to rise.

We were frightened. How big were they going to become? Then, all at once, they rolled out of the pot into the fire. The chopped hare and carrots followed. Steam and ashes filled the room as the stew boiled over into the fire, putting it out. Frankie turned and dashed out of the house. He'd heard Mum coming up the path.

'I'm off!' he shouted.

'Wait for me!' I cried, grabbing hold of the back of his gansey.

We were scared but we didn't get far: as we ran round the corner we collided with Dad. Now we're really for it, I thought.

'Well, well, well, and what's this all about?' he asked, looking down at us both.

I told him breathlessly how we'd tried to help Mum with the dinner. Frankie didn't say a word, he just looked at the floor and kicked the stones. Then I began to cry. But Dad only smiled down at me.

'Come along now, and you, Frankie.'

I felt a bit safer now my dad was there. The three of us went inside the house where Mum was standing by the wall with the cane at the ready.

'Not this time, Polly,' Dad said, taking the cane away from her. 'They only wanted to help you and give you a surprise.'

'Surprise? Surprise!' she blustered. 'Yer call this a surprise? Look at all the mess they've med.'

She was waving her arms about, indicating the state of the room. She didn't stop yelling.

'No dinner fer anybody today. I've got no mower money to buy any.'

'I have,' said Dad gently, in an attempt to calm her down. 'I've had a sub off the gaffer.'

This seemed to please Mum; at least she altered her tone and set to to clean up the mess while Dad lit the fire again. Then Mum took the pot and the remains of the hare and swilled it under the tap to save what she could: she didn't believe in wasting anything.

'Wasn't we lucky we run into Dad?' Frankie whispered to me.

I nodded in reply and we began to see the funny side of the affair but we didn't laugh for long. Mum and Dad had fish and chips while Frankie, Liza and I had to eat the hare that had been rescued from the floor.

Chapter 5

Christmas 1911

When Christmas came, Frankie, Liza and I went into the 'better' district which was not far from our school where there was a pub called the George and Dragon. This was a large public house with a long mixed bar, a gentleman's smoke room, a bottle and jug department, and a 'snug' for ladies only.

We all knew when Dad went there to have a drink with his mates because I always had the job of pressing his best suit and his white muffler. When Mum went there with any of the neighbours she always wore her Sunday best, a stiffly starched pinafore which she took great pride in ironing, especially the lace edges. Her hair would be plaited round over each ear, instead of the usual bun on top. She always tried to make an impression. I can remember her saying, 'We're as good as this lot 'ere, even if we ain't got much.' The kind of people Mum was talking about were mostly shopkeepers and independent, but the folk who lived in our district were happier in their own little local, the Golden Cup. They used to say, 'We feel at home here; the gaffer and the missus are like us.' How true that was: they both drank like fish too! Their moods were unpredictable, though. They would sometimes join in with their customers and sing, or alternatively throw them out if they'd had enough. This usually happened on Saturday night when a burly, punch-drunk barman was employed for the purpose. Then there'd be a free-for-all – spittoons and sawdust flying everywhere. You never saw a pub empty so quickly as when someone peeped round the door and warned them that the cops were on their way.

The night before this particular Christmas Eve it was snowing and freezing hard when Frankie, Liza and I hurried along the street to sing carols. The shopkeepers were busy in their windows putting up their decorations ready for the Christmas spree. While this was going on, Frankie nipped smartly up the baker's entry and helped himself to a large, empty flour sack. This was to keep us warm while we waited for the shops to close and the pub across the street to fill with customers. The three of us sat on an empty shop step, huddled up close together with the sack over our heads to keep us warm. Although we were covered in flour we didn't mind as long as we didn't feel the cold. I was lucky; being the smallest, I sat between Frankie and Liza. Even so, my feet were cold and wet because my clogs were split at the sides and my clothes were threadbare.

At last we saw the lights go out in the shop windows. The street was deserted and dark now except for the lights that shone from the leaded windows of the George and Dragon, the knight in his brightly coloured armour making red, blue, green and yellow lights that glistened on the snow. We were just about to cross the street when we saw two shadows coming towards us. Quickly we dashed back to our hiding-place, but it was too late. Before we could hide our heads underneath the sack again, a man's hand dragged it from us. He struck a match and peered down at us.

'Well, well, well and what have we here? Three little orphans of the storm?' he chuckled.

We were too scared to move. We just sat there looking up at him wide-eyed. He called back over his shoulder, 'Aggie, is there any port left in the bottle?'

Aggie brought the bottle and said, 'It's time they were in bed and dreaming about Father Christmas.'

'Here, drink this.' He offered the port. 'It'll warm yer up.'

Frankie quickly took the bottle. I thought he was going to drink the lot but he gave Liza and me the bottle, and between us we finished the rest. There was only a drop for each of us which was a good thing because otherwise we'd have been tiddly. Anyway I felt warmer. Frankie gave him back the empty bottle after draining the dregs and saluted him gratefully.

'Thank you, sir. And a merry Christmas.'

The man put his hand into his waistcoat pocket and pulled out three pennies which he dropped in my lap.

'Do you want us to sing some carols?' I asked, hoping to return his kindness.

'Don't be silly; of course he don't!' said Frankie, giving me a nudge which nearly pushed me off the step.

His lady companion walked away as the man warned us to get off home before a bobby came along. But we had no intention of doing that.

'We ain't sat on this wet step just to go back home,' muttered Frankie.

So we pulled ourselves up off the step and walked a little way to hide in a doorway until they were out of sight. Then we dashed back to sing outside the George and Dragon. We were happy to have threepence and grateful for the port wine. It gave us Dutch courage. We could've faced anybody or anything that night, we felt so happy and warm inside. The other kids at our school never sang carols here, they weren't allowed to go near this pub. Their parents used to frighten them by saying the owners were wicked people who, just like George and the dragon and the Mormons who came along our street, carried little children off. I asked Frankie if it was true about the Mormons.

'Yer don't want to believe everything people say. Anyway, our parents don't want us, yet they don't want the Mormons to have us either. It don't make any sense to me.'

'Shut up!' spat Liza. 'Let's get on with the carols. It's getting late.'

We stood just inside the doorway out of the snow, wiped the snow and flour off our faces, and began to sing. But we couldn't hear ourselves above the noise of merriment going on inside, so Frankie pushed open the door a little and kept his foot there. We waited until the sound had died down, then we burst in with 'Hark, the Herald Angels Sing'. We sang at the tops of our voices to drown Liza who was off-key as usual. Then someone shouted from inside, 'Some bloody angels!'

'Close the door,' somebody else cried.

This dampened our spirits. Frankie retrieved his foot and we walked away. However, before we'd got out into the street a kindly little lady came up behind us and gave us a silver sixpence. She told us to return on Christmas Eve, then she popped back inside, leaving us dumbfounded.

'Who was she?' asked Frankie.

'She's George's dragon we've 'eard so much about,' said Liza.

I was a bit disappointed. I'd imagined her to be a large woman something like our mum. We were happy, though. We ran to the fish shop to buy a pennyworth of fish and chips which we thought was plenty to share between the three of us. We ate it as we walked slowly back home. When we arrived, Frankie ran straight upstairs and put the rest of the money in a tin box which served as our savings bank. He had a good hiding-place, no one knew where, not even Mum.

The table was strewn with coloured papers which Mum had left for us to make our paper trimmings that night. We cut them all into loops and Liza made the paste with flour and water. If this failed, Frankie said he would get a tin of condensed milk to mix it with. Frankie took a little, not enough for Mum to notice, and this did the trick, and it was nice to lick our fingers each time we stuck one loop inside another and so we made the decorations for the walls and pictures. We didn't have a real Christmas tree. We had to beg two wooden hoops off a cheese tub from the grocer's. We fitted these one inside the other and covered them with different-coloured tissue and crepe paper.

When Dad came home he said we'd done a good job and helped us hang the streamers across the room, high up above the clothes line: and to let people see we had some sort of tree, the paper Christmas tree was hung in the window from a nail. Every time we had a farthing or a halfpenny given us for running errands we bought white sugar mice and little chocolate Father Christmases and shiny, coloured balls and tinsel or any little thing we could afford. After we'd trimmed up the room, Dad gave us a penny each to buy extra gifts for the tree. Then, after drinking our cocoa, we went off to bed, happy and contented, knowing we had some money to spend and that we were going carol-singing again to earn some more. When it got dark the next night we got ready to go out to continue our carolling. Mum watched us with keen eyes as we donned our coats and scarves.

'And where do yer think you three are gooin' this time o' night?' she asked, sternly.

'We're going carol-singing,' Frankie replied, defiantly.

'That's all right,' Dad said, 'but be back in bed before we get home.'

'Yes, Dad,' we replied in unison.

We ran out and turned up the street towards the George and Dragon. I was glad Mum and Dad hadn't asked what part we were going to because this street was forbidden territory. When we arrived, Liza and I started 'Hark, the Herald Angels Sing' again, but we only got as far as 'Hark' when I felt a hard thump on my back.

'Don't sing that one,' Frankie said. 'You know what happened last time. Let's sing "Noël".'

Halfpennies and pennies came flying through the door and when I picked them up I counted tenpence ha'penny in all. We showed our gratitude by singing it again, only louder. But when

Liza reached the high notes she gave out an off-key shriek which brought George out with the warning to 'clear off'.

Frankie turned on Liza as we walked away. 'You spoil everything with yer cracked voice. I wish I'd brought one of Mum's gobstoppers along for you!'

We turned into our street where we thought we'd try our luck again. When we got to the Golden Cup, Frankie warned Liza to keep her mouth shut and pick up the money instead. We were unlucky this time, though. While we'd been up the street the other kids had been here, so we sang in vain. Next we tried the Mermaid, then the King's Head, but they told us the Salvation Army band had already called. We were reduced to singing for the passers-by, a few of whom gave us a penny.

By now it was getting late and we remembered we had to be in bed before our parents returned, but we decided to satisfy our hunger first. We went to the cow heel and tripe shop and bought three pig's trotters. Frankie hid the rest of our earnings while we sat munching away. Suddenly I remembered that Mum had told me that morning to mend a hole in my stocking. 'Don't forget to sew that 'ole or Father Christmas will leave yer nothin',' she'd said. But I was too tired now. Anyway, I thought, perhaps she'll forget about it.

'Ain't yer going to 'ang up yer stocking?' asked Frankie as we were undressing.

'In a minute,' I yawned.

'Never mind. I'll 'ang it up,' he said, as I climbed into bed. Liza and I watched him hang three stockings over the bedstead. Then he jumped into bed and after blowing out the candle we fell to sleep.

Next morning we woke early and wished each other 'Merry Christmas' before looking to see what we'd been given. Liza jumped off the bed and grabbed her stocking while Frankie looked to see what was inside ours. Liza had an apple, an orange, some mixed nuts and a bright new penny. Frankie had the same, but when I looked in mine there was nothing, only the hole. In the dark Frankie had hung up the wrong stocking.

'Never mind.' Frankie was trying to be sympathetic and wiped my tears away. 'You can share mine.'

'But that's not the same. Mum's never loved me. I don't know why, Frankie, I always do as she tells me and I always try to please her,' I cried.

'Come and dry your eyes. It's Christmas Day. Anyway we've got our money-box hidden away for the holidays,' Frankie said cheerfully.

Liza didn't say a word. She was busy sucking her orange, sitting up in bed. So I sat up beside Frankie at the foot of the bed and he shared what he had with me. This was the one morning in the year we had to stay in bed until Mum called us downstairs. So after eating our Christmas fare we got back under the bedclothes to keep warm, planning what we were going to do with our savings.

All of a sudden we were startled by Mum's voice. 'Yer can get up now!'

We dressed quickly and went downstairs. Mary, Jack, Dad and Charlie were sitting at the table ready for us to join them. Mum was standing over a big fire frying eggs, sausages and bacon in a pan.

'Merry Christmas,' we called out to them all. They each returned the greeting except Mum. She turned round to face us and waved the fork at the bowl of water for us to get washed.

' 'Urry yerselves. We're waitin' to 'ave our breakfast.'

After falling over each other to get to the bowl first, we sat down in our usual places on the sofa which was drawn up to the table. Dad, Jack, Mary and Charlie each had an egg, two sausages and a rasher of bacon. On our enamel plates was half a sausage, half an egg and a piece of fried bread. By the side of my plate was a small packet wrapped in tissue paper. I smiled across at Mum. I thought, she's not forgotten me after all.

'Thank you, Mum,' I said as I opened it.

She didn't turn an eye, only said, 'Yer can look at it when you've 'ad yer breakfast.'

I didn't want any breakfast, I was too anxious to see what was in the small packet. So while Mum wasn't looking I slipped my fried bread and sausage under the table to Frankie. Then I finished my half egg but I daren't leave the table until everyone else had finished.

'Can I please open it now, Mum?' She didn't answer, so I presumed she meant me to and I eagerly unwrapped it and dropped the paper on the floor. It was a matchbox but when I opened it and saw what was in it I burst into tears. Inside was a little ball of black wool and a darning needle. I stared hard at it. My sister Mary came round the table and picked it up.

'How could you do such a thing to her?' she said. 'What's the reason?'

All eyes were on Mum now as I blubbered.

'That's 'er punishment fer not doin' as she was told!' Mum answered sharply.

Then Mary and Mum started to quarrel, and between my sobs I heard Mary accuse Mum.

'You've never loved her. But she'll know why some day!'

Mum walked over to the fireplace and Dad joined in.

'Now, Mary, let's have no more of this. It's Christmas Day, remember?'

Jack went out and Charlie followed, banging the front door behind him. Dad patted me on the head and said softly, 'I'll be back when you've settled your arguments.' Then he too walked out.

Frankie and Liza just looked at Mum. I didn't know what they were thinking but I knew why she'd given me the needle and wool. I went upstairs and took off my stocking and was beginning to darn it when Mary came in. She unfastened her trunk and took out a box of lace handkerchiefs. 'Here you are, Katie,' she said. 'Here's my present for you.'

I thanked her with a sob and a smile.

'Don't take Mum to heart too much, Katie. She didn't mean anything.'

I knew she was making excuses for Mum. I knew Mum didn't love me from piecing together bits of conversations I'd overheard, and now this morning I'd heard Mary say so to Mum.

'Mary,' I asked as I put on my stocking, 'do you know why Mum doesn't love me?'

'She does, in her funny way,' she said gently.

'She can't do or she wouldn't do and say the things to me that she does. Won't you tell me why?' I sobbed.

'When you're older,' she said. Then she went downstairs.

'That's all I get off you grown-ups: "when yer get older",' I answered angrily, following her.

Mary whispered something to Mum and then got her work-box out. She called me over to show me what was inside. I soon forgot my troubles as she showed me the presents the friends she worked with had given her. I couldn't believe my eyes: there were two rows of pearls, a row of blue glass beads, some more hankies and lots of other trinkets. There were also pretty Christmas cards with real lace round the edges. Before Mary closed the box she put the pearls round my neck. I saw Mum look, so I unfastened them quickly and gave them back.

'Now you just put them back on. They're yours, from me to you,' Mary said to my immense surprise and joy.

'Thank you, Mary.' I threw my arms round her neck and hugged her.

During all this time Mum never said a word until Mary left the room, then she said, 'Come on. 'Urry yerselves up, the three of yer. Yer gran'll be waitin' for yer.'

I was eager to go, so was Frankie, but Liza couldn't care less one way or the other. Anyway, Mum made her come along with us whether she wanted to or not. Frankie and Liza had Christmas cards in their hands to give their school friends, but I had mine in a surprise parcel for Granny. Our granny lived about twenty minutes' walk from our house – that was if we ran all the way, which we had to do that day because the snow was freezing underfoot and we wanted to keep warm. When we arrived, Frankie knocked on the door with his foot and we heard the heavy bolts being pulled back. Then she peeped round the door.

'We've come to wish you a merry Christmas, Granny.'

She glared at us. She didn't look very pleased when we handed our Christmas cards to her.

'What's there for me to be merry about?' She shook her head and dislodged some paper curlers which whirled to the floor. 'Anyway, come inside an' warm yer feet, yer must be afreezin',' she said, hobbling over to the fire.

I looked round the room. There wasn't much fire in the grate to warm us and there was nowhere to sit. Frankie rushed to sit on the only, backless, chair. Granny sat in her rocking-chair, and Liza dashed for the stool.

'Yoo ain't sittin' theea!' she screamed out at Liza. 'That's Katie's seat.'

'You don't like me, do yer?' Liza put out her tongue at Granny.

'No, I don't! Yer a little telltale,' she said, looking away.

'An' I don't like you!' said Liza, shrugging her shoulders.

But I don't think Granny gave Liza another thought because she turned to me. 'You sit in me rockin'-chair, Katie.'

It was a big old chair. It had to be big for Granny because she was a large woman like Mum, and when I sat down in her chair I felt lost. Whenever Granny sat in it the chair creaked, squeaked, rocked and rolled as she hummed to herself. I always expected her to tip over backwards, but she never did: she must have timed those rusty old springs to a fine point. All in all she was a very funny old granny. Sometimes she would be very kind to us, and other times her entire manner would change. She had her moods, just like Mum.

I sat trying to rock myself, but the chair was too heavy for me to get even a squeak. She stood by the table trying to untwist the paper curlers from her black hair. Then I remembered her present.

'Here you are, Granny, I've bought you some real hair curlers for Christmas.'

'Thank yer, I'm glad someone thinks about yer old granny.'

She took the box from me. Then she looked up at the alarm clock, which had only one hand and half a finger.

'Ain't it about time yer went now? It's getting late.'

We'd only been there about five minutes, but she could see we were already fidgety to be going. As we made for the door she said to Frankie and Liza, ' 'Ere y'are. 'Ere's a new penny for yer.'

I felt dejected again when she said she'd not got one for me, but then, as if from nowhere, she produced a cardboard box tied with real pink ribbon.

'And that's for you,' she said with a smile.

A lump came to my throat and tears started to flow, and I threw my arms round her waist.

'Be orf with yer at once. I'm 'ungry now and me cat wants 'is breakfast too. An' don't untie that ribbon now. Wait until yer get 'ome. An' yer can tell yer mum yer old gran don't forget yer, even if she does.'

I wondered then if she knew about the hole in my stocking, for Mum had always said she was an old witch. I felt sorry for Granny living in that old hovel all alone with her mangy old cat.

We ran all the way home, eager to see what was in the cardboard box. When we got indoors I untied the ribbon carefully because I wanted it for my hair. Then Frankie and I tore the wrapper to see what the present was. When I removed the lid there inside lay the biggest golliwog I'd ever seen, a lovely Christmas card and a note which read, 'This is for Katie which have made all myself.' I hugged it and kissed it and tears of delight ran down my face and dropped on to the golly's.

'She might have put a few marbles in the box for me,' said Frankie, beginning to sulk. But when Liza saw my present she just said, 'Phew,' and walked away with her head in the air.

'She's only jealous,' said Frankie, smiling.

The golliwog was made out of a black woollen stocking and filled tight with straw. She, for I had decided that it was a lady, had red wool for her lips and two linen buttons for her eyes and on the top of her head was real, curly black fur. I was proud to think that Granny had made this with her own two hands. I carried her nearly everywhere and I treasured her for years.

That was one Christmas I'll never forget. Frankie even said I could have his new penny, but although I was grateful for his offer I only wanted my golliwog because this was the first one I had ever had of my own. I hadn't even had a doll to play with when I was younger. Liza told Mum later that afternoon what Granny had made for me but she didn't ask to see it, and I could tell she wasn't interested. All Dad said was 'That's very kind of her.'

Christmas afternoon, Frankie, Liza and me went to a tea party at the Salvation Army Hall where there were other little girls like me with real dolls, but theirs weren't as big as mine, so there and then I decided to name her Topsey.

Chapter 6

My Grandparents

My Grandma Hannah, Dad's mum, was an eccentric, lonely old woman, poor but very proud. Her house was built on the same pattern as ours which meant there were no repairs done and she couldn't afford to improve it herself. Anyway, she used to say, 'I ain't spendin' any of my money to clean this place: it's the landlord's job.' She was a stubborn old woman, but I loved her. I believe if the house had fallen down she wouldn't have cared. She was very defiant and independent. Although she was well known in and around the district, she would never have anything to do with the neighbours. She hated gossiping tongues.

Often she could be seen and heard smacking her lips as she sucked a lozenge drop, or a pear-drop, on her toothless gums. She knew, too, how many were in a two-ounce paper cone. When she sent me to the little sweet shop she always counted them, and gave me one.

'That's for bein' honest,' she would say.

She usually wore an old black alpaca frock – which had seen better days and always swept the pavement – with a black bonnet and knitted shawl. On her feet were elastic-sided boots and she always carried a strong crooked stick. Many of the kids from my school called her an old witch, but if she happened to hear them she'd curse and threaten them with the stick. God knows what she would have done if she had caught one of them, for she feared no one.

Whenever I saw or heard any of the kids shout after her, I would await my opportunity and as soon as I saw my chance I would fight like an alley cat. But sometimes I got the worst of these battles, for I had my mum to contend with as well. But she was my granny and I loved her. Many times when my mum wanted me out of the way I used to go to Granny's and do little jobs, like fetching a quarter of a hundredweight of coal in a trolley, or going to the butcher's for three pennyworth of bits (scrag ends), or to the grocer's for two pennyworth of bacon bones.

'An' tell 'im not ter shave all the bacon off the bones,' she used to say.

She was stubborn, too, and very seldom paid her rent. One day I happened to be there when the rent man knocked on the door, and as she made her way towards the stairs she whispered, 'Tell 'im ter call next wick an' I'll 'ave summat for 'im then.'

I don't know whether he saw her through a wide crack in the door, but as I gave the message he called out, 'And see that yer do, or it's the last chance!'

But Granny was not on her own – several neighbours got into arrears too. The rent in those days was only 3s. 6d. a week, and if they couldn't pay something off the arrears, many had the bailiffs. Often I'd seen people bolt their doors on the inside and lie quiet until they passed. But at the first chance, the bailiffs would take off the door and carry it away.

I remember one bitterly cold foggy night, our door was taken away and my dad nailed up a piece of sacking, and when my brother Jack came home he mistook it for the door and fell head-first into the room. Later, Mum managed to make a bundle for the pawnshop, and with a loan from my married sister the door was soon back on again. But some were luckier than others – they did a moonlight flit. It often used to surprise me that my granny never lost her door; she was even more stubborn than my mum.

Whenever any bills were pushed under her door, she would tear them up and throw them in the dustbin. Other bills she would roll together and lay in the fender ready to put under the wood sticks to light the fire, and if some were soft paper she would fold them away, for her bum paper. She never wasted anything.

Sometimes on my school holidays I'd go and run her errands and sweep and dust the old well-worn furniture, which she didn't have much of. Often, I would see a mouse scurry down a hole in the wainscot. But I was never afraid of them, neither was my granny, for I was used to seeing both mice and rats, and many times I got into trouble when I put a few crumbs down by the hole.

One Friday afternoon I came home from school with a rash on my face and arms. I couldn't stop my nose running, and I was feeling sick. No one was at home, so I made my way to my granny's house. As soon as she saw me she cried, 'Wipe your snotty nose!' I wiped it with a piece of rag she pushed towards me. But when she took a second look she asked, ''Ow long 'ave yer 'ad that rash on yer face?'

'Since yesterday, Granny,' I replied.

''As yer mum seen it?'

'Yes, she said it's a cold I've got.'

'Don't look like a cold ter me!' she answered. 'Anyway,' she added, 'yer betta come over by the winda where I can see yer betta.'

As I stood in the light, she told me, 'Pull yer frock up an' tek yer drawers down, while I 'ave a good look at yer.' After inspecting my bum, and then my back, she turned me round to inspect my belly. Suddenly she tut-tutted and announced, 'I thought as much! You've got German measles,' and as I began to cry she said, 'You can't goo back 'ome now in this cold night air, yer betta stay 'ere in the warm where I can keep me eye on yer.'

'But Mum will be wonderin' where I am,' I replied.

'If I know anythink about yer mum, she won't care, as lung as she knows I'm lookin' after yer. Now cum on, wipe yer nose, yer stayin' 'ere!'

I'd never stayed at my granny's for more than a couple of hours when I helped her and ran her errands, so I looked forward to staying. She made me a makeshift bed on an old horsehair sofa she kept in her bedroom.

After lighting the fire in the old iron grate, she gave me a cup of watered-down warm milk, covered me over with an old grey blanket, and as she tucked it round me she said, 'Now yo'll be all right. I shan't be lung, I'm gooin' ter the chemist an' get yer some saffron tea, then I'll call an' tell yer mum where yo are.'

That small bedroom became very warm; I quickly fell asleep, but soon I was awakened by my mum prodding me.

'Cum on! I knew I'd find yer 'ere! An' wot's them spots on yer face?' she added.

'Granny says I got German measles,' I managed to say as tears fell.

'Well, yer betta get dressed an' cum 'ome, an' I'll get the doctor.'

Just then, Granny walked in. 'Yo'll leave 'er where 'er is, Polly! Yer wanta kill the child? Yo ain't tekin' 'er out of 'ere in this cold night air!'

'Very well,' I heard Mum reply as she went down the stairs, 'but if anythink 'appens to 'er I won't be responsible. Yer know yer spoilin' 'er,' she added.

'She'll be betta looked after in my care than in yowen!' I heard Granny reply before the door slammed.

During the day, Granny put a paper blind up to the window to keep the light from my eyes, and that half-light I had to contend with until I was better, except at night when she lit a piece of candle. Ever since I can remember I was always a nervous child with a very vivid imagination and, being undernourished, I wept at the least thing.

As I began to feel better and saw the rash was disappearing, I told her I wanted to go home and back to school. She stared hard at me. 'Yo ain't fit enough yet!' she snapped. 'Any'ow, we'll see wot the docta ses when 'e come!' I could see she was angry as she added, 'Ain't I looked afta yer betta than yer mum?'

'Yes, Granny, but I'm missing my schooling,' I replied as the tears began to fall.

'Now, I don't want any blartin'! If you'll promise to lie quiet I'll tell yer some funny stories.'

I loved her when she didn't lose her temper with me, but she had changeable moods, like Mum.

Often when she sat on her bed facing me, telling me fairy stories, I would fall asleep. One night I asked her if she remembered her mum, when she was a little girl.

She replied, 'It's a lung story, Katie luv; when yer older I'll tell yer.'

'But didn't you ever go ter school?' I asked, for I knew she couldn't read or write.

'No,' she replied. 'I 'ad ter goo into service. Now goo ter sleep.'

But one night she did tell me that her mother used to hide her away in the attic when she heard the Mormons were about.

When I asked her to explain why, she said, 'They carried little girls away and took 'em ter Salt Lake City.'

I was just about to ask more questions when she shuffled her way down the stairs to make my nightly cocoa. She seemed to be such a long time coming back that I wondered if she'd gone out and left me alone – everything seemed so quiet, and I was scared as I watched the flickering light of the candle making ghostly shadows on the bare whitewashed walls. My imagination got the better of me. Just as that small piece of candle burnt itself out, I began to scream.

As soon as Granny came into the room, she yelled, 'Now wot's the matter with yer?'

'The candle's gone out an' I thought you'd left me,' I whimpered. When she had lit another piece, she glared down at me.

' 'Ere's yer cocoa!' she cried as she slopped the cup down on the chair beside the sofa. 'Now,' she added, 'I want no mower silly screamin'! An' don't be such a big babby!'

As soon as I had finished drinking the cocoa she took the lighted candle, and as she shuffled her way towards the stairs I became scared of the dark again, but when I asked her to leave the candle she grew angrier.

'I ain't leavin' no light!' she shouted. 'Yo've slept in the dark befower, now get ter sleep!'

'But I'm frightened of the dark now, Granny, please leave the candle,' I pleaded.

'No, and I mean no!' she yelled over her shoulder. 'An' if yer don't lie down now, the bogeyman will come an' get yer!'

That was the worst thing she could have yelled at me. When I heard her footsteps on the stairs, I covered my head with the old grey blanket and cried myself to sleep.

As soon as I was well again, I went back home and the next day I started back to school. But I never forgot my granny's warning – it was still there in the back of my mind. I wasn't afraid when I was back home, where I slept with my sister and brother. Nevertheless, I was still afraid to be out in the street when it was dark.

Almost everyone in our neighbourhood thought it was best to steer clear of Granny when they saw her coming towards them down the street. She was a holy terror! But all the kids, especially her grandchildren, loved marching along with her when, some months later, she decided to join the Salvation Army. Sometimes she let me carry the tambourine while she waved the banner and we all sang 'Onward, Christian Soldiers'. You'd have thought that Granny really was 'marching as to war'. Everybody looked out to see her with her head held high and her voice above all the others.

She knew they were watching, but didn't care a jot, she just gave them a haughty stare and sniffed between hymns.

I was never able to keep pace with Granny's big strides and when I fell behind she'd snatch the tambourine from me and urge me on. 'Sing up, little soldier,' she'd cry and tap me on the head with the tambourine.

Soon, I'd grow too tired to stay in the band, and cold and hungry as a rule, I'd wander back home. On this particular occasion it was getting dark, and when I got indoors I found Dad dozing in his chair by the fire. There was no other light in the room, just the flickering flames of the burning coals. I tiptoed quietly towards him and whispered in his ear, 'Are you awake, Dad?'

He sat up and yawned. 'Where's the other two?' he asked, meaning Liza and Frankie.

'Still with Granny in the band,' I answered.

He twisted round in his chair and told me to get the bottle off the shelf and fetch him a pint of beer.

'And hurry yerself before yer gran gets here. You know how she sees the beer bottles about.'

'Yes, Dad,' I replied. He handed me tuppence and I ran off to the pub. The lamplighter was just about to enter and noticed me.

'That for yer dad?' I nodded. 'Very well, I'll get it, littl' un.'

I waited outside and kept a look-out for Granny but there wasn't a soul about. At last he emerged with the pint bottle. I thanked him and he gave me a humbug and told me to hurry home before the froth went off it. As bad luck would have it, I spotted Granny in the distance. My heart nearly stopped beating. I doubled back around the square to get indoors first. I stumbled inside the room, nearly dropping the bottle.

'Quick, Dad!' I blurted out, 'Granny's coming up the street.'

He snatched the bottle from my hand and took a quick gulp, then hid it in the sink behind the curtain. He flopped down in his chair and I sat cradling Topsey on Neddy. We were both hoping and praying that she hadn't seen me, but she had eyes like a hawk's and must have spotted me in the street because she came into the room sniffing the air and made a dive straight for the sink, hauled out the bottle and held it away from her as though it were about to explode.

'What's this?' she cried out and waved the bottle with the remainder of its contents under Dad's nose. Dad just shrugged his shoulders and said it was cold tea.

'Don't yer tell me more of yer lies!' she shrieked. 'Yer wicked, the lot on yer. Yer'll never goo ter 'eaven. 'Ell's the place fer yow.' She began pouring the beer down the sink. Then Dad lost his temper. Jumping up from his chair he stood beside her and shook his fist.

'Now look here, Mother, I've just about had enough of your tantrums. Now I'm warning you. While you're in my house you'll behave or you can go back to your own bloody house now!'

All the time Dad was shouting at her she kept marching up and down, waving her arms in all directions and knocking over everything in her way. Dad caught her by the shoulders and began to shake her. When he released her, she straightened her bonnet and walked to the door with her head thrown back.

'I'm gooin' back ter the Mission Hall and pray ter the Lord ter wash yer sins away,' she declared.

'Yer better ask Him to wash away yours too while you're at it. Don't think I ain't seen yer sitting on the stairs having a sly drag from my pipe. Mission Hall my foot!' he shouted after her as she disappeared into the yard.

'Can I come with yer, Granny?' I pleaded.

'No yer carn't. Yer as bad as 'im for fetchin' it,' she said, pushing me to one side, and looking down her nose at me.

But that didn't deter me, I intended following at a safe distance. She turned down the street, passing the churchyard and the Mission Hall. Then I couldn't believe my eyes – she marched straight into the pub! I waited for about half an hour for her to emerge but I was shivering with cold, and when it began to rain I returned home to tell Dad. As soon as I got indoors I blurted out what Granny had done.

'Yes, I know,' he answered calmly. 'She's there washing away her sins with gin.'

'But Granny's religious, Dad.'

'You'll understand one day. Now get the bottle and fetch me another pint before she comes back.'

When Dad had an extra drop of drink he always talked to himself. I made up my mind to ask Dad about it the first chance I found. Two nights later my opportunity arose. Dad was sitting in the chair by the fire dozing off, when I whispered nervously, 'Can I fetch you another drink, Dad?'

'No,' he mumbled between yawns, 'I've had enough tonight.'

I could tell by his voice and the smell on his breath that now was the time to ask about Granny.

'What yer standing there for?' he asked, smiling at me.

'I was listening to you talking about Granny. Did you have a dad?'

He stared hard at me, no doubt wondering whether to tell me about his family or not. He could probably see how interested I was, and after a bit he said, 'Make me a nice cup of tea.'

I made the two mugs of tea and watched Dad light his pipe. I was pleased with myself. I hadn't annoyed him and when I handed him his tea he told me the story in between puffs of his pipe.

'Now, Katie, I hope you'll understand why yer granny is like she is. Yer mum knows, but she loses patience with 'er. Me father joined the Salvation Army band when we were very young.'

'Who's "we", Dad?'

'Me and me two brothers. Now don't interrupt.' He stopped to yawn before continuing. 'He asked yer granny to join with 'im but I remember 'er saying she didn't believe in "blood and fire" praying.

She was just happy to stay at home and look after us. But one night 'e went out and never came back.'

His voice drifted away and he began to nod off to sleep again. So I gave him another nudge to rouse him once more and he opened his eyes blankly. 'Oh yes,' he said, 'you might as well know the rest. Yer granny went to the Captain and asked if anyone 'ad seen 'im. But 'e told 'er that Dad 'ad run away with a Sister called Agnes. Me mother never really got over the shock. She loved Dad and so did us three boys. 'E was our only breadwinner and although the Captain came round to try and help us, yer granny was very proud and stubborn. She wouldn't accept charity from no one. So when 'er savings had gone she had to let us go to the workhouse. She even went from town to town with the Salvation Army trying to find 'im, but she never did.'

'What became of yer brothers, Dad?'

'Arthur went to Australia, and George died when 'e was ten,' he answered sadly, and a tear appeared in the corner of his eye. I had tears flowing from my own and I couldn't ask him anything else. We were both upset but I hoped he would tell me more some other time.

'Now think what I've told you and be kind to your gran. And yer'd better clear the table and get up to bed before your mum comes home.'

I never knew my mum's parents, yet often when she and Dad came back from the pub at night they'd sit talking by the fire, not realising I was in the room, and I would hear snatches of conversation. One night Mum talked about the workhouse where she was born and put into service when she was thirteen, and another time she described how cruel her mother had been. And I wondered if she was tainted the same, for when anyone was cruel people used to say, 'They can't help it, it's in their blood.' As a child, brought up in ignorance, this puzzled me somehow.

When I asked my brother Frankie, he said he didn't know either. Now my brother wasn't so nervous of Mum as I was, so he decided to ask her if we had any grandparents or uncles and aunts on her side. One night, as Dad and Mum came in from the pub, Frankie decided to do it then and there. As soon as they sat down, he piped up at once, 'Mum, where's our other grandad an' gran'ma?'

'Why do yer wanta know that all of a sudden?' she cried.

'Well, all the other kids in the yard 'ave 'em, an' uncles an' aunts.'

Suddenly she got up out of the chair and slapped his face. 'Yo' wanta know *too* much. Anyway, yo'll be none the wiser fer knowin'. Any'ow, they're in 'eaven, God rest their souls,' she added.

It would have been wiser if Frankie had left it at that, but he was sulking now. As soon as he saw Dad go upstairs, he cried, 'How do yer know they're in 'eaven? They might be in the other place stokin' up the fire fer yo.'

Mum flew at my brother and gave him two more hard clouts across his face. 'That one's fer yer bloody cheek, an' the other's fer speakin' bad of the dead!'

Why our parents never talked to us about their parents we could never understand. When we asked any kind of question, we *should* have been told, but it was always 'Yer know enough to goo on with', or 'Kids should be seen an' not 'eard.'

My brother and I, the first chance we got, we always cleared out of Mum's way, especially when things didn't go right. We had more fun and affection with our little school friends with whom we played in the side streets.

Those iron posts were fun for us girls and boys, swinging a piece of rope over the iron arm that jutted out beneath the gas-lamp. And if we couldn't manage to find a piece of rope, we would tie together plaited straw from empty orange-boxes and swing around backwards, forwards, backwards, forwards, ten times, then others in line took their turn. Or you would see the lads sitting on the edge of the pavement beneath the light from the street-lamp, reading their swapped comics, or telling dirty stories, or skimming used tram tickets, to see who could skim the furthest.

Sometimes when our parents were out, the gas man would call to empty the pennies from the meter. We would watch him tip the pennies on to the table and count them – sometimes there would be a penny or tuppence over.

'Now give this to yer mum,' he'd say.

But this was *our* little treat – until we were found out.

I remember our gas meter was fastened to the wall, halfway down the cellar steps. I could never understand why our mum was the only one to put the pennies in the meter when at other times she was too scared to go *near* the cellar.

Some nights we would be sitting by the fire, when all at once we would see the gaslight begin to flicker. As soon as Jack, my eldest brother, came home, Mum would ask him if he could spare a penny.

'Wot, agen!' he'd cry. 'There must be summat wrong with that bloody meter. It must wait for me,' he added angrily.

'It only wants a penny in, Jack. I'll give it yer back later,' she replied.

'I've 'eard that befower! But it's funny ter me it wants feedin' wen I cum 'ome. Any'ow,' he added, 'I don't think yer gettin' enough gas for the pennies yer put in, yer betta see the gas man agen.'

'I will,' she replied. As she picked up the penny he'd slung on the table, she walked towards the cellar steps and dropped the coin in her black apron pocket. Mum knew Jack had been afraid to go down the cellar since he was bitten by a rat. As soon as the gas flared up again she came into the room, all smiles.

Then one night, I happened to be alone in the house when all at once the light began to flicker. I knew soon I'd be in the dark and I was scared. Suddenly I thought of the rent money Mum always kept in the empty tea caddy on the mantelshelf. Quickly, I took a penny and went down to the cellar. But try as I could, I couldn't get that penny in the slot, until I heard several clicks and another penny that was already wedged in fell. I put the other penny in, then when I turned the knob again and heard it fall, I realised why Mum always went down to the meter. She'd put a penny in, turn it halfway, therefore she'd get only half the gas. Having pocketed Jack's penny, she'd finish the first penny already there.

I never told her how I found out. But that same night, as we sat round the fire, I was watching Mum looking up on the wall waiting for the gas to flicker, when all at once Jack said, 'Did yer tell the gas man about the meter, Mum?'

'No, I dain't. Why?' she replied, still glancing up at the gas mantle.

'Well, it's funny you don't ask me for a penny ternight.'

Suddenly I piped up, 'There's no need, Jack, *I've* put a penny in.'

Mum stared hard at me, daggers drawn, as she demanded, 'An' where did yer get yer penny from?'

'I was afraid to be in the dark, so I took a penny out of the tea caddy. But I couldn't get it in at first, because there was already one stuck in the slot.'

Mum never said another word, but next day she gave me a thrashing with the cane. When I asked what it was for, she said, 'That's fer tekin' a penny from the rent without askin'.'

But I wasn't all that green. I knew the real reason.

Chapter 7

The Mousetrap

Frankie and I were always hungry and looked forward to going to school where each morning, before we started our lessons, we were given two slices of bread and jam and a mug of cocoa. After leaving school at twelve o'clock, we would all rush home hungry for our next feed, which might be scratching stew, or any other kind of food hashed up from leftovers from the days before.

Frankie and I even begged for food sometimes outside the factory gates as people left. Each night before going to bed we had a piece of bread and dripping, while Mum and Dad sat down to bread and cheese and a Spanish onion. Our mouths would water at the very thought of it. Dad also had his usual pint of beer, with a good head of froth on top. This was called 'The Long Pull', and in those days it cost tuppence.

One night, while Mum and Dad were out, Frankie whispered, 'Katie, I'd luv some of that cheese.'

'An' me,' I replied. 'But Mum alwis locks it away.'

'Ah, but I know 'ow ter get at it,' he replied, winking at me.

'No, Frankie!' I cried. 'Mum's sure ter find out, an' if she does she'll kill us both.'

'If 'er does find out, I'll tek the blame, Katie, an' say it was me, but you'll 'ave ter put yower 'and down inside 'cause yer 'and's smaller than mine.'

The following night, as soon as Mum and Dad were ready to go out, Mum told us to hurry ourselves and eat our bread and dripping and get off to bed. 'An' mind yer don't drop any of them crumbs on the flowa, we've got enough mice runnin' around the rooms.' Then they left the house, and we knew they wouldn't be back till after the George and Dragon closed at eleven o'clock. Frankie pulled out the top drawer of the sideboard and told me to feel down inside, where I'd find the chunk of cheese. After putting my hand down to the ledge below, I just managed to lift the cheese out. As I trembled all over in case Mum and Dad came home early, Frankie sorted in the drawer for a sharp knife, then carefully cut us each a thin sliver. I put the rest of the cheese back, and he pushed the drawer in.

This went on for three nights. Mum never said anything, so we felt safe.

Then one night, as we sat eating our meagre supper, we saw Mum unlock the sideboard door, and as soon as she put the cheese on the table she yelled, 'Sam! You'll 'avta get me another mouse-trap!'

While she was cutting the cheese and onion, I could feel her eyes on us both. Later, when I whispered to Frankie that I thought she knew it was us, he replied, 'Don't be daft, she thinks the mice 'ave bin at it, any'ow she would 'ave said.'

We didn't try again until that piece of cheese had been used up. The following weekend Mum bought a larger piece, so we decided to try our luck again. But at the last moment I got scared: 'We betta not, Frankie. I've still a feelin' she knows it's us, the way she looks at us.'

' 'Ow can she, when she's got the key? Cum on, don't be scared. Tell yer wot, we'll just 'ave a nibble around the edges an' when she sees teeth marks, she'll think the mice 'ave cum back agen.'

So out came the top drawer again and out came the cheese. I began to nibble one side and Frankie nibbled the other. But when he held the cheese and gazed at it longingly, I heard him say, 'It would be worth a beltin' from Dad to 'ave a good bite at it.'

'No, Frankie! No! Put it back, please,' I cried.

'OK. It was just a thought,' he replied, grinning at me.

Quickly I snatched the cheese from him and put it back where I'd found it. As soon as the drawer was pushed in, we went up to bed. That night I lay awake thinking he might go back downstairs and risk a thrashing by eating a lump. After hearing him get out of bed to use our makeshift bucket for a wee, I couldn't settle until I felt him crawl back to his place at the foot of the bed.

The following night we tried again, but as I felt around the ledge I began to scream – my finger was caught in a mousetrap. I pulled my hand out and ran around the room, screaming for all I was worth, with the mousetrap hanging from my finger.

'Frankie! Frankie!' I kept screaming. 'Pull it off! Pull it off!'

As soon as he released the spring I saw blood on the trap where my finger had been. After he had found a piece of rag and wrapped my finger, I began to weep.

'She'll know for sure now it's us, when she sees the trap,' I sobbed as my tears fell.

'Don't cry, Katie, I'll put it back an' if 'er does find out, I'll tek the blame, but try an' 'ide yer finger, an' don't say nothink.'

Then came that Friday night, which was our bread, brimstone and black treacle night. (This was what Mum called our physic.) As we sat at the table, I tried my best to hide my finger beneath my pinafore. Mum opened the sideboard door, then threw the cheese and the trap across the table.

'Them bloody mice 'ave bin at it agen, Sam!' she yelled.

'Ain't yer caught 'em, then?'

'No! But wotever it was must 'ave bin caught, 'cause theas the trap with blood on it.'

I wished the floor would open up and I could vanish as I saw Mum notice my finger.

'Wot yer bin up ter?' she cried.

Before I could open my mouth, Frankie said, 'It was an accident.'

'Wot yer mean, an accident?' she demanded.

'I 'it it with the 'ammer.'

Dad glared at him over the top of his paper. 'Wot did yer say?'

'Katie was 'oldin' me fire-can an' while I was knockin' a nail in the 'ammer slipped.'

'I'll knock a bloody nail in yow, me lad, if I see yer with another fire-can – now get yer grub down yer! An' get up them stairs, the pair of yer!'

We didn't need telling twice.

Next day my finger began to throb and was very painful. I was too scared to tell my mum, or even show it to her, but I had to show it to someone. The only person was Mrs Taylor, our kind neighbour. I knocked on the door, and as she opened it and glanced down at that piece of filthy rag round my finger I began to weep.

'Wot's the matter, luv? Wot yer done? Yer betta cum in an' tell me.'

As she sat me down on an orange-box I cried, 'I've done a terrible thing, Mrs Taylor, an' I'm afraid me mum and dad's gooin' ter find out an' me finger's painin' me summat awful.'

'Now wipe yer eyes an' tell me all about it.'

When I told her she cried, 'Yer wicked, wicked wench! Ye'll both be punished as sure as God made little apples! Now stop yer blartin' an' let me get that filthy rag off an' see wot yo've done.'

I began to scream with pain as she tried to snatch the rag off, but the blood had dried up and it was stuck. I was ready to run out, but she held me firm, and when I'd calmed down she got some hot water and salt and after bathing the rag came off. As soon as she saw my finger all bruised and bent she exclaimed as she crossed herself, 'Mary Mother of God, the end of yer finger's broke!'

'Can yer mend it, Mrs Taylor? It's 'urtin' summat awful.'

'There ain't nothink I can do fer that! Yo'll afta go ter the 'orspital an' get it seen to.'

'Can yer cum with me, Mrs Taylor?' I pleaded. 'I'm afraid of 'orspitals an' doctors.'

'I can't, luv, I've gotta get me washin' finished ready for the pawnshop, but I'll get our Minnie ter tek yer.'

'If I goo, yer won't tell me mum what I've told yer or she'll kill me?'

'Yer poor wench, I understand. I won't say a word, now sit thea while I put a piece of clean rag on, then afta yer drink this 'ot cuppa tea I'll call me niece.'

I thanked her and waited while she went to call her niece. Minnie Taylor was twelve, two years older than me. I was glad she was coming with me, for I was too scared to face a doctor on my own.

'Cum on, Katie, I ain't afraid of bloody doctors nor 'orspitals,' she cried as soon as her aunt was out of hearing.

We hurried up Spring Hill towards Dudley Road Hospital and came to the rusty wrought-iron gates. Minnie tried to push them open, but they were locked. Even the gates scared me. I was about to change my mind and turn back when a tall elderly man dressed in a long white gown, looking very stern and forbidding, came down the path. As he made his way towards the gates he bawled out, 'Wot yo two kids want?'

I was too scared to answer, but Minnie was scared of no one. She shouted through the bars, 'It's me friend 'ere, Katie. I've brought 'er ter see yer, Doctor.'

'I ain't a doctor! I'm the lodge-keeper. An' yer can't cum in 'ere!' he snapped.

'But we've cum a lung way, so yer betta open these gates an' let us in, 'cause me friend 'as broke 'er finger and the doctor's gotta mend it.'

'Yer can't cum in 'ere unless yer mother brings yer.'

'But I ain't got a muvver,' she replied.

'Well, tell yer friend ter tell 'er mother ter cum.'

'She ain't got a muvver either,' she lied. 'So yo'll 'ave ter let us in.'

'Not until an adult cums with yer.'

'Adult? Adult? Wot's them?' shouted Minnie.

'Yo'll soon find out when I open these gates an' clout yer bleedin' 'ear'oles. Now bugger orf the pair of yer!'

As soon as I saw him start fumbling for his keys, I was ready to run, but Minnie stayed to give him a bit more cheek. 'Bugger orf yerself, yer miserable old bleeda!' she yelled as she stopped to put her tongue out at him. We saw him put the key into the lock. We ran as fast as we could.

Mrs Taylor said when we got back, 'Never mind Katie, luv, it'll 'eal up in time an' if you'll cum in every day after yer leave school I'll bathe and dress it for yer.'

As soon as Frankie saw me he asked how my finger was. I told him it seemed a bit better now Mrs Taylor had treated it, and he yelled, 'Yer dain't tell 'er wot 'appened, did yer?'

'Yes, Frankie, I 'ad to,' I replied, as tears ran down my cheeks.

'Now it'll be all over the street, an' Mum an' Dad will 'ear about it.'

'Nobody will know, she's promised not to tell anyone,' I whimpered.

The following Monday morning while I was at school my teacher noticed the rag on my finger. When I told her I'd broken my finger, she said, 'Well, you'd better have a note and have it treated at the clinic.'

That afternoon I went reluctantly to the school clinic in Great Charles Street. This was where children went with all sorts of complaints, even to have their heads shaved for lice. But when I got to the door and saw a woman coming out holding a bloody rag to a little boy's mouth, my courage failed me. I turned back, and as I came down Great Hampton Street I called at Snape's the chemist's. With the few pennies I'd got hidden down my stocking I went up to the counter and asked for a finger bandage and some lint. 'That'll be fourpence,' Mr Snape said.

'But I only got threepence, can I bring yer the other penny next week?'

'Sorry, me dear, I'll 'ave ter cut the lint in half,' he replied.

As soon as I got home I hid the lint and bandage until I was alone. Each night I bathed my finger in salt water, then wrapped it.

My teacher, I'm glad to say, never questioned me when she saw my finger wrapped in a clean bandage.

As I grew older I was no longer scared of my mum. I remember the day I was eighteen. I thought now was the best time to tell her how Frankie and I stole the cheese. Imagine my surprise when she said, 'I knew it was yow two.'

'Yer knew? All them many years ago? An' yer never said a word?'

'No! Because I set the trap fer yer, an' thought you'd bin punished enough. Now you've got the end of yer finger broke ter prove it.'

Ever since I can remember my mother and I were never very close, but after she told me about that night I wondered how cruel she could be.

Often, when I'm trimming that fingernail, I remember how that mousetrap clung to it.

Chapter 8

Frankie Goes to Hospital

I used to like helping people, running their little errands for them or doing small jobs, but the farthing or halfpenny or piece of bread and jam that I usually received as a reward was an added incentive. Better than these, though, was a little love, a kind word or small affection, that was all I needed really. I remember one day Dad sent me to the home-made-sweet shop to fetch a pennyworth of pear-drops. Eager to please and hopeful of reward I ran all the way there and back. I even left Topsey behind. When I returned, breathless, he gave one to Frankie, one to Liza and one he placed in my pinafore pocket, or so I thought. Then we dashed off to school. During break I put my hand in my pocket for the sweet but I was surprised to find that there were two. I ate one and although I was tempted to eat the other I didn't. I wanted to impress Dad with how honest I was. When I returned, Dad was dozing by the fire. So I tiptoed up to him and pushed the pear-drop under his nose, waking him up. He sniffed and opened his eyes.

'Dad, you gave me two pear-drops by mistake, so I've brought you the other one back.'

He yawned lazily and pushed my hand away. 'Go out and play.' He seemed unconcerned at my exemplary behaviour.

I felt dejected. If only he'd thanked me or given me a pat on the head or just a kind word I would have been proud and happy. It took me some time to forget that incident and my childish hurt. I was too young to understand my own feelings and the strange ways of adults so I bestowed my love on Topsey.

I wandered out, hugging my golliwog, to look for Frankie. I found him sitting on the pavement with the other boys and girls. I soon won some marbles and even a few 'glarnies', larger and brighter than ordinary marbles, much to the delight of my brother who squatted nearby, watching me beat the boys and hugging my Topsey. When I'd cleaned out the opposition and we were about to leave, Jonesy and Freddie who lived in our yard began to jostle Frankie.

'Look at 'im. The silly little Topsey,' they taunted.

This angered Frankie who flung Topsey at me and jumped up so violently that one of his braces snapped. The other boys backed away apprehensively. They were alarmed because they knew what Frankie might do. He was a tough lad, not easily frightened, and on this occasion his tormentors thought better of their challenge and ran off. Frankie never looked for trouble. He didn't have to, trouble found him. Frankie's annoyance subsided and then I noticed that he was shivering. His trousers were wet through from sitting on the moist pavement and he began to sneeze. I told him I thought he'd caught a cold and that, worse, Mum wouldn't like the look of his trousers. But he wasn't worried about that.

'Well, she ain't going to see them, is she?'

Nor did she. Each time Mum was about he contrived to face her and edge about backwards, which aroused no suspicion because there was precious little room to do anything else in our tiny room. The following morning he was slow to get up and looked very pale when he came down. He assured me he was all right so off to school we went and after eating our school breakfast we parted to go to our separate classes.

Out of all the girls in my class I was the one picked to do odd jobs. I suppose I was thought to be trustworthy and reliable. Anyway, each Friday afternoon I had to wash out all the ink-wells ready to be filled on Monday morning. I did other jobs as well, and the one I preferred was emptying the flower vases ready for the fresh ones our teacher brought each Monday morning from her garden. Secretly I thought it was a wicked waste to put them in the dustbin when some were still fresh and I sorted out the best ones and hid them behind the school door until it was time for me to go home. Mum was usually pleased with the flowers when I gave them to her for her to put in a jam-jar and stand them on the win-dowsill for the neighbours to see.

On this Friday afternoon I was taking the ink-wells to wash when I happened to look over the partition to see what Frankie was doing. As soon as I saw him I could tell something was wrong. He was sitting at his desk with his head on his arms. I was so alarmed that I forgot for the moment where I was and gasped aloud, 'What's the matter, Frankie? Are you ill?'

I dropped the ink-wells with a tremendous clatter, which I was oblivious of, and strained to see Frankie whose head was being lifted by his teacher. My own teacher had come over and was trying to drag me away but I resisted her defiantly and remained looking through the glass partition. Frankie's face was covered with what looked like bright patches and he looked quite ill. By this time Liza had come over to see what the matter was and the rest of the class took the opportunity to break our regimented routine. They crowded round, standing on tiptoe, craning their necks to see Frankie and pulling faces at the boys. Liza and I were too upset to join in the noisy chaos. We were intent on watching Frankie who was being carried out to the corridor by the master.

'What's the matter with my brother?' I wept.

'I believe he has a fever. Is your father at home?' the master asked.

'Yes, sir, I think so. If he isn't, I know where I'll find him.'

'Run along then and tell him to come at once!'

I was off like a shot. I didn't need telling twice. I only paused to pick up the flowers, then off I ran home, leaving Liza to wait there. I burst into the house, throwing the flowers on the table and breathlessly pouring out my story to Dad. He hurried along to the school as soon as he heard what was up and I trailed behind, trying to keep pace with him. The schoolmaster had a few words with Dad who picked Frankie up in his arms and then carried him home while I was sent to fetch the doctor.

When he arrived the doctor examined Frankie and said he would have to go to the hospital at once because he thought it was scarlet fever. We waited anxiously for the ambulance and I cried bitterly as he was driven off with Dad. I had to wait for Mum to come home to tell her what had happened, but she eventually came in just as Dad returned alone. I just sobbed as Dad told Mum that there had been no empty beds in the hospital and that Frankie had been taken to the infirmary instead. The worst news was that nobody would be allowed to visit him for a week, until it was discovered whether he had scarlet fever or not.

When it was clear Frankie's illness was not infectious, Liza and I had to attend school again, but I wasn't able to concentrate on my lessons. I was glad when the following Friday, as I was gathering the ink-pots, my teacher put her hand gently on my shoulder and told me she'd given this job to Minnie Taylor. I wasn't sorry; it was a dirty job anyway and I always received a scolding from Mum when I came home with ink on my pinafore and all over my hands. I looked up into her glasses, perched on the end of her nose, and asked about the flowers. She looked surprised, but agreed.

'Yes, you may do that if you wish,' she answered kindly. 'And how is your brother getting along?' she added.

'He's still very ill, Miss.'

'Never mind, we'll all say a prayer for him. Now run along and change the flowers.'

Off I went to pick over the flowers and discard the dead ones. I returned home with the others and gave them to Mum for her and Dad to take to Frankie with a get-well note from me when they visited him on the next Sunday afternoon. On Sunday I waited at home and prepared the tea for Mum and Dad.

'He's been put outside on the verandah,' Dad told me when they returned.

Apparently he was very pale and the matron had said he needed plenty of sun and fresh air. When Mum had gone indoors the neighbours began to flock round, asking Dad all sorts of questions about Frankie and the infirmary and the nurses and if he had seen so-and-so in there. Dad elbowed his way through them, muttering that Frankie was clean and comfortable. He never had much to do with our neighbours because he thought they gossiped too much, which was the truth, and on this occasion they wandered up the yard noisily speculating on matters of health and illness. With their shawls pulled tightly round their heads and shoulders they formed a ring, and I hovered on the periphery to listen to them, and you should have heard them, nodding their heads and thinking the worst.

' 'E ain't got enough flesh on 'is bones to keep 'im warm,' said one.

'Poor lad. I don't think 'e'll come out agen, do you?' said Mrs Taylor to Maggie.

'I don't know,' she answered, shaking her head.

'Oh!' wailed another, ' 'e must be a-dyin'.'

I couldn't bear to hear any more from these ragged, ignorant women. The tears ran down my cheeks and I put my fingers in my ears and screamed at them, 'Yer a lot of wicked old witches!' then ran indoors.

'What's the matter with 'er?' Mum asked Dad, and I told them.

When she heard what they were saying, Mum made to dash out into the yard but she was restrained by Dad who told her not to be a fool and that it didn't make any difference. Fortunately, when she did get the door open they'd scattered.

Not much was said that night. We had a late tea but I wasn't hungry and Dad didn't go out but read his paper while Mum sat stitching a patch on a sheet. After Liza and I had washed the dishes, I took my candle and went to bed and prayed as I had never prayed before.

'Please, Jesus, save my brother. Don't let 'im die and please show me a way to go and see 'im and also forgive these wicked people who are telling lies. Also forgive me if I have sinned. Goodnight, O Lord, and God bless everyone. Amen.'

I crept into bed but I couldn't sleep. I kept thinking of a way to see Frankie. Whatever would I do if he died? I thought. Just then Liza came into the room. She too was weeping as she knelt down to pray for Frankie. I looked at her with some surprise. I hadn't thought she cared, but apparently she did because when we got into bed we threw our arms round each other and cried ourselves to sleep.

Next morning, very early, I awoke and lay there puzzling how I could get inside that infirmary when suddenly I remembered the gully that ran along one of its walls. The next afternoon, when teacher let me out early, I made my way to the infirmary. I found the gully, but each time I tried to climb the wall I slipped back again, taking the skin off my knees. I made several attempts, but my clogs wouldn't grip. I took them off and walked along to where the wall was lowest and, leaving my clogs at the bottom, I scaled the wall in my stockinged feet. Then I was inside the grounds.

I could see several beds outside on the verandah, so I crept over and peered at the faces of the people lying there, but I couldn't see Frankie's until I came to the last bed outside the ward. I stood and looked at his pale face.

'Frankie,' I whispered. 'It's me, Katie.' But he didn't hear me because he was fast asleep. I was just about to kiss him when a nurse appeared from nowhere and saw me.

'What are you doing here?' I was afraid then. I threw the six daffodils I'd brought from school on the bed and ran back to the wall. I climbed back over as quickly as I could, put my clogs on and ran home. I was disappointed but determined to try again.

The following afternoon I asked my teacher if I could leave early. She said I might but only after I had got all my sums correct. This seemed like an impossible task but with the help of an older girl who sat next to me I did. So off I went to try my luck again at the infirmary. First I peeped over the wall to make sure no one was about, then I took off my clogs once more and climbed over. I couldn't see Frankie anywhere and had no idea where he could be. I was beginning to worry when a young man in bandages on the verandah hailed me.

'Who are you looking for, my dear?'

'My brother. 'E was here yesterday and now 'e's gone.' I was almost in tears by now.

'Oh, you're the little lass that was here yesterday. He's been taken into the ward. If you peep round the door quietly before the sister comes you will see him. He's in the last bed on the right.'

'Thank you, sir,' I replied with pleasure.

I wiped my eyes on my sleeve, and peered into the ward. There were about a dozen beds on each side but Frankie's didn't seem to be there. Men and boys were sitting up in bed blocking my view so the only way to see if he was there was to pluck up courage and run down the ward. I saw no nurses or doctors about so I ran in. As I did so my stockinged feet slipped on the polished floor. I skidded, bringing a screen down on top of me. I struggled to push the screen aside and getting to my feet I saw that I was next to Frankie's bed and I slipped quickly in. I heard the man in the next bed say, 'Poor little sod,' and he smiled at me as I turned in his direction. The rest of the patients were laughing at my comical entrance but I only had eyes for Frankie, who was sitting up in bed sucking an orange. In my excitement to see that he was well, I jumped on to him, hugging and kissing him. He was happy to see me, too. But the sister and matron were not; they had come to see what the commotion was all about. They had to drag me away from him: I wouldn't let go. Eventually each took an arm and hustled me along the ward. As I was ejected, I could hear Frankie's voice. 'Don't worry, Katie. I'm coming 'ome tomorrow.'

They pushed me outside without saying a word. It wasn't the way I'd come in, but through the front gates. I didn't care. I was happy now. God had answered my prayer and Frankie was coming home again. I still had to walk round to pick up my clogs from where I'd left them, but when I got there, I couldn't find them. Someone had stolen them. So it was with tears in my eyes that I slowly walked home in my stockinged feet. I knew Mum would cane me hard for this. It would make no difference explaining. Still, I thought, it would have been worth it, so it was an added bonus when I met Mrs Taylor.

'Whatever are yer doin' with yer clogs off?' She smiled when I told her what had happened. 'You'd better come with me and see if our Min's old 'uns' ll fit yer before yer mum finds out.'

'Thank you, Mrs Taylor,' I said, and followed her.

She sorted them out from a lot of other clogs and boots in the bottom of her cupboard. I tried them on but they were too big, so she packed the toes with paper and that did the trick. Then she gave me a sweet and sent me off.

'Yer better get 'ome now before yer mum misses yer.'

I thanked her again and asked if she wanted any free errands run for her. I don't think anyone ever found out about the clogs: it remained a secret between us.

The next day was Saturday and Dad got ready to fetch Frankie home.

'Can I come with you, Dad?' I asked eagerly.

'Yes, but you'll have to wait outside the gates, and you can't take that with you,' he said, pointing at Topsey.

I laid her down on the sofa and tagged along with Dad. He gave me Frankie's clogs to carry, wrapped up in an old comic, while he took the clothes. He stopped to have a quick one at the pub, not long, though it seemed like hours to me. I kept looking through the door and calling to him to hurry, but he just ignored me. At last we were on our way and it was not long before we arrived. Dad took the clogs while I waited outside the gates. I walked up and down the pathway to keep warm. I felt tired and hungry but excited in anticipation of seeing Frankie. The waiting seemed to last for ages then eventually I heard the familiar sound of Dad's hob-nailed boots and the clatter of Frankie's clogs coming down the path. I ran towards him as he came through the gates. The visitors turned to look at us and smiled as I threw my arms round his neck and kissed him several times.

'Come on, don't eat him,' Dad said kindly.

I asked Frankie if I could carry his parcel and was curious as to what was inside. 'I'll show you when we get home,' he told me, winking.

It seemed a long walk home from the infirmary and Frankie began to lag behind. Dad looked back and when he saw how pale he was he put his hand into his waistcoat pocket, took out two pennies and we boarded a tram: a penny fare for him and a halfpenny each for us two. Mum was waiting indoors with a roaring fire and the kettle singing on the hob. She greeted Frankie gruffly.

'Well, and 'ow did yer like the nurses looking after yer?'

'Smashing! It was better than here,' he replied without thinking. Mum and Dad glared at him.

'Well, you know what I mean,' he added quickly.

I turned to him. 'Did you really like being in the infirmary, Frankie?'

'Yes, everybody was kind. I didn't have to bath myself and even the patients gave me sweets, fruit and comics. And the nurses tucked me up!'

I asked him what happened to the comics and he reached down his trousers and pulled them out.

'Put them under the bed with the others,' he hissed.

As I went upstairs Mum shouted, 'What 'ave yer got there?'

'They're only my comics,' replied Frankie.

When I returned, Mum and Dad had gone out so we sat in their chairs. They wouldn't be home again until late, so we kicked off our clogs and pushed our feet towards the fire. Then Frankie told me all about what went on in the infirmary. He wanted to be a doctor when he grew up. I told him I thought that would be great, if I could be a nurse too. At least I wouldn't have to climb the wall to get in, I said, and we burst out laughing again at my antics. We were so happy to see each other. We wanted things to stay like that for ever. We had no idea then what the future would hold for any of our generation.

Then our elder sister Mary came in. She hugged Frankie. 'I'm so glad you're home again.' She had tears in her eyes: in those days hospitals were places to fear.

Frankie had never had so much fuss made of him in his life before. He was lapping it up. I asked Mary where Mum and Dad were.

'They're down the local. We're all going to celebrate your home-coming tonight, Frankie.'

'Where's Liza then?' I asked.

'She's down at Granny's but she'll be home later.'

She sat down in the armchair with Frankie on her lap and began to sing in that sweet voice of hers which we all loved to hear, except Mum of course, who was jealous because Mary could reach the top notes and she couldn't. She was too ill-educated to know that Mary was a soprano and that she was a contralto. Mum was a good singer, but when she tried to reach Mary's top notes she made an awful noise. Mary stopped singing soon after because Liza had come in and she was always off-key when she joined in. She too only had eyes for Frankie.

'Hello, are you better?' she asked, and kissed him too.

He looked surprised and so did Mary. They hadn't expected any fuss from Liza but I thought that perhaps she'd changed for the better.

Mum and Dad stumbled in. 'You can all stay where you are,' Dad managed to say as we all jumped up in surprise. Then we all experienced something new. They stood up while we sat down. 'We're all going to have a sing-song tonight,' Dad said.

Dad gave us children some port wine and we all waxed happy and merry. Mary drank stout and Mum had gin. Dad poured himself some ale. Then we each had to sing in turn. It was only on very rare occasions that we sang together – at weddings or christenings and sometimes when our aunty came to visit us, which wasn't very often. On this occasion Mum and Dad were so pleased to have Frankie back that they declared a general celebration. Mum got out the gobstoppers that were kept on the shelf for special occasions and gave one to Liza in case she joined in.

Mum did 'Nellie Dean', and we all joined in the chorus. Liza joined in as well, off-key. Mum stopped at once and shouted at Mary, 'Give 'er another gobstopper. I don't know who 'er teks after. Not me!'

As Mary pushed it into her mouth, Liza grinned at Mary and sucked away to her heart's content. Mum gave Liza one of her hard stares before she started again. We all sat quiet while Mum finished her song, then Dad said it was time for Mary to sing a duet with him. She sang her favourite, 'Annie Laurie', and Dad harmonised. It was beautiful to hear their rich voices, Dad's baritone and Mary's soprano. When they'd finished, I asked Dad to sing my favourite.

'What's that?'

'You know, the one you sing in the pub, "A Soldier and a Man".'

I always called it 'my song' because I knew the tune and most of the words. I'd heard Dad sing it so often when he wanted a few coppers for a pint.

'Very well,' he said and cleared his throat with a swig from the bottle. Then he thrust out his chest and was about to begin when Mum's fist came down with a bang on the table, causing everything to shake and rattle.

'Now give order! All on yer, while yer Dad sings 'is war song.'

Dad looked at each of us in turn, then rose to his feet, and with his back to the fire he began to sing. I gazed at him, fascinated. He gave the song all he'd got.

> 'A soldier stood upon the battlefield,
> His weary watch to keep,
> While the pale moon covered his mantle o'er
> A soldier who needs a sleep.
> "Ah me," he cried,
> With tearful eyes,
> As he called to God above.
> "I am far away from my children dear
> And the only ones I love."
> But as the bugle sounds
> He turns once more, amid the shot and shell.'

But he never finished the rest of the song that night. He said it was too sad and brought back too many memories. I always pictured Dad in the Boer War standing on the top of a mountain, alone and sad, and I loved to hear him sing because it always made me weepy. Dad's song ended our evening because Frankie and I were sent to bed. Liza was still sucking her sweet when she joined us soon after. As we climbed into bed Mum shouted up to us, 'Yer can 'ave a lie-in later, bein' it's Sunday.'

Then the stairs door closed with a bang. Our privilege was a mixed blessing because if we made use of it we'd miss our meagre breakfast and have to wait until dinner-time to eat.

Monday morning came all too soon and we had to return to school. I watched Frankie with envy as he cleaned his teeth and washed himself with scented Erasmic soap someone had given him while he was in hospital. I was proud, though, to think he looked and smelled better than anyone else in our school. We settled down into our different classrooms, but halfway through lessons I was eager to see how my brother was faring on his first day back. So while my teacher was writing on the board I tiptoed to the glass partition and peeped through. His teacher was making a fuss over him. I asked myself why he was having all the attention. I felt sorry for myself because I was always ignored. Then I heard my teacher's voice boom out so loud that it startled me. I walked slowly back to my place and sulked. It was then that I had an idea.

'I don't feel well,' I whispered to Nelly, who sat in the next desk.

'What's the matter, Katie? You look pale.'

I didn't answer. I just lay my head on the desk and pretended I was ill. I thought that if I could convince my teacher, I might get a little affection and perhaps go to the infirmary. I lifted my head and whispered to Nelly to tell the teacher I was feeling sick. I sprawled back on the desk and waited.

'Please, teacher, Katie's ill.'

However, I began to be afraid when I heard the heavy tread of the teacher's feet coming down the classroom towards me.

'Sit up and pay attention,' she said angrily.

I didn't move a muscle. I meant to carry out my plan now at all costs but when she caught hold of my hair and lifted my head up roughly, I began to tremble inside. I must have turned pale in earnest then.

'What's the matter with you?' she asked sharply.

Then I put my hand to my forehead and lied for all I was worth.

'Please, teacher, me 'ead and throat hurt.' The next thing I knew she called out to Liza to come to me. She saw that by now I was trembling all over but she did not realise the cause. I wished I hadn't started the deception.

'Take her home, and if she's no better your mother had better call in the doctor.'

With that she turned to the rest of the class and brought the cane down with a loud swish. It was difficult to remain calm and take no notice as I walked slowly out of the classroom with Liza. I must have put on a good show because Liza appeared to believe that I was ill and she put her arm around my shoulder and helped me home. She'd never shown such kindness before. I hoped Mum would be home and I was pleased when I could see the welcoming smoke from our chimney. Then I remembered that today was the day for scratching stew and I began to anticipate it with pleasure. When we entered, Mum's first reaction was to ask why we were home so early. I just looked at her, feeling sorry for myself, while Liza told her about my sudden illness and being sent home to see a doctor. When Mum heard all this she turned on me and let fly.

'An' now what's the matter with yow? Don't yer think I've 'ad enough with yer brother bein' ill an' only one pair o' 'ands 'ere ter do everythink?'

Oh dear, I thought to myself, when's she going to stop? My head really was beginning to ache now and I wished I hadn't started this pretence. But I'd gone this far and had to continue. I began to whimper.

'My throat's sore, Mum, and my head aches.'

'Sit down theea!' she cried out and pushed me down into Dad's armchair. 'An' open yer mouth wide! Wider.'

Trembling with fear I slowly opened my mouth a little way as she returned with something from the cupboard. I regretted trying to deceive everyone, it wasn't worth the trouble.

'Come on, open up agen!' she screamed in my face as she leaned over me. I opened wide, there was no escaping.

'I feel better now, Mum,' I cried, and struggled to get up from the chair. But she prevented me.

'Old 'er 'ands down,' she told Liza.

Then I was told to open my mouth again as wide as I could but she had to slap my face before I'd opened it wide enough. I watched her make a funnel with a piece of newspaper; then she emptied some sulphur powder from a jar and blew it into my throat. I coughed and spat it out immediately but she made sure the second time. She held my nose with her finger and thumb, squeezed hard and blew down again. I had to swallow it this time. She blew so hard I was knocked breathless and I thought I was going to choke.

'That'll learn yer a lesson not to play the fool with me. Now get yer dinner 'an then get ter school before I blow some mower down yer.'

I couldn't eat a bite; my throat was really sore and felt like sand-paper. My head hurt terribly and I had to admit to myself that my plan had failed miserably. I determined there and then to run away from home and become a nurse when I was old enough.

Chapter 9

Granny Moves In

Each Friday night Liza, Frankie and I had to stay up later than usual. This was not a treat, far from it. We had to blacklead the grate and the big iron kettle that stood on the hob, as well as rub off any soot on the enamel teapot that stood beside it. On the other hob was a battered copper kettle which had a hole in the bottom; Mum never threw anything away. She said Dad would mend it one day, but he never did, and we still had to polish it. Jutting out from the top of the grate was a large meat jack which always held our stewpot. I called it the witch's cauldron. We had to scrub the deal-topped table, the stairs, chairs and the broken flagstones, brown as they were from years of hard wear. The soda we used hardly touched them; the only things that were cleaned were our hands.

Standing each side of the fireplace were two wooden armchairs, one for Mum and one for Dad. We children were never allowed to sit in these unless given permission to do so, but we did make good use of them when Mum and Dad were out at the pub. Our usual seat was the old horsehair sofa under the window. Someone had given this to Dad in return for doing odd jobs. It replaced the wooden one which was chopped up for firewood. Only the legs were spared because Dad said they might come in handy for something one day. Every corner of the house was cluttered up with odds and ends. Our sofa was moulting badly and had bare patches all over. We nicknamed it 'Neddy'.

Beside the table were two ladder-backed chairs, one for my brother Jack and the other for Mary. There had been three but after Charlie and Dad had a row over money, Charlie left home, and Dad burnt the chair. There was also a three-legged stool under the table; on its top stood our large tin washing bowl. Set into the wall beside the fireplace was a long, shallow, brown earthenware sink. We only used this for putting dirty crocks in because we had no running water indoors. On the other side of the fireplace was an alcove behind the stairs door where the old rotten mangle was kept; this was a permanent fixture. We had orders that if anyone called we had to leave the stairs door open to hide our laundry from view.

The fireguard, round the fireplace, was always covered with things airing or drying, especially when the lines across the room were full. Around the mantelshelf was a string fringe with faded coloured bobbles and on the shelf were two white cracked Staffordshire dogs and several odd vases which contained paper flowers and pawn tickets. Hanging high on the wall above was a large photograph of our granny. We'd have loved to have got rid of it, but didn't dare. When you stared at it, the eyes seemed to follow you round the room. The effect was heightened at night when the paraffin lamp was lit. This was the only picture in the room with the glass intact. Mum in particular objected to it.

'I carn't see why yer don't 'ave a smaller picture of 'er. It takes up too much room.'

'No!' Dad would reply. 'Nothing's big enough for me mother. It stays where it is.'

'It'll fall down one of these days, you'll see,' Mum replied.

'Not if yer don't intend it to. But I'm warning yer, Polly!' He wagged his finger at her in admonishment. So there the picture stayed.

We also had to dust all the pictures and knick-knacks that hung over the walls. There were three pictures, 'Faith', 'Hope' and 'Charity', as well as a print of 'Bubbles' – the advertisement for Pear's soap – and many photographs of Mum's first-, second- and third-born, all dead and gone. Underneath these were the death cards and birth certificates of the others, and photographs of relatives framed in red and green plush. They were so faded you had to squint to recognise who they were. There were even paper mottoes stuck to the wall which announced such sentiments as 'God Bless This House' and 'Home Sweet Home'. I could never understand why they were there: our house or home was far from happy.

On the wall opposite was a picture of Mum and Dad taken years ago on their wedding day. Mum looked happy, wearing leg-o'-mutton sleeves with her hair parted in the middle. She was smiling up at Dad who stood beside her chair. Dad had one hand on her shoulder and was standing erect like a regimental sergeant-major. His hair was dark like Mum's and was also parted in the middle, with a kiss-curl flat in the middle of his forehead. His moustache was waxed into curls at each end. He held a bowler across his chest. Now as it happened this was the very same hat which had pride of place on the wall, just low enough for me to dust. One night I happened to knock this hat on the floor just as Mary entered. As I stooped to retrieve it she said, 'You'd better put that back on its nail before Mum comes in.'

So I snatched it up and, as I put it back, I replied, 'It's no good. It's going green.'

'Yer'd better not let Mum hear you. She 'appens to be proud of that. It has a lot of memories for 'er.'

I went on working around the room; then I noticed that Mary was smiling. 'What are you smiling at, Mary?'

'Come and sit down and I'll tell you about it.'

I sat on Neddy as Mary began her story.

'Now that billy-cock–' she pointed towards Dad's dilapidated hat, '–that hat has sentimental value for Mum. About the time when she started having the family . . . I'll tell you all about it, but only if you don't laugh and can keep a secret. Every twelve months Mum gave birth to a baby and when it was a few weeks old Mum and Dad went to church to have it christened. They thought they'd gone on their own. They never saw me watching them. I used to hide behind the pillar. Now when the parson took the child off Mum he'd sprinkle water on its forehead and then it would cry and water would come out the other end. When the parson had finished the christening and handed Mum the baby she'd sit down in her pew and change its nappy. Well, it was then that Dad was at the ready. Taking off his billy-cock he'd take out a dry nappy and put the wet one inside the hat and then when he replaced it on his head, they'd leave the church and go in the pub to celebrate. You see I always followed them, just like you do.'

She gave me a sly wink and we both burst out laughing.

'Phew!' I cried, holding my nose.

Then she left and I finished my chores. Although the house looked and smelled better it was not fresh air, it was carbolic soap and Keating's Powder. In the end I was almost too tired to crawl up the attic stairs and fall into bed. I just peeled off my clothes and was asleep immediately. I didn't even say my prayers.

Friday wasn't the only day I had chores to do. Saturday was my day to get up early and be down to riddle the overnight ashes and put the embers in the steel fender ready to place on the back of the fire when it was lit. It was also my job to make a pot of tea and take a mug for Mum and Dad.

Mum's temper wasn't always at its longest first thing in the morning. She'd yell at me, 'The tea's too 'ot!' or 'It's too cold!' or 'Not enough sugar in it. You ain't stirred it up!' She'd find fault with anything. This particular morning I was saved from her nagging, but only for a short time. Just as I was about to take the mug of hot tea upstairs, a loud knock sounded on the door. I lifted the corner of the curtain and peeped out. It was only the postman, who was a cheery man with a smile for everyone he met.

'Good morning, Katie, and how are you this bright, cheery morning?'

'Very well, thank you, Mr Postman,' I replied.

If only everybody in our district was as pleasant, life would have been much happier. He asked me to give a letter to Dad and returned down the yard. He'd only just stepped down from our door when Mum shouted, 'Who's that bangin' on the dower this time of the mornin'? Carn't we get any sleep around 'ere?'

She'd forgotten that she woke everybody, singing and banging at the maiding-tub at six o'clock every Monday morning.

'It's the postman, Mum. He's brought a letter for Dad,' I called back from the foot of the stairs.

I put the letter between my lips and turned to get the mugs of tea. I hurried up to the bedroom where I found Mum sitting up in bed. I put the mugs down on the cracked, marble-topped wash-stand and had the letter snatched from my lips.

'An' about time too!'

'It's for Dad,' I said, loud enough to wake him.

'I know, I know,' she repeated. 'An' where's me tea?'

'On the table,' I answered timidly.

I made to go downstairs, but she called me back to read the letter. I watched Dad stir and yawn as I fumbled with the envelope. I was glad he was awake; it was his letter anyway. But he waved me away.

'Oh, read it, Katie, and let's get back to sleep.'

It was from Granny and although her spelling was bad I managed to read it out. 'Sam an Polly, I'm not well in elth me ouse as got ter be fumigated The Mans bin an ses Ive gotter move for two weeks so Im coming ter you Ill bring wot bitta money I got an Im goin ter joyn the salvashun army an Ill bring me rockin chare an me trunk so Ill see yer all tomorra so be up early. Hannah.'

She didn't ask if she could come, she just assumed she could. When I'd finished reading the jumbled and nearly illegible writing, Mum jumped up with a start.

'Good God above!' she cried, waving her arms about. 'We ain't 'avin' 'er nuisance agen, are we?' She glared at Dad, who was still lying on his back. He wasn't asleep. Who could be, the way Mum was raving? But he did have his eyes closed. He was thinking about how to deal with Mum.

'Yow asleep, Sam? Dain't yer 'ear wot I said?'

'I heard yer,' he shouted back and opened his eyes wide. 'The whole bloody town can hear when you start.'

'Well, what can we do?'

'It's only for two weeks. Nobody will take her, so we'll have to do the best we can,' Dad replied.

They must have forgotten that I was still standing at the foot of the bed. I watched them both lay back again and stare up at the ceiling deep in thought. Then suddenly Mum shot up out of bed. I'd never seen her move so quickly, nor look so misshapen as she did then, standing beside the bed in her calico chemise all twisted up in the front. I'd never seen her without her whalebone stays which she laced so tightly she looked like a pouter pigeon, her heavy breasts pushed up high. I never knew how she got all that flabby flesh inside those stays. I had to put my hand over my mouth to keep from laughing out loud. As she leaned over the bed and shook Dad, her belly wobbled and her bare breasts flopped out of the top of her chemise.

'Sam!' she shrieked. 'Wake up!'

'Stop bawling. I'm not deaf.'

'I wanta knoo where 'er's gonna sleep.'

I thought it was about time to go downstairs before they noticed me giggling. 'Shall I go and make some more hot tea, Mum?' I managed to say. She yelled at me to shut up and clear off as she tried to cover herself with her shift. This was the chance I'd been waiting for, so I fled downstairs, but still strained to hear what was being said.

'Now listen, Polly, and calm down. You know she'll help. She'll bring you some money for her keep and if you don't tell the relief officer we'll be all right.'

'But where d'yer think she's gonna sleep? She carn't sleep with us. It ain't decent.'

'I'll sleep on Neddy for the time being so don't worry about me.'

I took two more mugs of tea up and put them on the table, anticipating the usual grumbles from Mum, but she and Dad just lay there looking snug and warm. She pulled the clothes around her and turned to Dad.

'Do yer think the bed'll 'old us two? She's sixteen stone. I'm sixteen stone an' that meks us . . . er . . . er . . .'

I could see she was trying to puzzle out how many stones they would both be. Suddenly she sat up in bed. Sticking her two hands in front of her face and spreading her fingers apart she began to count. 'I'm sixteen and sixteen makes seventeen, eighteen, nineteen . . .'

'Sixteen and sixteen makes thirty-two,' I said, trying to help.

'I count my way then I know I'm right,' she snapped.

Dad lay back smiling and let her get on with it. Up went the fingers again and she counted on each finger again and again until eventually she yelled, 'The bed'll never 'old us!'

Dad and I collapsed in laughter as she tried with her hands to demonstrate the combined weight.

I found Frankie and Liza washed and dressed when I got downstairs. I was pleased because I could see that my brother had lit the fire and had put the kettle on to boil. Mum and Dad were not long following. We pulled our chairs up to the table and waited for our breakfast which turned out to be a burnt offering of toast; however, the tea was fresh, as I'd just made some more. Usually the leaves were used over and over again until they were too weak to stand the strain, then they were thrown on the back of the fire. Nothing was ever wasted if it could be reused, not even water or paper. We seldom had enough to eat. Sometimes we sat like three Oliver Twists, although we didn't dare ask for more. In fact, if we ever refused to eat anything that was placed in front of us, it was taken away and we had to eat it next mealtime, by which time we'd be so hungry we'd be glad of it. After our burnt toast, Dad told Mum to get the bedroom ready and he pinched her bottom as she rose from the table. She waved his hand away and warned him not to do it in front of us children. They both seemed happier. He pushed her gently up the stairs and turned to wink at us. I thought, if only they were always smiling or acting this way our lives would be much happier.

As we stood washing up the mugs and enamel plates we could hear the iron bedstead being dragged along the bare floorboards towards the wall so that Granny wouldn't fall out of bed. This was only the preliminary to a hectic tidying-up operation and although we'd cleaned the night before, we had to get out the carbolic soap and begin again. Mum was always one for making an impression when Granny called, but I couldn't see why because Granny's house was far more cluttered than ours. Dad cleared out and Frankie and I were left singing as we dusted and scrubbed. When Liza joined in Mum yelled at her to stop her 'cat warlin'. I think Liza was expecting another gobstopper but if so she was unlucky. We all fell silent and I thought maybe Granny would bring a little cheerfulness into our home now she was going to join the Salvation Army.

Very early next morning, before anyone was awake, I heard a loud knock on the downstairs door and before I could get out of bed a louder knock and three taps on the window pane. I woke Frankie and Liza with a good hard shake and we lifted the window to see what the racket was all about. As we leaned over the window-sill to look down into the yard below we saw Granny at the door, calling and waving her arms in all directions.

'Ain't nobody awake yet! 'Ave I gotta stand 'ere all day? I'm freezin' an' if nobody lets me in I'm comin' through the winda.'

She sounds just like Mum, I thought. Before anyone could get down to let her in, she tried to push up the window. Turning to the little man who'd brought her things on a hand-cart, she shouted for assistance. He looked too scared to move. Then Granny saw the bucket of rainwater that Mum kept for washing her hair. She promptly tipped the water away, turned the bucket upside down, and pushed the window up and stepped on to the bucket. Suddenly, as she was halfway through, disaster struck. The sash-cord broke and the bucket slipped, leaving Granny pinned half in, half out, by the window frame. She began to kick her legs in a vain attempt to free herself but she only succeeded in showing the neighbours her pantaloons. For the first time we experienced a temper worse than Mum's. She swore till the air was blue. Proof, I thought, that she needed to join the Salvation Army.

Dad popped his head out of the window and called down angrily, 'You'll have to wait, Mother, while I slip me trousers on.'

When he came downstairs and saw the plight she was in, he lifted the window but he was too quick. Granny fell out backwards, rolled over the bucket and landed in a puddle of rainwater.

'An' about time too,' she bawled while he struggled to pick her off the floor.

'I'll get meself up,' she muttered.

By this time Mum's head had appeared at the window and the neighbours too were peering down at the commotion.

''Annah!' Mum shouted. 'Yer'll wake up all the neighbours.'

'Wake 'em up! Wake 'em up!' she shrieked, struggling to her feet.

She turned round and waved her fist at the amused onlookers and bellowed at them, getting redder and redder in the process.

'Look at 'em! The nosy lot of idle sods.'

All the time she'd been carrying on, the little old chap was standing still, waiting to be paid for his labours. Suddenly she turned on him, leaned against the cart and sniffed.

'Don't stand there all day. 'Elp me off with me trunk an' me rockin'-chair. An' mind 'ow yer 'andle me aspidistra.'

He couldn't manage the trunk nor the rocking-chair, but Dad soon came to the rescue. Meantime Granny felt inside the bosom of her frock, sniffed a couple of times and pushed a silver sixpence into his outstretched hand. He looked down at it disdainfully and mumbled a barely audible 'Skinny old Jew'.

'What did yer say?'

'I said, "Thank you",' he answered meekly.

'Dain't sound much like "thank yer" ter me,' she retorted.

Scratching his head, he wheeled his empty cart away and said to Dad in a louder voice, 'I feel sorry for yow, mate,' but Dad ignored him.

The neighbours closed their windows. The fun was over for them but for us the trouble was only just beginning. We dressed hurriedly and dashed down to see Granny. She looked huge standing beside the trunk. We hadn't seen her for some time and it was easy to forget her size. She wore a black taffeta frock almost to her feet, black elastic-sided boots and a battered black woollen shawl. Her lace bonnet, also black, was hanging from ribbons on the back of her neck where it had slipped while she'd been trying to climb through the window. Her hair, too, was dishevelled, but what I noticed most was the large raised lump on her behind. I poked Frankie and he whispered, 'Ain't she got a big bum.'

'That ain't her bum. It's a bustle,' I replied as he started to snigger.

Liza too stared at Granny, but Granny paid us no attention until she suddenly straightened herself up to her full height of six feet, pulled her shawl around her and addressed us. 'Don't just stand theea gorpin'. Come an' give yer ol' gran a kiss.'

I closed my eyes and lifted my face up sideways for her to kiss my cheek. She must have read my thoughts because she just pushed me roughly away, with a slap, and bent to peck Liza and Frankie's cheeks. As I walked off clutching Topsey she asked what I was holding.

'It's the golly you made me, Granny,' I replied.

'I don't remember mekin' that.' She shrugged her shoulders and dismissed me.

'Now, now, Mother. You gave it to her last Christmas. You must have forgotten.' Dad attempted to pacify her.

'Er's always forgettin',' Mum piped up.

'Put the kettle on, Polly, and we'll all sit down and have a cup of tea.'

This was Dad's favourite tactic when he saw a quarrel brewing. He drew Gran's rocking-chair towards the fire. Granny sat down and rocked in the creaking chair. With hers in the middle and Mum's and Dad's chairs on either side of the fireplace no one else could feel or see the flames. I picked up Topsey and sat with Frankie on Neddy to await my tea. When it was made, Granny's was the first cup to be filled. Then she took a sip and spat it back out.

'What yer call this?' she spluttered, pulling a face at Mum.

'It's yer tea. Like it or lump it.' This was a favourite retort.

'Tastes like maid's water ter me.' Granny could give as good as she got.

We looked at each other; we all knew what Mum's tea was like. The pot had been stewing all morning and Dad told me to make a fresh one. As I squeezed past Mum to empty the tea leaves into the spare bucket, I heard her whisper to Dad, 'Thank the Lord we've only got 'er fer two weeks.'

The following Saturday afternoon Mum said they were going to the Bull Ring to do the shopping. This was our marketplace, where everything was sold cheap. There was the fruit and vegetable market, the fish market, the rag market and the flower market, all next to each other; and on each side of the street were barrow boys shouting their wares.

Dad asked Granny if she would like to go as well, but she said no, that it was too noisy, and that there was too much swearing for her liking. I could tell by the look on Mum's face that she didn't want Granny to go but Dad asked anyway.

'No. I can find summat betta to do with me time. Anyway I'm gooin' ter see the Captain of the Salvation Army,' Gran replied when pressed.

'Come on, Sam, before she changes 'er mind,' Mum said irritably.

As he was leaving the house, Dad said, 'Now if you kids behave yourselves I'll bring yer back a little present from town.' Then off they went, slamming the door behind them.

Granny put on her bonnet and shawl and went off to the Salvation Army Hall without a word to us. We were at a loss for something to do, then our eyes alighted on Granny's trunk. Frankie heaved open the rusty tin lid and we peered eagerly inside to see what secrets it held. We were disappointed to find only a pair of white pantaloons, a long, black lace frock with a bustle, a pair of button-up boots and a pair of whalebone stays like Mum's. We lifted them out to see what was underneath. It was then that we discovered Granny had been in the Army before. There was a tambourine, a uniform, and a bonnet with a red ribbon with 'Salvation Army' written on it. Underneath these was a bundle of old papers tied with string. We were about to start returning these things to the trunk when I hit on an idea to amuse ourselves until the grown-ups returned.

'Let's dress up and pretend we're in the band,' I said. The other two agreed.

Frankie fetched Mum's broom handle and tied the pantaloons on to it to represent a flag. Liza put on the bonnet and carried the tambourine and I put on the long black frock with the bustle. When we were ready we marched up and down the yard. Frankie waved the flag, Liza banged the tambourine and I dragged the bustle behind me. We sang 'Onward, Christian Soldiers' as we marched back and forth. All the neighbours turned out to see what all the noise was about. They joined in too. People sang a lot in those days. The children joined our band and we paraded up and down. Frankie's pantaloons bellowed out in the breeze as Liza's tambourine kept the beat.

We were having great fun until Liza gave one hell of a scream, dropped the tambourine and ran into the house. Frankie and I were scared stiff, thinking it was Granny or our parents come home early. Frankie dropped the broom and followed Liza into the house. I tripped over the long frock in my anxiety to follow them. Everybody was giggling, thinking it was all part of the act. When I did manage to get indoors I saw Liza was standing on Neddy still screaming and pointing at the bonnet. We couldn't understand what she was screaming about until she flung the bonnet violently at Frankie. I stooped down to pick it up when I was startled by a mouse which suddenly ran out across the floor. Frankie and I tried to catch it but the mouse was too fast for us. Like a flash it ran down a hole under the stairs and was gone. We must have caused quite a commotion because people had gathered round our door to see what was happening. They disappeared quickly enough when I told them what it was, though. I couldn't understand why they were so squeamish; they had plenty of mice of their own.

We managed to quieten Liza down eventually. Then we packed Granny's belongings back into the trunk, but we had a good look to see if we'd left any other little friends behind. Then we fastened down the lid just as we'd found it. We'd only just put the things away and set the kettle on the stove when the door opened and Dad walked in.

'Yer been good kids?' were his first words.

Frankie said we had, and warned Liza with a look.

'Well, here you are.' Dad handed me a box. I couldn't believe my eyes when I opened it. There, sitting on some straw, was a tame white mouse with tiny pink eyes.

Chapter 10

Off to the Farm

One morning there was a loud knock on the door. Mum jumped up exclaiming loudly, 'Now who can that be this time a mornin'? Bloody pest, whoever it is.'

'Well, go an' see,' Dad told her.

Shrugging her shoulders, she shuffled to the window and lifted the curtain to peer out. 'It's Mrs Nelson, Sam.'

'Well, call her in then, don't leave her standing there.'

Now Mum was a real artist, she could change her mood whenever it suited her. She opened the door and greeted Mrs Nelson cheerily. 'Good mornin', Mrs Nelson. An' 'ow are yer? Come in.'

Mrs Nelson lived over near the churchyard and did a lot of work for local charities. She was also better off than most and helped those in need. She was small and round as a barrel.

'Good morning, everybody,' she bellowed to us in her deep, manly-sounding voice.

We all returned the greeting, except Granny who looked up and merely grunted. Dad drew up my brother's chair and wiped it with his newspaper.

'Please sit down,' he said.

'Would you be interested to go hop-picking for a few days in the country?' Mrs Nelson said. 'I believe the change and the fresh air will do the children good. Transport's laid on and sleeping accommodation's free.'

We all looked at each other. 'I'll 'ave ter let yer know,' Mum answered pleasantly. 'An' thank yer fer askin' us,' she added.

'I must have yer answer this evening at the latest,' Mrs Nelson told her, and then rolled out.

As soon as she'd gone, Mum turned to Dad, beaming all over her face. 'It'll do us the world of good. Don't yer think, Sam?'

'You can go, and the kids, but not me.'

'Well, yer carn't, can yer? You've got yer job ter goo to.'

Then, banging her mug on the table Granny exclaimed, 'An' who d'yer think's gonna look arta 'im an' me?'

'Yes, you can come too, 'Annah. You can earn as well as mek yerself useful,' Mum said and rushed out of the house without stopping to take off her apron or put Dad's cap on. 'I shan't be long. I'm gooin' ter tell Mrs Nelson we're gooin',' she called back over her shoulder.

While she was out Dad gave us three a lecture. 'Mind yer manners, and don't forget to address the farmer as "sir", and no climbing trees or scrumping apples. Anyway, I don't have to tell you how to behave. Yer mum and granny'll see to that. And you, Katie, if you don't like it, just write me a note and I'll fetch yer back.'

He didn't seem too cheerful. In fact he looked a bit down in the mouth as we ran out. We rushed along the yard to tell the other kids we were going hop-picking with them. They'd all been before, either potato-, pea- or hop-picking, but this was a new experience for us. All our neighbours and their kids were busy as bees, dodging from place to place, getting the clothes off the line and fetching their buckets and bowls from the wash-house. Everything in our district was done on the spur of the moment; you were never given a date. It was 'make up yer mind' or 'it's now or never'. We weren't sure whether we were going or not until we heard Mum call us indoors to tell us we'd have to start getting things together for ten o'clock in the morning. She began at once snatching down the clean clothes from the line around the room and giving out orders to us to fold up what we needed.

'Come on, 'Annah, get a move on,' she shouted at Gran, who was trying to do her best but badly.

'Oh, back-peddle!' Granny shouted back, and threw down the towel she was trying to fold and stormed upstairs.

Mum handed me the list Mrs Nelson had provided, with all the instructions printed on it. First on the list was a towel, followed by soap, clean clothes, cups, frying-pan, bucket, bowl and other articles that we'd need. And underlined at the bottom was 'NO PETS, CATS OR DOGS'. We were busy collecting things together when Granny came downstairs.

'I thought we goin' 'op-picking!' she said, looking at the jumble of utensils on the floor. 'I ain't carryin' none of them,' she added.

Just at that moment Mrs Taylor called in the door. 'What time are we going, Polly?'

'Ten o'clock in the mornin', prompt. An' if yow ain't ready, Mrs Nelson said she'll leave yer be'ind,' Mum replied.

'We'll be ready.' She ran off to tell the others.

While us children were doing our best to help, Mum was losing patience with Granny. She wanted to wear her uniform and take the tambourine along too. But after sharp words, Granny got her way. I managed to smuggle Topsey inside the bucket and covered her with Liza's clean knickers. When everything was ready and pushed into a corner for us to pick up next morning, Mum flopped down into her armchair.

'I'm done in,' she puffed.

Dad, Mary and Jack had left the house before Mum called us downstairs the next morning. We jumped down the stairs two at a time. A few minutes later Granny came down already dressed in her uniform and bonnet with her tambourine clutched in her hand. We each had something to carry. I hung on to the basket and

Frankie and Liza carried the tin bowl and the other odds and ends. Granny, true to her word, just carried the tambourine. We had our mugs tied with string round our necks.

After Mum had taken a last look around to see if we'd forgotten anything we were ready to join the others in the yard to wait for the cart to pick us up. With us was Mrs Taylor and the little twins, Joey and Harry, wearing their everyday suits which had been starched and mangled. Mrs Buckley was dressed up to kill in her dusty, black velvet coat with a hat that looked more like a plate of withered fruit. Every time she moved her head, I thought it would fall off. She had her eldest girl and boy with her who were busy scratching their heads. Then there was Mrs Jones and 'Pig's Pudding Face', her son. She was gossiping with Mrs Phipps who was one of Granny's neighbours. She kept getting out of line to show off her moth-eaten fur coat which she always wore on special occasions, no matter what the weather. This day promised to be hot, the sun was already shining and Mum saw an opportunity to get in a dig.

'Where yer think yer gooin', ter the North Pole?'

They all turned to stare at Mrs Phipps's coat, but she threw her head back proudly and breathed defiance.

'It's real skunk!'

'Smell's like it, an' all,' Mum shouted back in triumph, and held her nose.

'Now then, you two!' Mrs Nelson yelled like a sergeant-major. 'Get in line, all of yer, and let's have some order!'

Mum and Granny pushed everyone closer together and got us three to the front of the queue so that we'd get in the cart first. Just then we saw two shire horses pulling a farmer's cart down the street. I wondered how we were all going to get in but we did, with a squeeze. Mrs Nelson urged us to hurry and the driver dismounted from his high perch and tied the reins to a lamppost. He looked a typical farmer with an old dusty cap, corduroy trousers, a fat face and wiry, grey hair like a halo. He gave a jolly laugh and scratched his head as he spoke to us.

'Well, what a motley crew.'

He dropped the back end of the cart which smelled like a pigsty and he apologised for not having had time to clean it out. I don't think any of us minded much really. We were all too happy to be on our way to the country. Granny was the last on board and stood looking at the cart, sniffing.

'I ain't gooin' in theea,' she protested to the driver.

'Well, by the look of yer, you'd better sit up front with me.'

This pleased Granny. She beamed, but when she tried to climb up, she slipped backwards. Everyone was tittering as they watched her capers. Several times she tried to lift herself up into the passenger's seat, but failed.

'Come along, Grandma, we'll be here all day,' the farmer said, getting behind her and heaving her bottom up with his shoulder. Granny gave him a dirty look for pushing her that way, but he just sat there in the driver's seat gathering the reins and the whip.

At last we began to move. By the time we'd reached the end of the street we'd begun to sing, even Liza. And Mum only put her hand on her shoulder and said, 'Yer'll 'ave ter yell, I ain't gooin' back for no gobstoppers.' Everyone seemed happy, even Granny who was banging her tambourine.

It seemed hours before we saw any country lanes or green fields and, when we did, I thought it was a wonderful sight. I wished I could go on riding for ever. After what seemed like hours, we started getting restless but the driver wouldn't stop till we reached a water trough where we could water the horses. Luckily we rounded a bend and came upon a public house which had a trough outside. The farmer spurred the horses on with the whip which made Granny hold on for dear life, because when the horses saw the water glistening in the sunlight they broke into a gallop, throwing us all on top of each other. The little twins began to bawl as they'd wet their trousers but nobody paid them any heed. We stood around on the grass verge waiting for the farmer to come back from the inn. It wasn't long before I saw him returning, carrying a large enamel jug.

'Get this down yer!' he cried, and handed us the jug filled with cider. 'Then let's be going.'

Mum was the first to drink. Then the other women followed and finally it was the turn of us children. Granny snatched the remains of the cider from the farmer's hand and, pointing at her Salvation Army uniform, said angrily, 'Don't let these fool yer, mista. I've gotta swolla as well!' And with that she emptied the rest of the jug.

Frankie was told to take the jug back to the inn and when he returned we were pushed back into the cart and Granny was once more heaved up next to the driver; and so we continued our long, cramped journey. Everybody dozed off, doubtless suffering from the effects of the cider. I strained to keep awake because I was inquisitive to know what was happening and where we were going. After a while the driver turned the horses sharply to the left and they broke into a trot, the cart rocking from side to side. I held on to the open lathes until the driver pulled the horses to a dead stop and I could see we'd arrived at our destination. We were in a farm-yard.

'We're here!' I screamed. 'We're here!'

We all tumbled out of the cart, dishevelled, dirty and hungry, with an avalanche of tin bowls, mugs and buckets. Mum, Granny, Mrs Buckley, Mrs Phipps and Mrs Taylor with the twins dragging behind made a dash to sit on a low wall that ran along the side of the farmhouse. Frankie, Jonesy and Annie ran off to explore, with Liza tagging behind. I was too bewildered to move. I'd never seen a farmhouse or a farmyard – especially one with live pigs! The only ones I'd seen were dead ones hanging outside the pork-butcher's shop.

I spotted a water pump and realised how thirsty I was. I ran towards it, took the mug from round my neck and pumped for dear life. But when it came, the water gushed out so quickly that I was soaked to the skin. I put the mug on the ground and held my head under the tap so that trickles ran into my mouth. It tasted like wine. Then, taking off my woollen stockings and clogs I stood in the water, happily bathing my feet.

I was so happy jumping up and down in that cool, clean water that I didn't notice two black and white sheep-dogs and several ducks waddling towards me, followed by a lame pig. They'd decided that they were thirsty too. When I saw them I hopped out of the basin, afraid of what they might do to me, but they were friendly enough and seemed more interested in drinking than they were in me. So I helped them and pumped some more. Then suddenly they scattered. They'd seen the farmer and our driver coming towards us.

Mum came running. 'Goo an' find yer brother an' Liza!' she shouted, and pushed me along.

I ran down the yard. The cobblestones were hot and covered with the muck of farm animals. When I eventually got to the end of the lane, I saw Frankie and the rest coming along.

'Come on, you lot!' I yelled. 'Mum's sent me for yer. The farmer's here an' yer know what that means.'

But they weren't interested in what I was saying. They were only interested in telling me where to go scrumping later!

We gathered round to hear our instructions. The farmer introduced himself as Farmer Onions which caused some tittering amongst the boys, then told us to go and wash ourselves before going to the kitchen. We all took turns pumping, but most of them only splashed their faces. Granny was last but she was too busy shooing away the ducks to have much of a wash.

Farmer Onions emerged from the house just then and told us

our meal was ready. We followed him into the kitchen where the first thing we saw was a large, stony-faced woman of middle age staring through us all as if we weren't there. But she couldn't out-face Mum who went boldly up to her and, putting on her best tone of voice with aitches in the wrong places, said, 'Good hafter-noon, Mrs Honions.'

Mrs Onions said nothing, but her eyes spoke volumes. She beckoned us to follow her into a larger kitchen where we could smell bread baking. I glanced around and saw several hams and strings of onions hanging from the ceiling. The shelves around the kitchen were full of all kinds of stone jars of home-made jams, honey and preserves, labelled with dates written on. There were slabs of cheese and butter and lots of other good things to eat. In the middle of the red-tiled floor stood a white wooden table with cheese scones, chunks of new bread, butter, pickled onions, cakes and buns together with a large jug of cider. We stood drooling as we waited for the word to start. At last in a gruff voice Mrs Onions spoke. 'Be yer gypsies?'

'No, we ain't!' piped up Granny and gave her a filthy look.

'Well, whatever yer be, I hope yer be better than the others we've had here.' Mrs Onions said no more but beckoned us to be seated and left us to help ourselves.

'An' about time too,' Granny said ungratefully.

We all made a mad dash for the food. We didn't even wait to sit down. We were ravenous, for we hadn't eaten all day and it was now late afternoon. We soon made up for lost time, though. What we couldn't eat we filled our pockets with for later. Mrs Taylor even found room for some down the twins' trousers.

Mrs Onions came back carrying a large enamel jug of warm milk, straight from the cow. It was delicious. I'd never tasted any-thing like it before, neither had the twins. Their mother had to take it away from them when she thought they'd had enough, but they wouldn't let go until she had given them a couple of smacks.

The farmer's wife looked on and frowned as she stood beside the table with her arms folded across her heavy bosom. 'Well if yer be ready, farmer is outside waiting to give ye all the instructions.'

We all filed out. I was fascinated by the kitchen and the food and because I was looking round I was the last to leave. Looking into that stern face, I said, 'Thank you, Mrs Onions,' and ran out scared.

The farmer gathered us all together and asked us if we'd had enough to eat.

'Yes, sir. Thank you, sir,' we chorused.

'Now it's too late to go picking tonight so I want each of yer to take a sack, and two for you,' he said, pointing to Mrs Taylor who had the twins. 'Then follow me.'

We picked up our sacks from a pile that stood against a wall and followed behind. Frankie and I looked at each other, wondering where he was taking us. We had the idea we'd be sleeping on the logs in the farmhouse, but he was leading us to a large barn across the meadow. Inside it was very warm and stuffy. There was only one small window to let in the light, which was dusty and dirty and covered with cobwebs. At the top end of the barn were piles of clean straw, a broom and a long, heavy rake. There was also a clock and a ladder which hung from hooks on the wall. Overhead was a loft with more hay and straw.

'Now, Sunny Jims,' the farmer yelled out to Frankie and Jonesy, 'get the broom and clear a space for yer mothers and fill yer bags with straw.'

Granny turned to the farmer. 'What's the bags gotta be filled for?'

'They're yer sleeping bags to sleep on,' he snapped. 'An' that's where yer sleep!' he added, pointing to the bare floor.

'I ain't sleepin' on no straw. I'm gooin' 'ome,' Granny said.

'Please yerself, old woman,' he answered, and walked out and left us to our fate.

This was our first disappointment. We were a long way from the farmhouse and miles away from home. I was getting homesick already. This was the first time in my life I'd been away from home. But I tried not to dwell on these thoughts and busied myself helping people fill their sacks. I sat on my straw bed beside the twins and remembered what Dad said before we left.

'Yes,' I said to myself. 'I'll write tonight when they're all asleep and I can post it in the morning.'

Suddenly I heard Granny throw her tambourine at a mouse that scurried across the corner where the rubbish had been swept. 'I never ought to 'a' come,' she sobbed.

Mrs Jones and Mrs Phipps went over to her and tried to comfort her, but she pushed them away. 'It's all yower fault. Yower used ter this. I ain't!'

Then Mum took charge and called us together. 'Now,' she began, sitting on an upturned bucket, 'I want yer all ter be'ave yerselves, an' let's 'ave no mower arguments.'

I smiled to myself for it was always Mum who started the arguments and the present occasion was no exception. She stood up and went across to Mrs Phipps and Mrs Jones who were always in league together.

'I wanta ask yow two what 'appens now?'

'The farmer will tell yer that when he wakes us up in the mornin'. I know we'll 'ave ter mek our own tea an' buy our vittles from the stores,' said Mrs Jones.

'What with?' Mum interrupted sharply, losing her temper.

'With the money we earn pickin' the 'ops,' Mrs Jones yelled back, equally annoyed. 'An' if yer wanta know any mower ask the farmer!'

Mum cooled down for a while, but not for long.

'Don't we get any grub from the farm'ouse?'

'Oh, no,' Mrs Phipps replied. 'Only yer first meal, what we've already 'ad.'

Mum looked amazed. So did Mrs Taylor. Then all of a sudden Mum burst forth, hands on hips:

'Then in that case yer betta empty yer pockets an' let me 'ave the grub yow all 'elped yerselves to.'

'What d'yow want it for?' Mrs Phipps ventured meekly.

'What d'I want it for?' Mum was getting angrier. 'It's to keep it safe in case we goo 'ungry.' Mrs Taylor handed Mum her share but Mum told her to keep it.

'Yow keep yowers. Yer'll need it fer the babbies.'

'Thank yer, Polly,' she replied and after putting the food in a box, she lay down beside the twins.

We pushed all our utensils into a corner until we'd sorted ourselves out and, while I was shaking out the worn, grey army blankets to cover us, everyone shook out their straw beds.

'Frankie, bring me that bucket an' bowl,' called Mum.

Suddenly I thought of Topsey hidden beneath the clean knickers inside the bucket. Before Mum saw me I snatched her out but then Jonesy grabbed the bucket and bowl and threw them across the floor to Mum. They clattered to her feet and Jonesy shouted, ' 'Ere y'are, yer greedy old sod!'

At this Frankie gave him such a hard clout that he fell over backwards, nearly landing on top of Granny. 'Shut yer mouth, Pig's Pudding Face!'

I watched Mum untie the bowl from the bucket. All eyes were on her. She was in a real temper and doing things at double pace. She threw the clean knickers across to Liza who could take the credit for thinking of packing them. Then she gathered all the broken food together and rolled it up in a towel, placed it in the bowl and stood the bowl in a corner of the barn, away from us all. She took the bucket and placed it upside down over the bowl of food. Next she marched off into the yard and returned a few minutes later with the biggest and heaviest stone she could carry. This she dropped heavily on top of the bucket. Then she slapped her hands together with satisfaction.

'That'll keep the grub safe from the rats until we need it.'

We all smiled at Mum's performance, and she smiled too when she surveyed her handiwork.

'Now I think we all gotta goo out an' explore. It's too light yet an' too early ter get ter bed.'

Granny was first to respond. 'Yow ain't leavin' me be'ind.'

Mrs Taylor said she couldn't leave the twins in case the rats nibbled them.

'Rats don't eat everything that's moovin',' Granny replied. 'Any'ow, what's the other kids dooin'? Carn't they mind 'em?'

So us kids were left behind to look after them. In any case we all knew where our mums were going to 'explore'. They were looking for the nearest pub which, as it turned out, was the one our driver had stopped at earlier, the Pig and Whistle.

After they'd gone the boys decided they were going to scrump some more apples. This left only Liza, the twins and myself. So Liza and I decided to look around outside while the twins were asleep. It was still very light. According to the clock, it was seven o'clock, so there was plenty of time to explore. When we got outside we noticed a large shed with a stove-pipe coming out of the roof. We looked inside and saw a rusty, round iron stove in the middle of the floor. Against the wall was an old, worn, marble-topped table and an earthenware sink like ours at home.

'This must be the place where we've got to cook our meals,' I said to Liza.

'Well, let's clean it up,' she replied.

Liza began sweeping and I looked around and found a rusty tin bowl behind some baskets, and a wet rag, and then ran down the yard to the pump. I kept my eyes on the cows across the meadow while I filled the bowl and then hurried back. When we'd finished sweeping the dust away, we decided we'd better look for Frankie and the others. However, I remembered the twins and decided to stay with them while Liza went off. I was scared to be left on my own, so it was with great relief that I heard Frankie and the rest running along the gravel path. I was never so happy to see them and threw my arms round my brother and burst into tears.

'What yer cryin' for?' he asked. 'Look what I brought yer.' He pulled up his gansey to reveal several red, waxy apples. His pockets were bulging fit to burst. The others had plenty too, which they shared out. What we couldn't eat there and then we hid under our straw beds for later.

By this time it was beginning to grow darker. The night was very warm and still, and Liza said she thought we were in for a storm. I started to get nervous again and imagined all sorts of things that could happen to us. Then I heard the sound of heavy footsteps on the path outside. I crouched behind Frankie who'd taken hold of a rake in readiness. At that moment a deep voice boomed out, and into the barn strode the farmer.

'No need to be afraid of me. I've brought you a lamp.'

We watched him light it and climb the ladder to fix it high on the wall, out of reach. Then he asked where our mothers were.

'Gone for a walk,' Frankie replied quickly.

'Well, Sunny Jims, tell yer mums or whoever's in charge, there's only enough paraffin in the lamp to last another two hours. See you're all up early in the morning.' Then off he went into the darkness.

We could only just see our beds in the dim light. I glanced up at the clock again. It said five past nine and Frankie, Liza, Annie and Jonesy had all stretched out for the night, fully clothed. I was hoping and praying Mum and the others would return soon. I suppose I dozed off at last. Suddenly I was awake again, and could hear voices in the distance. To my great relief I heard Mum's voice singing above all the others.

'My ole man says folla the band', rang out, followed by a chorus of 'An' don't dilly-dally on the way.' I could hear Granny's tambourine distinctly, keeping the beat. They were all drunk; I could tell by the way they were all laughing. I'd been amused by their capers when I was younger, but now I was nearly ten years old, and I no longer found them funny. They all looked stupid, and I hated to see people like this, especially Mum. They were all too drunk even to undress and they just picked their places and went to sleep.

Mum lay at the top end of the barn, Granny next, then Mrs Phipps, Mrs Jones and Jonesy, Mrs Buckley and Annie and Freddie, Frankie and Liza, Mrs Taylor and the twins, and finally me. It was very warm and stuffy and there seemed to be no air at all. I wept. I felt so unhappy and miserable. I wanted to be home with my dad and Mary. I determined to write a letter to Dad and with that thought in mind I felt better and, hugging Topsey, I fell asleep.

I was woken by a loud crash of thunder and several flashes of lightning which illuminated the whole barn. Mrs Phipps and Mrs Jones sprang up at once. Mrs Jones was evidently frightened because she ran round the barn crying and crossing herself.

'Mother of God, save us all!'

'Shut up, yer stupid fool. Yer wanta wake up all the rest?' yelled Mrs Phipps.

Everybody was restless now. They tossed and turned but eventually when the thunder died away they all fell sound asleep again. However, the storm returned with a vengeance. There was lightning and thunder, and hailstones that hit the corrugated roof so hard that I thought it would fall in. There was another loud crash and a third which seemed to shake the barn – at that point everybody woke up. I watched Mum between the flashes of lightning as she fumbled around for the candle and matches. Swearing, she lit the candle and placed it on the stone that stood on the bucket. Granny too was cursing and saying she wished she hadn't come. Frankie and Liza got up and took the ladder down from the wall, propped it against the loft and climbed up into the darkness out of everybody's way.

After a while the storm abated and all that I could hear was the sound of snoring once more. I lay there thinking about Dad and what I should put in the letter, and what with these things on my mind, the heat and the lack of air, I couldn't sleep until Mrs Taylor turned over and whispered that she'd open the barn door to let a little cool air in. I didn't answer, but she knew that I was awake. She opened the door a few inches and lay down again with a sigh. Soon she too was snoring and with the light breeze on my face I finally drifted into an exhausted sleep.

Chapter 11

Country Adventures

It was just breaking dawn when I heard a cock crowing in the distance. I sat up and rubbed my eyes and looked up into two big brown doleful eyes looking down at me. I fell back and screamed for all I was worth, waking everybody. Mum was the first to my rescue, treading over everyone, before she could push the cow through the door. But it wouldn't leave. I clung to Mrs Taylor who was guarding the twins. She was as scared as I was. We stared, horrified, as Mum tried to get the cow to budge but it only glared at her and mooed loudly. I started to cry, trembling with fear.

'Shut yer blartin'!' Mum yelled, and began rolling up her sleeves as if she really meant business. 'I'll soon settle 'im.'

She wasn't afraid of the cow but nor was the cow afraid of her. They faced each other. Mum 'shoo-shooed', and the cow 'moomooed' back. They were holding quite a conversation but the cow had the advantage of size and with an extra-loud moo it stepped closer. Mum ran back to the corner of the barn and grabbed a rake. Just as she was about to attack, the barn door was flung wide to reveal the farmer standing there with a stout stick in his hand. Glaring angrily at Mum, he snatched the rake from her and bellowed, 'Cows won't hurt yer!'

Then he hit the beast hard on its rump and it backed slowly out to rejoin the others. The farmer looked around the barn and informed us gruffly that he'd lit the fire in the shed and that we could get water from the pump and milk from the farm. The baskets for the hops were in the corner of the shed and we were expected in the field 'when yer ready'. With that he turned and stalked out.

Then Mum took over, giving orders to pile up our straw beds on top of each other in the corner ready for the evening. By the time this task had been accomplished we were beginning to get fidgety for the toilet but no one seemed to know where one was. Little Jonesy was crossing his legs and Joey pulled the hem of his mother's dress and complained, 'Me wants a two-two.'

Frankie and Jonesy had already vanished after complaining of belly-ache, evidently the result of all the sour apples they'd eaten the previous evening. Mrs Taylor picked up the twins, one under each arm, and went outside. I followed. There, at the back of the barn, we found a long wooden shed which I hadn't noticed before. There was a door at each end of this structure with a wet cardboard notice on each which read 'MEN' and 'WOMEN'. While Mrs Taylor held each twin in turn over a piece of newspaper, I entered through the door marked 'WOMEN'. There was a stone floor covered with wet lime, the result of water leaking through the roof. From one end to the other was a long wooden seat in which were three round holes. Behind the seats was a tarpaulin sheet. Curious, I lifted it to see what was behind but I dropped it quickly when I saw the two bare bottoms of Jonesy and my brother. They both turned round and, when they realised that it was me, burst out laughing. I went all hot and felt so ashamed. I ran out, nearly knocking Mrs Taylor over. She was on her way to dispose of the newspaper parcel. I watched as she disappeared through the door of the boys' side but I was too late to tell her. I waited to see what would happen, when all at once I heard Jonesy say in a loud voice, 'Yer can come an' sit on the 'ole next to me if yer like.'

'Yer cheeky bleeda,' was her startled reply.

The next thing I heard was a loud slap. Then she chased him outside, still with his trousers round his ankles.

'Come now, Katie.' Mrs Taylor took my hand. 'There's nothing to be ashamed of. We've got to put up with what we find in a place like this.'

'I wish I was home,' was all I could say. I told her I was going to write to my dad and tell him everything and that when he collected us perhaps she and the twins could come too.

'We'll see,' she whispered softly. I liked Mrs Taylor. She was the only one who ever really talked to me and she'd helped me when I'd lost my clogs and caught my finger in the mouse-trap.

At last we went into the shed to wash and get something ready to eat. But before we could do this, Mum said we had to pool what little money we had. I gave the only penny I'd been saving for some sweets. Mrs Taylor said she'd only got the rent which had to be paid when she returned home, but she would willingly give some of that until then. Granny hesitated to give her share until she saw Mum glaring at her, then she threw a shilling down on the table.

'An' I want it back!'

Altogether there was four shillings and twopence three far-things. Mum gave Annie a pencil and paper and told her to write down what we wanted from the general stores down the lane. ''Alf a pound a cheese, 'alf a pound a marg, three loaves, an' don't forget the mek weights. A quarter a bacon, an' see it's lean. Two ounces a tea, a pound a sugar, an' a tin a 'Andy Brand.'

'What yer want tinned milk for when we can 'ave fresh from the farm 'ouse?' Granny wanted to know.

'It's ter shove on the twins' dummies ter keep 'em quiet,' Mum snapped back and she began to count on her fingers how much the food would cost: but after getting herself into a muddle she pushed Annie away and called for me to reckon it up. I told her it all came to one shilling and three halfpence.

'That's right,' she answered, defying the others to deny her ability to add it up herself. But she hadn't a clue whether it was right or wrong: she could only trust to her fingers. I was still standing, waiting, while she sat fumbling with the money in her lap as though she didn't want to part with it; then after a while she told me Annie could fetch the food while I went to the farmhouse for the milk. I didn't wait for any more orders. Grabbing hold of the twins, I dragged them after me as I rushed out of the barn.

It was a lovely, warm, sunny morning and the cobbled path looked clean and fresh now that the heavy rain had washed all the animal dung away. I skipped along happily with the twins following closely behind. I felt a tug at my frock and when I turned round the twins were trying to attract my attention to a little pig with a limp and some ducks approaching us. I became nervous again for I remembered what Granny used to say when we ate pigs' trotters at home.

'Kids who eat trotters or cows' meat are 'witched. An' animals are like elephants, they never forget.'

She often said she never ate meat of any kind but we knew she did if she thought no one was watching. She also used to frighten me with the story that cows tossed you in the air if you wore red drawers. As a result, I was terrified of almost any animal with four legs. With this in mind, I dashed off, only slackening my pace after I'd run some distance. When I looked back I could see the pig had dropped behind, so I reached the farmhouse safely. I knocked on the door, and the farmer's wife came almost at once.

'Please. My mum has sent me for some milk,' I said timidly.

She looked down at me and asked if I had something to put it in. I'd forgotten to bring any kind of vessel, so I told her Mum hadn't got a jug and would she please lend one. She disappeared into the dark depths of the kitchen and returned a few moments later with an enamel jug filled with milk, still warm from the cow.

'Here yer be,' she said, handing me the large jug. 'And tell yer mum to let me have the jug back.' She didn't seem to look as stern as when I had first seen her. She really smiled broadly and asked if I was getting on all right. I nodded, and then asked her boldly what was wrong with the little pig's trotter.

'Yer mean Hoppity. There's nothing wrong with his leg now, but he did cut it on some barbed wire. My little granddaughter plays with him sometimes and wraps a rag round it. Now be off with yer before the milk gets cold,' she said, returning to her sharp manner. 'I'm busy.'

I thanked her for the jug and went off to pick up the twins but when I looked over to the wall they were nowhere to be seen, nor were the ducks and nor was Hoppity. I thought the worst. There was only one place to look: the pigsty. And that is where they were. They were sitting in the midst of the filth, still sucking their dummies and stroking Hoppity. I rushed in and hauled them out and dragged them across to the shed where I knew Mum would be waiting impatiently for the milk. But before we'd gone three strides Hoppity began to follow. We ran and arrived back to find Mum in an awful temper. She scolded me for being so long but I knew it was hopeless trying to explain.

Mrs Taylor snatched the twins away from me and began to wash them down while the others sniffed the air. This didn't stop them continuing to eat their bacon sandwiches. Mum was cooking my pieces of bread in the bacon fat. Mrs Taylor filled the twins' titty bottles with the rest of the milk. I was surprised that they guzzled it so readily because I wasn't aware that they'd ever tasted cow's milk before.

When we'd all finished eating, the farmer came along with his horse and cart to take us to the hop field. The cart was similar to the one we'd come in, but larger, with plenty of room for us and all the baskets. The farmer threw the baskets in first and then told us to jump up after. We all climbed in one by one, except Granny. She wanted to ride up on top with the farmer, but he wouldn't hear of it and insisted that she had to ride with the rest. So after a few moans and groans Mum pulled her inside and they embarked on their first trip to pick hops.

Mum and Mrs Taylor had decided that Liza and I should stay behind to look after the twins so we waved the others out of sight and returned to the shed to clean away the crocks. While we were busy, Liza told me how Mum had taken down her bloomers and smacked her bare bottom in front of everybody.

'Not in front of Frankie?' I said, shocked.

'Yes. And Jonesy,' she replied. 'They didn't even look away. They just laughed. But I'll get my own back when they return,' she said darkly.

'I don't like it here, do you, Liza?' Then I told her I was going to write to Dad to fetch us home.

'When?'

'Now. As soon as I can find the pencil and paper he gave me.'

After fumbling in my pockets I found the paper and envelope and a stub of pencil. My letter went something like this.

Dear Dad,
We are all very unhappy here. Will you come and fetch us
home? Mum and Granny and Frankie and the rest have
gone to the hop field and left Liza and me to look after Mrs
Taylor's twins. Liza is trying to comfort them while I write
this letter. Please, please fetch me back home or I shall run
away. I'm afraid of the cows. One came in the barn this
morning and if the farmer hadn't come in when he did, the
cow would have tossed Mum in the air. And there's a little
pig here called Hoppity and he follows me everywhere I go.

So please come and fetch me home as soon as you can. I
don't know this address, only that the farmer's name is
Onions. Mrs Nelson will give you our address.
love, Katie

This was the first letter I'd ever written and I was hoping it sounded convincing. Liza read it and put it in the envelope and addressed it.

'Where's the stamp?' she asked.

I fumbled around again in my pockets. Then I realised Dad hadn't given me one. 'Now we carn't post it,' I told Liza.

'Yes we can,' Liza said. 'But we'll have to take a chance whether Dad gets it or not.'

She held the envelope and in the top right-hand corner she pressed her wet, dirty thumb. 'There you are,' she said, smiling at her handiwork. 'The postman will think the stamp's fallen off. If he don't, Dad'll have to pay when he gets the letter. But we'd better not tell Mum you've written to Dad or we'll cop it.'

We gathered together Joey and Harry, and went off to post the letter in the letter-box outside the stores. Then we gazed into the shop window. There was almost everything imaginable there to make your mouth water, or so it seemed – cakes, jam tarts and all kinds of sweets. But we hadn't got a halfpenny between us – at least we thought we hadn't until Joey said, 'Me got penny, Tatie. To buy yoo sweeties.'

We didn't bother to find out where he'd got it from, but grabbed it from him and entered the shop. Once in the stores, we had no hesitation in asking the lady behind the counter for two liquorice laces.

'Let's see the colour of your money first,' she said, peering accusingly at us.

Liza showed the penny and she promptly gave her the two long strips of black liquorice. She glared at us all the while.

'Where yer from?'

'Onions's farm,' snapped Liza. 'An' we want a coupla bull's-eyes with the change.'

Bull's-eyes were what Mum called gobstoppers, and gave to Liza when she tried to join in the singing. When we left the shop, the twins were chewing on the black strips and we followed behind sucking a bull's-eye each. I always liked these sweets because they lasted a long time. While we sucked them we took them out of our mouths now and again to observe their changing colour. Liza and I skipped merrily down the lane and the twins followed up behind with more liquorice around their mouths than in them.

It was a very hot day and the bad weather of the previous night had quite disappeared. Liza suggested we go exploring. We walked along the quiet lanes for about a mile and didn't meet a soul, only the cows in the fields. Soon the twins grew tired and decided that they'd had enough so down on the grass verge they flopped. I must say I was surprised Joey's little bowed legs had carried him that far. Liza and I pick-a-backed them, but we soon wearied of this. They were small for their three and a half years, but they were still heavy if you tried to carry them as we were doing. We decided that we'd have to return to the barn.

Soon we were completely lost, afraid and on the verge of tears. All the lanes looked the same to us. There was nothing but fields and meadows – not a house or a human being in sight. My clogs had rubbed holes in my stockings and made blisters on my heels. Liza was complaining about the heat. We decided to sit down by the wayside, remove our clogs and rest. Perhaps someone would come along and show us the way. The twins began to grizzle.

'Me is 'ungry, Tatie.'

'An' me's wet me trousers.'

Soon we were all in tears together. We were hungry, tired, lost, and not a little miserable. We endeavoured to pacify the twins with a lullaby but they continued to sob until eventually they fell asleep.

Liza and I huddled together on the verge and slept as well. We must have been there for hours because the next thing I knew was a horse neighing and loud voices. Then somebody was shaking us.

'What yer all doin' 'ere? Wake up. Wake up, the pair on yer.'

I can't remember ever being so happy to see and hear my mum bawling at me. Liza and I quickly got to our feet and the twins were snatched up by Mrs Taylor.

'Oh, my poor little babbies. Whatever are yer dooin' 'ere?'

But we were too relieved to answer her and we just gazed at Granny and the rest of the hop-pickers who were standing among the baskets on the cart. They all looked surprised to see us, even the farmer.

'Come on,' he called. 'Jump in, all of yer. I'm late already.'

So Mum pushed us roughly aboard the cart and told the farmer that she'd walk, and off she went with Mrs Taylor and the twins. It was then that it dawned on us. We were only a few yards from the farm and we hadn't realised it. In our panic we must have walked round in a circle.

The farmer dropped us off, and then went over to Mum and paid her the hop-picking money for her and the rest of the women. This provoked a lot of grumbling from Granny and the others because Mum was in charge. But they needn't have worried. She shared it equally amongst them – all except Annie and the boys, who had to be content with a penny each for their troubles. Mum called me over to do the counting. When I'd completed this by a feat of mathematics, she wasn't satisfied with her share which she'd already calculated on her fingers, so I was ordered to do it all over again.

'All bloody day for two bob each?' she said to Mrs Phipps.

'Well, we do get twopence more than the other farm we worked at, dain't we, Mrs Jones?' she asked. 'An' we do get paid every day.'

Mrs Jones nodded her head in reply, but Mum wasn't satisfied. She shouted across the barn to Granny and the rest, still glaring at her two shillings.

'We worked like bloody Trojans fer this!' She spat her words out with contempt. 'If that bloody farmer thinks I'm pickin' 'is 'ops all day for two bob, 'e's off 'is rocker.' She was livid, and paced up and down.

'Yow tell 'm, Polly, I ain't doin' any mower!' Granny sobbed. 'Send somebody to the stores and let's 'ave summat ter eat. I'm clammed. I wish I was back 'ome. I was allus sure of a pot o' stew.'

'Oh shut up, 'Annah! We're all clammed,' Mum snapped back. 'Anyway, let's goo to the shed an' 'ave a cup a tea while one of yer fetches some food.'

'I'll goo,' Mrs Jones volunteered quickly.

'No!' shouted Mum. 'I don't trust yer.'

So Liza and I had to go instead, and by the time we returned the tea was ready in the pot. I still had to go to the farmhouse though, as we had no milk. The twins dragged along after me. Before we'd gone very far we saw little Hoppity in front of us. Joey and Harry ran up and stroked him. They thought he was a kind of dog and they tried to climb on his back. I was afraid the pig might turn nasty but they didn't turn a hair; they were enjoying themselves and so apparently was the pig. It was then I found enough courage to stroke him myself. He was just a friendly little pig. I noticed that the dressing had come loose so I wrapped it back on for him and from that moment we became friends. He trotted along behind us and when we got to the farmhouse the farmer's wife told us not to encourage him or he would follow us everywhere. I smiled and thanked her for the milk, and the pig followed us back along the path towards the shed. But didn't come in. He stood outside and would have nothing to do with anybody else, only the twins and me. In the end the only way I could get rid of him was to throw an apple as far as I could and hope he wouldn't return for more.

It was about eight o'clock and the evening was still warm and light. We had our share of fried bacon, mugs of cocoa and fried potatoes. Mum, Mrs Phipps, Mrs Jones, Mrs Buckley and Mrs Taylor washed and combed their hair ready to go to the pub again. The other kids had already vanished across the field to do their scrumping. I knew I would be left alone with the twins. I filled their two empty medicine bottles with what was left of the cow's milk and fastened the teats on the ends. I lay down beside them and they sucked their milk while I sang a lullaby until they fell asleep. I felt so unhappy and miserable that I considered running away. But where could I have gone? I was miles from home and I couldn't even walk to the farm to ask the farmer's wife if I could stay with her because I was too afraid of the cows. I could still hear their lowing in the fields. All kinds of things crowded into my mind, but above all I thought I must not leave the twins. I put my arm round them and cuddled them until I dropped off to sleep. This didn't last long. Liza and Annie and the lads woke me up when they came bounding in and dropped their pile of apples and carrots on the floor. We gorged ourselves, knowing our mothers wouldn't be back before closing time.

When the boys had had their fill they climbed the ladder to the loft and settled down for the night. Liza and Annie made their beds on the other side of the twins. It was really dark now and I could only just make out the time by the dusty clock on the wall. It was ten thirty.

It was very warm in the barn with the door closed and very humid as well. I tiptoed to the door and opened it to let in some air. As I did so I heard singing in the distance, and I was relieved to hear Mum's voice way above the others. But as I stood in the doorway waiting for them to arrive I became aware of male voices too and when they all drew nearer I could see Mum, Granny and the rest arm in arm with four men. The smallest of the four was holding Granny up, while the other three were trying to push past

Mum into the barn. They were dishevelled, ragged and swearing loudly and they each brandished a bottle of beer.

Mum pushed the first one outside. 'Thank yer for seein' us 'ome. But that's as far as yer goo,' she said firmly. But they wouldn't budge.

The leading one stood there and seemed most aggrieved. 'What d'yer tek us for, missus? We've treated yer all night. Come on, let's open a bottle inside.'

Then he pushed his way inside and the other three followed, waving their bottles in the air. Then the little bearded man grabbed Granny round the waist and dragged her on to the straw, nearly landing on the girls as they rolled about. Mrs Phipps, Mrs Jones and Mrs Buckley were struggling to free themselves and Mum was giving a right and a left to another fellow's belly. Before he could get a grip on her, she lifted her heavy foot and landed a kick in his groin. He let out a yell and fell to the floor, clutching his private parts and, as he laid there groaning, the contents of his bottle poured out beside him. Mum clapped her hands and grinned.

'That's number one settled.' Mum was really enjoying herself and so were the boys, who were laughing fit to burst in the safety of the loft. However, Liza and I were scared. We were in the thick of the skirmish and didn't think it was funny at all. We crouched in the corner with Mrs Taylor and the twins, who were crying loudly, and watched as Mum caught hold of the little man by his beard and dragged him off Granny, down whose throat he'd been trying to pour more beer. Mum held him firmly and then threw him through the door. He was probably glad to leave!

Mrs Phipps, Mrs Jones and Mrs Buckley were still struggling with the other two burly fellows. These blokes obviously had no intention of leaving the women and things seemed to be getting rougher. As Mum made to help, the men lashed out at her and she fell over Granny who was lying on the straw exhausted, but with sufficient energy to swear at the interlopers. Mum was unable to get to her feet. Each time she got up she was pushed down again. I shouted out to Frankie to come down and help, but he was already sliding down the ladder with Jonesy and Freddie close behind. They jumped on to the largest fellow's back and pummelled him and they were soon joined by Mum who'd struggled to her feet. Meanwhile Mrs Jones was standing in the corner, crossing herself and praying. 'Mary, Mother of God, save us!' she kept crying out.

Meanwhile the second man was chasing Mrs Phipps and Mrs Buckley round the barn, when suddenly we were all plunged into darkness. The lantern and our supply of paraffin had burnt itself out. Liza, Annie, Mrs Taylor and I were still crouching out of the way, afraid for our lives. Mrs Phipps yelled out and fell, with the man on top of her. Then the big fellow shouted, 'Come on, George. We'll settle this lot tomorrow night.'

Mrs Buckley crawled to the upturned bucket and lit the only piece of candle we had left. We could see George getting to his feet. Mum rushed at him and his friend came to his rescue, but Mum was afraid of no one, not even the devil. She lunged at them both and knocked one fellow down and then Frankie tried to come to her aid with the hay-fork. He rushed at them but the fork was too heavy and he tripped over the chap on the floor. He pulled himself to his feet and when he saw that Mum was not going to stop he dashed outside and at last the big fellow decided he'd had enough, too. He helped the first fellow Mum had floored, who appeared to have fallen into a drunken stupor, to his feet, and they limped out. Mum slammed the door and pushed its wooden bar into place, and slapped her hands together in a gesture of having polished them off.

'Well, that's the end of that!' she cried in triumph.

Frankie and Jonesy climbed back into the loft and we emerged from our hiding-place. The barn was a shambles. Straw and empty bags were strewn about amongst the broken beer bottles. We all set about refilling our beds but it was impossible to see, so we girls clambered up to join the lads in the loft. The women below began to quarrel. I could still hear their efforts to scrape together some straw when I heard Mum's voice.

'I wish to God we 'ad a light in 'ere to see what we're doin'.'

Suddenly her prayer was answered. The farmer stood in the doorway with his lantern lighting up the whole barn. He gazed at the scattered straw and then looked at us all hard in turn. 'What's been going on here?'

Mum put on her look of surprised innocence.

'Nothin', sir,' she replied, giving him the benefit of one of her smiles.

'What do you mean nothing? I want an explanation!' He was angry. 'The place is a shambles and I could hear the noise all the way down the lane. Come on, who's going to own up?'

No one spoke. We all stared at him, afraid of what he might do. Then after a few seconds he spoke. 'Very well. You all leave in the morning.'

But as he turned to go, Granny burst out with sobs. 'It worn't us, sir. It was them men from the other field who followed us 'ere.'

Mum stood in front of Granny and said she didn't know what she was saying. 'A bit funny in the 'ead, sir,' she said, putting her finger to her forehead.

The farmer glared at Mum. 'I'll talk to you lot tomorrow. And see that you've all got yer belongings ready to clear out!'

When he went off, leaving us in the dark again, the quarrelling started in earnest.

'Yer dain't 'ave ter tell 'im, 'e'd 'ave found out anyway. The way yow carried on with all yer 'ootin' an' ravin'.'

'Oh, lie down, yer silly ole fool, an' get ter sleep!' Mum yelled.

Then Granny laid down on the straw again. Soon everybody was snoring but I just lay there praying that my dad would fetch me home as quickly as possible. It was pitch dark now and quiet but for the sound of a steady succession of women using the bucket. I resolved to run away as soon as it got light and with that thought I must have drifted off to sleep.

Chapter 12

Hoppity Goes Missing

I was woken by Frankie shaking me. I looked around sleepily and realised that it was long past dawn, in fact it was ten o'clock by the clock on the wall. When I was fully awake I could hear that there was a storm overhead. It was thundering and lightning and raining in buckets. All thought of running away was out of the question. We couldn't even get to the shed to see if there were any scraps or leftovers from the previous evening. Instead we set about rousing our mother who made loud complaints about the weather and their headaches. Granny was the last to rise and was the loudest complainer.

'I want ter goo 'ome. If nobody comes ter fetch me I shall die 'ere!' she sobbed.

'Don't cry, Granny. I've written a letter to Dad to come and take us home,' I confided in her. This seemed to pacify her and she pulled me to her.

'God bless yer, me wench.'

But I recoiled from her. The smell of stale beer on her clothes made me feel sick. I felt miserable because the rain had prevented me from running back to Birmingham, but I consoled myself with the thought that Dad might come after it had stopped. By now everybody was up and the twins were yelling to be fed, but their mother couldn't be bothered with them. I looked away. I knew how they felt; I was hungry too.

Mrs Taylor was not the only one in a temper. Everybody was in the same mood. They were getting in each other's way as they tried to clear away the half-empty bags of straw. We were really fed up, particularly with the rain, and every few minutes someone would stick their head out the door to see if it was easing off.

Mum asked Granny and the rest to pool what money they had left to buy some more food from the shop.

'I carn't, Polly,' said Mrs Jones, 'I've only a few coppers left.'

Mum, hands on hips, glared at Mrs Jones and it was then that I noticed for the first time that she had the biggest black eye I'd ever seen – and I'd seen a few in my time! There were always drunken brawls in the street. Mum grew red in the face giving out instructions.

'All on yer!' she commanded. 'Yer'll 'ave ter doo yer share! An' another thing. We've got ter get our chattels together. Yer knoo what the bloody farmer said.'

To which Granny responded, 'Talk a the bloody devil an' 'e'll be bound ter appear.' At that, all eyes turned to the barn door and everyone lost their tongue in amazement as they saw the farmer standing there. He gave them all an icy stare before he broke the silence.

'Well? And what have you all got to say for yourselves?'

No one answered. Not even Mum. Then he called us to him and continued in a gentler tone. 'Now I want you to listen carefully. All of yer. I been over to my brother's farm and I've found out what happened last night. Now if you'll promise not to go to the local I'll let things pass. But I warn you all, if you do go you'll be sorry!' It was then he caught sight of Mum's face and saw her black eye and his face broke in a broad smile. 'Well, I see you won a medal too! There'll be no picking today,' he continued. 'The ground's too wet.

But see you're up bright and early in the morning. I want double-pickings tomorrow.'

We felt a bit happier now we knew we weren't going to be turned out in the rain. Mum collected the few coppers the others had placed on the table.

I jotted down the things we were to get from the shop as Mum dictated them, and Liza found an old basket to carry them in. We also took two sacks to cover our heads and shoulders from the rain. Then, carrying the basket between us, we skipped along the lane.

When we got back to the shed everybody was doing something, even the kettle was boiling on the stove and the pan was ready with a lump of lard melting, to fry the bacon. The table was laid ready with tin plates and mugs. The twins were seated on up-turned boxes, rattling away at the mugs with their spoons. After a while we sat on the floor – there wasn't enough room to sit at the table – and our meal, which Mum had rationed out, was presented to us. There was only enough food for breakfast and we still had the rest of the day to get through before we could pick more hops and earn more money.

At last we went back to the barn. Mum, Granny and the other women stretched out and took a nap, while Liza and the children played a guessing game. At about seven o'clock it finally stopped raining and since it was still light we decided to go out while the adults were still sleeping. We didn't get far enough, because Mum woke up and called to us, 'Where do yer think yer all gooin' to?'

At that the other kids ran off, leaving me. 'Yer better goo to the farm'ouse an' get the milk,' Mum ordered.

I collected the jug from the shed feeling very miserable. Nobody seemed interested in me until there was a job to be done. I took the jug and trudged reluctantly to the farmhouse, hoping that at least I might meet Hoppity, but he too appeared to have forsaken me.

Mrs Onions was sweeping pools of rainwater away from the

door as I approached. She looked up and fixed me with a glare.

'Well!' she said sharply, 'I see you've come for some more milk.'

'Yes, please,' I replied timidly, and handed her the jug.

'This is the last yer get without money. Yer better tell yer mother I want paying at the end of the week.'

'Thank you,' I whispered, but as I was creeping away she called me back.

'Just a minute. You wait there while I wrap a parcel for you.'

She returned with a parcel wrapped in newspaper inside a large paper bag. She also gave me two rosy red apples which I was tempted to eat there and then. I couldn't really understand Mrs Onions. One minute she snapped at me, the next she smiled and handed me a present.

'Off yer go now and don't forget the money for the milk.'

I thanked her again and hurried back to find a bustle of activity as the table was prepared for tea. Mrs Taylor took the milk from me and I handed the parcel to Mum.

'What yer got there?' she wanted to know.

'Mrs Onions gave it to me and she says she wants paying for the jugs of milk.'

'Well she can wait till we goo to work tomorra,' Mum snapped and the rest, who'd gathered round to watch her unwrap the parcel, nodded in agreement. Everybody's face changed and their eyes lit up as Mum placed on the table a dozen buns, a big lump of cheese, a lump of best butter, a slab of currant cake and a piece of fat bacon.

'She ain't so bad after all,' Mrs Phipps said as she stared hungrily at the contents of the bag.

I thought so too. Grown-ups were changeable creatures when they wanted to be. They all bustled about like busy bees, getting everything laid out in apple-pie order. Mum told me to call the other kids in. I spotted them coming over the field, their pockets bulging with booty. They could hardly believe what they saw on the table. It was laid out with everything we had. And when we'd eaten, we thought it was the best feed any one of us had had for a long, long time. We even had the best butter on our bread and a bun each as well. The adults had fried bacon and cheese sandwiches. Then Mrs Taylor asked me to go for a drop more milk. I told her what Mrs Onions had said about paying but she insisted. 'Well yow tell 'er it's fer the twins. They won't sleep without their bottles. I'm sure she'll let yer 'ave some till I can pay 'er.' With that she pushed the empty jug into my hand.

I began to weep. How could I ask for more milk when the woman had been so kind and given me all that food? I began to walk slowly towards the farmhouse when I noticed a van drive up and stop near the door. When I saw who got out I dropped the jug and ran as fast as my thin little legs would carry me. It was my brother, Jack.

'Jack! Jack! Oh, you've come to fetch us back home!' I cried out and tears welled up in my eyes.

'All right, let goo.' He smiled at me clinging to his trouser-legs. I let go and hung back while he knocked on the door.

'Anybody in?' he called out, but there was no reply. There was no one about but Hoppity who came running towards us on his three legs. I was happy and excited, telling my brother that this was Hoppity who followed me wherever I went.

'Funny little pig,' he said, lifting his flat cap and scratching his head in wonderment.

'You've got him tamed all right.' I didn't like the look he gave the pig when he said, 'You'd look nice on the table, Hoppity.' Then he added, seeing the look on my face, 'I'm only kidding. You know I wouldn't do that.' But you never knew with my brother Jack. Then he said, 'Jump in the back and show me where you're staying.'

While Jack parked the van at the back of the barn I ran to tell Mum the good news.

'Mum, Mum!' I cried excitedly. 'Our Jack's outside. With a van. He's come to take us home!'

Mum jumped up, knocking the box she was sitting on flying against the wall, and rushed outside to meet Jack. She threw herself at him, almost smothering him as she kissed him.

'Where've yow sprung from?' she cried out.

Jack replied in his usual joking vein, 'Well, old 'un, I've come ter fetch yer 'ome.' He very seldom called her Mum or Mother.

'Thank God y've come. I've 'ad anough of this 'ole,' she declared, indicating the farmyard in general with an expansive gesture.

It was then that he noticed her black eye.

'Who give yer that?' he asked, pointing at her face.

'I fell over in the dark an' 'it it on the wall,' she lied.

Granny jumped up and screamed out, 'No she dain't! Tell 'im the truth!'

Mum walked away, giving Granny a filthy look. Then Mrs Buckley asked how everybody was at home and if her husband and children were all right, but before Jack could answer Mum butted in, 'How's yer dad, Jack? An' 'ows Mary an' Charlie and 'ow's everybody copin' with the rest of the kids?'

While they were all trying to get a word in edgeways, I put the kettle on to make Jack a cup of tea but when he noticed what I was doing he said he had something better in the van. He went out and came back with a pint bottle of whisky. The women's eyes were glued to the bottle. Nobody wanted tea now. Frankie and Jonesy were hoping Jack would give them some too, but Jack was adamant. They were too young and the whisky was too precious to be wasted on them. So the tea came in useful after all. We kids drank it.

After a while, when all the chatter had died down and the crocks had been cleared away we retired to the barn. 'Mower room ter move about in theea,' Granny said.

We led the way and when Jack entered he began fuming.

'What a bloody place to sleep. I'll have a bloody word with the farmer.'

'It's better than some barns we've slept in, ain't it?' said Mrs Phipps.

'Yes, that's right,' Mrs Jones replied, trying to look indignant. 'Anyway we ain't gooin' 'ome till the end of next week.'

'You please yerself what yer do.' Jack was annoyed. 'I'm teking my family out of this place first thing in the morning.'

Frankie piped up, 'I want to stop with Jonesy. I like it here.'

'You'll do as you're told.'

With that Jack gave him a good back-hander that made him sulky for the rest of the evening. I would have loved to tell Jack a lot of things that had been going on, but I knew I'd better be quiet while Mum was around, so I cuddled up next to the twins. Just as I was dropping off, I heard Jack and Mum talking.

'Where yer gooin' ter sleep, son?'

'I'll muck down in the van. Now, don't forget.' His voice dropped to a whisper. 'I'm going to have a drink at the Pig and Whistle. Get some sleep and I'll wake yer when I get back.'

'All right, son, an' mind 'ow yer goo,' she whispered in reply.

I heard the van drive away; then Mum lay down and went to sleep. Everybody was quiet now. I got up off my bed and tiptoed over to Frankie and whispered in his ear, 'Are you awake, Frankie?'

'What yer want?' he mumbled, and struggled up.

'Jack's gone to the Pig and Whistle and I'm afraid the men might set on him, Frankie.'

'Oh, go to sleep! He can take care of himself. Anyhow I don't care about him any more.'

And with those words he turned his back on me. I felt so unhappy I wanted to cry. My mind was like a maze. I imagined all sorts of things were going to happen before Jack could get us safely home. But Frankie was right. He could take care of himself. He was six feet tall and as strong as three men. I still wished I was back in my bed at home. Dad had said the country air would do us good but it only seemed to have made us all quarrelsome and miserable.

I don't remember how long I slept, but I woke up and could hear voices in the barn.

'Are you awake, old 'un?' I heard Jack whisper. 'Come on, we ain't got all night. I want to get away before it gets too light.' I could tell by the tone of his voice he'd had plenty to drink.

'There's only a few more things to get out in the van now,' I heard Mum reply. Then Jack told Mum to get some sleep and he'd wake her up at dawn – and not to forget the pills.

'Yer betta 'ave 'em now,' Mum whispered.

'Only give 'im one,' I heard her say.

Then Jack put the candle out and disappeared. I couldn't think what was going on. What were they plotting? My eyes ached and at last I fell asleep again. It was just breaking dawn when I woke again in time to see Mum and Jack carrying armfuls of straw and empty sacks out to the van. Then they returned and whispered to Gran to get up and go to the van.

'What's 'appenin'?' she mumbled as Mum led her outside still half asleep.

'Hush. We're tekin' you 'ome. We don't want to wake any of the others.'

I jumped out of bed quickly, thinking they were leaving me behind. I grabbed Topsey in one hand and my clogs in the other and ran outside and stood by the van. They weren't leaving without me, even if I had to hang on the back.

'I'm glad you're up and ready,' Jack said. 'You can keep an eye on Gran while we go and get Liza and Frankie.'

There was no great need to watch Gran: she was already snoring. After a couple of minutes, Jack came out with Frankie who was still protesting about having to leave, but when Jack raised his hand to him he soon scrambled aboard.

'Come on, old 'un,' Jack hissed to Mum, 'we'll have to hurry up before it gets too light.'

They've just gone for a wee, I thought. But after they'd been gone quite a time I began to worry. By the time I heard them coming back, everyone else had fallen asleep. When the door opened I could see Jack with Hoppity in his arms. The little pig seemed to be sleeping as well.

'Where yer found him?' I managed to splutter.

'I've bought 'im off the farmer for yer.'

I stared at him wide-eyed as he continued, 'He told me he was always running away and getting lost and said you might like him. Now move over while I put him down.'

I moved across to accommodate the pig and Mum, but apparently she was riding up front with Jack. I was glad of that. But I wasn't very happy about the pig beside me. Anyway, Jack placed him on the straw and whispered, 'Now listen carefully. I don't want anyone to know I've bought him. Not even Liza, Frankie or yer gran. This is our secret. I'm going to hide him until he wakes up. Then we'll make him a sty in the yard. Promise me now that you'll keep our little secret.'

Jack started the van and when we reached the open road we speeded up. I tried to sleep, but I could hear Granny's snores and the pig's grunts. Liza and Frankie slept on like the babes in the wood. It was still very early in the morning and the lanes were misty and quiet. All I could hear was the occasional noise such as the bellowing of cattle, and later the clanging of a tram bell in the distance. At last the van halted in our yard. Jack opened the doors and whispered instructions to me to make no sound. I watched him lift the sleeping pig in his arms and carry him into the house. Mum followed behind with an armful of straw. Jack lifted the old bit of sacking off the cellar grating and carried the pig down into the darkness. I stared and wondered. Why were they hiding him in the cellar if they'd bought him? It didn't make sense. I assumed they'd explain to me later, and in any case the cellar was the only spare room we had.

There was no one at home when we arrived and the house was cold, so I was soon busy chopping sticks to make the fire with. I was itching to tell the others what Jack had bought for me, but Jack guessed that I was about to tell Frankie and he shook his head at me. Mum began bustling about, making a meal, and we sat down to our breakfast – all, that is, except Granny. She was sniffing and sneezing in the corner and seemed to have a bad cold.

'Come on, Gran,' Jack chivvied her, 'yer breakfast's ready.'

But as she tried to stand up, she swayed and was only saved from falling into the fire by Jack's timely intervention. We were concerned, but Mum, predictably, was unmoved.

'I 'ope I ain't gooin' ter 'ave 'er bad on me 'ands. I've enough ter do round 'ere as it is.'

'I know I ain't wanted,' Granny cried between sniffs. 'I'll be gooin' back to me 'ouse in the mornin'.'

But she didn't leave the next day, nor the next, nor the one after that. She was quite ill and I was given the job of looking after her.

We finished our meal, and Jack returned the van after I'd helped him clean out the bits of straw. When Jack handed me a silver sixpence I could hardly believe my eyes and stared at the coin in amazement.

'That's for being a good girl,' he told me. 'But don't forget our secret.' He winked. I nodded but I wanted to tell someone, Frankie for example, because I knew he could keep a secret. But I had crossed my heart and promised. I dropped the sixpence down my stocking and went indoors. I knew it was no use asking Mum to explain why it had to be a secret. She was busy combing her hair and arranging it in different styles to hide her left eye, which had now turned yellowish. She turned round from the cracked mirror and glared at me.

'Don't stand gorpin'! Call Liza to come an' 'elp fill the copper. I want ter get the washin' done before yer dad gets 'ome.'

Liza was nowhere to be found as usual, so I took the bucket and went to the tap in the yard to fill it. This was Monday morning – Mum's washday, and most other women's too. Maggie was standing by the tap with her own bucket as I approached.

' 'Ello, Katie,' she greeted me – in some surprise I thought. 'When did yer come 'ome?'

I told her we'd arrived early that morning.

'All on yer? But where's Mrs Taylor and the others?' she asked. 'They ain't bin ter collect their kids they left be'ind yet!'

I explained that we'd returned alone, and this aroused her curiosity. Mrs Huggett came hurrying down the yard. 'What d'yer think, Nell?' Maggie said. 'The others ain't come back yet.'

She turned to me again for an explanation as though it was my fault. I was about to reply when I saw Mum dashing towards us. I could have laughed out loud. She looked so comical, marching along with Dad's flat cap pulled well down over her left eye. She snatched up the half-filled bucket and marched back towards the wash-house, glancing back over her shoulder and calling out, 'They're stoppin' a few more days if yer want ter know. We've 'ad enough of it!'

'An' so 'ave we 'ad enough!' Maggie shouted back at her. 'It's took me an' Billy, an' the rest of the good people round 'ere to feed 'em.' But Mum wasn't listening. So they went off to the neighbours to spread the news and gossip about it. 'Never agen!' I heard one of them say. 'The little buggers 'ave eat us out of 'ouse an' 'ome.'

This was the first Monday I'd seen Mum washing alone at the washtub. The women always did their washing in pairs, but on this day the rest were too busy pulling everybody to pieces. Mum was pleased because it gave her more time to get the clothes dried and into the pawnshop before Dad returned for his meal. Once or twice I went upstairs to keep an eye on Granny, but she was fast asleep and peaceful. I also ventured down the cellar stairs to see how Hoppity was. He too was asleep and although I did think he might be dead I could see the rise and fall of his belly. I had a sudden thought. What if he woke up and wanted a drink? So I emptied the soapy water out from the only tin bowl we had, and filled it full of fresh water for him.

Later, in the warm of the late evening, I helped Mum fold and mangle the dry clothes and while she was away at the pawnshop I set to and peeled the potatoes. We were having a treat that night – corned beef and mash. I placed a clean newspaper on the table and arranged the tin plates. The potatoes were already cooked when Mum came in with her apron full of goodies. Two loaves, margarine, a tin of condensed milk and, of course, the corned beef.

Mum counted the plates and then said to me, 'Mek yer gran some more gruel. Do 'er more good while she's in bed.'

I made it, and when I took it upstairs I found she was still sleeping soundly. So I left her meagre meal on the marble-topped table in case she woke and was hungry. I felt sorry for my gran. She seemed to be unloved, just like me. I heard Jack's footsteps outside the door.

'Wipe yer feet!' was Mum's greeting.

When Jack saw the cap over her eye he burst out laughing.

'Yer better put it on straight before the old man comes in. 'E'll notice it anyway. Yer carn't hide an eye like that.'

'Sit down, an' stop yer staring, all on yer!'

She was in an awful mood. Mary wouldn't be home till late, so I sat on her chair next to Jack. Frankie and Liza sat on the other side of the table and we waited for Dad to come in. Soon we heard him scraping his boots on the mat and Mum began slapping mashed potatoes and paper-thin corned beef on to the plates.

Dad looked round at us all and said, 'I'm glad you and the kids are home, Polly. I've missed you all.'

Mum was careful to present her unbruised cheek for him to kiss for obvious reasons, but his attention was caught by the cap. 'Yer want to get yer cap straight, Polly. You look like an out-a-work navvy,' he teased.

'Navvy am I now?' She straightened herself to her full height but her quick temper had found her out again because Dad saw her eye for the first time.

'How did yer get that?' he demanded.

'I fell down,' she snapped back at him. 'Now sit yer down an' get yer supper before it's cold.'

He left it at that, and went to the sink to wash his hands.

'Where's the bowl, Polly?' he asked.

'On the stool under the sink where I always keep it,' she answered impatiently.

It was then that I forgot my promise and blurted out, 'I'm sorry, Mum. I took it down the cellar to give Hoppity a—' But I didn't get any further. Jack gave me such a hard dig with his elbow that I screamed with pain.

'What's going on 'ere?' Dad demanded of Jack as I began to weep.

Mum tried to change the subject and told Dad to get on with his dinner while she fetched it.

'No yer don't! I want to know what's going on first.'

He stood beside the table in his shirtsleeves waiting for an answer. He was in a temper by now. His face was red and he banged down his fist like a crack from a gun. The potatoes jumped into the air and rolled on to the floor. At that moment there was a knock at the door and voices called for Frankie and Liza. They could see that something unpleasant was about to happen, and they guessed that they were better off out of it, so they ran out before anyone could stop them. I stayed behind because I wanted to see what Dad was going to do with Hoppity when he found out about him.

'What's all the secrecy about the cellar, and why did Katie take the bowl down there? You may as well tell me because I intend to find out.'

Jack and Mum looked at each other, but neither of them said a word. Dad could see that they weren't going to speak so he went to the door and peered down into the murk.

'What's that down there?' he asked. 'It looks like a pig!'

'Well, Dad, it's like this.' Jack kept stealing a glance at Mum for support. I could see how nervous they looked. 'I was going along the lane to have a drink at this pub, the Pig and Whistle, when I saw this little pig.'

'So it is a pig then, is it?'

'It's only a little one. He was hurt. Someone had put a rag around his leg so I picked him up and put him in the van and drove down towards the farmyard and left him there. But when he started to scream I decided to . . .'

'Go on. You decided what?'

'To give him a couple of sleeping pills. You know the rest.'

I jumped and began to pummel him furiously with my fists. 'You lied to me! You lied to me! And I promised . . .' I screamed. And the tears streamed down my face. Dad lifted me into the air and flopped me back into the chair.

'Now you be quiet. I'll 'ear what you 'ave to say later.'

I'd never seen Dad in such a bad temper. He turned on Jack. 'And what do you intend to do with it?'

'I thought we 'aye 'im for the table or sell him.'

At this, Dad brought his fist down again with a thump. ''Ave yer gone mad?' he bawled. 'I don't want any part of yer thieving ways. I'm warning you, if that pig or whatever you call it ain't out of this 'ouse when I come home tomorrow night I'll throw you out with it . . . for good!'

'Don't be too 'ard on 'im, Sam. 'E was only thinkin' of us,' Mum said, weeping some more.

'You can turn yer tap off, Polly. I suppose you've lied as well about that black eye,' Dad said. He turned his back on her.

Then Jack promised he would ask his gaffer to lend him the van again and make some excuse to take the pig back as soon as it was dark.

'Who else knows about this, Polly?' Dad asked.

'Only me, Jack and Katie.'

'What about Frankie, Liza and Mother?'

'No. They don't know. They just slept in the van,' she replied, wiping her eyes on her apron.

'Well, where's Mother now?' Dad wanted to know.

'She's upstairs asleep.'

Dad stared at her. 'I suppose you've given her a tablet, too?'

'No,' Jack answered for her, shaking his head. 'I took her upstairs. She's got a bad cold.'

'I don't wonder at it. I warned yer not go in the first place, but I never thought you'd do this.'

Jack tried to calm him down and repeated that he'd sort things out. Dad was still very angry. 'Don't yer forget what I've told yer. That pig goes back to the farm.' Jack didn't say anything. He just gave me a look good enough to kill, then banged the door behind him, and rattled the window frame.

Dad's face was still grim and he told me to sit in the chair. 'Now, Katie, yer sure Granny nor Frankie nor Liza don't know about the pig?'

'Yes, Dad, they were fast asleep.'

Dad opened the door and called out for Frankie and Liza to come inside. They both looked puzzled and wondered what had been going on, but they were used to quarrels and few secrets remained secrets very long in our close little yard so they weren't very bothered.

I got the small brush and shovel that were kept in the fender and cleared up the mess. While I emptied the remains of our meal on to the fire, Liza helped Mum to prepare some cheese and onions.

Mum didn't say a word but instead she slapped everything down on the table until Dad could stand it no longer and warned her to make less noise and let him read his paper in peace. When we'd all eaten our supper of dry bread and cheese Frankie and Liza went to bed, leaving me to clear away the supper plates and lay the table for the morning. I was about to reach for my piece of candle and follow the others when Dad stopped me.

'Before you go I want another word with yer.'

What does he want now? I thought. I stood at the foot of the stairs wishing I was in bed. Butterflies fluttered about in my stomach and I was scared.

'Now, Katie,' he said quietly, 'I want yer to keep this a secret – about yer brother and this pig.' I kept nodding my head as he continued, 'Jack'll take it back to the farm where it came from or 'e'll be put in prison if 'e's found out. So you understand why yer not to tell a soul?'

'Yes, Dad,' I nodded. Then suddenly I remembered how Hoppity was always getting lost.

'Dad, I think Jack'll get him back before 'e's missed because 'e was always wandering off and getting lost.'

'How do you know?' Dad asked.

'Mrs Onions, the farmer's wife, told me.'

Dad smiled and said he hoped Jack would get him back in time.

Frankie and Liza were asleep. I sat down on the bed to undress. Then, as I removed my stocking, I discovered the tanner Jack had given me. I placed it on my hand and wondered if I should give it back. But I took a second look at it and resolved to keep it as payment for the lies I'd been told. As bad luck would have it, as I was blowing the candle out the sixpence fell and rolled down a crack in the floorboards. There was nothing I could do in the dark, so I crept into bed and wept. I felt sorry for myself; everything seemed to happen to me, but I consoled myself with the thought that I might find the sixpence in the morning.

I was first down next morning after Dad and Jack had gone to work. I lit the fire and filled the kettle ready to put on the hob. Then I went down to the cellar to take a last look at Hoppity. I was sorry for the little pig and wondered what would happen to him. When my eyes grew accustomed to the dark I could see that he wasn't there. All that was left was the straw he'd lain on. Jack must have taken him in the middle of the night, and I was glad really for all our sakes. Perhaps there would be no more rows now. And there was none, for a while at least.

One afternoon, not long after our return from the country, Mum, Liza and I entered our yard to be greeted by a tremendous commotion. There in the middle of the yard were Mrs Phipps, Mrs Taylor, Mrs Jones, Mrs Buckley, Mrs Huggett and Maggie Bumpham and a few more besides from the next yard, all nattering away, nodding their heads together. Jonesy and Freddie, the twins and Annie, were running around listening to the conversation as they played. However, as soon as they heard Mum's heavy tread they turned their heads and stared at us. Mum seemed to know at once that they were talking about us. They moved away when she marched up to them. Standing with her hands on her hips, her head thrown back, she shouted out for them all to hear, 'What yer gotta say, yer say it to me face!'

All the kids scattered when they saw Mum but none spoke. Everything went dead silent as Mum waited for someone to speak. Then Maggie moved away from the rest and said from the safety of her doorstep, 'Do yer really want ter know, Polly?'

'What yer think I'm waitin' for?' she replied angrily.

'Well, these lot 'ave told me yow've pinched a pig but I don't believe 'em, Polly,' she stammered. Mum glared at her, knowing she was as big a gossip as the rest, but Maggie went on to finish what she had to say. 'An' the farmer's goin' ter 'ave yer all arrested.'

It was clear that Mum had to deny it there and then to save us from prison. 'Yer must be mad, the lot on yer! They can come an' search my 'ouse as soon as they like. We ain't got no pig. 'Ave we?' she said turning to me.

I noticed how pale she'd gone but I kept up the act.

'No, Mum,' and Frankie called out, 'Yow lot 'ave pinched it and are trying to blame us.'

Mum shut him up with a clout across his face but that didn't stop him sticking his tongue out at them. Then Mrs Phipps spoke up for all the others.

'Well, Polly,' she began timidly, 'what was we to tell the farmer? You left while we were fast asleep. Dain't they, Mrs Jones?'

'Yes,' came the reply. 'And yower Jack made sure we would get to sleep when he give us that whisky.'

'Believe what yer like!' Mum shouted back.

But as we turned to enter our house, Jonesy shouted out, 'I bet it's yower Frankie that's pinched the pig!'

At this there was a scuffle and a fight broke out, as Frankie pitched in and soon they were rolling on the ground. Mum stepped in and dragged Frankie off because he was holding Jonesy down and it was obvious he'd had enough. But that didn't stop her giving Jonesy an extra-sly dig before parting them.

News travelled quickly in our neighbourhood and when Mum gave me sixpence to go to the grocer's to get some vegetables every-one glared and whispered as I passed. When I entered the shop it was full of women chatting. I stood just inside the door and watched them and listened to snatches of their conversation.

'Common lot, them 'op-pickers,' I heard one say.

'Wonder who they were?' said another.

'Don't yer know? They live up the top end.'

'I hear they stole a pig.'

'Yes, an' it only 'ad three legs.'

'Somebody told me they'd tried to chop the other one off!'

'Did yer know the police are goin' ter arrest 'em?'

'Serves 'em right. They ought to get life.'

I was so scared I didn't wait to hear any more but backed quietly out of the shop and, still clutching the bag and the sixpence tight in my hand, I ran crying back home. I tumbled through the door and began gabbling my story. Mum looked pale when I told her word for word what had been said.

'It's that Mrs Phipps and the Joneses that's got all this about. Now listen to me, Katie. Jack's took the pig back during the night. The farmer is sure ter find 'im an' nobody will be any the wiser. So if anybody asks yer about it, yer don't know anythink. Understand? If you don't we'll all goo ter prison.'

'I won't say a word, really I won't. Really,' I sobbed.

'Now wipe yer eyes before the others come in. And give me the sixpence. I'll goo ter the shop meself.' Then she went off with the bag under her arm. I hoped and prayed that afternoon that my brother really had taken the pig back to the farm, but I had my doubts.

Two days later, Mum said she had to do some shopping. I busied myself tidying up the house when I became aware of Mrs Jones talking outside the door.

'That's the house. They live there, mister.'

There were three loud raps on the door. I went to the window and lifted the corner of the curtain. I saw a policeman and a man in plain clothes who I later discovered was a detective. He wore a collar and tie and a bowler hat, like Dad's on the wall. I trembled when I realised who they were. Slowly, I dropped the curtain and crept down to the cellar to hide, but they continued knocking. I was terrified they'd find me and take me away, so I crouched in the darkest corner I could find. I was so scared by now that I'd wet my bloomers.

Then I heard a deep voice above say, 'Very well. We'll call again,' and their heavy tread on the cellar grating as they walked away from the house. After a while I came out of the cellar and could hear the neighbours and their kids outside our door. Off down the broken stairs I went again, too scared to cry.

Just then, I heard Mum's voice bellow out, 'What's gooin' on 'ere?'

'Two policemen 'ave been to see yer,' Mrs Buckley informed her, smugly.

'What yer bawling about? Clear off before I throw this bucket of water over yer all.'

There was the sound of general scattering footsteps. They knew well that Mum meant what she said. Then the door slammed and I came up to find Mum slumped in the armchair, crying into her apron. When she heard me come in she jumped up from the chair with fright.

'Where've yow sprang from?' she asked. 'Yer nearly frightened the daylights out of me.' Then, quite unexpectedly, she did what I'd always wanted her to do: she drew me to her and hugged me, and with our arms round each other we both wept. I was weeping because I was happy and felt safe at last in my mother's arms, but I knew she was weeping over Jack. She told me he'd been arrested and would be tried the next day. I plucked up courage and asked what was going to happen to us. I pressed her to assure myself that everything would be all right.

'What are we going to do to help him, Mum?'

' 'E's goin' to deny 'e ever seen the pig, and I think that's the best way out.'

I looked at her, surprised. 'But, Mum, he did,' I exclaimed. 'You know he did and I know he did. It will be worse if he tells lies.'

Then she sat me down in Dad's chair and faced me. 'Now, Katie, listen to what I'm goin' ter say. Jack is your brother and my son an' we've talked this over before he was arrested. That's the best thing to do an' he might well get away with it. Now, Katie, promise me you won't say a word about this to anyone.' Her eyes were full of tears as she pleaded, but I didn't ponder too much on the significance of what was happening. I was too happy and felt on top of the world at the thought that Mum really loved me, so I promised. Then she sat me on her lap once again and kissed me.

'Yes,' I said again. 'I'll even lie if I have to.' I felt I was really wanted at last and would have done anything.

Dad came home later that evening looking like thunder. He neither spoke nor appeared to notice us, but flung himself into his chair. When I went out into the yard for a bowl of water for his wash they started arguing. I heard, 'It ain't my fault the gaffer's put our wages down and put us on short-time,' then I entered.

I watched Mum's eyes raised to the ceiling. Then she erupted. 'Oh my God! Double trouble!'

Dad sat down calmly, lit his pipe, then asked me to give him his specs and began to read his paper. Mum went red in the face as she tried to control her temper. 'Yer don't care, do yer? An' what about poor Jack?'

'Poor Jack!' he burst out. 'I've heard all I want to hear about poor Jack from my workmates. And I'll tell you another thing. He don't darken this door again while I'm here. Now, I don't want to hear any more about poor Jack.'

I thought how unkind and hard he was to talk to Mum this way. I felt so sorry for her, she was very upset. She'd been crying on and off all day. I tried to say something, hoping it might help, but I couldn't get my words out and began to cry too. My eyes were sore and my head ached and I didn't want to be around when Granny returned home because I knew there'd be more trouble. So I told Mum I didn't feel well and asked if I could go to bed.

'Yes, Katie. An' be up early in the morning,' she replied pleasantly.

I lay on my back staring at the ceiling, wondering why Mum was being so kind to me. Things were suddenly changing in unexpected and inexplicable ways and I was no longer being beaten and shouted at. I tried to fathom it out, and then suddenly everything fell into place like pieces of a jigsaw puzzle. I sat up in bed. Yes, that's it, I thought. Mum knew I'd been awake that night in the barn when they were planning what to do and that I'd heard them scheming to drug Hoppity with sleeping pills. Then I felt very miserable again. I also knew how she'd come by that black eye. Yes, that was why she was so nice to me. She was afraid I might tell Dad the truth. But while I kept my promise she would think twice now before hitting me again. The knowledge of this secret between us made me feel happier and with this comforting thought I fell asleep.

Chapter 13

Our Jack's Trial

After Dad had gone off to work next morning we got ourselves ready to go to the courts to see our Jack's trial. I watched Mum in the mirror putting on her Sunday best, her stiff, starched pinafore, over her shabby alpaca frock. Then she twisted her hair into a bun on top of her head and reached for Dad's flat, grey cap that was hanging behind the door. She put it on the bun and glanced in the mirror to see how she looked. All at once she snatched the cap off and slung it across the room.

'That don't look right,' she said, completing her preening.

Granny too was busy getting dressed. After she had put on her uniform she tied on her bonnet. Mum saw what she was doing. 'Yow ain't gooin' in that get-up. Put summat else on.'

'No!' Granny shouted back, 'an' yer carn't mek me. An' I'm gooin'. I'm one of the witnesses.'

Mum didn't answer, she just shrugged her shoulders, tut-tutted and shook her head. Liza and me were already waiting to go, but Frankie too had to give a finishing touch to his wiry hair with a dab of dripping from the basin. Then off we went, closing the door behind us.

We knew everyone in the district, and they knew us, so the incident of Jack and the alleged theft of the pig was the topic of the hour. However, we never expected the scene that greeted us outside. All our neighbours were there dressed to kill and waiting to follow us to the courts. There was Mrs Phipps with the same old moth-eaten fur coat which was supposed to be real skunk. She also had a flat cap on. She was talking quietly to Mrs Buckley who had on her black, dusty velvet coat which brought her in a steady income from the tuppence fee she charged when she loaned it out for funerals, and she had her old, flat straw hat with the wax fruit on top. Mrs Jones wore a boater on her red hair and a brown, coarse-looking frock which dragged to the floor. All the while she chatted with her two friends she kept swinging an orange-coloured boa round her neck, and the loose feathers flew everywhere. They stopped whispering when they saw us. Mum stared at them.

'Yow lot ain't comin' with us,' she cried out haughtily, throwing her head back.

'But we're witnesses. Yer carn't stop us. The copper came an' told us we 'ad to goo an' give information on what we know. Dain't 'e, Mrs Jones?'

'Yes,' said Mrs Jones meekly. 'An' if we don't 'urry we'll be late.'

'Plenty a time,' Granny told them. 'Yow can goo in front.'

I could see she didn't want to walk with them either. Nor did I. To my mind they were three gossiping, spiteful old women and I was scared to think what they might say if they were called to give evidence. So off they went, leaving us behind.

When we arrived at the courts, Granny and Mum were out of breath. We struggled up the steps and entered a spacious hall. I looked around and noticed four glass doors leading into different courtrooms. Mum was already peeping through the first one when a policeman crept up behind her and tapped her on the shoulder. She turned round and told him who we were and whose case we were concerned about. He asked us to follow him and he ushered us into courtroom two. We trailed in, in single file, with Granny bringing up the rear. When the policeman saw Granny's Salvation Army uniform he spoke to her very politely.

'This way, madam.' And he took her arm and led her to a seat.

The trial was in progress, but I didn't listen to what the judge was saying because I was too busy looking at the people round me. On the left side was the farmer and his wife and the farmer's brother, the man who'd taken us to the hop fields in his hay cart. Next to him sat a middle-aged man, very smartly dressed, in top hat, black cape and with a silver-topped cane. Then I saw my brother, looking as charming as ever as he stood in the dock. My gaze settled on the judge who peered sternly over the top of his spectacles. He towered over us in an upright, high-backed chair. Below, sitting at a long, oblong table, were several sombre-looking men, writing down what everyone was saying. The voices seemed to echo in this dismal, dark, dusty room with its oak-panelled walls. Mrs Phipps, Mrs Jones and Mrs Buckley sat in the row behind us. I'd never seen them sit so quietly.

When Frankie saw Jack he jumped up, waved and called out, 'Hello, Jack.' Everybody turned their heads just like they do when watching a tennis match. It went dead quiet for a couple of seconds. Then the judge broke the silence. His voice boomed out to the constable standing by the door.

'Remove that lad at once!'

Frankie didn't wait to be removed. He ran out, and Liza followed him. I would've liked to have gone too, but I couldn't move. Once more there was silence, but just as the judge began to speak again Granny decided she wanted to go to the lavatory. She moved towards the door quickly and asked the constable where it was and I saw him smile as he whispered loudly that she'd find it in the hall. It was clear that the judge was not amused. He sat bolt upright in his chair and frowned at us over his glasses. I followed Granny out. The hall was nearly empty now, apart from the old policeman darting about from one room to another. Frankie was sitting on a bench reading a comic. We couldn't see the lavatory anywhere. Then Granny spotted another door tucked away in a dark corner.

'What's it say on theea?'

'Private Chambers,' I answered.

'Well goo an' ask 'em if I can borrow one of 'em or I'll burst in a minute,' she complained, holding herself.

I was just as ignorant as she was. I thought they were chambers like the one we had under our bed. I was just about to ask a policeman, when a young lady came out of the courtroom. She could see Granny crossing and uncrossing her legs and said, 'It's over there in the corner. Mind the steps.'

Granny dived down the half-dozen steps for dear life, but when she tried the door it was locked from the inside and smoke was coming over the top of the door. Granny banged on the door and yelled out, ''Ow long yer gooin' ter be?' She was hopping from one foot to the other, but there was no reply. 'If yer don't 'urry up I'll do it on the floowa.'

I was scared stiff in case she did and I knew Granny might. Then the door opened and Granny rushed past the previous occupant, nearly knocking her over, flopped down on the seat and kicked the door shut. I couldn't look at the woman, I was so ashamed. When she started to ascend the steps I looked at her and saw the back half of the prettiest drawers I'd ever seen. I was fascinated by this but felt too shy to tell her. Yet if I didn't she'd be out of the door and it would too late. When she reached the top step I ran up after her and cried out, 'Lady, you've tucked your frock into the back of your drawers.'

Like a flash, she pulled the remainder of the dress out and when she turned to thank me I could see it was Mr Skinny-Legs's wife. I hadn't recognised her at first, she looked so pretty in her blue dress with matching gloves and a pretty blue picture hat with lace trimmings. She thanked me kindly and asked how Jack's case was going. I said I didn't know and then, struck with curiosity, asked why she was here too.

'I came to see Jack, but I'm afraid I'm too late. Anyhow, I'll wait outside until we know the result.'

I was just going to ask how she knew about our troubles when Granny emerged from the cubicle. 'Don't yer let me see yer talking to that brazen 'uzzy,' she said, dragging me out of the doorway.

I had to obey and we returned to the courtroom, Granny to be escorted by the policeman to her seat, and me making my way as best I could to my place on the bench. Mrs Jones was in the witness-box giving evidence. There seemed to be something different about her, but I couldn't put my finger on it. It wasn't her clothes because I'd seen her dressed in these same clothes as far back as I could remember. She looked pale against the orange boa.

'No, sir,' I heard her saying to the judge.

'But you said you saw the prisoner that night with the van.'

She didn't answer, but began to fidget. Then she burst out, 'Phew! It's 'ot in 'ere!'

She pushed her boater back on her head and I could see why she looked so strange. She was wearing a big red wig and as she pushed the boater back the wig went with it. People in the court began to titter.

'Silence!' the judge boomed. He turned once more to Mrs Jones and told her to listen to him. 'Now, did you see the prisoner at any time with the pig?'

'No, sir. After I 'ad the whisky I fell asleep. Yer see I was worn out an' tired. I'd bin . . .'

'That will be enough,' the judge interrupted, drumming his fingers. 'We're getting nowhere. You may stand down.'

'Thank you, sir,' she said, getting down from the box. 'I wish I could tell yer mower but the truth is I don't know mower.'

He waved her away and called out sharply to the constable at the door.

It was Mrs Phipps's turn. All eyes followed her as she made her way noisily towards the witness-box. She climbed the steps and stood waiting. She looked very frightened, and held the rail to steady herself. I'd seen her and Mrs Buckley having a nip or two of gin from a medicine bottle before they went in. The officer handed her a Bible and asked her to read the words that were written on a card. Everyone was so quiet now you could have heard a pin drop as he waited for her to begin.

'I carn't read,' she said in a hoarse whisper.

'Very well. Repeat after me.'

She repeated what he said word for word. Then she kissed the Bible and handed it back and looked across at the judge.

'You are Amelia Emily Phipps?'

'Yes, sir.' She nodded vigorously.

'Now, did you, on the night in question, see the prisoner with—'

'Can I sit down, sir?' she interrupted. 'Me legs are killin' me. Yer see I've got varcus veins an' if I stand too much they'll bust. I'll show yer if yer don't believe me!' she babbled, hitching up her frock at the same time.

The judge looked across at her and cleared his throat noisily. 'Sit down and answer the questions.' He was red in the face and as he frowned his shaggy eyebrows pushed his glasses to the tip of his nose. He looked over the top of them at us lot in the court. 'Silence!' he shouted. 'Or I'll clear the court.'

Silence descended once again and he began slowly and deliberately: 'Now, Mrs Amelia Emily Phipps, I want you to tell me in your own words, and truthfully, what you saw on the night in question. Did you see the prisoner with the pig?'

'No, no. I dain't. I only told 'im I thought Jack 'ad took it.'

'You're a liar,' the farmer shouted across to her.

Suddenly there was a sharp crack as the judge brought down his gavel on to the desk in front of him. He banged it down several times before he got any kind of order.

'Now,' he said, addressing Mrs Phipps. 'I want you to tell me in your own words, and truthfully, what you saw on this particular night. Did you see the prisoner or anybody else with the pig?'

'No, sir! No, sir!' she repeated, and shook her head so fiercely that the cap seemed about to fly off.

'Did you tell the farmer that you knew who had stolen the pig?'

'No! No! I dain't. I only told 'im I *thought* Jack 'ad took it.'

Again the farmer called her a liar. Again the judge struggled to re-establish order.

'Now,' he said to the farmer, 'if I don't get some kind of order I shall dismiss the case at once.'

There was dead silence once more, not a whisper from anyone. Then glaring at her, with the gavel still clutched in his hand, he waved Mrs Phipps from the witness-box. 'Step down! I'll question you again later.'

He blew his nose hard, making a noise like a trumpet. Then he called the farmer to the witness-stand. Again the judge blew his nose and cleared his throat.

'Are you Mr Henry William Onions?'

'Yes, sir,' he answered.

'Now do you recognise the prisoner?'

'No, sir,' he answered at once.

'No? You mean to say that you don't know him?'

'I've never seen him before.'

The judge started drumming his fingers hard, with obvious impatience. 'If you say you have never seen this man before, how is it that he is charged with stealing the pig?'

The farmer jumped up and pointing across at Mrs Phipps shouted, 'She told me. She said she saw him put it in the van.'

All eyes turned in her direction as Mrs Phipps jumped up and denied his accusation. Once more the gavel banged down with enough force it seemed to split the desk.

'Put that woman outside!' the judge instructed the constable at the door.

She was led out and Mrs Buckley and Mrs Jones walked out in sympathy. Mum, Granny and I sat very still, too scared to move. I was trembling and so afraid that I might be called next to answer their questions. How could I lie to such a flint-faced man? His eyes penetrated you when he looked at you.

Then he sat back in his high chair and fixed my brother with his cold stare. 'Now, begin at the beginning.'

Jack looked handsome as he stood up to his full height and began. 'My father received a letter from my sister Kathleen to say would he fetch them all home as they were sleeping all together on bags of straw and they were all hungry. This is the letter, sir,' Jack said, and handed it to the constable to give to the judge. He read it and placed it on the desk and then spoke slowly.

'You were saying?'

'They were very short of money and food and—'

'That's a lie!' the farmer shouted. 'The missus gave—'

Down came the gavel again. 'Silence!' The court resounded. 'If I have any more interruptions I shall close the case.'

The farmer sat down, looking furious. Then the judge told Jack to continue. He sounded to me as if he'd rehearsed the answer over and over again. He spoke easily, without hesitation.

'My father asked me to fetch them home. I asked my boss if he would kindly lend me the works van, which he did. So that same night I drove to the farm, but when I knocked at the farmhouse door there was no answer. Then I drove up to the barn and found my mother and her friends. I told my mother I had come to take them back home.'

'Go on,' the judge said, looking Jack squarely in the eye.

'I drove the van along to the Pig and Whistle to have a drink of cider, and to see if I could find out where the farmer was, but when

I inquired no one knew. The first time I saw him was when I was arrested, sir.'

'What happened after you left the public house?'

'I drove back. Everyone was asleep bar my mother. I asked her to wake my granny and my two sisters and brother. Then we all got into the van. That's the God's truth, sir.'

I waited for him to explain how the pig came to be in the van but he didn't mention it.

'Why didn't you wait to see the farmer and explain why you were taking these people away?' the judge asked.

'I hung about until after midnight, sir, but we had to go. I had to be in work by six o'clock the next morning and I'd promised to take the van back.'

The men in black who sat round the table were writing down what he said, word for word. Then the judge stopped drumming his fingers and stroked his chin. He looked first at Jack, then at the farmer and then round the room at the rest of us. I knew, and so did my mum, that Jack had lied and that if he were ever found out we would all go to prison. If only my dad was with me I would have felt safer. I knew I wouldn't be able to face that man's steel-grey eyes without speaking the truth. So I made up my mind to dash out, but just as I started to get up off the bench Mum caught hold of my plaits and pulled me down again. I prayed to myself and began to cry.

The judge was speaking again. 'Do you wish to question the . . .'

The farmer was angry now, and he interrupted the judge again. 'If he ain't had my pig, well, who has? Tell me that!'

Once more I put my hands to my ears as the gavel banged loudly. The judge had finally snapped and he was furious. 'Case dismissed. Clear the court!'

My prayer had been answered and I didn't have to give evidence. I didn't stay to see the people leave. I flew out of there as fast as I could. I saw Frankie in the hall talking to the woman with the pretty frilly drawers and when she saw me she asked how my brother had got on. I told her the case had been dismissed. She smiled at me and sat down beside Frankie who was more interested in his comic than in Jack's fate. Then I saw Jack, Mum and Granny, beaming big smiles, coming towards us. Jack had eyes for no one but his fancy piece, as Granny called her. Almost at once I felt that I never wanted to see him again and I couldn't stop myself tugging at his coat tail and upbraiding him.

'You lied, Jack. I won't ever believe you again.'

But he only grinned at me and put his hand in his trouser pocket and drew out a handful of change and selected a silver sixpence for me. He pushed it into my hand and it occurred to me that this was the second sixpence he'd given me. The other one was still under the floorboards beside my bed. This second gift made me even madder. To think he couldn't trust me to keep his secret without bribing me. I looked down at the sixpence in my hand and wondered what I could do with it. Then I heard Jack say, 'Come on, Lil. Let's go across the road and have a drink.'

Then I decided. I threw the sixpence down and called after Jack, 'I don't want yer sixpence, and you can have the other one back when I find it!'

I watched it roll across the floor and before Mum could stoop to retrieve it, Frankie had beaten her to it. He put it quickly in his pocket and ran off. Granny, who hadn't noticed what had happened, said she was going after Jack to have a gin to warm her up. However, Mum wasn't interested. She dragged me by the hand down the street. Passers-by could hear every word she uttered in her harsh, loud voice.

'What yer do that for? Come on! You bin 'iding money away from me, ain't yer?'

'No. I ain't yer,' I mimicked.

By now people were stopping and staring at Mum who was shaking me violently. But I didn't care any more what she said or did because I'd found the courage to answer her back. Suddenly I broke away from her and shouted that the sixpence was under the floorboards and then I took to my heels and tore down the street. Mum didn't follow me, but turned and marched off into the pub.

It was late in the afternoon by this time and I was hungry. I regretted throwing the sixpence away. Still, I think I'd have tossed a sovereign back at him, if Jack had given me one. Anyway, it was idle speculation to think about the tanner because Frankie had probably spent it by now. Then I had a thought: I would stand outside Mrs Gingold's window and if she saw me she might give me a twist of batter scratchings. I hurried along and turning the corner, I came face to face with Frankie eating fish and chips which he'd bought with the sixpence. My eyes fixed on them and my mouth began to water.

'Here, have a chip.'

I grabbed a few before he changed his mind, and stuffed them in my mouth. He was annoyed. 'Here, have 'em all,' he said, handing me the remains. 'I'll go back and get some more.'

I sat down and finished them off and it didn't take long either. I was so hungry I even licked the vinegar off the paper. Then Frankie came back and let me help him with the second lot.

Frankie still had tuppence left and that he shared with me too. I felt better when my belly had stopped rumbling. We strolled along together and Frankie didn't say a word. I was glad, really. I thought that at any moment he would ask me about the pig. Then Jonesy ran up and they went off together, leaving me standing alone. There was nothing left to do except return home to face Mum. If there had been any other place to go I would have gone willingly. But I knew that wherever I went in our district people would ask me all sorts of questions, and I had no idea how I would answer them. When I got indoors there was nobody there, so I sat down to wait for Mum. I'd only been there a few moments when I heard a noise like boards creaking and I dashed upstairs.

'Is that you, Mum?'

'Yes,' she called back. 'Come up 'ere. I want yer!'

When I reached the attic door I wasn't surprised to see that she'd lifted the boards.

'Where did yer say it was?'

'There.'

I pointed to the one beside the bed where there was a large crack. I knew she wanted the sixpence badly. She went on her hands and knees as best she could. The loose board came away in her hand when she tugged at it, for it was rotten and half eaten away. She felt around in the open gap but didn't find the tanner until she'd placed several piles of fluff and dust beside the bed first. I went back downstairs, wondering if all mothers were like mine. I knew we were living through very hard times, but we were a little better off than some. My dad was working, after all, but you only had to mention money and Mum was all ears. She counted every penny on the fingers of her left hand. When it came to farthings I always did the reckoning, but the Lord help me if she discovered I'd made a mistake. She followed me downstairs and when I looked at her I could see she was pleased with herself.

'Get the bag and fetch some stewin' meat and vegetables. We'll 'ave a nice pot o' stew fer yer dad when 'e comes 'ome.'

She never bothered about us kids all day but it was always the same, 'yer dad must 'ave this', and 'yer brother must 'ave the other', until I was sick and tired of the sound of her voice.

Then I saw her self-satisfied grin and I said defiantly, 'No! I'm not going! That sixpence belongs to me.'

Like a shot she raised her hand to strike me, but before it came down I backed away. 'If you dare hit me again, I'll tell Dad, Mary and everybody else about that night in the barn and about the pig!'

She turned pale and her hand dropped to her side. Flopping down in the chair, she demanded, 'Come 'ere!'

'No!' I gripped the door knob, ready to run out.

'Come 'ere,' she said, 'I'm not gooin' ter 'it yer any more.'

Slowly I edged towards her. She changed her tone of voice and smiled at me. 'Get me yer dad's cap off the door, an' the bag. I'll goo meself.'

I couldn't believe my ears. I had actually defied her and she'd done nothing to me. Quickly I reached down the cap and handed her the shopping bag and, keeping my distance in case she changed her mind, I watched her push the cap on the back of her head and march out without another word. I was sure she was going to punish me when she returned but I determined to disappear until Dad came home. Frankie and Liza always did that and got away with it. Then I thought, if I don't have my punishment she'll never forget. She always said, 'There, that's what I owe yer,' when you were least expecting it. That was one reason why I was always nervous. I was sure she didn't love me, and at times I think I hated her, although at others I was sorry for her. After all, I was lucky to have a mum of any kind, some kids round our way had no mother at all.

After she'd left for the shop, I tried to think what I could do to please her. Then it dawned on me that I needn't bother. I had the secret of why she had a black eye and I knew all about the pig. It was this secret that stopped her from hitting me and she was afraid I would break my promise and tell Dad. I realised that I had a weapon to defend myself with and I made up my mind to use it whenever I needed to.

I jumped up from the chair but I sat down again quickly. I could hardly see. There were little flashes of light in front of my eyes. I felt sick and there was a nasty taste in my throat. I rushed for the bowl but it had dirty clothes in it. I couldn't use the sink either, it had the crocks in it, so I rushed outside with my hand to my mouth. I didn't want to retch in the yard in full public view, so I ran down towards the lavatory. But Frankie and his friends were kicking a can about and I felt too weak to brazen my way past them. I leaned against the wall and Annie Buckley approached me.

'What's the matter with yower Katie, Frankie?'

'Yow ain't 'alf white!' I heard someone say.

Then the gang round me parted and Maggie Bumpham pushed her way towards me. 'My God!' she said, but her voice sounded far away. 'Yer look as if yer dyin' an' yer white as a ghost! What's the matter with yer?' She put her hand on my forehead and roughly pulled my eyelids apart and peered into my eyes. She propped me against the wall and fetched out a backless chair for me to sit on. The flashes subsided and I became aware of my surroundings. Maggie pushed my head back and poured salt water down my throat. The kids crowded round to watch the performance. I lurched out of the chair and tried to spit it out but I'd already swallowed most of it. I tried to run away, but before I could, she grabbed me and told Jonesy and Frankie to hold me down. Then, while I struggled, she pushed her grimy fingers down my throat as far as she could. I thought I would choke. I heaved twice. Then the only meal I'd had that day slid down the drain. I felt better when my stomach had emptied and the flashes subsided.

I looked to Frankie for sympathy but got no support.

'You shouldn't 'ave bin so greedy with the chips,' was all he said.

They continued playing their game and I walked indoors. I looked in the bit of cracked mirror on the wall. I was still very pale but I felt better when I sat back in Dad's chair. Soon after Mum walked in. She looked tired and harassed and she didn't look my way. She knew I was there but she didn't speak, and had her back to me. She tipped the food on to the scrubbed table top. I watched her sorting things out.

'Mum,' I said. But she didn't answer.

'Mum,' I repeated. 'I'm sorry. I won't tell anyone or say a word to Dad. Really I won't, Mum.'

Then she turned and faced me. 'What yer bin dooin'?' She saw how pale I was. 'Are yer sickenin' fer summat?'

'I've been sick, Mum,' I said.

But I said nothing else, only that I was feeling better.

'Very well. You can 'elp me get yer dad's tea ready.'

'Can I peel the potatoes, Mum?' I asked, eager to make it up with her.

'No! I want 'em cut thin. Yer can scrape the carrots while I skin this rabbit.'

I watched her hang the rabbit by its two back legs from a convenient nail and with two deft tugs she had it skinned. I began scraping the carrots at one end of the table while she chopped up the rabbit into small portions at the other. I didn't look at her, but I could feel her eyes on me all the time. When she'd completely dismembered the rabbit and it was in the pot she sat down and called me over to her. Now I'm for it, I thought.

'But I haven't finished the carrots yet.'

'Never mind about them. I want ter talk ter yer.'

I slowly edged round the table towards her.

'Now,' she began looking me straight in the eye. 'Yer remember what yer said this afternoon? About 'ow yer was gooin' ter tell yer dad?'

I was too afraid to answer, so I nodded several times and all the time she fixed me with her stare.

'An' do yer remember yer made me a promise not ter tell yer dad?'

I nodded again.

'Well,' she continued. 'I'm gooin' ter promise yow this. If yer'll keep yer promise not to say a word to 'im or anybody else about the pig or anythink what's 'appened, I'll never 'it yer again.'

I threw my arms round her and said all in a rush, 'I'll never tell a soul, cross my heart, Mum, and hope to die!'

'All right! All right! she answered and impatiently pulled my arms from round her neck and waved me away.

It was not many minutes before Dad came in, closely followed by Frankie, Liza and Granny. Dad washed his hands as usual, picked up his newspaper, took the spectacles I handed him, and proceeded to settle in his chair without a word. I could see he wanted to be left alone but Mum was very fidgety and kept glancing across at him. Then she could contain herself no longer and she burst out with the news.

'He got off, yer know!'

Dad carried on reading.

'Sam!' she persisted, 'our Jack got off, yer know. I told yer 'e never kept that pig. 'E took it back ter the farm.'

Dad slowly looked up over the top of his glasses and stared coldly at Mum. 'I don't want to hear another word about Jack or the pig.'

Then, pushing his glasses back on to the bridge of his nose, he recommenced reading his paper. But Mum couldn't leave well alone. She thought Dad should hear about the court hearing. When Mum was excited about anything she kept on and on until she got every little detail off her chest.

'But, Sam,' she began, but got no further. Dad slapped the paper down, pushed his chair back, and went across to her.

'Now look here, Polly. I don't want to hear any more. I've already heard enough from outsiders. Now get my supper ready, I'm clammed.' I watched him take down the lavatory key and go out into the yard to find a refuge.

After he'd gone out Granny came in and started questioning Mum. 'What's all this fuss about? I knew Jack wouldn't pinch a pig. That farmer's took 'im for somebody else. Still, I'd like to know who did take it, wouldn't you, Polly?' She rambled on and on.

'No I wouldn't!' snapped Mum. 'An' don't yow start!'

Then Granny's temper really exploded. 'Nobody tells me anythink that goos on in this 'ouse. I'll be glad when I can goo back to me own place. An' yer keep yer supper. I'm goooin' ter bed!'

'You're not going anywhere, Mother!' Dad said as he entered. 'You'll sit down with the rest of us and eat. Now, let's not hear another word. And you, Katie, call Liza and Frankie in. It's about time they were here.'

We all sat down round the table and while Mum dished out the food, Granny sat with a self-satisfied smirk on her face. Not another word was spoken and later, when Jack came in, Dad didn't even look at him. In fact he didn't speak to him for days, and each time he returned Dad would deliberately walk out and go to the local for a drink.

Chapter 14

Granny's Funeral

It was a cold, wet, wintry day in November 1913 when the undertaker brought the coffin with Granny inside it to our house. Before he arrived Mum made us children bustle about making the place 'spic-an'-span' to create a better impression on the visitors who were expected to drop by to pay their last respects to the memory of a notable local character. The house was buzzing from early in the morning. Mary had taken the day off work and had washed the curtains but for lack of time to dry them properly had hung them back up wet. The blinds were drawn to darken our downstairs room where the coffin rested on the table in front of the range. Jack and Charlie had turned up and were shuffling about, getting in everyone's way, and Dad lit the candles so that the flickering glow shed an eerie light. My attention was attracted by Granny's big black eyes staring down from her photograph on the wall. To my childish imagination it seemed as if she was still alive to what was happening and was showing her disapproval. I hadn't noticed this picture much while she was alive, but now she was dead it seemed as if her eyes sparkled with the same vitality that they had appeared to possess when I had seen her lying cold on her straw mattress a few days earlier.

Granny had originally come to stay with us while her house

was being fumigated but that had been months before and there was no excuse for her to continue living in our overcrowded home. She was a contrary old woman and a match even for our mum, so it was little surprise to me when one evening after a skirmish Mum had blown up at Dad with more than her normal vehemence.

'I can't stand any mower of 'er. She'll 'ave ter goo,' she stormed as soon as he got through the door. As usual he tried to smooth things over, but Mum was adamant.

'I mean it this time. I can't stand 'er. If 'er don't goo, I goo!'

Looking back with seventy years' hindsight, Dad might have been wiser to have accepted this offer, but things were different before the First World War and couples might quarrel and argue all their married life, as Mum and Dad did, but rarely separated and never divorced. As bad luck would have it, just as Mum was shouting, Granny walked in and surprised them.

'What's all the row about? 'Ave yer med up yer minds ter be rid of me?' she demanded. Dad must have recognised the inevitable so he began gently.

'Polly an' me think it's best fer yer ter go ter yer own 'ouse now it's ready,' he told her firmly.' But I could see he looked sad as he added, 'I think it'll be fer the best fer all of us.'

'Oh!' she cried, beginning to gesticulate as she did when excited and then to square up like a boxer. 'I know when I ain't wanted. No, I can 'elp meself.'

She turned round and stormed out and I followed her as she marched down the street to Mr Kiniver's 'hire shop' where you could rent a horse and cart for two hours for one shilling. The boy in the stable said that Mr Kiniver was out at a funeral and was not expected back until late.

'Can't wait!' Granny told him. 'I want a loan of one of the 'orses and a cart, now.'

The lad was obviously frightened and backed away from her.

'Giss yer shillin' then,' he managed to mumble. He came forward warily and took the coin she offered and then he went off to one of the stables to fetch the horse and cart. The flat cart was none too clean but Granny didn't seem to mind and was only anxious for the horse to be hitched to it. When this was accomplished she took the reins and walked the old horse down the street. This was by no means an easy feat and she soon attracted an interested audience who speculated loudly about her intentions.

'Where's 'Annah gooin'?' asked one of another.

'I bet yer that Polly's told 'er ter goo,' said another.

'Where's 'er got that old nag from? It oughta be in the knacker's yard,' exclaimed a third.

As they gossiped noisily I followed Granny who was pulling the reluctant animal towards our house. The horse's hooves and the iron cart rims made a terrible clatter on the cobblestones but at last silence fell as she came to a halt outside our door. The neighbours and their children crowded around to see what was going on and to hear the conversation between Granny and Dad.

'There's no need to get that old nag, mother,' he said. 'I would 'ave helped yer move yer trunk and chair if yer'd waited.' He spoke quietly, but Granny wanted to create a scene.

'Get me things on the cart,' she ordered him loudly.

Dad went indoors and brought out her belongings and placed them as she directed. I knew he didn't want her to leave but I also knew that he hated the constant uproar of quarrelling, so what was he to do? All he wanted was a bit of peace and quiet.

'Well, I'm off now,' she yelled and glared round at the neighbours with her finger on her nose. Then she tried to heave herself up on to the driving seat but couldn't manage without Dad's help. However, when he tried to assist her she pushed him away indignantly. 'I don't need any 'elp from yow. I can get meself up.' And she did.

Dad returned to the house but I remained to watch her, seated now erect and looking proud, whip in one hand and reins in the other, for all the world the expert driver as she prepared to move off.

'Gee up now,' she cried, clicking her tongue at the old mare who just turned her head and stared at Granny.

'Gee up! Gee up!' Granny repeated but it was no good, the horse stood still.

Crowds were gathering by now, and many were laughing with amusement. Granny paid them no heed. She reserved her temper for the horse. She yanked the reins and brought the whip down hard upon its bony rump. The toothless old mare only turned her head and gave Granny what seemed like a horsey laugh too.

Granny decided to dismount, which she did with some difficulty on account of having to keep her frock pulled down to hide her torn drawers. Once on the ground again she tried pulling the horse, but still it would not budge an inch. At that moment I spotted Jonesy throw a stone which caught the animal on the rump and caused it to rear up. Jerking the reins out of Granny's hand, it galloped off, leaving Granny standing in the road waving the whip and cursing.

She appealed to the onlookers for help. I would have given anything to have been able to do something, particularly since nobody else seemed interested in assisting, but Granny was a difficult person to help and I was young and afraid of horses. Then Mr Mitchell the muffin man came to the rescue. He jumped off his cart which was nearby and ran after the runaway. He soon had it back with Granny's belongings intact, and I could hardly believe my ears and eyes when I heard her thank him and allow him to lift her back on to the driver's seat, in gratitude for which she kissed him on the cheek.

'Yer'll be all right now, mother, off yer goo.' He gave the horse a gentle slap and the old grey mare, the cart, Granny and her possessions went slowly on their way. However, before she'd gone many yards she recollected herself and turned to the bystanders.

'Yer a lotta nosy parkers. Yow'll never goo ter 'eaven. None on yer!'

When I returned indoors Dad asked me if Granny had got off all right. I thought he looked upset, so I didn't mention the pantomime I had just witnessed and instead offered to make him a cup of tea. He nodded and returned to his chair while I stoked the fire.

'I want yow and Frankie ter pay yer Granny a visit every Sunday and let me know how she is. Do you understand?' he said, and I replied that I would. But each time we called she wouldn't answer the door although we could see the curtain move so we knew she was at home. I told Dad and suggested that if he called she would open up, but he said, 'No. I don't think so. She'll come round if she wants anything.'

So our house got back to normal and our life carried on as before. Then one cold afternoon later that winter when we were all huddled round the fire for warmth from the snow falling outside, Dad sighed, looked at his mother's photo and said, 'Perhaps you could take yer granny a lump of coal in yer cart, Katie?'

'Goo on then, get yer coat on,' Mum told me, and then I was sent down the cellar for the fuel. One lump Mum told me to fetch. But I thought to myself, I'll take two when she isn't looking, which I did. Dad saw what I had done but he covered the coal with an old sack, winked and whispered, 'Good girl.'

Granny lived about half a mile away, in a narrow street with drab shops dotted between the houses, which were one down and two up, like ours.

Arriving at her house I found a crowd of people outside her door. In the middle of them were Mrs Phipps and Mrs Taylor, our neighbours, sitting on the step crying. I asked them to move so I could take the coal into Granny's house.

'Yower Granny won't need that where 'er's gone to,' Mrs Phipps said.

'Where's she gone to then?' I asked, wondering what she meant.

'She's dead. Don't yer Mum know? Everybody else does,' Mrs Taylor replied.

'That's right. She's 'ad 'er chips this time,' Mrs Phipps added.

'I don't believe yer,' I exclaimed.

'Come 'an see fer yerself. I'll tek the coal.' And so saying she helped herself.

I didn't want to go in. I was so shocked I just turned tail and ran home as fast as I could. I stumbled across the threshold but before I could say anything Mum shouted at me, 'Where 'ave yow bin all this time? An' what yer cryin' for now?'

'Granny's eaten some chips and now she's dead,' I stammered, tears dripping off my nose.

'What yer talkin' about? An' where's that lump of coal?' she yelled, shaking me.

'Mrs Phipps took it. She said Granny wouldn't need it where she was going.'

'Oh! She did, did she? Well, we'll see about that.'

She slapped Dad's flat cap on the top of her bun and marched out of the house. She thought more about losing the coal to Mrs Phipps than about Granny, it seemed to me then, but I expect it was the shock that caused her to react in that way. She wanted me to accompany her but I hung back, afraid that she'd find out that I had taken two lumps of coal.

'Come on. An' don't 'ang back theea. An' bring yer cart along with yer. I might need it fer summat else beside the coal.'

I snatched up my doll, Topsey, and laid her in the cart and ran after Mum who was halfway down the street before I caught her up. When we arrived at Granny's house Mrs Phipps and Mrs Taylor were still standing outside gossiping with the neighbours. Mum went straight up to Mrs Phipps and demanded to know what she meant by saying Granny had had her chips.

'She's dead, Polly. I come in this mornin' to see if she wanted anythink, an' there she was, stiff an' cold.'

This made me shudder but I was brought back to my own worries when I heard Mum demand that she gave the lump of coal back. At that Mrs Phipps began to back away from Mum's fierce stare.

'Oh, I forgot about that. Now she wunt want it, will she?'

'No, she wunt, will she,' mimicked Mum. 'Well goo on 'an fetch it.' Mum was insistent.

I watched and held my breath, but to my relief she only brought one lump out of her bag, and that the smallest of the two, which she gave to me and I put it quickly into my cart.

Granny's neighbours were still looking on, watching for further developments, because they all knew Mum's temper. But Mum just gave them one of her black looks and elbowed her way past the two women and went into Granny's house. I followed and peered round. Everything was so still and quiet and there was dust everywhere. I wondered why this should be when Granny was so particular, but I was soon roused from my thoughts by Mum.

'Katie, I want yer ter stay 'ere with yer Gran while I goo out an' get Mrs Taylor. An' don't let anybody in. I don't trust 'em.'

To make doubly sure of this she turned the key in the lock as she went out. At this I was more frightened than ever. Granny was seated in her rocking-chair facing the fireplace, but her back was to me and I could only see the paper curlers she had in her hair. There was something strange about these and they seemed to scare me though I could not take my eyes away. I put my hands over my eyes to shut out my fears: I'd never seen a dead person before. But after a bit my curiosity got the better of me and I spread my fingers slowly to peep through. Then I crept forward to look at Granny. I wished I hadn't. I started back terrified. Granny was staring at me with her eyes wide open. I literally jumped for joy when I heard that key turn in the lock and saw Mum and Mrs Taylor enter with another woman. As they banged the door shut, the vibration set Granny's chair rocking and I put my hands over my eyes. But Mum wouldn't have that.

'Yer don't 'ave ter look if yer don't wanta,' she said sharply, pulling them away.

'We're gooin' ter tek 'er upstairs an' lay 'er out,' she said.

I felt safer now that they'd arrived and I was curious to see what she meant by 'laying out'. So, avoiding Granny's staring eyes, I watched Mum, Mrs Taylor and the big-bosomed woman they called Aggie lift Granny with some effort out of her chair and up the creaky stairs. They stripped off Granny's clothes and then washed her all over. Then Aggie dressed Granny in a brown calico shift which she had brought with her and they laid her back on the straw mattress and covered her with a sheet.

Downstairs Mum flopped into Granny's chair, heaved a sigh and exclaimed, 'My God, she was 'eavier dead than alive,' and her companions nodded in agreement.

When they had gone I was surprised to see her lock the door again. Then she returned upstairs with me close behind. We entered the room and Mum began to look round, but my eyes were drawn to the bed. I let out a shriek. The sheet had slipped off Granny's face and I was horrified to see that her eyes were still open.

'What's the matter with yer now?' she demanded, shaking me.

'I want to go home.' My voice was trembling now.

'Get outta me way. An' wait,' she muttered irritably, pushing me to one side.

Mum went over and I gazed on as she replaced the sheet and then rolled Granny on to her side and began feeling under the mattress. At last she found what she'd been looking for. It was a small, battered tin money-box. She opened it and took out several half-crowns, silver threepenny pieces and some pennies. There were some faded letters but she wasn't interested in those and shoved them back in the tin unopened. Then, pocketing the money, she placed the box back underneath the straw mattress and rolled Granny on to her back again.

I squatted on the stool at the foot of the bed while Mum searched the drawers, from one of which she pulled a bottle of gin. She consumed the contents quickly before replacing it as she had the box. Amongst the assorted contents of the other drawers she found another small box. Her eyes lit up when she opened it and found it full of farthings. These she slipped in her pocket, then she tidied the stuff away. As she was poking about for more loot I glanced back at Granny and saw that the sheet had moved again.

'Mum, Granny's watching you,' I sobbed.

'Don't be silly. It's only the sheet that's slipped. I'll soon fix that.' And with that she took two of Granny's pennies from her pocket, put her fingers on Granny's eyes to push her eyelids down and placed a penny over each eye.

'That'll keep 'em shut,' she said with satisfaction and replaced the sheet. At last she stopped searching and said, 'Come on, there's nothing mower 'ere.' But I was already fleeing downstairs to the door.

When we emerged we found the neighbours still standing around discussing what had happened, but Mum just pushed her way through them without a word. However, we hadn't gone more than a few yards when she stopped and turned around.

'Where's the cart with the coal in? Yer betta goo back an' fetch it. 'Ere's the key,' she said, fumbling in her pocket.

I stood and looked at her, petrified. I could no more return to that house alone than face the devil.

'No! No! No!' I screamed and ran off down the street.

When I got in I found the house was empty and the fire nearly out. It so miserable. I was cold and wet. I pulled down my damp bloomers and changed them for a warm, dry pair that were hanging on the line over the fire. Then I just sat on the floor and wept for Granny, and for myself. I was deep in thought when I heard Mum's unmistakable heavy tread coming towards the door. I thought, I'm for it now, but all she said when she'd bustled in and taken the coal from the cart, was, ' 'Ere yar. Tek 'old a this an' mek tha fire up before yer dad comes in.

I was only too happy to be busy breaking the coal up with the hammer, pulling out the drawer pan and stoking up the fire with the bellows. Soon Dad returned. I could tell immediately by the look on his face that he knew about Granny, for news travelled fast in our district and nothing was secret for long. I ran over to him.

'Dad!' I cried. 'Granny died from eating chips. Mrs Phipps said so. Shall I die too?'

'No,' he replied. 'It's just a saying.'

'How did she die then?' I asked.

'She was just getting old,' he said sadly.

Now I was talking to Dad I wanted to tell him about how Mum and I had found Granny and what wicked things Mum had done, but I knew Mum's eyes were on me so I thought better of it. Whether she ever told what she'd found I never discovered, but for my own part I only wanted to forget the whole frightening incident. But I never did. That episode has lived with me all my life.

When Dad had eaten his tea I heard him ask Mum if she'd kept the payments up on the insurance policy.

'Course I have,' she told him. Mum didn't believe in paying any premiums for herself, though. 'Why should I waste a penny a week? I shan't be 'ere ter spend it,' she always said. No matter how Dad tried to explain the principles of insurance to her she didn't want to know. That was how she was. She always looked at every farthing twice before parting with it.

Mum got me to reach down a tall vase from the mantelshelf.

From this she drew the policy and Dad went off to take it to the agent.

Mum took down two more vases and started sorting out a pile of pawn tickets. Some she discarded and threw into the fire, others she kept.

'I'll be able ter get some of these things out,' she mumbled. 'An' I must set a good table for the funeral.'

Just then there was a knock on the door. Mum lifted the corner of the curtain and peeped out to see who it was. It was Mrs Jones, Mrs Phipps and Mrs Taylor.

'An' what der yow three wanta borra?' she inquired sarcastically.

'Can we speak to yer, Polly?' Mrs Phipps asked, ignoring her last question.

Mum opened the door to them. 'Well? Spake up then.'

'We're very sorry about poor 'Annah passin' on, so we thought we 'ad better come to pay our respects.' They stood there with their aprons to their eyes. But Mum knew them for crafty rogues and she hadn't forgotten the coal. She probably knew too that they had been none too fond of Granny when she'd been alive. She made to close the door on them when Mrs Phipps added, 'We're gooin' from dower to dower ter get a collection up for a few flowers. Is that all right with yow, Polly?'

'That's the least yer can do!' Mum replied and stared at them hard and long.

'Well,' Mrs Taylor said. 'We'll do our best, Polly.'

Then off they went but I had noticed that Mrs Taylor was really crying. I liked her. She was always kind to me and she was the only neighbour Mum could really trust.

When Dad returned he didn't speak a word to either of us. He just sat in his chair and gazed up at Granny's picture in its faded gilt frame.

'May God rest your soul, Mother,' I heard him say to himself at last. 'If only I'd 'elped you more you might still be 'ere.' And he put his face in his hands and sobbed. Mum went over and tried to console him but he pushed her gently from him. I suppose his grief was a personal thing which he could not share with anybody.

So that was how we came to be sitting in the darkened room with Granny's coffin on the table, waiting for the neighbours to come and show their last respects. I remember the undertaker asking if anyone wanted to see her before she was screwed down and the people filing past one by one, their heads bowed. Some shed real tears too. Some of them I had never seen before and some were there to satisfy their curiosity. Wreaths and flowers were piled up outside in the yard, waiting to be heaped on the coffin. I remember going upstairs while they were looking at the corpse and writing a note with trembling fingers. It went something like this:

Good bye Granny and God bless you. And please forgive
my Mum.

I really did love you and so did my Dad. XXX

I rolled this message into a little ball and returned downstairs. Dad was still standing by the coffin and I whispered to him, 'Dad, can I have another look at my granny?'

He nodded and turned away, and while the others' attention was elsewhere I put my hand down inside the coffin until I felt Granny's cold fingers. My stomach went all queer inside but I managed to push the message between her icy fingers and kiss her forehead before I pulled my hand away.

'Goodbye, Granny, I'll try to be a good girl,' I sobbed before I stood back for the undertaker to screw down the lid.

I was pleased he hadn't seen the note or the tears that I left behind on my granny's face. I wiped my eyes and felt a bit better, knowing that Granny was taking my message with her to heaven.

Then I wandered outside to look at the wreaths and the Salvation Army Captain touched me on the shoulder.

'Katie, will you tell your father I'd like to speak to him?' he asked me.

'Yes,' I said. 'Will you come inside?'

I thought I ought to ask him. I could see the neighbours looking curiously at the big box he had with him. I heard him say to Dad how sorry he was about Sister Hannah and how he'd have liked to have seen her before she was screwed down. Then he handed the box over, saying, 'Here's the crocks I promised to lend your wife . . . and some extra food. It's not much but it'll help.'

It was amazing how people did rally round at times like this. They didn't bother much at other times unless asked, and then they often had to think twice. But now the Captain was on his knees beside the coffin praying. When he'd finished he stood up and asked Dad the time of the funeral so, he said, he could be there with the other brothers and sisters and the band. Mum kept out of sight until he had left, then down the stairs she came, all dressed up in a long black taffeta dress, which rustled when she moved. She wore new black button-up boots and on her head was perched the largest black hat I had ever seen with a black bird on top.

'Now 'ow do I look, Sam?' she asked as she stood preening herself. Dad didn't take a bit of notice but Mary stared at her.

'Anyone would think you was going to a weddin' instead of a funeral,' she let out. 'Disgustin' I call it.'

I looked at Mum and thought, if only she was as nice as she looked maybe all our lives would have been better. But I knew this was wishing for the impossible.

Mary was dressed as usual, for she always wore a black tam-o'-shanter and a black coat. Dad, Jack and Charlie just wore a black armband each with their Sunday suits, and I was dressed in a white lace dress with a wide black sash of silk ribbon. I also had real boots for the first time. I remember the argument there had been too between Mary and Mum over keeping her wages back that week.

'What about buying the kids some clothes?' Mary had said. 'Instead of spending all the insurance money on yerself.'

But Mum's reply had been, 'I'll see what I've got left when I've got the grub in.'

'I shouldn't bother yerself if I were you,' had come the reply. 'I'm keeping my wages to buy them some myself.' So that was how I came to have a new dress and boots and a real ribbon for my hair instead of the usual string.

By this time there was quite a crowd gathered in our little room. There was Mr Phipps, Mr Jones, Mr Smith, Fred the lamplighter and another of Dad's drinking pals, all having a drink and talking quietly. They were to be the pall-bearers.

When we went out the sun had come out and the horses' coats shone like black silk. They were so different from the dustman's horses and those that pulled the water carts. Then the bearers carried the coffin out and the Salvation Army band struck up with 'Nearer My God to Thee' just as we climbed into the carriage.

We passed along slowly so that the cortège could be seen and all could have a last look at the coffin. I looked through the window and there were people lined up on both sides of the street, the women with black aprons and the men with their caps and hats off, bared heads bowed as we passed. Even the dustcart and the dray-cart pulled over to one side. Shops had their blinds drawn down and the shopkeepers stood in their doorways as a mark of respect. I saw some of my school friends on tiptoe, straining their necks to see.

The church bell was tolling mournfully as the carriage entered the cemetery gate. We stopped outside the church door and the driver handed us down. There seemed to be crowds of people lined up on each side of the door and lots were already seated inside the church waiting for the coffin to enter. Just inside the vestibule there was coconut matting, and seeing this Mum looked about then began to wipe her feet. I thought she was never going to stop until I heard a woman say, 'I see 'er's still showin' off.'

At this Mum turned round and gave her a dirty look before she moved along with Dad, followed by the rest of us. However, it was obvious that she was intent on making a spectacle of herself. She wanted to be noticed in all her finery and as she walked up the aisle she kept stopping to give a little cough on the back of her hand and looking from side to side. Dad simply pushed her forward but I heard him whisper, 'Move along, yer 'olding up the service.' She moved but she still kept glancing about. She would touch her hair then fiddle with her hat and pretend to straighten her dress.

Everybody's eyes were on us, especially on Mum. Then I heard someone say, 'It's disgraceful the way she keeps standin' there preenin' 'erself.' Then another joined in. 'Who does she think she is? The Queen of Sheba?' Finally Dad pulled her down into her seat. Then everyone fell silent as the preacher entered and the service began. When it was over we filed out to the accompaniment of the organ. There were people from everywhere in the district standing around that wet, muddy graveside that day. The preacher delivered a sermon during which everyone stood still, until he picked up a handful of earth and spoke in a deep voice: 'Ashes to ashes. Dust to dust.' Before he could continue, little Jonesy chipped in: 'An' if God don't 'ave yer, the devil must.' All heads turned as his father gave him such a clip that he landed in the muddy, freshly dug grave behind him. The preacher held his hands together and looking skywards said, 'Forgive them, Lord, for they know not what they do.' Then, walking away in disgust, he said, 'I've never come across such a disgraceful congregation in all the years I've given burial services.'

Jonesy was still struggling to get out of the grave, and this he managed only with his father's help, after falling back in once. By now some were laughing openly, but Mrs Jones did not think it was funny. She turned round angrily: 'It's no laughin' matter. We might 'ave 'ad another funeral,' she wept.

When we arrived home Mrs Taylor was there in Mum's starched white apron, ready to serve. Mum had given her permission to wear her pinafore. At that time it was a tradition that when someone in a family died there was always a bow of black ribbon draped over the top of their photograph frame. But we had had to make do with black crepe paper, which was the next best thing. It was also said that if the bow should move of its own accord after it had been draped it was a bad omen. While we had been out Mrs Taylor had placed the paper in position.

I had never seen such a mouth-watering display of food on our table. There was cheese, pickled onions, corned beef, cottage loaves, pig's pudding and even a gallon jug of ale. After they had consumed all they could the guests began to leave, saying what a good send-off Mum had given Granny. Mr and Mrs Jones apologised to Dad for their son's behaviour and promised that he would get 'what's comin' to 'im when we get 'ome'. After they had all left – Dad too – Mum hung Granny's death card beneath her picture then went off to join the others in the local. Now that the house was quiet Liza, Frankie and I sat round the fire with the leftovers.

'Tell yer what,' I said, 'I'll bring in some of the other kids and Jonesy can imitate the preacher.'

I went into the yard, rounding up those I could find. I knew Mum and Dad would be out until late drowning their sorrows. The pubs didn't shut until eleven o'clock so we would have a good three hours' fun.

I had to go to the next yard to fetch Jonesy. I didn't like him much because he was a terrible liar but it wouldn't have been fun without him. I knocked on his door and when he answered I could tell from his face that he'd been crying. I told him our plan but he was none too eager until I told him we were going to play at funerals and that Frankie wanted him to imitate the preacher; then he came along at once.

'I'll tell yer what the bloke said if yer'll all be quiet,' said Jonesy. With that he pulled Dad's shirt off the line, put it over his head and, pushing his arms through the sleeves, picked up the Bible which was on the sideboard. 'Ashes to ashes, dust to dust,' he intoned, just like the preacher had. We roared with laughter. Then he put his hands together and continued. 'Forgive them Father, for they know not what they do. But my dad said, "I know what I'm gooin' ter do when I get 'im 'ome."' He changed into an imitation of his dad. But Florrie Mitchell from the next yard was not convinced.

"E dain't say that did 'e?'

''E did!' he replied angrily. 'An' I've got the marks to prove it.'

With that he replaced the Bible, tore off the shirt and dropped his trousers. We could see the red marks when he bent over but that was not all we saw. We burst out giggling at the sight of his bare bottom and we were still tittering when the door burst open and Mrs Taylor entered. Seeing Jonesy she cried out, 'Pull yer trousers up yer dirty lad.' But he was out the door, tripping over them in his anxiety to avoid another whack.

'Yer mum asked me to call in and clear away the crocks and tek the chairs outside ready ter goo back ter the Mission 'All,' Mrs Taylor said.

We were happy helping Mrs Taylor tidy up. She was different from the other women. She was always ready to do odd jobs for anyone in need. She bustled round finishing her jobs and was just about to leave when she noticed that the crepe paper had slipped from Granny's frame. She stood on the stool and reached up to replace it, and when she stood back down again she bent over and whispered to me, 'That's a bad omen, luv. I should get up ter yer bed before there's any more trouble.' I was really scared at this. 'An' remember to be careful what yer say or do, fer yer Granny's eyes will be on yer in the future.' Then she went off.

I tried to remember what my sister Mary had said about ignoring old wives' tales and I tried to put them from my mind, but after that I often caught myself glancing at Granny's picture and it seemed to me that her black eyes came alive and followed me round the room.

Chapter 15

Mary's Wedding

One day, a few weeks after Granny's funeral, Mary came home earlier than usual from work. I heard her tell Mum the news that she was getting married.

'Why dain't yer tell me before?' Mum said loudly.

'Yer don't 'ave ter shout so loud. I can 'ear yer. You knew I was getting wed. I told Dad weeks ago.'

'Yower like the rest on 'em,' Mum replied irritably. 'Yow tell yer dad everything but I'm the last to be told.'

'Oh be quiet and sit down,' Mary yelled back. 'I tell yer lots of things but you never even listen. You always say "shut up" or you've got no time or "tell me later". You aren't interested.'

'Don't yer give me any of yer lip!' Mum started going red in the face. 'Yow ain't too old ter 'ave yer face slapped!'

But Mary was no longer scared of Mum; she stood up to her and matched her temper. 'Strike me if you dare! I don't fear you any more. You can't push and slap me around like you do her,' she said, pointing her finger at me. 'But don't forget, she'll grow up one day too and then yer'll be sorry.'

Mum went quiet for a moment but then she started on Mary again. 'I suppose yower in the family way, is that it?'

'That's 'ow your dirty mind works. Yer'll 'ave ter wait an' see won't yer?'

They were still arguing when Dad came in. 'What's all the shouting about? I could 'ear yer 'alfway down the street.' He loathed the constant uproar of our house and only wanted peace and quiet.

'It's 'er,' Mum told him, pointing at Mary. 'She wants ter get married.'

'Well, what about it?' Dad answered. 'She's old enough to make up 'er own mind.'

'But 'er Gran's only bin dead a few weeks. And I shall miss 'er wages when she goes,' moaned Mum.

'That's all yow ever think of,' Mary retorted. 'Money! Money! Money! Yer'll 'ave ter drink less beer then, won't yer.'

Dad put his hand on Mary's shoulder. 'Now, now, Mary. You mustn't talk ter yer Mum like that. Anyway we'll try to manage. I'll put a few more hours in at work.'

However, Mary was still upset and sulking and with a 'so long' to Dad she walked out, head held high, just like Mum. I didn't want to stay so I followed her and asked if I could go along with her. After some hesitation she agreed, and taking my hand we went off to her young man's house. Albert his name was, and he greeted her with a kiss when he opened the door to us. He didn't give me so much as a glance. He only had eyes for Mary, especially as she immediately burst into tears.

'Now what's the trouble?' he asked, getting out a white hand-kerchief. When she'd finished telling him he went wild.

'You're not to go back to that place any more! An' I don't want anything from that house or yer mother,' he told her.

'But I've already bought the new bed, Albert,' she sobbed.

'Never mind about that. You can leave it. We're going to start afresh. My mother will take care of you while I get the house together,' he said, embracing her gently.

Albert's father was a bookmaker and they were partners in the business. Sometimes Albert's mother helped with the book-keeping in a side room she called 'The Den'. She was a kind woman and whenever I called with a message she would sit me down and fetch me a biscuit or a glass of milk. She was smartly dressed, different from the other women in our district, but then she could afford to be because they were very comfortably off. She was generous, though, and helped anyone that was really in need – if she liked them, that is. Our mum was not one of these and she knew it, but the knowledge didn't bother her; she couldn't care less whether she was liked or not.

When Mary came in from work the day after the row she told Mum that she and Albert had had a talk and that she was going to stay with his parents for a bit while Albert sorted out a house.

'That's nice,' Mum said sarcastically. 'They can afford it with all the money they tek off people, can't they?'

Mary resisted the temptation to answer her back and after a moment's silence Mum continued. 'Yer won't want yer bed then, will yer Mary?' she spoke slyly.

'No, I won't. Albert's told me to leave it.'

This pleased Mum, until I made the mistake of asking Mary if I could sleep in it. Mum scowled at me when Mary said I could have it.

'Huh, we'll see!' Mum shrugged noncommittally. 'When's the 'appy day then?' she asked.

'It'll be soon. I'll let yer know in plenty of time,' Mary answered.

'But yower gooin' ter get wed from 'ere, ain't yer?' Mum asked anxiously.

'Yes. That's the usual thing, isn't it?' said Mary gulping down her tea. I could see she wanted to leave and soon she pushed her chair back from the table and stood up to go. But Mum put her hand on her arm.

'Will yer 'elp me out? Yer know what I mean. With a little money, so's I can give yer a decent wedding.'

Mary knew what she meant all right. She wanted to show off in front of the neighbours. Mary didn't want the wedding from our house, but she was prepared to concede, and promised she would speak to Albert and see what could be done in the way of money. With that she lifted the latch, but before opening the door she turned to me and asked if I would like to go shopping with her.

'Can I, Mum?' I asked eagerly.

'I s'ppose so, but don't be back late,' she said grudgingly.

I was really glad to be going out with Mary instead of Mum; I don't think Mary had ever asked if she could take me with her before. We boarded a tram which was a treat on its own for me. Finally we got off in a street with enormous shops with beautiful window displays: I could have stood gazing at them for hours, but Mary pulled me away. Liza and I had wanted to go into the big shops in New Street and Corporation Street for ages but we'd never dared to pass the attendant who stood in the doorway ready to shoo small children off. But I wasn't afraid now with my big sister, and while Mary tried on garments I stood gazing in awe at all the sumptuous clothes that hung in the display cases. I would have loved to touch them to see what they felt like but I could see out of the corner of my eye that I was being watched. So I sat down on a chair that stood by the counter and looked around the shop while waiting for Mary to emerge from behind the colourful painted screen where she was trying things on. Finally she came out carrying a long white veil and dress over her arm. These were wrapped up together with a pair of white satin shoes. Then we left the shop.

By now it was getting late and I began to worry. 'We told Mum we wouldn't be late and it's getting dark,' I mumbled.

'Never mind about Mum. You're with me and you'll go home when I take you.' She was firm. 'Would you like to come with me to Albert's?'

I forgot my fears when she said this and we made our way to Albert's house. 'Hello littl'un and how are you?' Albert asked pleasantly when he opened the door.

'Very well, thank you,' I answered shyly as he patted me on the head.

'Well, love,' he said to Mary. 'Did you tell your mother?'

'Yes,' said Mary. 'I've explained everything. But you must understand, Albert, I have to get married from my home. And we must both help Mum to do the honours. I promised, so if we give my parents some money towards the expenses it will make me very happy.'

'Say no more about it now. We'll see your mum and dad together and make all the arrangements.'

They hugged each other, and then Mary and I went home. Mum was waiting up for us when we got indoors, but before she could speak Mary began telling her about the agreement she had with Albert to pay for the wedding and this took the wind out of her sails. 'You'll see Albert when he calls tomorrow and he'll give you enough money to get the food and whatever else you want.' So saying, she turned abruptly to go upstairs.

Mum was satisfied with this. She started talking excitedly. 'I'll mek this the best weddin' in the district,' she blustered, but Mary wasn't interested and climbed the stairs without another word.

Next day Mary took Frankie, Liza and me to the shops to buy us some new clothes for the wedding. Liza and I had white satin dresses and shoes with bows on, and Frankie had a suit of small grey and white checked material with a cap to match and a pair of new boots. After the shopping spree Mary took us to a little tea shop for tea and cakes and then we returned happily with our presents.

Mum was pleased as punch when she found that Mary had bought us new clothes, but she was not so pleased when Mary told her she couldn't see them until the day of the wedding and took them straight up and locked them in her trunk. We all knew why: left with Mum they would have been in pawn before we had the chance to wear them.

I never knew how much Albert and Mary gave Mum and Dad, but they threw money around like water; as Mum had said, she was going to give Mary the best turn-out in the district. She and Mrs Taylor went around the shops ordering what they thought was necessary and Dad and his cronies, Fred the lamplighter and his workmate Willie Turner, went along to the Golden Cup to order the drink. When she returned from the shops, Mum told me to accompany her to the Captain's to ask if we could have the Mission Hall for the wedding. She was disappointed when he told her he was sorry but it was being used for band practice that day. This put Mum in a terrible temper and to make matters worse, when we got home Dad and his friends were there pouring out beer from bottles. I could see at once that they had all had a skinful. This made Mum livid.

'Now what's wrong with yer? Can't a man 'ave a drink ter celebrate?' Dad asked, continuing to pour the beer. ' 'Ere, 'ave one an' shut up.' He pushed the mug under her nose.

Mum took the mug from him but she didn't drink it. She slapped it down on the table, spilling some of its contents. 'I wanta know whater we gooin' ter do. The Captain can't let us 'ave the 'all for me daughter's weddin'.' She sagged into her chair and sobbed.

Fred went over to her. 'Can I make a suggestion, missus?' he asked.

'Anythink as long as it'll 'elp us out,' she wailed through her apron.

'Why don't yer 'ave yer celebrations in the yard? It's big enough and besides yer'll be near the closets when yer need 'em.' He laughed, as did Willie and Dad, but Mum wiped her eyes and smiled.

'Now why didn't I think of that?'

On reflection, though, she doubted if she'd got enough crocks or cutlery and 'what was they going ter sit on?' After a pause for thought she told Dad that he must go and ask the Captain if he could let them have some cups and saucers and whatever else was available, even if they could not have the hall. Dad was less than enthusiastic about this suggestion.

'No, no, go yerself if yer want 'em. Yer never took the last lot back. 'E 'ad ter come an' fetch 'em.'

'Oh well,' she answered, 'I'll goo meself. Yow carn't do anything in that state any'ow.'

She drank down the remains of the mug of beer and off we went again to see the Captain.

'I've come ter ask yer, if we carn't 'ave the 'all, would yer be kind enough ter lend us some crocks an' chairs? Yer see, we're gooin' ter 'ave the party in the yard after the weddin'.'

'I'm very sorry,' he answered sharply. 'I shall be needing them all for the meeting.'

'But what am we gooin' ter do?' she wailed tearfully.

After pausing for a second he must have relented, because he told her that if it was any help she could borrow benches and tres-tle tables.

'That'll do.' She brightened up visibly. 'I'll send somebody to fetch 'em in the mornin'. Yer see it's tomorra the weddin'. An' yow come yerself if yer like.'

When we got back home Dad's mates had left and he was snoring in the chair. Mary was there too. Mum told her about the changes in the arrangements but Mary wasn't at all pleased. 'Whatever are yer talking about? I thought everything was arranged for using the Mission Hall?'

Mum tried to calm her but Mary was not impressed by the thought that the money for hiring the hall had been saved. In the middle of the fuss Dad woke up.

'What's all the bloody shouting for now?'

'We carn't 'ave the use of the 'all, Dad, and we carn't 'ave the celebrations in the yard neither! Whatever will Albert's people think?' Mary sobbed.

Mum chipped in with, 'They'll 'ave ter think what they like. The stuck-up lot!'

Mary was now in tears. 'I wish I hadn't agreed ter get married from 'ere. In fact I wish I wasn't getting married at all.'

Dad put his arm around her shoulder. 'Now Mary,' he said, 'dry yer eyes and listen ter me. It's yer weddin' day termorra and we all want ter see yer 'appy. Yer mum's done the best she can under the circumstances.'

'But Dad, I feel so ashamed to think that Albert's parents will 'ave ter mix with our kind of neighbours, and you know what Mum's like when she's 'ad a few drinks.' Mary glared at Mum who was pretending not to listen.

'Leave everything to me, Mary. I'll keep yer Mum and everyone else in order.'

But I knew that was easier said than done. It would be as much as Dad could do to keep himself in order after he'd had a drop too much. Dad was a jolly chap sober, or could be, but when he'd had a few he thought himself a bit of a lady-killer. Mum knew this too, which was why she always kept an eye on him when he was the worse for drink.

Mum went out to the yard, waving her arms about and giving directions to the neighbours. 'I want this 'ere,' she said, pointing. 'An' I want that there,' indicating where the chairs and tables were to go. 'An' bring some crocks, an' knives, an' forks an' anything else we can use.' She was not asking, she was demanding; but they were all used to her ways and were probably scared of upsetting her in case she changed her mind about the invitations.

I slipped away before she spotted me and went to look for Frankie, but I could find neither hide nor hair of him, nor of Liza either. I finally came to the churchyard, Titty-Bottle Park, where there were literally dozens of kids running about the tombstones.

Frankie and Liza were there with some of our friends, who gathered round to hear me excitedly telling my tale.

'Better than the Mission Hall,' Frankie said. The others agreed that it would be more fun to eat in the yard.

It was bright and early next morning when, with a clatter of buckets and bowls, we started to swill down the yard. The lavatories also had a birthday, and Dad left ours unlocked with plenty of fresh newspaper on the nail. The women even cleaned their windows. This was a red-letter day indeed. The clothes lines were taken down and rolled up by the dustbins, together with the props. I couldn't remember such a bustle and hubbub in our yard before. Everyone was singing a different song out of tune and taking no notice where they were throwing the water. Several people ended up with wet feet and all the cats vanished and even the kids who were trying to help got the odd clout for 'gettin' under our feet'. Eventually Frankie and I were called in by Mum and told to wash and change as it was nearly time to go. But it was worse in our house than in the yard. We were all at sixes and sevens, getting in one another's way. Mum and Mary kept calling for this, no that, yes that, to be brought upstairs. It was pandemonium.

Then to top it all, two of Mary's friends squeezed in with several more parcels. They were what were then called 'buxom young women' and I thought them very pretty. They had come to help Mary dress but there was no room at all when they started busying themselves. Still, they were efficient. They put the parcels on the table and tidied the room while Frankie and I sat on the sofa and watched. Then brother Jack strolled in and he wasted no time in chatting them up. He joked and play-acted, then put his arm round one's waist and kissed her on the cheek. This started them both giggling and they fled upstairs in hysterics. But they were no strangers to Jack because he called out 'See yer later, Molly' as took his leave.

After a while Mary came down with her two friends. Molly removed the rags that Mary had put in my hair and it fell down in ringlets. Then she helped me put on my white satin dress, after which I pulled on my shoes. Frankie dressed himself, and he looked smarter than I had ever seen him in his check suit, waistcoat and matching cap. Liza looked good too. Then Mum came rustling down the stairs in her almost-new taffeta dress with its leg-o'-mutton sleeves. I could hardly believe my eyes. She looked years younger. Her hair was done on top like a cottage loaf with bits dangling around her ears, in which she had long red glass earrings, and peeping out from under the long russet-coloured dress were her brand-new button-up boots. She twirled around the room and preened herself in the glass until Frankie could contain himself no longer.

'If yer don't watch out yer'll crack that mirror.'

Mum scowled at him and slapped him hard across the face. He wasn't bothered. Mum returned to the mirror and replaced strands into the bun which had become dishevelled during the twirling. Then, looking satisfied with herself, she marched out into the yard to see how well her orders had been carried out and to show off her fine clothes. We followed. All eyes turned, filled with admiration and envy. Even Dad looked at us proudly as he paused in his job of putting up the bunting.

All our playmates crowded round to marvel at our get-ups and touch our finery, but Mum soon put a stop to this and sent us indoors. 'Goo inside, we don't want their dirty maulers on yer clothes.'

The young women had come downstairs and Dad, who had already had a skinful, addressed Molly in a jovial manner. 'Why 'ello Molly. I didn't know yow'd bin invited.' Then he pulled her towards him and asked her to give him a kiss, but she pulled away quickly when she saw Mum's scowl.

Just then Albert put his head round the door and Mum turned her wrath on him. 'Out! Out! Get out! Don't yer know it's bad luck ter see yer bride before yer married?'

Albert was probably as glad as Dad to do as he was told and leave and I noticed that Mary's two buxom friends slipped out after them. But Mum's attention was elsewhere. When Mary came down, she was all smiles. 'Are yer ready now, Mary me luv? We'll be late if we don't 'urry.'

I could hardly believe my eyes. Mary looked a picture, radiant, all in white. Over her orange-blossom headdress she had a long flowing veil which flowed down her back; her dress of white satin rustled and crinkled as she walked. She seemed to glide on her little satin-shod feet. As I watched her I thought Granny would have been proud if she'd been alive to see Mary now. I glanced up at Granny's picture and for once she seemed to be smiling.

Dad came in and I was struck by how handsome he was with his moustache freshly waxed and his hair brushed flat and parted in the middle. He wore his best suit which had been redeemed from the pawnbroker's and was freshly cleaned and pressed. He even had on a collar and tie, which I'd never seen before and which he would tug at every now and then as if it were too tight. When he had finished looking in the mirror to put in his buttonhole rose, it was time to go.

Mary picked up her bouquet of white roses from the table and placed her hand through Dad's arm. He looked at her proudly then they turned and we walked out into the crowd. Confetti showered down on us and congratulations were shouted from all directions. Then the people moved aside and we passed through the smiling, cheering crowd.

This was not a wedding such as we see today This was an old-fashioned wedding. There were no wedding cars nor yet carriages. The church was within easy walking distance of our street so everyone went on foot. It was a warm May day and everybody seemed to be out in the street or standing on their steps. There was quite a procession by the time we got to the church, St Paul's, and as we entered the organ played 'Here Comes the Bride'. We walked down the aisle and the church seemed really awesome.

Mary and Albert had more confetti thrown over them as they stood on the threshold of the church after the service. Mary was kissed and hugged by her workmates and Albert's back was slapped and his hand shaken by his friends.

When we reached our yard again I could see that Mrs Taylor and her friends had worked hard. The trestles had been put up and were covered with white tablecloths of American oilcloth. They were piled with corned-beef sandwiches, cheeses, sausage rolls, sliced pickled onions, beetroot, all kinds of pickles, watercress, pig's pudding and every mouth-watering delicacy you could think of. And standing in the centre was a two-tiered, iced cake. At one end of the table there were four stone gallon jars of ale, bottles of stout, gin and whisky. There was room on the benches for twenty guests each side, facing each other. We children had a table to one side to ourselves on which were laid out bottles of pop, cakes, buns and bread and jam.

While the adults sat on their forms we sat ourselves down on an assortment of broken chairs borrowed from the neighbours. There was a plate, knife and fork and a paper napkin for everyone. Some, the lucky ones, had a glass for their drink but the rest had to make do with a cup or a mug. After we had settled down, brother Jack stood up and banged the table and called for order for Dad to say grace. Everybody bowed their heads, then as he said 'Amen' they dived into the 'eats'. You would have thought some of them hadn't eaten for days, but then perhaps they hadn't. Many seemed not to know what the knives and forks were for and took the napkins for handkerchiefs.

Mrs Taylor kept an eye on us, ready to rap our knuckles if we got too greedy. As everyone feasted themselves Mum went round with the drink, pouring out gin and whisky or stout as they preferred, making sure to test them all as she did so, while Dad and Fred did the same with the ale. Things were beginning to hum when I noticed Albert's mother get up from her seat and go over to Mary. 'Fred and I will have to leave now as we have to catch the early train in the morning, Mary,' she said. 'But we'll see you as soon as we get back from our holidays. In the meantime, I hope you and Albert will be very happy. You have my blessings, my dear.'

'Thank you, mother,' replied Mary with tears in her eyes. 'I didn't want the weddin' this way.'

'I quite understand,' Mrs Lewis assured her. They embraced briefly and I heard her say quietly, 'Remember I shall always love you and if there's anything I can do or that you want, don't be afraid to come to me.' And with that she and her husband left.

Soon after this Mary and Albert slipped away unnoticed except by me. I didn't want Mary to go because I thought I wouldn't see her for a long time, and I ran over to her and pleaded, 'Where are you goin'? Ain't you stayin' till the end of the party?'

'No, Katie,' they answered in unison. 'But,' Mary continued, 'you can come and visit us when we've got settled in.'

'But remember,' said Albert, 'only you and Frankie, mind.' And they picked me up in turn and gave me a kiss.

Nobody seemed to miss them, only me. I tried to get Dad to tell me where they'd gone but he was tipsy and only laughed and said they'd gone on their 'funnymoon'. They were all pretty well oiled by then so I went back and sat with the other children. Battling Billy was attempting to sing one of his war songs and Maggie was merry too; if he went too far she would have to help him indoors. Mum was leading the chorus and us kids were singing our own dirty ditties.

By now the barrel organ was in action, belting out 'Down at the Old Bull and Bush'; the noise was tremendous. When that number was over people started calling for order so that Mrs Buckley could do one of her songs. Unfortunately Mrs Buckley couldn't sing a note in tune; her throat sounded like it had gravel down it. There was nearly a fight when her husband heard Fred the lamplighter say to Dad that she sounded like 'a constipated canary'. The adults were beginning to get out of hand: some were dancing, having a 'knees up'; others were arguing with the organ grinder about what should be played.

Then the men got round to the subject of politics. 'Asquith should be shot,' someone suggested. 'This government's never bin any good,' another agreed. Others sprang to the defence of their rulers and the argument became furious until a heavy fist banged down on the table and bottles and food went flying. This started a real rough-and-tumble, with people falling or being pushed to the ground amongst the debris.

Frankie suggested that we gather up the bottles and hide them in the wash-house before they all got broken. We ended up with about a dozen assorted gin, whisky and stout bottles. When we emerged, two women were pulling each other's hair and screaming at each other while the men tried to part them. Mum was not taking part. She stood there with hands on her hips, glaring with a face like thunder. However, the disturbance didn't last long because just then there was a cry of 'Hey up! Here's the cops!' They were not joking. It was not only the cops but the Black Maria as well. Dad pushed Mum indoors and Frankie and I followed quickly. Then Dad shot home the bolt, though this didn't stop us opening the window to see the end of the rumpus. We saw Maggie drag Billy from under the table where he was on his knees praying for 'the good Lord to send down lightning and scatter all these wicked people'. The police took one look at him and decided to leave him for later. But while they were hauling various protesting individuals off to the police wagon Maggie got him indoors. Then in a few minutes they were gone and quiet descended on our yard – but not for long.

Just as we'd closed the window and were breathing a sigh of relief there was a loud knock on the door. We looked at each other, scared, thinking it was the police come back for us. The door rattled and the pictures shook. Granny's crepe paper slipped over one eye and she seemed to be saying 'Serves them right.'

Mum whispered, 'That's another bad omen.'

'I don't think it's the police, Polly,' Dad said. 'Yer better see who it is.'

It turned out to be Mrs Taylor. 'Yer tryin' ter knock our bloody door down?' Mum shouted. 'What yer want?'

Mrs Taylor stood there sobbing. You could hardly make out what she was saying. 'P-Polly, S-Sam, 'ave yer seen me three young uns? I carn't find 'em. I've looked everywhere. Whatever shall I doo?' she wailed.

Dad and Liza went inquiring door to door while Frankie and I used this opportunity to see if our bottles were safe in the washhouse. They were, and so were Mrs Taylor's twins, Joey and Harry, and little Billy. I tried to lift Joey into my arms but he wriggled on to the slack and ashes on the floor and started giggling. I couldn't understand what was wrong with him until Frankie pulled out the other two from behind the boiler and found them in a similar state.

'They've bin drainin' the dregs outta the bottles. They're drunk!' he cried.

We stood them up. They were filthy with coal dust. We tried to get them to the door but they kept falling about. They looked really comical, and Frankie and I were in fits of laughter trying to help them. Then I spotted Dad down the yard and called out to him. He and Mrs Taylor came tearing down the yard to see what was up.

'Whatever's up with 'em? They're filthy!' he said.

'Yer'll 'ave ter carry 'em, Dad. They're drunk,' Frankie told him.

Then he caught sight of the empties and saw what had happened and began laughing as well. He tucked a twin under each arm and took them home, where we helped to wash and clean them before they went to bed. When we got in there was no tea waiting for us. Mum was asleep in her chair, snoring. However, we were not hungry for once, so we didn't mind going to bed.

Thus ended Mary's wedding day. The party did not continue after the police raid. I suppose you could say that the occasion went with a bang.

Chapter 16

Rosie

Our living-room, like many rooms in our district, was not even large enough to swing a cat. So in very warm weather my mum, like the rest of the neighbours, would bring out one of the old backless wooden chairs, and peel and scrape potatoes into the tin bowl. These potatoes were a luxury for Sunday dinner. Other days we had fried leftovers. Some Sundays she would make believe she had a joint of meat to carve. She would bring out the carving knife and sing at the top of her voice so that all the neighbours could see her sharpening the knife on the window-ledge. Over the years that sandstone window-ledge, as well as the step, looked more and more like a half moon.

Mum would buy the cheapest and smallest potatoes she could find. She always said they stretched further, but many were too small even to scrape and were tipped into a bucket of water. I had the job of swishing them around with a broken brick until the skin came off. Mum would also sit outside on the step shelling the peas. Once, and only once, did I sit on that step beside her, but when she caught me pushing a few peas into my mouth she knocked me flying.

Another time, she said I could have a few empty shells. Others she saved to put on the back of the fire. Nothing was ever wasted in our house. Those pods tasted delicious after you took the outer skin off, but some I saved.

I would hang each pea shell from a line tied to the lamppost Then I'd call out, several times, 'Pin a pick, pin a pick, one pod for a pin, and two for a safety pin.' Kids would find pins from somewhere and pick the ones they fancied.

Another time I would cut pictures from newspapers. I had a craze for saving pins, hairpins too, but I found that other kids had the same idea – until one day I stood on the orange-box from the corner of the attic and climbed into the loft, where I found lots of odds and ends and a large old book covered in dust. When I blew the dust off, I saw it was a Bible. As I mooched around on my hands and knees, I came across a coloured picture book. I hid them under my bed. The first opportunity I had, I cut out all the coloured pictures and placed each one inside the pages of the Bible.

Next day was Saturday, and while Mum and Dad were shopping in the Bull Ring, I took the old backless wooden chair outside. Sitting down with the heavy Bible on my lap I began to cry out, 'Pin a pick . . . come and pick yer own coloured picture. Two for a safety pin.'

Soon there were several kids with their pins trying their luck – one brought a hairpin and another even brought me a hatpin. Those who drew a blank were unlucky, but I'd let them have two tries. If they failed again, I would show them which page to stick the pin in to save any squabbles. That day I was doing a roaring trade. I had quite a large cocoa tin full – until little Rosie Pumfry, who lived opposite, came running towards me holding two safety pins up in the air. She was about eight, three years younger than me, very small but very podgy, with little red fat cheeks and corn-coloured hair. She was an only child.

As soon as I took the pins and showed her where the pictures lay, she ran down the yard as if someone would stop and take them from her. She had been gone only a few minutes when I saw her mum dragging young Rosie towards me. Rosie was trying to stop her ragged drawers from falling down and I guessed then where the two safety pins had come from. As Rosie's mum came near me she yelled, 'Now, you can just give me back them safety pins befower I clout yer bleedin' ear'ole.' I was often scared of this hard-faced little woman, but I found enough courage to say, 'Well, Mrs Pumfry, yer can 'ave yer pins back if yer give me me pictures back.'

'I put 'em on the fire, an' I ain't gooin' from 'ere till I get my pins,' she yelled.

I was really scared now, and I knew that all the kids were gathering around to see what was going to happen. But someone must have run to tell my mum. As soon as she came and saw the commotion, and heard what was going on, she called all the kids together, then tipped the full tin of pins on the floor. I began to cry when she told them to help themselves. Suddenly there was a free-for-all as the pins began to vanish. Mum handed two safety pins to Mrs Pumfry, and I saw her drag little Rosie home, her dirty drawers falling about her ankles as she wept.

Mum snatched up the Bible and pulled me indoors. As soon as she had slammed the door she threw the Bible on the table, then flung me across the room. 'Werd yer gettit?' she yelled.

'I found it in the loft, Mum,' I managed to answer.

'You tellin' the truth?' she replied, glaring at me.

'Yes, Mum.'

'Whose is it, do yer know?'

'No, Mum, I don't know whose it is.'

'Could be yer granny's, 'er was always 'idin' things away from me, but if it is, she's gooin' ter haunt yer for stickin' pins in that Bible.'

Suddenly I shouted loudly, 'But I dain't stick pins in it!'

'Don't yer dare raise yer bloody voice ter me, yer cheeky little varmint!' she yelled as she slapped my face. 'An' now, yer can get that chair in what yo've left outside, an' yer can tell them pin-pinchers what's listenin' outside me dower if they don't clear off, I'll be cummin' out an' chuck a bucket of water over 'em, an' it won't be only dirty water I'll be chuckin', either!'

They must have heard the warning. As soon as I opened the door they fled.

As I pushed that old wooden chair under the table, she began to bawl again: 'Now! Yer can goo an' put that Bible back where yer said yer found it, till I'm ready ter call yer down! An' yer can stop yer blartin'.'

As I turned to go up the stairs, she caught me putting my tongue out. She was ready to hit me again, but I was too quick. Before her hand came down, I snatched the Bible and fled up the stairs.

But I knew I'd get my punishment later, even if it was several days later – she never forgot.

After I had put the Bible back in the loft, I lay down on the flock mattress and cried myself to sleep. I didn't even feel my sister Liza get in beside me. But when morning came and we were on our way to school, Liza asked me why I'd been crying in my sleep.

When I told her what had happened she said, 'I knew it was Gran's Bible, she told me to 'ide it away before she died.'

'But why did she want to 'ide it away?' I asked.

' 'Cause me mum always 'ated seein' anythink of me gran's lyin' about.'

Mrs Pumfry, Rosie's mum, was a small woman in her mid-forties. Her greying hair was always pulled tightly over her ears and set in a bun in the nape of her neck. Her small dark eyes seemed to stare out from her angular features and her thin lips drooped down at the corners, which made her look discontented and older than her years.

Whenever I happened to see her out in the yard, I would run back into the house and hide, for I was afraid of her since taking the two precious safety pins from Rosie. But I hid once too often.

When Mum asked me what was wrong I told her why I was afraid and what Mrs Pumfry might do to me.

'No need ter be afraid of 'er!' she exclaimed. ' 'Er bark's worse than 'er bite, so the best thing yer can do is ter knock on the dower an' say 'ow sorry yer are.'

As I stood wondering whether to go or not, Mum yelled as she pushed me outside, 'Goo on! An' do as yer told!'

When I knocked on the door, there was no answer. I was relieved in one way, but as I walked away I looked across the yard and saw Mrs Pumfry in the brewhouse, standing over the copper. stirring the clothes over with the wooden boiler stick. As she wiped the hot steam from her face I blurted out quickly, 'Mrs Pumfry, I'm sorry I took those two safety pins off Rosie, but I didn't know they 'eld 'er drawers up.'

'No 'arm done, love,' she replied. 'But if you would like to 'elp me with the wringer . . .' I knew now I was forgiven. I also helped her to peg the washing out on the line across the yard.

Mrs Pumfry said I could call for Rosie any time. But whenever I did call, I could never understand why her mother always made me wait outside. Never once did she ask me in, nor any of her neighbours. They used to say she was stuck up because she owned a piano, yet no one ever heard it played. (People were lucky if they owned an old gramophone.) Plenty of gossip went around – people would say she wasn't married, a spinster left on the shelf with Rosie. But whatever she was, she always ignored everyone, whether she heard them or not.

She went to church on Sunday mornings and evenings and sometimes of an afternoon to prayer meetings, and during these times Rosie was left alone to play with us children in the yard. This gave scope for more gossip. Talk went on: she must be meeting a 'fancy man'. Although there were plenty of Peeping Toms looking through their curtains, no one ever saw her bring anyone to the house.

One chilly afternoon I saw Rosie sitting on the doorstep crying. When I asked her why, she replied, 'I forgot to say me prayers last night an' me mum punished me.'

'Never mind, you go inside an' get warm, an' if yer want me to I'll come in an' stay with yer till yer mum comes 'ome.'

She stood up, nodded and wiped her eyes on her sleeve. I took hold of her hand and as we stepped inside, I realised that in all the three years they had lived there this was the first time I had entered her home. At once I noticed it was almost dark inside. The gas was going out.

'Do yer 'ave a penny for the meter?' I asked.

'Yes,' she replied. 'Me mum always leaves one on the shelf.'

After putting the penny in the meter, we came up the cellar steps into the living-room. I was surprised to see what a nice tidy room it was – not like our room, all cluttered up with everything in the wrong place. I noticed too that everything was old and well worn, but clean and highly polished. What caught my eye most was the old piano against the wall facing the door. It had a roll-top lid, and two iron candle brackets jutting out from each side of the wooden music frame, and on the back of these was fretwork with faded red satin showing through. Also two rusty pedals. But for all that, I wished that I owned it. There was a piano stool beneath with an embroidered top, also faded and old.

'Does your mum play it?' I asked as I stared at it.

'No,' Rosie replied. 'She only opens it to dust and polish it.'

'Don't you play it neither?'

'No, I don't know 'ow to, any'ow Mum won't let me, even if I wanted to. She always keeps it locked.'

'But why does she keep it if it's never played?'

'She says she wouldn't part with it because it belonged to me Granny Pumfry. 'Ave you gotta piano?'

'No, we've only got an old gramophone with a brass trumpet. But that belongs to me brother Jack. 'E won't let us play it neither.

But more often than not it's in the pawnshop, and Jack always carries the needles with him, and the soundbox.' I told her how one day while he was out he forgot to take the soundbox. I looked everywhere for a needle, even a used one, but he must have put those away too. I was alone in the house, so I decided to get the chopper and chop a darning needle in two. With a bit of a struggle the needle snapped in two, so I put one half up the soundbox. I placed the soundbox on the record and as I turned the handle it gave a couple of moans and then the needle snapped and the soundbox fell on my brother's favourite record and cracked it. My mum must have been upstairs. Suddenly she came flying down. There was no time for me to run, so I got a walloping, and another when my brother Jack saw his favourite record in three pieces. After that, he always carried the handle and the soundbox with him, even if he was only going to the closet, to work, or out late at night, tomcatting.

Me and the rest of the kids in the street had lots of laughs when we put tissue paper over a comb and held it to our lips and hummed a tune. We called it a jew's-harp. The real jew's-harp is five thin bits of wire stretched across a small piece of plywood which cost threepence, which we couldn't afford, so that was our next best thing.

I left before Rosie's mum came home, but Rosie promised me she would try and find the key, then she would open the piano up and I could play.

One afternoon I was teaching her to play hopscotch, when all at once she stopped in the middle of the game and told me where her mother had hidden the piano key. 'Would yer like ter come and play a tune on it?'

'What if yer mum comes 'ome and catches us?'

'She won't be back till five o'clock,' replied Rosie.

As soon as Rosie turned the key in the lock the piano lid rolled back with a few squeaks. But I was disappointed to see not black and white ivory keys but instead, staring at me, old and broken keys yellowed with age, like an old man's discoloured teeth – some missing too. I tried my one-finger exercise, 'God Save the King'. It was then that I realised that some of the keys were dead as well, but after trying further up the scale I managed to finish part of the tune. When Rosie asked if I could play something else, I said I'd never had the chance. 'But I could if I 'ad plenty of practice,' I added.

'Well, if you'll come an' stay with me when me mum goes out you'd be able ter come an' practise.'

Each time the opportunity arose, I would go and play it while Rosie stood by to watch, and it wasn't long before I could play our national anthem with both hands. Rosie and I were delighted, although it sounded out of key at times. Rosie made sure to lock it up and put the key back where she had found it, until the next time.

One Saturday afternoon I was surprised when Rosie's mum knocked on our door and asked to see my mum. I was scared. Had she found out about me going into her house and opening up the piano? Guiltily I tried to hide, but it was too late. Mum had already called her in.

'Mrs Greenhill,' I heard her say, 'I was wondering if you could keep an eye on my Rosie for me. You see I 'ave to go to my brother's funeral today and I won't be back till about six o'clock.'

After she'd gone, Mum said, 'Blimey, that's one out of the book. Fancy 'er comin' ter ask me! Anyway, Katie, you can both 'elp me in the brew'ouse.' After we had helped Mum we left to go out to play, and Rosie suggested I should practise on the piano. There was still a good two hours before Mrs Pumfry was due home, so we had plenty of time. But when we got indoors Rosie couldn't find the key anywhere. We tried prising the lid open with a knife, but the knife snapped. Then all at once she said, ' 'Ere it is, it was right at the back of the drawer beneath the knives an' forks.'

I banged on those keys for all I was worth. Afterwards I opened up the piano stool and saw several faded pieces of music sheets. I took one out and tried to read the notes, but it was all Chinese to me. The only thing I could understand was a piece called 'Rock of Ages'. Another was 'Abide with Me', and another was 'Onward, Christian Soldiers'.

I knew all these tunes off by heart, as we had sung them many times in Sunday school and church. But I made believe. I took each piece, propped it up on the music frame in front of me and pretended to play from the music, and as I began to play by ear I felt marvellous the way my fingers went over those keys, but making plenty of mistakes when I struck the dead ones. I was very excited, and so was Rosie – she even called in some of the kids who were playing in the yard to listen to me. But when the time for her mum to come home drew near, Rosie locked up the piano and out we went to wait. We were afraid the kids would tell on us, but Rosie said if they did she wouldn't let them come in her house again.

One Saturday afternoon while Rosie's mum was out I started practising again. I know it must have sounded awful to some people, but I enjoyed it, so did Rosie and the kids. It seemed that all the kids in the street came that day to sing. But when they tried to dance as well they cried, 'Carn't yer play summat else, we carn't dance ter that!'

After a few more tries I managed to hit the keys, and found I could now play (after a fashion) 'Any Old Iron' and 'Knees Up Mother Brown'. All the kids began to sing and dance around the yard with Rosie. It was bedlam, with some kids taking turns looking out for Rosie's mum to appear and to warn us in time. But no one cared – even the 'looker-out' joined in, which was a mistake. As soon as someone shouted out that Mrs Pumfry was coming down the street the kids scattered, leaving Rosie to run in and warn me. But before she and I could close the lid, Mrs Pumfry almost fell into the room.

Kate's mother (seated) and eldest sister Mary (standing right) with Mary's daughter and baby granddaughter in 1932

Kate's brother Jack (seated far left) in the army in 1914

Kate's father (standing fourth from left) outside the 'George and the Dragon', Albion Street, 1921

Kate's brother Charles
holding her first born son,
Camden Street, 1922

Kathleen Dayus in 1933

The Bull Ring was, and remains, the market where Brummies go for a bargain. This shows the view from the High Street looking towards St Martin's-in-the-Bull-Ring as it was in 1895, with the market stalls in the shadow of the church.

The heart of Joseph Chamberlain's remodelling of Birmingham was the Council House, seen on the left here. Colmore Row, which stretches into the distance, was cut through an area of poor housing and its inhabitants moved into areas like that Kate grew up in, immediately to the north and west.

Number 1 Court, Camden Drive was identical in every respect to Number 4 Court where Kate's family lived. Five three-floor, three-room back-to-back houses faced the communal toilets and wash houses, across the back-to-back houses.

This court at the rear of Holland Street was typical of thousands in the densely-populated central wards. The galvanised iron bath hangs on a hook and the milk churn and barrow suggest that the family had a small milk round.

Two women in the Flower Market, one of Birmingham's central markets not far from the Bull Ring, photographed in 1900.

Black country hop-pickers at Little Witley, Herefordshire, in 1896. The photography captures both the community spirit and holiday atmosphere of working excursions like those taken by Kate's family into the countryside.

These ragged, barefoot 'children of the poor' were photographed on an outing by the charitable Cinderella Club to Sutton Coldfield Park. Like Kate, they can have had few opportunities of a good meal or a sight of the countryside.

Flower-sellers near the Bull Ring, 1896.

Whenever a Victorian or Edwardian photographer set up his cumbersome tripod a crowd of curious onlookers gathered to enjoy the experience of being photographed although they can rarely have seen the results. Here such a group of children and shop assistants are gathered outside shops in Great Hampton Street, one of the main thoroughfares which bounded the area of slums and workshops where Kate's family lived (1901).

Surprisingly few photographs of Birmingham's metal-working trades have survived. This one of brass bedstead makers taken in 1905 shows the cramped work space and laborious nature of the job.

St Paul's churchyard, seen here at the end of the nineteenth century, was the 'titty-bottle park' of Kate's childhood. The church was designed by the Wolverhampton architect Roger Eykyn in 1777 when St Paul's Square was the fashionable home of merchants and manufacturers. However, long before Kate knew it, the area had declined socially and the houses had been converted to small jewellers' workshops, which they remain to this day.

'You wicked, wicked pair!' she yelled as she snatched up the sheets of music and banged the lid down. I was trembling now with fear, and so was Rosie. As tears ran down her cheeks, her mother yelled again: 'An' what 'ave I told yer about that piano! Never ter be opened! An' where did yer find the key?'

'In the back of the drawer, Mum,' whimpered Rosie.

'Well, in future it goes in my pocket. And as for you!' she added, turning on me, 'I don't want ter see you in my 'ouse again! Now clear off!'

I didn't need telling twice. I fled.

I never did enter that house at number fifteen again, but Rosie and I were still friends.

When I told my mum later, she just scolded me and said that Rosie could come in our house any time. I was pleased about this, but it wasn't the same, for I loved any kind of musical instrument, and I vowed when I was old enough to get married the first thing I would buy would be a real piano.

But my big ideas never materialised until 1950, after my second marriage. Then I had two!

Chapter 17

The Facts of Life

Our next-door neighbours, Mr and Mrs Buckley, had a daughter named Sally who had been staying with an aunt for a year or so. She was three years older than I was. She was mysterious about herself but had plenty to say on the subject of her boyfriends. I was impressed by her self-confidence; I'd never had one boyfriend, let alone as many as she'd had. She used make-up and bleached her hair and was a very attractive girl. The neighbours held their noses in the air when she went out dolled up. Everybody seemed to shun her but I felt sorry for her and we became close friends. However, she didn't suit Mum. The first time she found us chatting in the yard she rushed up and dragged me away.

'Don't yer 'ave nuthin' ter do with that brazen 'uzzy!' she warned me.

'Why? What's she done?' I asked angrily.

'Never yow mind what she's done. Yer'll find out when yer older,' she ranted. 'She's the talk of the district. After anythink with trousers on, or off! Don't ever let me see or know yer've 'ad any-thing to do with 'er agen.'

Saying this to me was like holding a red rag to a bull: the more anyone told me not to do a thing, the more I tried to do it. So we continued to meet on the sly. I bumped into Sally one evening when I was out fetching Dad twopenn'orth of twist. We greeted each other and were soon chatting. She asked me if I'd like to meet her current boyfriend and I agreed.

'There's two really,' she said, winking. I didn't understand what she meant by this but she smiled and asked if I would like to go to the 'flicks' the following Saturday. I agreed and we arranged to go to the second house. I would have to wait until Mum and Dad went out to the pub so we couldn't make it to the first. The second house finished at ten so that would give me plenty of time to get home before my parents.

Saturday afternoon arrived and I had the house to myself to get ready. I sorted through my frocks but could find none that fitted me; I'd outgrown them all and was waiting until I'd grown into Liza's cast-offs. I tried hers on anyway and after rummaging about for a bit I found one I liked. But it was too big in the bust and too long. I put it back in the trunk, disappointed that there was nothing right for me to wear and wondering what I was going to do, for I wanted to go out with Sally. I decided to go round to her place to see if she had anything I could borrow. Sure enough she offered straight away and gave me some lipstick as well.

'Yow 'ave ter look nice for the boys.' She nudged me, and I, innocent enough to think I could have a boyfriend like her, accepted the dress and the make-up. She was combing out her blonde hair and pouring a colourless liquid from a bottle over her head. She noticed my interest and offered me some.

'It'll make your hair blonde like mine.'

I thought her hair was a lovely colour so I took the remains of the bottle and the other things, thanked her and returned next door. There was still no one home so I was safe to carry on with my experiments in dressing like an adult. The dress was a little too long and fitted tight across my bosom. My breasts were developing fast and I was ashamed to see that my nipples showed through the material. I couldn't wear it so I returned to Sally's. When I showed her she lent me a silk shawl to drape round my shoulders and over my breasts. I returned home to admire the effect. I thought I was the cat's whiskers. Then I began combing my hair, wondering if I dared use the peroxide. I was just about to drip it on the top of my head as I had seen Sally do when, from nowhere, a hand knocked me to the floor, spilling the contents of the bottle. I was taken completely by surprise to find Dad standing over me. I was petrified; I'd never seen him like this.

'I'm warnin' yow, my gel, if I catch yow with that stuff agen I'll cut all your hair off and I'll put this strap across yer back!' he bawled. With that he snatched up the bottle and flung it through the open window into the yard. 'I'm off now,' he continued, 'ter meet yer Mum, so when yer've cleared up yer can get ter bed.'

With that he left, slamming the door behind him. This meant that they wouldn't be back before the pubs closed, but I also knew that if they knew who I was going out with they would have locked me in. I fussed about, preparing myself, washing, combing my hair and putting on my borrowed finery. When I'd completed this process I turned to the mirror to look at myself for a last time. Then I received a shock. When Dad had knocked the bottle out of my hand some of the bleach must have spilled down my face because my right eyebrow was blonde. I'd no idea how I was going to deal with this until my eyes settled on the grate. Then it came to me. I spat on my finger, rubbed it in the soot, then applied it to my eyebrow so that although it was not too convincing at close range, from a distance it looked natural enough. Then, after I'd made sure that I'd left no telltale traces, I was off.

There was nobody about to see me knocking on Sally's door. We took off down the back alleys and finally, by the roundabout route, we reached St Paul's churchyard where we were to meet the boys. Sure enough they were there and the smallest was introduced as my date. He was not a bad looker, I thought, and shook hands as he told me his name was Freddy. 'Frederick the Great, that's me,' he said with a chuckle. He placed his arm round my waist, which gave me a pleasurable feeling I'd never experienced, and then we set off to the picture house. He did all the talking. I was very shy but his mischievous grin put me at my ease and we strolled along behind Sally and her beau. We'd hardly gone halfway when it began to rain and we had to run the rest of the way to queue under shelter. Just inside the foyer there was a long narrow mirror with an almost naked woman painted on it. How shameful, I thought. I glanced at my reflection to admire the effect and then I got my second shock that evening. The rain had smudged my sooty mascara and it was streaked down my cheek. I looked away quickly. Frederick the Great had been straightening his tie but now he turned round to look at me and called to Sally and her friend. They all burst into laughter. I was angry and embarrassed in equal measure and hated them. I just turned and ran off. They deserved each other, I thought.

When I got indoors I was still so upset that I tore off the frock, ripping a sleeve in the process, but I didn't care; I was so angry. I rolled it up into a ball and pushed the shawl and lipstick inside the bundle, then I went to put it on Sally's step. As I dodged down the yard I noticed the broken bottle of peroxide lying in the drain. Picking it up, I rolled that up with the bundle too. I put it on the step, knocked on the door and ran back home.

I was surprised to find Liza sitting up in bed reading one of her romances. 'What's the matter with yow?' she said when she saw my tears. I had to tell someone so I told her. When I'd finished we began to see the funny side of it and ended up laughing.

My first experience with boys was not a great success but it wasn't the last, and later I found myself in worse scrapes than on that first occasion. I had nothing further to do with Sally but she didn't seem to be bothered when I passed her in the street without speaking. In the end I thought it was a good job that I'd cut her dead because I began to pick up the gossip about her and found out that she'd left home when she did because she was pregnant and had had a baby. She was what was known as 'a bad lot' and several times later I saw her standing in alleyways, always with a different man. Mum summed her up when she said, 'Any man can have her, with or without his trousers down.'

This experience renewed my curiosity about the facts of life. All I knew were the half-truths and lies that children were told in those days. I was afraid to ask Mum any details of where babies came from and the word 'sex' was considered a dirty word in our house.

When I saw my first period I was scared to death. I ran all the way home from school thinking I was going to bleed to death. I burst into tears when I saw Mum, and told her what had happened. But all the explanation she gave me was, 'Now yow keep away from the lads an' never let 'em kiss yer or the next thing yer know yer'll be 'avin' a baby. Then God 'elp yer.'

I pointed out that I kissed Frankie but she dismissed my puzzlement. 'That's different. 'E's yer brother, ain't 'e. Now be off with yer, I'll see ter yer later. An' don't forget what I've told yer! Keep away from the lads.'

I was perplexed. If only someone would explain these things to me, but I was too shy and scared to ask. I determined to overcome my embarrassment and go and ask Mrs Taylor. Perhaps she could tell me why I was bleeding. When I told her she just gave me a piece of clean rag and said more or less the same as Mum had.

'Is it true?' I asked her. 'Will I have a baby if a boy kisses me?'

'Well, it's a start,' she answered, smiling, 'but when yer grow older you'll find out.' This was clearly little help either.

I knew when people were married and slept together a baby usually followed, but this didn't enlighten me about the facts of life. In fact, for a while I was almost as afraid of boys as I was of horses and cows. As far as my education on the subject was concerned I was reduced to listening to gossip in the hope of learning more.

I was in the yard one day when all the women were gossiping and Mrs Smith from the next yard happened to pass. 'Hello Nell, I see yer've bin eatin' new bread agen,' Mrs Phipps called to her. 'Yes, an' it's all me own,' she replied, smacking her belly as she walked by. Then Maggie said, 'Did yer know Mrs Buckley's balloon's up agen?' 'Yes, we 'eard,' replied Mrs Jones. Mrs Phipps gave Maggie a cold look and said, 'Why is it yer've never 'ad your balloon up, Maggie?' 'That's my affair,' Maggie replied. 'Any'ow my Billy ain't got much, an' what 'e 'as got 'e's keepin' it fer 'imself.' And they all burst out laughing.

I didn't make much of this but Mrs Smith's daughter was a friend of mine. Her name was Nellie and she was in the same class as me at school and her family had not long moved into the neighbourhood. I was attracted by her outspoken ways. Sometimes after school I would visit their house and she would show me all her nice clothes. Nellie promised me one of her old dresses when she had a new one. Then one afternoon Mrs Smith came in and found us and asked who I was.

'It's Katie, my school friend,' Nellie replied.

'Well, sit yerself down, Katie. Don't be shy, I'm not going ter eat yer,' she said, busying herself untying the parcels she had with her.

She was a pretty woman and would have had a good figure had she not been pregnant. She had a pleasant disposition and always had a twinkle in her eyes. She had a soft voice and always put me at my ease. We watched her untie the parcels which turned out to contain pretty blue woollen baby clothes.

The next parcel contained a new dress for Nellie. It was bright pillar-box red with a white lace collar and cuffs. When her mum undressed her to try it on I couldn't take my eyes off the lovely white underclothes she wore. I turned my head away then, because

Mum always said it wasn't decent to watch people undress. Evidently Mrs Smith thought differently.

'Don't be shy, Katie,' she said. 'Yer can turn round now.'

Nellie looked sweet in her new frock. Then she asked her mum to find something for me. Mrs Smith went to the wardrobe and brought out a yellow dress with pretty flowers and leaves all over it.

'Take your dress off and try this on. It should fit.'

I must have looked embarrassed when she handed it over because they both turned their backs while I slipped my old dress off and put the new one on. After fastening all the buttons up the front I said meekly, 'You can turn round now.' I felt great when Mrs Smith said I looked pretty and that I could keep the dress. I was so overwhelmed that I started to cry.

'What's all this for?' she asked kindly.

'Mum will never let me keep it. I've only got old ones an' this one will go to the pawnshop.' I wiped the tears with the back of my hand.

'Never mind that. Wipe yer eyes and then we'll go upstairs and see what else we can find,' Mrs Smith soothed me.

Nellie had a pleasant bedroom all to herself. If I had a room of my own, I thought, I would knit and knit to make it as pretty as this. We girls sat on the bed while Mrs Smith sorted out some underclothes for me.

'Now, don't be shy. Yer can undress in front of Nellie and me,' she said. 'But if yer like we'll go downstairs.'

'I'd like Nellie to stay,' I whispered. I was shy of undressing in front of adults. So Mrs Smith left us alone and I stripped off in front of my friend although I made her turn away when I came to my combs. Then I dressed in the vest, bloomers, camisole with pink ribbon threaded through the top and bottom, a pretty lace underskirt and finally the yellow dress. I felt like a princess.

'You look lovely, Katie,' Nellie said. 'Let's go an' show Mum.'

They both enthused over my new look and I became weepy and wailed that I couldn't keep them.

'But they're yours to keep, like I told you,' Mrs Smith said gently.

'No, they'll end up in the pawnshop,' I sobbed.

'Oh, no they won't. Nellie, you go upstairs and bring down Katie's clothes,' she said.

What was she up to? I wondered. She wrapped them up in a parcel and took them out to the dustbin. She was about to pop them in when we heard the strains of the rag-and-bone man's cry. Round the corner he came, pushing his handcart with balloons flying high. She gave him the bundle and he opened it to examine the contents.

'What yer want fer these, Mrs?' he inquired.

'Oh, just give the kids a balloon each,' she told him.

'They're only worth one,' he grumbled.

'Right! I'll put them in the bin then,' she replied, but before she could get them off the cart he handed us the balloons.

Then, with many thanks to Mrs Smith, I left for home, anxious to tell Mum about my good fortune. Mum stared at me, dumbfounded, until she recovered and found her voice.

'Who's got yow all dressed up?' she demanded, shaking me.

'Mrs Smith gave them to me,' I told her.

'An' where's yer own?' she snapped.

I was too scared to admit to her what had happened to them, so I said Mrs Smith would tell her. Now our houses backed on to each other, with only the party wall between, so she just picked up the poker from the fender and started banging on the wall so that the plaster showered a cloud of dust in the room.

'Are yow theea, Mrs Smith, cos if yow are I want some words with yow!' she bellowed.

Mrs Smith came immediately, with Nellie behind her. Mum had found her mistress in Mrs Smith. She drew herself up to her full height, hands on hips; quite a figure. 'An' what's the matter with you?' she asked sarcastically. 'Yer trying' ter knock the 'ouse down?'

'Where's me daughter's clothes yer've took off 'er? I want 'em back.'

Mrs Smith was unimpressed by Mum's overbearing manner, she simply grinned and replied calmly, 'Sorry, my dear, you'll have to ask the rag-an-bone man for them.'

'WHAT!' yelled Mum.

'Yes,' Mrs Smith nodded. 'They weren't worth keeping so I swapped them for a couple of balloons.'

Mum's face reddened visibly. She continued to splutter and threaten. 'I'll 'ave the law on yer.'

'Come on you two,' Mrs Smith said to us. 'I never 'ave anything to do with trash if I can 'elp it.'

I went round to their place again and we had toast and tea with real cow's milk, not the Handy Brand condensed milk we always had at home. After tea we went out to play. I was afraid to go back home for fear of the trouble I'd be in from Mum. When I left Nellie I went to several pubs looking for Dad but nobody had seen him, so, as it was getting late, I turned to go home. As I dragged reluctantly along past Mrs Smith's house again who should come out, deep in conversation with Mrs Smith, but my dad. They were smiling and when Mrs Smith saw me she called out cheerily, 'It's all right, Katie, I've explained to your dad.'

'Come on, Katie,' he said. 'Let's face the music.'

Before we'd set foot over the doorstep Mum had started. 'What yer think about 'er round the back? Tellin' me what ter do with me own kids. She wants ter look after 'er own.' She stopped to draw breath which gave Dad his opportunity.

'Now yow be quiet, Polly. Yow don't want all the neighbour-hood round yer door, do yer?'

'Oh, she's told yow the tale 'as she?' Mum didn't miss much

'Only the truth, and I admire her for it. She's one person yow can't push around like the rest of yer cronies.'

Mum could see she was getting nowhere so she tried shedding

a tear or two. This was an old ploy when she couldn't get her own way. Dad was having none of this.

'Yow can turn yer tap off, I'm going up to bed and you, Katie, better get off too,' he said, handing me a saucer with a stub of candle on it. I didn't wait to be told twice and I made myself scarce.

After that Nellie and I became close friends and so did her mum and my dad. Mum never said a word when I invited Nellie into our house but I could tell she didn't like her. We sang together and Dad sometimes gave us money to go to see a picture at the Queen's Hall. When Nellie's mum was very large and the baby was due she wouldn't let Nellie go far in case she needed her to fetch the midwife. All this time I still wondered about the origin of babies, and one night I raised the subject with Nellie. I began by asking her if she liked boys. She said she did 'a bit' but she was also afraid of them 'a bit' as well. I asked why and she gave me a reply I hadn't expected.

'Well, my mum told me not to let boys fondle me or kiss me now I've started me periods, otherwise, if I did, I'd soon be having a baby.'

I told her my mum had said the same. 'My mum says she don't want me growing up like Sally Buckley.'

'Do you know 'er?' she asked in apparent surprise.

'Everybody knows 'er,' I said. Then I told her about the date at the pictures with the two boys and about the disaster with the bleach.

'How lucky you were,' Nellie laughed. 'Yer never know what would 'ave 'appened if it 'adn't rained.'

'Nellie,' I said, 'd'yer know where babies come from?'

'Course I do, silly. Don't you?'

'No.' I shook my head, a bit shyly.

'Well you know when mothers get fat and their stomach sticks out like a balloon? Well, they carry that for nine months, don't they? Then when the time comes their belly goes pop with a bang and the baby pops out.' That seemed to make sense to me. 'Tell yer what,' she offered. 'When my mum's about to have her pains I'll call for yer and we'll sit on the stairs and listen.'

Although I was anxious to be there I didn't get the chance because Mrs Smith gave birth to a baby girl in the early hours of the morning later that week. We were both disappointed but Nellie said we could wait until the next time.

I also wondered about why we never saw Nellie's dad and eventually I asked her about him. Nellie rounded on me angrily and asked me why I wanted to know. Then I told about the tales the neighbours were telling about her mum and her men friends. She replied that she knew where he was but she didn't want to discuss it. 'What my mum does is her affair.' She was adamant. She must have known what her mum was up to but I didn't question her any more on the subject.

We were still at school when, later that year, the First World War broke out. We were in standard seven, the highest class, which meant we could leave school early, when we were thirteen, which would be another eighteen months for me. We were both monitors and I helped the teacher with the younger children, teaching them how to knit socks and balaclavas for the soldiers at the Front. We put little messages in them wishing the Tommies 'good luck' to cheer them up. I loved knitting and do to this day. I won first prizes for the best garment and for the most knitted in my class. The only thing I didn't like was the monotonous khaki wool. One day I asked the teacher if it wouldn't be more patriotic to knit some items in red, white and blue. She smiled at this and said if I wanted a change I could knit up navy blue wool for the Royal Navy, which I did. I won another prize for this as well, and I was presented with a beautiful work basket lined with red satin by the headmistress, Miss Ford. I had to stand in front of the whole school which gave me ample opportunity to observe the envy on some girls' faces because knitting for the troops was a popular pastime then. In fact, everybody seemed to be busy finding some job to help with the war effort, except Mum who continued to clean at the Gingold's chip shop.

My two eldest brothers, Charlie and Jack, volunteered for Kitchener's Army as most boys of their generation did. Even Dad tried to enlist. He told the recruiting officer that he'd been a sergeant in the Boer War and boasted that he knew more about the Army than all these whipper-snappers who were waiting to join with him. He was told to strip for a medical examination but he wasn't up to scratch and failed, and so never got his chance. Nevertheless he was determined to do his bit, making shell cases in the casting shop. This was more patriotic than wise because he had to work long hours and came home coughing; you could smell the sulphur on his clothes. But he said he didn't mind as long as he was helping the war effort, and anyway it would all be over in six months. Little did we imagine then that the war would last until November 1918.

Frankie left school and Dad found him a job with him, fetching and carrying sand for the men. He was a strong, healthy lad and as pleased as punch to be working with Dad. He began to put on airs and think he was a grown-up who could boss us around until Dad checked him for it. Liza left as well and got a job on the munitions with Sally Buckley, which boded no good. There were rows at night over her staying out late with Sally. Mum always stood up for Liza, her longtime favourite, telling Dad she had enough sense to know what was right and wrong, but I doubted she did. Dad wasn't convinced either.

I wanted to help too but I was still too young to leave school. There was work for everyone. People were doing all kinds of jobs to earn money; even the married women who could get nothing before were able to take in washing for the posh folk whose maids were earning more in a week in the munitions factories than they could in a month skivvying. Mum would have none of this: she was not going to do other people's dirty washing and she stayed at the fish shop all the war years.

It was ironic that now everybody in our district had plenty of money for food they couldn't obtain it because everything was rationed. Still, this left all the more to spend on drink. The pubs were doing a roaring trade, what with this new-found prosperity and the constant flow of soldiers on leave with money to spend and precious little time to get rid of it. There was plenty of scandal about the Australian and Canadian troops being out with other men's wives or, worse, being seen in doorways or entries with them while the blackout was on. Women whose men were away at the war were still having babies. Several times I was given money to go to the chemist's for bitter aloes or pennyroyal or a bottle of gin from the outdoor. Miscarriages procured in this way often led to death or malformed births.

Brother Jack wrote each week while he was in training on Salisbury Plain with the Royal Field Artillery. Mum always opened the letters but I had to read them for her. He would write that he was 'doing fine' and that the war would be over soon. I knitted him socks and slipped packets of Woodbines in with them.

Another incident which sticks in my memory from those final years at school concerned a friend of mine, Nelly Mitchell. I'd discussed the mystery of childbirth with her as well and she'd offered, like Nellie Smith, to call me when her mother, who was pregnant, was about to give birth. I was playing jackstones in the street when she ran up with the news that she was going for the midwife. We ran and knocked on the midwife's door and she called out for Nelly to run and get newspapers and hot water ready.

When we got to Nelly's the fire was low, but while she was collecting newspapers I filled the kettle and using the old leather bellows stoked up the heat. Mrs Bullivant was the only midwife in our district and if the women couldn't afford her the neighbours helped, a practice which often ended in tragedy. As Mrs Bullivant, carrying her bag of instruments, mounted the stairs, Nelly's mum began to cry out in agony. We looked at each other, scared stiff, but we followed Mrs Bullivant upstairs. She was a small, round woman with eyes that seemed too small for her face which was flushed red; it was as much she could do to struggle up, rolling from side to side and, I noticed, smelling of drink. When we followed her into the bedroom she ordered us out, saying it was no place for kids. We went outside but could still see because the door didn't quite close. As soon as she thought we were out of sight she reached under her apron and produced a small bottle from which, tipping back her head, she took a swig. Then she replaced it and went over to see to Mrs Mitchell who lay on the top of the bed dressed only in a calico nightgown, groaning as she writhed about. Then the midwife lifted up the gown and rolled her roughly on to her side. I almost screamed when I saw the largest bare belly I'd ever seen in my life. The belly button was protruding and it looked ready to burst. I'd seen enough. I didn't want to wait for the baby to appear through the navel. I tried to back down the stairs but as Nelly kept hold of my frock to prevent me, we crashed against the door and ended in a heap on the floor. I expected a slap but Mrs Bullivant just stepped over us saying she'd be back later, after she'd attended Mrs Groves who was having her first. Then she was gone.

Nelly begged me not to leave her, and plucking up courage I stayed. Nelly held her mum's hand while I dipped a sponge into the cold water jug and mopped her brow which was sweaty from the pain she was in. I became frightened; I thought she was going to die and I felt sick. It was the first time I'd seen anyone in labour and I made a silent vow that when I was married I wasn't going to have any babies if this was how you had to suffer. A few minutes later, when Nelly was preoccupied, I'm sorry to say my cowardice got the better of me and I crept out of the room, down the stairs and ran off home.

For hours I couldn't put those dreadful cries out of my mind and

I imagined that with every breath my own stomach was swelling and about to burst. I had a nightmare that night which ended with me rolling out of bed and landing on the floor where I was sick. Next morning I cleaned up the vomit and got myself ready for school but I still had a nasty taste in my mouth and I was hot and achy. When I peered at myself in the mirror I screamed. My eyes were puffed up and my face was covered with red spots. My scream brought Mum up to see what was wrong and when she saw my face she ordered me back into bed. I had measles and had to stay isolated in the darkened room for two weeks.

I was dosed with saffron tea which tasted foul and I couldn't see anybody. By the time I'd recovered I was skinnier than ever, having been rationed to an orange a day. After a few days I was allowed downstairs and began to eat proper meals again, and two weeks later I started back at school.

On my way there the first morning I noticed that Nelly's house had a 'To Let' sign in the window. I ran to catch Liza up and when I asked her where they were she hesitated before replying.

'She's dead,' she said. I was dumbstruck.

'Who? Nelly?' I stammered. Then Liza told me that Mrs Mitchell had died in childbirth and that Nelly herself had been taken to Wolverhampton to live with an aunt and uncle. I felt miserable and blamed myself even more for not staying that night or fetching a doctor. I was too upset to go to school. I went and sat in the churchyard and wept for Mrs Mitchell and Nelly and prayed for myself to be forgiven and for them to be looked after. I was not missed that day either at school or at home. I didn't forget Nelly who had been a good little friend to me, and eventually we did meet up again, several years later.

Chapter 18

My First Job

At Christmas 1916 when I was nearly fourteen I was preparing to leave school. The Great War was still going and there was still plenty of work for young people in our district. I got an inkling of what was in the wind when I came home early from the Band of Hope and overheard a conversation between Mum and Dad.

'She don't look strong enough ter work on a press,' said Dad.

'But that's where the big wages are, on munitions,' Mum told him. 'Anyway,' she continued, 'we'll soon fatten 'er up if we give 'er plenty ter eat.'

'All right,' Dad said, 'I s'ppose yer know what's best for 'er.'

'She's gotta earn 'er keep like the rest of 'em,' Mum concluded.

I was amused when I was given two thick slices of bread and half a cow heel before I went to bed but I didn't take long to devour it. This was a treat and no mistake and I sucked all the bones clean I was that hungry. I was even offered more, and I could see the writing was on the wall. Every mealtime for the next few weeks it was as if I was being fattened up for the slaughter. I had as much as and more than I could eat for a change. And I was putting on weight so fast that my clothes wouldn't fit. I was also getting taller. Mum said she couldn't afford to buy me a new frock and that I would have to have one of Mary's old ones cut down. She cobbled it together with black thread so I felt a proper charlie, but she said it would have to do until I earned my first week's wages.

I wasn't going to wait until then. I'd been saving pennies and halfpennies up for ages for this moment. Next day when the house was empty I bolted the door and ran upstairs to the attic. Pushing the iron bedstead across the room I got on my knees and with a knife prised up the floorboard and pulled out a mice-nibbled newspaper package. I emptied its contents on to the bed and counted out three shillings and ninepence-halfpenny, all earned running errands. I put it in my rag purse, replaced everything, unbolted the door and went off down the street to an old woman who sold second-hand clothes from her front room.

When I got there I looked through the window and there as luck would have it was the prettiest pink crepe de Chine blouse I had ever seen. It had lace trimmings on the cuffs and round the high collar, and down the front it was fastened with six round pearl buttons. I had to have it. I pushed open the door and went in, a rusty bell clanging a warning to the owner. At first I couldn't see her and assumed she was in the back but then I saw her sitting on a stool sewing, amidst heaps of old clothes. Suddenly she looked up, glared at me and shouted, 'What der yer want, comin' in 'ere like that?'

'H-how much is that blouse in the window?' I managed to stammer.

'Who wants ter know?' came the reply.

'Me,' I said. 'I want ter buy it.'

She stared at me in disbelief until I shook my bag and she heard the chink of coins. That livened her up and she grinned a gummy smile and said, 'Ter yo' it's 'alf a crown.' She then proceeded to extol the garment's virtues and the 'fine lady' who originally owned it. However, I had to explain that although I liked it I couldn't afford that much because I wanted to buy a pair of boots as well and all I had to spend was three shillings and nine pence-halfpenny. I explained that I wanted it for an interview for a job because I was leaving school and she began to soften.

'All right,' she grinned, 'yer can 'ave a pair of second 'and button-up boots an' the blouse for three an' ninepence an' I'll throw in a camisole. Now come on through the back so's yer can try 'em on.'

I held on to my money though until I'd satisfied myself the clothes were worth what she wanted for them. She handed me the camisole which was frayed and yellow with age but which looked clean, then she shuffled through to the window to fetch the blouse. I was pleased when she handed it to me to see how nice it was, and when I tried it on it looked better on me than it did in the window. So she wrapped them both up in some newspaper. I next tried on several pairs of boots until eventually I found a pair that fitted. They were a bit down at heel but with blacking I could see they would look better than the ones I was wearing.

'Yer got a bargain,' the old crone cried, counting the pennies. 'Now be off with yer before I change me mind!'

All I had left was a halfpenny, but I was pleased with my purchases which I hid under the straw mattress until I needed them. The following Friday I shook hands with my teacher for the last time, listened to her lecture on 'my new life', was handed a book for good attendance and walked home feeling grown up, at the tender age of fourteen.

When I got in I showed Mum my book and told her what the teacher had said but she didn't seem interested. All she said was that my sister was coming to tea and she wanted me to do some errands.

'I want yer ter go ter Jefferson's an' fetch two ounces of tea, two pounds of sugar an' a tinna condensed milk. Oh, an' 'alf a loaf, an' see it's new. An' don't forget me change.'

I remember Mr Jefferson vividly. He was a short, fat man with a red face and a bald head. He reminded me of Humpty-Dumpty. He kept a well-stocked, tidy shop where you could buy almost anything. I ran all the way to the shop and rushed in, pushing open the frosted-glass door and making the bell clank noisily. I went straight up to the counter. I climbed on the hot-water pipe that ran along the floor and peered over the top where I could see Mr Jefferson's bald head. I blurted out my order without drawing breath and jumped down to the floor.

He glared at me over the counter and said, 'Be quiet, an' wait yer turn.' Then for the first time I noticed three well-dressed women looking daggers at me.

When I got back Mum was in a lather again. 'About time,' she said and snatched the bag off me. Just then Mrs Taylor tumbled into the room and Mum looked up with a glare on her face.

'Yower Mary ain't comin' terday, she told me ter tell yer 'er mutha-in-law's took bad.' She collapsed breathlessly into a chair.

' 'Er thinks mower of 'er than she does of me,' Mum fumed, sitting down in the other chair. I could see signs that they were going to be some time nattering so I crept up to the attic and rummaged through Liza's trunk. I found an old, long black hobble skirt which I knew she didn't want because she'd grown out of it. With the hem turned up and some elastic in the waist I thought it would be just the thing to go with my blouse. When I heard the two women leave a little later, I went down and set to with a needle and thread. I took some elastic from a pair of bloomers and pretty soon had a serviceable skirt to go with the other things.

On the following Monday morning Mum gave me tuppence for a bath at the public ones in Northwood Street where I went now that I was 'a big girl', and sixpence for my medical which I had to have before I could work in a factory. I bundled up my new clothes and set off. It was heavenly to stretch out in such a big bath and soak in gallons of hot soapy water; I could have stayed there all day, but I knew I had to go out and look for a job before long. I stepped out of the bath and dried myself and admired myself in the mirror; I'd certainly filled out. I felt so clean and fresh. I put on my stockings, clean bloomers, my camisole and skirt then my blouse. It felt a bit tight when I fastened all the buttons up but I thought, I won't burst open if I don't breathe too deeply or thrust my chest out. Then I buttoned up my boots which were now polished and I felt ready to face the adult world. I folded the old clothes into a bundle and standing on the lavatory seat I pushed them behind the iron cistern. Then I walked out into the street. Imagine my surprise when the first person I bumped into, practically on the steps of the baths, was my old friend Nelly Mitchell.

We threw our arms round each other and exchanged greetings. She told me she was in lodgings round the corner. I asked her why she hadn't been to see me before but she said she'd only been there a few days and had only just moved from her aunt's in Wolverhampton. Her aunt had died and now she was with a friend and looking for work like I was. We walked along arm in arm exchanging news, oblivious of anything else. Then I noticed how well dressed she was and she told me about the good times she had with boys. It seemed so exciting, but my first thought was to find a job. Then as luck would have it we turned a corner and saw a notice on a factory gate which read: 'WOMEN AND GIRLS WANTED TO LEARN PRESSWORK'. I knew it was tough, manual work, swinging the handles of the heavy mechanical presses which were used to stamp out metal components, but many young girls like us were doing this sort of work because so many men were away at the Front.

'You go in and ask first, Katie, while I wait here. Then you can let me know how you got on and I'll go in after.'

Up the narrow stairs I went, trying to avoid slipping on the grease which covered them. I reached the top and pushed open the door and found myself inside a small cubicle just big enough to hold two people. I tapped the wooden panel and suddenly a small trapdoor shot up and I jumped with fright as a woman's face and shoulders appeared in the gap.

'What yer come for? The job is it?' She had to shout to make herself heard above the noise of the presses in the room behind her.

I was suddenly nervous. Why, I wondered, didn't Mum come with me for the interview like other mothers did? Now I was fourteen I had to stand on my own two feet, she'd said. I stared at the woman's stern face until I found the courage to speak.

'Yes, ma'am,' was all I could manage. She eyed me up and down and asked me my age.

'Fourteen. I left school last week,' I told her.

'An' yer sure yer want ter work on a press?' she asked.

'Yes, we do,' I answered without thinking.

'We, who's we?' she snapped gruffly.

'My friend Nelly. She's downstairs.'

'Well, send 'er up. Let's take a look at 'er.' Then the trapdoor slammed shut.

I ran and fetched Nelly and we both returned to the cubicle. Up shot the door again.

'So you're Nelly?' she snapped. 'Well, yow'll do.' She had to bellow.

She gave us a note pad to write down our names and addresses and when we handed it to her she told us to return at eight the following morning with our birth certificates and medical certificates. 'An' I mean eight, not five past!' she shouted.

'Yes Miss,' I replied while Nelly tried to peer over her shoulder into the workshop beyond.

'Yower ter call me Madam. I'm the forewoman,' she snapped.

'Yes Madam,' I replied timidly. With that the trapdoor shut again and we were alone in the cubicle.

'I don't like 'er, she's an old battleaxe,' said Nelly as we made our way down the iron stairs and back into the street. Then Nelly asked about the pay. I had to admit that I'd forgotten to ask. 'Well, you'll 'ave ter go back and ask 'er then, won't you,' she snapped.

When I entered the cubicle the trap sprang and Madam appeared wanting to know what I wanted.

'Please Madam,' I asked, ''ow much will the wages be?'

'Twelve an' six a week, eight o'clock till six and one o'clock on Saturdays. Yow get fifteen minutes for lunch and one till two dinnertime and yow'll clock in and out. I'll put yow right, an' if yer be'ave yerself an' work 'ard you get a rise to thirteen shillings at the end of the month.' And with that the trap closed again and her hard face was gone.

I thought on twelve and six I would be rich in no time. Mum could have ten shillings and I could have the half-crown for myself. I could do a lot with that much. But when I told Nelly she didn't seem very pleased and suggested that it was not wise to take the first job that offered itself but to look around for something better.

'But Nelly,' I told her. 'She's got my address an' if my mum finds out I'll be in trouble.'

'Yer Mum won't find out an' anyway she won't mind more money.' With this I had to agree.

We went off down the street in high spirits, looking in all the shop windows, planning what we would spend our money on. Then we thought we'd better look for an alternative job. By now it was one o'clock and the boys were coming out of the factories. They began to whistle at us and although I didn't want anything to do with them, Nelly stopped to talk to them. I went round the corner and waited for her. Eventually when Nelly appeared she said she'd made a date with one of them. I was shocked at her brazenness. How could she? I thought. She was only the same age as me but a lot more forward.

We stopped at several other workshops that were advertising for women and girls, but none of them wanted to pay more than ten or eleven shillings and one small place only seven and threepence with overtime. So we decided to take the first job at the factory in Vittoria Street.

Then we thought about going for our medical. We walked along the street, arm in arm, as the trams clanged past, their bells ringing. Posters were pasted up everywhere there was room. Life-size posters of Kitchener looked down on us, proclaiming 'Your Country Needs You'. There was the odd Union Jack, and hand-painted slogans saying, 'Down with the Hun', and 'Votes for Women', and rude ones like, 'Fuck the Kaiser'. I was shocked when I saw this. Bad language was frowned on even in poor households. Finally we arrived at the clinic. There were several women waiting with their daughters. They stared at us; we were the only ones without our mothers. We watched the steady stream go in and come out until it was our turn, when Nelly pushed me in front as the voice called loudly, 'Next!'

I steadied myself and entered; I was very nervous. The doctor was sitting at his writing table. Without looking up he said, 'Sit down!' He was a thickset man, very dark-skinned with wavy black hair. I couldn't make up my mind what nationality he was but he wasn't English. When he'd finished writing he suddenly swivelled round in his chair and stared at me, and his black eyes seemed to look through me. He stood up and bent over me and with his pen he lifted up my plaits.

'I ain't got ticks in my hair, doctor,' I told him. He didn't answer but instead shone a little light in my ears. 'Hm, hm,' he repeated. 'Hm, open your mouth and put out your tongue.' I did as I was told. When he was satisfied with that he took his stethoscope and put it to his ears. Nobody had told me there'd be all this rigmarole. I thought he just asked you questions and you paid the sixpence for your medical certificate; I had already put it on the table. I was beginning to wonder what he was going to do next when he snapped at me:

'Open your blouse!' I was rooted to the spot with fright; I wanted my mum or Nelly to walk in to come to my aid. 'Come along, open your blouse. I can't stand here all day,' he said, becoming impatient.

Slowly I fumbled with the first button, then the second, but I was not going to open my blouse any further than that. I felt unclean as he looked at me and the next thing I knew he had pulled my blouse open wide and the lovely pearl buttons had gone pop, pop, pop and were rolling about the floor. I was unable to move, terrified of what was to come next. Then he put his cold hands down inside my camisole and lifted out my bare breasts. He felt them for some time, then with another 'hm' slowly returned them – but not before he'd smiled and squeezed them. I slapped his hands as hard as I could, and clutching my blouse fled out of the room with 'Next!' echoing in my ears. I had no time to tell Nelly who was through the door in a flash and I collapsed on the bench in tears over my beautiful pearl buttons.

In no time at all Nelly emerged, all smiles. 'He's nice ain't 'e?' she said.

'No! 'E's not an' I don't ever want ter go through that again,' I replied still sobbing.

'Yer too modest,' she laughed. 'Anyway, 'ere's yer buttons an' yer medical certificate 'e gave me ter give yer.'

Birmingham's Jewellery Quarter near where we lived was an area of old Georgian and early Victorian houses that had once been fashionable but were now run down. As the tenants left the landlords would rent off the rooms singly to craftsmen in the many trades of the area. Workshops were built at the back of these houses and the whole area was a warren representing many of the city's 'thousand trades'. Some people in the district I knew let off their front room, undertaking outwork for the jeweller who moved in. All kinds of gold and silver objects were made there: diamond rings, tableware, anything you could think of in that line.

When I was a bit older I would go on a Friday night to a pub called the Jeweller's Arms with some of the girls I worked with. Many's the time I have watched the gaffers of these thriving little businesses exchanging hundreds of pounds or packets of diamonds in corners of this and other pubs in the area. The factory where Nelly and I started work was not far from this pub. It was called the Birmingham Brass Works. The front door led to a small office and the workshop was down the entry.

At five minutes to eight the next day we were standing outside the gate with several roughly dressed women. They pushed Nelly and me to one side when the gate opened, clocked in and went off up the yard, disappearing up the steps without exchanging a word. We were standing there, hesitant, when a voice boomed out, 'Follow me.' It was Madam, the forewoman, dressed in a khaki overall. She was elderly, tall and straight and very serious: I never remember her smiling. She showed us how to clock in with our timecard and then we followed her along the cobbled yard and up the greasy steps into the workshop.

The women who we'd seen previously were already busy operating the presses. At the end of the shop were smaller machines driven by an electric motor on the wall which worked the leather pulleys that ran along the ceiling. The workshop was dirty and reeked of oil. In the centre of the room was a large, battered pipe stove filled with glowing coke. Every now and then smoke billowed into the room and when it did Nelly and I began to cough, but no one else seemed to be affected. They just sat there busily swinging the handles of the presses.

We were each handed khaki overalls like the rest had on; mine came almost to the floor and my cap, when I tried it on, kept slipping over my eyes. The forewoman told me it was the smallest they had. Nelly was taller than me and had more hair to fill her cap with.

'Come along you two,' she snapped at us. 'You can work the guillotine,' she said to Nelly.

As soon as she had Nelly settled in she came back to me and showed me how to use the press to cut brass blanks from strips of scrap metal. I soon picked the job up but she came several times that morning to see how I was getting along.

'We don't want any scrap left,' was all she said. She examined the blanks that I had made and seemed satisfied, and that made me work harder. Then I noticed the other women along the bench were giving me black looks but I had no idea why.

At break time when I was standing eating my corned beef sandwich, one of the women shouted over to me.

'Yow've got my job, an' it's the best in the shop!'

They were all about to join in when Madam appeared and warned them if there was any more trouble they would be reported to the gaffer. They went on eating in silence. One of the women came over and offered me her place by the fire but I was too scared to move and anyway it was too late because just then the bell rang for us to start work again. I hadn't finished my sandwich so I wrapped it up and put it in my overall pocket. I was surprised I hadn't seen Nelly but I found out later that she'd walked out because she didn't like the place or the work. But I did. It was satisfying work cutting out the shilling-sized blanks and stacking them in three dozens. Afterwards I took them to the drilling machine where Minnie, the woman who had offered me her place, showed me how to drill four holes in them. I was proud to be doing my bit for King and country when I was told they were brass trouser buttons for the Army.

When one o'clock came and I was clocking out, Minnie came up to me and spoke. She was a small, thin woman, very pale, and came, she told me, from the Black Country. I asked why she couldn't get a job nearer home but she said she had seven children and a husband to keep and this was the best-paid job she could find. We became very friendly. She looked as old as my mum with her lined face but she told me she was not yet thirty. She explained why the other women were nasty to me. Apparently they were on piecework, although I hadn't realised this, and I had one of the best jobs.

That made me work harder. But when I got my first week's wages I received a shock. Instead of the twelve and six I expected there was only ten shillings and ninepence. I was too embarrassed to ask the other workers why so I plucked up courage and tapped on the office door.

'Come in!' came the voice of the Battleaxe from within.

I edged in timidly and asked if there had been a mistake in my wages.

'No!' came the reply. 'If you read the notice, you'll find it's correct.'

'What notice?' I asked; this was the first time I had heard about a notice.

'The girls will show you, now be off. Can't you see I'm busy?'

I went over to Minnie and asked her and she pointed to a notice on the wall at the end of the machine shop. It was small and splashed with oil and almost illegible but I could make this out:

STOPPAGES EACH WEEK
TO BE COLLECTED FROM WAGES

6d. FOR XMAS FUND
3d. FOR THE SWEEPER
3d. FOR THE LAVATORY CLEANER
6d. FOR THE TEA LADY
3d. FOR THE LOAN OF OVERALLS AND CAP

I thought about it and reasoned that since we all had to take our turn sweeping and cleaning the lav then next time it was my turn I would receive my fair share. When my turn did come I found that they were dirty, smelly jobs but I did them anyway thinking of my reward at the end of the week. But when the wages arrived I found the same amount as usual. I demanded an explanation from the other women but they just laughed.

'Silly girl. All the money's pooled together for our outing and Christmas party.' Unfortunately for me I went on neither.

When I returned home with that first week's wages I was afraid to tell my mum because I knew there would be hell to pay. She would have turned the workshop and the forewoman inside out, so I gave her the ten shillings that she expected and made do with the ninepence: not much for a hard week's work.

I went back on the Monday after I'd discovered my error over the deductions but I was determined to find myself another job. However, during the morning the forewoman came over to where I was pressing the brass buttons and offered to put me on piece-work like the others, although I hadn't been there as long as you normally had to have been for this to happen. She told me I could earn more money and I deserved it because I was a good little worker. When she'd gone the other women sent Minnie over to find out what she'd wanted and when Minnie told them they started to laugh and titter. I ignored them and set to as hard as I could; so hard that by the end of the week my fingers were bleeding from many cuts I had from the sharp brass discs. The others tried to compete, I suppose because they still resented me, but I worked even harder. I even slipped back in, unknown to them all including the forewoman, and worked through my dinner hour; at the end of that week I'd earned fifteen shillings and fourpence clear. I didn't tell the others but the following Monday the forewoman told me how pleased she was with my 'output'. I didn't tell Mum either; she still had her ten shillings and the rest I hid under the floorboards.

The following week the pace began to tell and I had to slow down because I felt tired and lifeless. All I wanted when I finished work at six o'clock was my bed. I was in more trouble at work as well. The women crowded round me, jostling me and shouting, making all kinds of threats. I had no idea why until Minnie told me that the piece rates were being cut and it was my fault. And sure enough at the end of the week all I had earned was seven shillings and threepence. It was not even the day rate. That was it! I decided there and then to leave, and I did. I was only glad I had enough to make up Mum's ten shillings.

I didn't move far because my next job was at a firm only a few doors away where they were advertising for a young girl to learn case-making. I went along the next Monday and rang the bell of the workshop which had been someone's front room. It was opened by an elderly man, small with a grey, pointed beard. On his head was a black velvet cap and round his waist a long, well-worn leather apron. He smelled horribly of glue, as did his little workshop. I told him why I'd called and after looking me up and down while he fingered his beard he took me inside where there was a long bench from one end of the room to the other on which were laid sheets of red- and blue-covered cardboard and plywood. Sitting at the bench with their backs to me were two women and a young man busily making boxes out of the cardboard. These, he told me, were jewel cases. I didn't get much chance to see what was going on here because he led me into a smaller room at the back which I could see had been somebody's kitchen. There was a gas stove with two pots of molten glue on it, and on the other side of the room was a bench with scissors, a tape measure and a small roll of velvet.

He told me I was to work here and that my job was to cut out the pieces of velvet and pass them through to where the women sat glueing. I enjoyed this job because although it was smelly it was clean and wasn't hard work. He said my wages would be fifteen shillings a week if I could be trusted and I did what I was told. I spent a happy month there until an incident happened that scared me off.

It happened one Friday night. The boss asked me if he could trust me to take a packet to a woman who would be waiting outside the Rose Villa, a public house on the corner of Vyse Street. With that he brought a Bible out of his desk and asked me to swear on it that I would not tell anyone what I was carrying or where I was going. I agreed and after I'd kissed the Bible he handed me a small leather 'dolly bag' which he said I was to give to a tall woman, dressed in a fur coat, who would approach me and say, 'I'm Di.' In return she would give me a packet which I had to bring straight back. I must, he emphasised, be very careful that nobody saw me hand the bag over. My immediate reaction was to be thrilled to be trusted with this important errand and when I said I would hide the leather purse round my waist under my apron he just smiled and told me to be off. Before I had even reached the pub the woman approached me and said the password. Then taking me by the hand she led me up an entry. I retrieved the purse from underneath my frock and in return for this she handed me a large flat envelope which I could feel contained banknotes. Then she was off, without saying another word. I retraced my steps as quickly as I could and found my boss waiting for me outside the workshop door.

'Good girl,' he smiled and whispered, taking the packet, 'Now come in an' warm yer 'ands while I make up the wages.' As soon as he'd disappeared upstairs one of the other women came over to where I was warming myself by the stove.

'I want ter warn yer,' she whispered, glancing towards the stairs. 'Yer don't want ter goo on them sorta errands.'

'Why?' I whispered too although I had no idea why.

'Yer know what yer was carryin'?' I shook my head. 'A bag o' diamonds. He's too scared ter tek 'em 'imself in case 'e gets caught or somebody knocks 'im down. Tek my advice, yow leave before it's too late or yow'll get caught or worse!' she hissed.

I was terrified. I didn't want to go prison or get killed, and as soon as he gave me my wage packet I was off, never to return there again. When I'd calmed down enough to open my wage packet there was the fifteen shillings I had been expecting and in addition a ten-shilling note and a message which read, 'Thank you, this is for you.' I wasn't sorry to be clear of whatever racket it was that they were up to, but the ten shillings helped me over the time until I found another job. I couldn't be out of work and I couldn't tell anyone why I'd left my last job.

I went to several factories asking for work; I'd decided I would be safer working with lots of people. I had a couple of jobs at factories in Frederick Street and Vyse Street, still in the Jewellery Quarter, but I spoilt the work, not being very experienced, and was given the sack. Eventually I settled for a job learning to enamel brooches and badges and motor plates at Fray's in Tenby Street North. It was an interesting job although all I was doing was learning how to 'lay on': that is, apply the powdered glass on the metal prior to firing in the kiln. I wanted to learn all the other aspects of the process from grinding the enamel to firing, filing and polishing, but I found out that I would have to spend three years laying on before I was likely to move on to anything else, and at that rate I would be middle-aged before I was expert in all the processes of enamelling. However, I was not to be deterred so easily and I decided that if I couldn't learn everything at one firm then I would move on and learn more somewhere else. That, in fact, is what I did. I changed jobs, making sure that when I moved I was taken on to be trained in a process that was unfamiliar to me, and in that way I picked up the entire trade bit by bit. In no time at all I knew it inside out, but I'd learned enough to make sure that it was never me who was responsible for getting the piece rates reduced again.

Chapter 19

Falling in Love

I had steady work in the enamelling trade until 1920. By then the War to End all Wars was over, but so too was the boom in the metal trades of Birmingham. It was no longer easy to flit from job to job until you settled for something you fancied. Plenty of people were laid off and many girls, particularly married women who had found no difficulty getting jobs in munitions and suchlike a year before, were now reduced to whatever odd jobs they could find. In short this was the beginning of the Depression which, unlike what many people think, began then and went right through until the Second World War brought another period of full employment to Birmingham. That time too it brought destruction of life and property in the Blitz. It was during those two decades of grinding poverty between the wars that I grew to womanhood, experienced love and marriage and children and had it all taken away, all my hopes dashed. I was brought to the very edge of complete and utter despair before I was able to drag myself back from the abyss of sorrow and re-establish myself and my family. But this is jumping the gun, and a lot happened to me and to Birmingham before that came about.

Mum was not so strict with me now I was contributing to the household. I placed my wages beneath the faded, bobbled mantel fringe every Friday night and I was free to go out to the pictures with the girls I worked with.

'Keep away from the boys,' she would warn me, wagging a finger at me as I was leaving. 'An' don't forget if yer bring any trouble 'ome 'ere I'll 'ave ter put yer in the workhouse.' She still enjoyed ranting, but I would shrug my shoulders now: it was an old record I had heard throughout my childhood. I needed maternal love and affection and I needed to understand what really happened between men and women, and what it was I was to avoid, but I didn't learn any of these things from Mum.

I worked with a lot of pleasant girls mostly my own age and I suppose you would say I was enjoying life. I was young, had money in my purse if I needed it and a sort of independence. I remember Christmas Eve 1919. Florrie, a girl I worked with, had invited me to a party at her mother's house. I'd saved a few pounds over the years since I'd left school and this particular Christmas I decided to celebrate by ceasing to be a regular customer of second-hand shops and splash out on some brand-new clothes.

I decided to go to the Bull Ring markets where the shops kept later hours. I caught a tram into the city centre and alighting from it bought a twopenny bag of roast potatoes to eat as I went along. The streets were crowded with late-night shoppers, young couples and the inevitable drunks weaving along the pavement. At the Bull Ring the barrow boys lined the pavements, naphtha flares casting an unnaturally bright light on their wares. There were crowds of people pushing and shoving, trying to get a bargain, and the noise was like a fairground on a Saturday night. The barrow boys shouted to outdo each other and the Salvation Army band was there too, competing for the attention of the people.

One of the barrow boys shouted at me, 'Come on duckie, fower a penny oranges, all sound', but I moved quickly on, clutching my purse tightly. When I reached the open-air fish market I saw two down-and-outs, disabled soldiers still in their khaki overcoats.

One, a man with only one arm, had a card round his neck saying that he had a wife and six children to support. The other was trying to play his concertina above the hubbub. When these two saw me stop and stare, the one pushed his cap towards me crying pitifully, 'Please 'elp an old soldier, missy.' I dropped a coin into the cap, wishing it could have been more, and then I went on my way to the little clothes shop I was heading for.

It was in Moat Row, near the Rag Market, and when I arrived I found the woman closing up. However, when she saw my tears she relented. 'Oh all right, wait 'ere while I lock up, an' then yer can come 'ome with me an' try a few things on.'

She was a small woman, not much bigger than me. She had untidy hair and a dress that dragged on the floor, and around her shoulders she swung a black knitted shawl while on her head she slapped a flat black straw hat. Then she set off wheeling a basket carriage full of clothing in front of her. I offered to help but she said she could manage. We were soon at her house and she kicked open the door and pushed the carriage inside. I followed her into the room which was piled so full of clothing old and new that you could hardly move. She asked me what I wanted and how much I had to spend. I had three pounds fifteen shillings and sixpence and I wanted a skirt, blouse, stockings and a coat.

'Can't let yer 'ave all them for three poun's fifteen,' she said.

'Well, that's all I've got. I haven't bin able ter save more,' I told her.

'Oh well, let's see what we've got,' she said, rummaging through things.

So instead of new I had to be content with nearly new, which is little different from second hand but sounds better. I tried on several pairs of shoes until eventually she let me have a new pair of black patent leather which were the only ones that fitted. I'd always wanted a pair of these since I'd seen a woman wearing some in Jefferson's years before. I also chose two pairs of lisle stockings, a black hobble skirt, a white satin blouse with a frill down the centre and a brown velvet cape. She threw in a dress that was frayed along the edge, saying that if it was cut and hemmed I'd be able to wear it for work. I was very pleased with my purchases, which she folded up for me and put in my string bag.

While she was doing that I opened my purse to pay her but when I did I couldn't believe my eyes. Inside there were only three pounds, two half-crowns and a sixpence. Where was the half-sovereign? She saw me fumbling and stopped what she was doing.

'What, yer mean yer ain't got the money?' she demanded.

Then I remembered. 'I must have given the half-sovereign to those two soldiers,' I said, getting very upset.

'What soldiers?' I could see that she didn't believe me. I tried to explain between sobs that I must have dropped that coin into the man's cap instead of the sixpence I'd intended.

'Yer wunt see that or them again. They're more likely ter be in the pub now suppin' ter their good fortune. Anyway dry yer eyes an' give me the three pounds. Yer can pay the other after Christmas.'

I gave her the money, and the two half-crowns I slipped back in my purse. Then after thanking her I made my way back through the heaps of clothes towards the door. She warned me not to stop or talk to anybody on my way home. 'Pretty little thing like yow shouldn't be down a rough quarter like this at night.'

The barrow boys were thinning out by now, sweeping their speckled oranges and apples into the gutter along with the other rubbish. I thought of when I was little when I would have been glad of these, and indeed there were some small children scavenging. I half hoped that I would see the two soldiers still begging when I reached the fish market but they were nowhere to be seen.

It was late when I got home and the house was deserted, the fire only embers. It seemed damp and cold and I set to to put some life into the fire with some wood and coal from the cellar. I found a penny and put that in the meter and got the kettle going and then went up and put my purchases in my trunk. I'd bought all my Christmas presents so there was nothing else I needed. I had got Dad a new clay pipe and an ounce of twist, a black apron for Mum, two packets of Woodbines for Frankie and a box of chocolates for Liza. For Mary I had a box of white handkerchiefs. Just as I was about to sit down Mum and Dad appeared, both well oiled. They pulled their chairs up to the fire and began singing 'Only a Rose'. I'd heard enough drunken singing on my way home so I went to go to bed. But before I'd got to the door Mum called me back and told me to hang up some holly she had bought and some 'mottoes'. As I was sticking the oval mottoes up I thought what it was to put up the message 'GOD BLESS THIS HAPPY HOME' in our house. There were not many happy homes in our area now that the war was over and there were so many unemployed. When I'd done this I grabbed some bread and pickled beef from the table and tiptoed up to the attic where I sat on my bed eating my meagre supper, listening to Mum and Dad's feeble attempts at harmony before getting undressed and popping into bed.

I was too old to hang up my stocking now I knew who Father Christmas was, but even though he was out of a job Dad gave me a shilling and a kiss. 'Thank yer me wench, just what I could do with,' he said next morning when he saw his present. Mum gave me a pair of fawn-coloured lisle stockings and a Christmas card with lace edging. Frankie had a tin of toffees for Liza and me. We thanked each other with kisses that were only exchanged in our house at the festive season. After breakfast Dad went out to find his mates and us three helped Mum clean the house and prepare for dinner. We had a stuffed goose and sausages and roast potatoes with Christmas pudding to follow. Mum couldn't afford to put silver threepenny bits in that year but I'd made the pudding and had slipped in four anyway. This meal was what passed for a real 'blowout' in 1919.

After we'd washed up the dirty crocks Dad produced half a

bottle of rum from the cupboard. He said he'd won it at a fair but although I could see Mum didn't believe him, it didn't stop her from helping him empty the bottle. Then they went upstairs to have a 'nap' as they termed it and I went up to get out my clothes in readiness for Florrie's party that evening.

First I put on the camisole, then clean bloomers, stockings and so on, until I was completely ready. Then I combed my hair, parted it in the middle and tied it up in a bun on top. I was ready to face the world. I looked in the mirror and thought I looked just 'swell'. My cheeks did look a little pale but since Liza always hid her carmine away I spat on my finger and rubbed some red off the wallpaper and rubbed it gently into my cheeks and lips. At last I had it right, I thought.

It was a cold frosty night that Christmas but I hadn't far to go. I was hurrying along past the George and Dragon when I heard the strains of 'The First Noël', and looking towards the pub doorway I saw six small, ragged children, four boys and two girls, trying to reach the top notes. I stood at a little distance – they hadn't seen me – and listened. It brought tears to my eyes, recalling as it did the night when Frankie, Liza and I, equally ragged and runny nosed, had sung carols on those very steps. Like us they were not having a lot of luck. So I opened my purse and gave them all I had with me, sixpence; a penny each, I thought, not much. I was late so holding my hobble skirt above my knees I hurried on. Lights were on in many houses and the sounds of jollity drifted on the night air; somewhere a gramophone crackled out a popular tune.

I could hear that Florrie's party was going with a swing before I reached her house. I knocked on the door but no one heard over the noise so I walked in boldly. As soon as I entered a chorus of voices sang out, 'A merry Christmas, Katie.' I knew most of the boys and girls from the works and I felt relaxed and at home in no time. Florrie introduced me to her mum, who was sitting at the piano about to play.

'Hello,' she said cheerfully. 'Go an''elp yerself to the eats and have a glass of port.' She had a pleasant smile and made me feel welcome. As the notes of 'Hearts and Flowers' sounded from the piano I helped myself to sandwiches and a glass of port as she'd directed. I stood by the piano listening to the tune and reflecting that Florrie was lucky to have such a nice mum and homely home. I thought, I can never ask her to my home, I'd be too embarrassed. I moved across to stand by the log fire which was blazing in the grate. After a minute or two Florrie's young man came up and invited me to have another glass of port, but before he could take my empty one, Florrie had whisked him away.

'Come on, we haven't finished our dance,' she pouted. I saw at once she was jealous but he ignored her for the moment and fetched me my drink. Then I was left to drink alone. Everyone was paired up and I began to feel left out. They were all dancing and nobody had asked me but I couldn't dance anyway, so I made the best of it and enjoyed the scene. I couldn't dance because I'd never been taught and was definitely not allowed to go to dance-halls. The second glass of port I could feel warming me, and I had another for 'Dutch courage'; then I had a fourth because by now I was beginning to feel merry. After that I became bright and gay and finally tipsy.

'I'll show 'em,' I thought, 'they'll regret ignoring me.' I walked calmly, not a bit unsteadily, over to the piano and requested Florrie's mum to play 'Annie Laurie' and I would sing. I had a good voice and as she called for quiet and the first notes sounded I let rip. When I had finished there were calls of 'encore', and as they pressed round me I felt dizzy and faint. One of the girls took me outside for a breath of fresh air and a glass of cold water. Then I went back in and sat on the plush green sofa.

I determined to leave as soon as I felt well enough. I was making my way over to the door when a young man in soldier's uniform came in.

'Don't go yet, Katie,' Florrie urged me as she dashed over to greet the newcomer. 'I want you to meet Harry's friend, Charlie.'

I looked up into his face and I knew in that instant that I didn't want to leave. As soon as he'd entered he removed his cap, showing his dark auburn hair. He had light blue eyes and a fresh, ruddy complexion and a few freckles. I thought him most handsome. I must have stood there staring, too shy to speak, but he soon put me at my ease.

'So, your name's Katie? I've seen you lots of times coming home from work but I didn't like ter speak to yer when you was with the other girls.' I felt myself go hot all over and blush at this.

'She's just leavin', Charlie,' Florrie called out, but I didn't want to leave now. I wanted to stay.

'Would you like me to see you home then?' he offered.

'I only live two streets away but if you don't mind you can see me part of the way.' I didn't want him to see the yard where we lived; I would have been too ashamed. When we got into the street we found it freezing hard and icy. Neither of us spoke as we walked along the pavement. I was too shy and perhaps he had nothing to say but every now and then when I slipped on the ice his arm went round my waist to steady me. To tell the truth I slipped purposely a couple of times so that I could feel the slight pressure as he gripped me. If it had been anybody else's arm I should have knocked it away, but each time he tightened his hold I experienced a certain thrill that I'd never known before. All too soon we reached the corner at the top of the hill which led down to Camden Drive where our yard was. He was as keen as any young man ought to be to see the girl he is escorting right to the door. However, I dissuaded him by telling him that I was not quite eighteen and that my parents would object if I was brought home by a boy.

'Can I see you tomorra night then?' he asked me and without hesitating I replied, 'Where?' We were looking straight into each other's eyes, the way only people falling in love do, as he replied, 'Outside the Mount Zion, seven o'clock.'

I knew the chapel in Graham Street he meant; I'd gone to Sunday school there as a child.

'Now, you're sure you'll be all right?' he asked, bending to kiss my cheek.

I felt a little disappointed he'd not taken me in his arms and kissed me properly but as I walked down the hill I heard his footsteps behind me, and as I turned he took me in his arms and squeezed me so hard I thought he would squeeze me to death. I was thrilled; I wanted to stay like that for ever. At last he released his grip and whispered, 'Good night, and don't forget your promise or I'll come knocking on your door.' With that he hugged me again and kissed me full on the lips, then turned to walk away. As I walked down the hill towards the Drive I felt I was walking on air; I was in love for the first time in my life.

The next night, Boxing Night, Charlie looked so handsome in his navy blue civilian suit, white shirt and dark tie, and as he doffed his cap to greet me I noticed his auburn hair highlighted under the street lamp. He kissed me on the cheek and took my hand. We walked and talked as young people have done since Adam and Eve. He told me he was twenty-two and lived with his sisters nearby in Nelson Street. We strolled along the Sandpits and went into a pub called the Stores. Everyone was singing and making merry and we joined in. Then all too soon it was eleven o'clock and 'Time gentlemen, please!' We stopped on the way home to kiss and cuddle and parted with a promise to meet again outside the Queen's Hall, off the Parade.

In the next few weeks we went for walks or to the pictures and each night before we parted we stopped to kiss and cuddle in an entry. In fact we stopped in one regularly near Stern and Bell's in Arthur Place, which was lined either side with larger, bay-windowed houses. It was an alley between two of these houses and at its end was Moseley's toffee factory. There was nowhere else to go and it was at least warm and out of the wind. One night we were seen together by my sister Mary who questioned me later. She wanted to know if I was going steady with Charlie. So I told her. I love him, I said, and when I was older I would marry him. She tried to warn me, tell me the facts of life, but I was too much in love with love to listen or care.

We were invited to a New Year's party where we both drank too much but we were so happy and so terribly in love nothing seemed to matter. Going home he stopped me and, putting his hands on my shoulders, sang, 'I'll take you home again, Kathleen'. He had a good voice and I shall remember his singing that song to my dying day. We sang together and laughed and giggled all the way to our courting place. That evening I forgot my sister's warning and we made love for the first time. We stayed there for a long time after, our arms around each other, huddled together until the thin light of dawn began to streak the night sky. Eventually we did part and I floated home without a care whether my parents were waiting up for me or not. When I got home and tried the door I found it bolted on the inside. They must have assumed I was already in bed so I was left with only one alternative; I had to lift the cellar grating and get in that way. I crept up the bare wooden staircase, hoping it wouldn't creak too loudly and wake Mum and Dad who were 'sending the pigs home to market', as they used to say. I quickly undressed and jumped into bed and had hardly hit the pillow than I was waking up the next morning.

As I awoke, what had happened the previous evening came flooding back to me. Now I finally knew the facts of life: there was no doubt in my mind at all where babies came from now, and I felt ashamed and worried in about equal measure. What if I have a baby and he won't marry me? I thought. There were girls in our neighbourhood who had babies and were not married. Would

Mum turn me out into the workhouse as she'd always threatened she would? All that day I was worried sick and when I met Charlie that evening I was that upset I broke down and cried. I hung my head, I was too ashamed to face him. But Charlie lifted my face to his and kissed my wet cheeks and smiled.

'Don't get upset, Katie. I really do love you an' as soon as we can save enough money, we'll put up the banns and in the meantime we'll save 'ard an' look for a 'ouse.'

Of course this was easier said than done. We met only at weekends, when Charlie took me to lodgings where he was staying since he had left his sisters'. That was only temporary while he sorted himself out after his discharge from the Army. I cleaned and cooked for him and was happy that we had things worked out between us. I managed to save a pound a week and Charlie likewise. I put it away safely and our savings began to grow. The first of February was my birthday: I was eighteen. I told Charlie I was going to tell my parents that I was courting but he dissuaded me, saying he would tell them himself in a while. I was reassured by this and each time his landlady was away at the weekend we made love. Towards the end of March I felt out of sorts, and one morning couldn't face my breakfast. I felt nauseous and frightened. I pushed my food away untouched and Mum noticed I'd turned pale.

'Wot's the matta with yow? Ain't it good enough for yer or summat?' she said.

'Yes, but I feel sick.' I knew that I was pregnant. I'd missed my period and now I was feeling sick in the morning. I wanted to confide in Mum but I was too scared: I knew she wouldn't understand. I should have brought Charlie home before so she could have got used to the idea of my getting married.

When I returned from work that evening Mary was waiting for me. Straight away she said, 'Mum says yer've been outta sorts the last few mornin's. What's the matter with yer?'

I just broke down and cried. 'I think I'm going to have a baby, Mary,' I wailed.

'Is it the young chap I've seen you with?' she asked, and I nodded my tearful reply.

'Then he better marry yer before Mum finds out. Or anyone else round 'ere for that matter, yer know how the tongues wag,' she added.

She made tea and we drank it. 'Now we'll talk,' she said sharply. 'An' stop yer snivelling.'

I told her all that had happened and when I'd finished I could see she was not impressed. 'You should both be ashamed! If it had been Liza I could understand but not you!' she said harshly. 'I warned yer, didn't I.' At that I flared up.

'Yes, you warned me, but too late!' I snapped back. 'I was always asking you an' Mum to explain things to me years ago, but no, you never did! "Yer'll 'ave ter wait until yer older", that's all I ever heard from yow. 'Ow old 'ave I got ter be, tell me that?'

'Well, why didn't you bring 'im home?' she asked.

'What! Bring 'im ter this hovel!' I shouted at her.

'Oh, well, I'll see what I can do to 'elp,' she said, getting up to leave.

Next night I came home from work to find Charlie, Dad and Mary already there, discussing me. I looked from one to the other, shaking in my shoes, wondering what was going to happen. But Charlie came over and put his arm round me.

'It's all right, don't worry, Katie. Your dad's given 'is consent, so we can get married in a few weeks' time.'

Hearing that I threw my arms round my dad and hugged him. There was no one like my dad.

'Be good to 'er, lad,' he told Charlie. 'She's a good girl. But I don't know 'ow her mother is goin' ter tek this,' he added.

'You leave 'er ter me,' Mary said firmly.

'Come along, lad. Let's go out an' 'ave a drink an' leave these two to sort things out,' said Dad.

'Mary, I can't face Mum. What am I goin' ter say?' I said as soon as they had left.

'You should 'ave thought of that before getting into this trouble! Any'ow you better slip upstairs and wait there while I try to explain.'

I rushed out of the room and hid. I would sooner have faced the devil than face our Mum. It wasn't long before I heard her voice below.

'Oh my God! Oh my God!' she shrieked. 'Whatever will the neighbours think?'

Then I heard Mary's voice, very angry. 'Never mind the neighbours as you call 'em. It's your daughter upstairs you've got to think about now, and stop crying. That won't mend matters.'

'I warned 'er, I warned 'er wot would 'appen if she brought disgrace on us,' she wailed.

'Don't be stupid, mother. And wipe your eyes, she's getting married in three weeks' time.'

'Who ses so?'

'Dad and the young man she's been going with. He seems a nice fella, Mum, and I know you'll like 'im too.'

'We'll see,' I heard her say more quietly before adding, 'yer betta call 'er down while I mek a cuppa tea.'

Slowly I crept down the stairs and finally stood facing Mum. It was then that I got the biggest shock of my life. She threw her arms around me, drew me to her bosom and wept.

'Why did yer do it? Why?' she sobbed. I was in tears now as well, thinking I'd been forgiven. I should have known better: Mum was never one to forgive or forget. She was like the weather and whenever we were alone together she kept harping on about the disgrace I'd brought to the family, and each night I cried myself to sleep. I felt I could never be happy there any more and on the following Friday, after placing my wages as usual under the mantel fringe, I put some of my belongings in my string bag and prepared to leave the house. Then, just as I was opening the door, in walked Mum.

'An' where do yer think yer gooin'?' she demanded.

'Charlie's. He's made arrangements for me with his landlady,' I replied at once.

'All right!' she snapped as she pushed past me. 'Yer can please yerself but wotever yer do from now on I wipe me 'an's on yer.'

I walked down the hill in tears. If only she'd offered to forgive me, taken me in her arms and meant it. That was the impossible, and it was not until later when I was raising my own family that we came to understand each other better and became a little closer as mother and daughter.

Chapter 20

Married Life

Charlie and I were married on 25 April 1921, by which time I was three months' pregnant. I would have loved to have been married in white with a flowing veil like Mary, but she had said that it would be a 'sin' and 'a mockery' and no matter how tightly I laced my whalebone stays, she said, the neighbours would know the truth when they recollected the date of the wedding. So I was wed in a pale blue frock and coat, both much out of date, with a blue straw picture hat and white shoes and stockings. I had begged Mary to lend me some money which I'd promised to pay back from my wages each week so that I could put on a better show on my wedding day. However, she refused, saying she'd enough money owing to her already. It was then she told me she was planning to go to America to make a fresh start, and this was another reason, I suppose, why she wouldn't lend me anything. Perhaps she thought I should be punished as well. In any case we quarrelled and were never truly close after that.

They did do us the courtesy of coming to the church though: Dad, Mum, my brothers and sisters, as well as a few of the neighbours and some of my friends from work. After the ceremony we received the usual congratulations and Mum was the last to kiss me. I noticed a real tear in her eye, but I was past caring then; I was what is known as 'a happily married woman'.

Charlie and I returned to our lodgings to pack our weekend case ready to catch the early train to Blackpool next morning. I'd saved the money to do this in a 'diddleum' club, run by a Mrs Chapman with whom I worked. I'd never seen Blackpool so we thought this would be a good idea for a honeymoon: we couldn't afford anything better.

The following morning, Saturday, found us waiting on the platform for our train when several women from my works, together with their men friends or husbands, appeared. They were already the worse for drink, rolling around and looking bedraggled, as if they'd not been to bed. Had the train not drawn up when it did we would have forgone the diddleum money and returned home.

'Good 'ealth, me wench,' one of the women cried out to us as she tipped back the contents of a bottle.

'Mind wot yer doin' ternight,' another shouted, amid howls of raucous laughter. The only two who were sober, I noticed, were two spinster sisters who lived in Sloane Street.

When the train stopped we jumped on and found an empty compartment. We pulled the blinds down, then we were alone and happy. We could still hear the off-key singing from along the corridor, but we weren't disturbed.

When we arrived at the boarding house we had to be shuffled about because there were too many guests and some had to go next door, but our landlady had the pick of the bunch before sending the others off. In our group there were the two maiden sisters, prim and proper, two women friends, Mr and Mrs Chapman and Charlie and I. The landlady was a small, plump, middle-aged woman; a typical seaside landlady. She motioned us upstairs and off we trooped. Our rooms were on the first floor; small bedrooms made from partitioning one large room into four with plywood walls. Although our room was virtually empty apart from the bed it was clean. The bed was only three-quarter size and stood in the middle of the room. There was a washstand by the window with a crock bowl and water jug on it and there was also a small piece of Sunlight soap and a threadbare towel. There were only nails on which to hang our clothes and no carpet or lino, just bare floor-boards. Yes, and beneath the bed there was the regulation china chamber pot. Pinned to the door were the house rules regarding lights out and breakfast time which was 'nine o'clock sharp'. Over the bed was another handwritten message: 'Please Be Quiet As Other People Want To Sleep'.

Before she left the landlady said, 'I'll send Fred up with your bag,' and as she opened the door she paused and said, 'You're the newlyweds?' We nodded and she left, smiling.

There was a strong smell of disinfectant about the room which seemed to emanate from beneath the bed. I turned down the bed-clothes and the mattress to check for flea or bug powder but everything, though threadbare, was clean. Charlie and I sat down on the edge of the bed and giggled. We'd expected something better than this but would make the best of it.

We settled down to wait for the supper bell, and while we sat there we became aware that every movement and word that went on in the rooms adjacent to ours were distinctly audible. Then the bell sounded and we went downstairs to see what was in store for us. We entered a large kitchen where the landlady was standing beside the large, black range and we got a good meal of roast mutton, carrots, cabbage, peas and roast potatoes. Fred and his wife sat down and had their meal with us and we had a pleasant conversation. When we'd finished the other guests asked us if we'd like to join them for a drink in a nearby pub but we couldn't afford to go drinking. Fortunately, before we could refuse Fred came to the rescue.

'If yer like ter stay in an' keep me an' the missus company we've got a drop in,' he offered.

Charlie and I were happy to accept because apart from any-thing else it was now raining heavily. Fred and his wife turned out to be a jolly couple and they made us feel very welcome, and as we sat round the range supping stout and ale we became very talkative. Fred regaled Charlie with his exploits in the Navy and Charlie in turn talked about his time in the Army while 'the missus' and I talked of our families and what I was going to do when I got a home of my own. We seemed to chat like this for hours until, when it was time to go to bed, I felt quite dizzy, not being used to drinking much. Charlie too, I could see, had had enough but we thanked them without difficulty and said 'good night'. However, when it came to the stairs I needed some gentle pushing from Charlie to get up. As soon as we had entered our room and lit the gas jet I flopped down on the bed. The others were already in their rooms, as the laughing and giggling we could hear testified, and when Charlie had removed his boots and trousers and was standing beside the bed in his shirt I was infected with the giggling too: I could see all he'd got.

'What's there ter giggle about?' he asked huffily. 'Get me the pot, I want ter mek water.' But before I could reach it he bent down and we both somehow managed to topple over. We lay there giggling hysterically as the floor began to resound with thumping on the ceiling of the room underneath ours.

'What's goin' on up there?' we heard Fred shout.

'Sorry ol' man,' Charlie replied, 'I 'appened ter fall over.'

'All right, but think of us what wants ter sleep,' came the annoyed response and we could hear our neighbours laughing at this exchange.

'I wonder just what they think we're up to,' Charlie said close to the partition.

We sorted ourselves out and I held the pot for Charlie to stop his making too loud a noise. I was embarrassed. I closed my eyes and turned my head and giggled and while he made water I must have raised the pot higher. I'd forgotten there was disinfectant in it and I suppose his penis must have dangled in, because the next thing I knew the pot and its contents went flying across the room.

'Oh my God! Oh my God!' he kept screaming as he shook it and chased me round the bed. 'I'll kill yer,' he shouted, 'I'll kill yer!' By the look on his face I could believe him.

Before I could reach the door it was flung open and there were Mr and Mrs Chapman and the two old maids, their eyes almost popping out as Charlie showed them what I'd done. I fled down the stairs and fell into the landlady's arms. She had to sit me down and administer whisky before I could explain coherently what had happened. Then she and Fred began to laugh but I'm afraid I couldn't see the funny side of the situation so she sent Fred up to see what could be done. He took a bowl of cold water and a sponge. When he returned, still smiling, he said there was no real damage done, only that the pot was broken and Charlie was a bit sore but that it was safe for me to go back upstairs. Charlie lay in bed, staring up at the ceiling.

I threw my arms round him and whimpered, 'I'm sorry, Charlie, I forgot there was disinfectant in the pot.'

'No good bein' sorry now. It could 'ave bin worse. Now get undressed an' get inter bed before yer catch cold, an' stop yer snivelling.' He sounded far from pleased.

I undressed slowly and lay nervously beside him. Then he took me in his arms and kissed my wet cheeks and I knew I was forgiven. That's how we lay, in each other's arms, until we fell asleep.

The next morning the landlady knocked on our door and brought our breakfast in on a tray. 'I thought you'd like ter stay in bed late.'

We thanked her as she left the tray at the foot of the bed. We sat up and I poured the tea as well as I could without spilling it. I asked Charlie if he was still sore.

'No, it's wearin' off a bit now, but we won't be able ter mek love until I've seen the doctor,' he said.

'But I wasn't thinkin' about that,' I replied angrily.

'Now, now, don't lose yer temper. Let me get back inter bed, it's freezin' out 'ere.'

And there we lay just huddled together to keep each other warm until the dinner bell rang. Then we hurriedly washed and dressed and went down to the dining room, not the kitchen as before, where we found that the others had already started theirs. I could see by their exchanged glances that they knew what had happened the previous night. So we finished the meal in silence and then it was time to get our things together to catch the train back to Birmingham. We'd not seen a great deal of Blackpool on our honeymoon except what we'd glimpsed after our arrival the previous afternoon.

We were lucky enough to have a compartment to ourselves again for the return journey and as the train puffed slowly out of Blackpool station I observed to Charlie, 'We never did see the sea, did we?'

'Never mind,' he answered, putting his arm round me. 'We'll come next year an' stay a whole week. I promise yer we'll 'ave a real good 'oliday.' But I was to be thirty years of age before I ever saw the sea: the only water I saw till then was the canal.

When we arrived home late that Sunday night our landlady greeted us with bad news. 'Yer'll 'ave ter find yerselves new accommodation,' she said. 'I'm sorry but I let the 'ouse ter me brother an' 'is family an' they want ter move in next week.'

Charlie called her a liar. 'Yer want ter get rid of us because my wife's 'avin' a baby,' he told her and she didn't deny it.

'Well, yer've got till next week anyway,' she conceded. All that week we searched desperately but furnished rooms were difficult to come by, particularly when the landlady found out I was pregnant. By the end of that week we were at our wits' end and there was only one thing to do as a last resort. We went to see Mum and Dad together and explained that in a few days we'd be out on the street.

Mum said she knew a Mrs Larkins who lived on the corner of Arthur Place next to the Leopard public house who had a furnished room to let.

We were able to take the room, which was very scantily furnished, for eight shillings and sixpence a week, but while we were there we saved enough to buy some second-hand furniture including a couple of chairs and a large oak wardrobe. There was a bed and a table and odd crocks that belonged to Mrs Larkins and we had to manage without other things until such time as we could afford them.

Now that I was living just a stone's throw from Mum and Dad they came to visit us often. Dad would call in at the Leopard for a pint and a game of dominoes while Mum dropped in to chat and tell me what to get for my confinement. We were closer now than we'd ever been and I was glad, because now I was going to have a baby I needed her more than ever. She told me she'd booked a midwife, who turned out to the same Mrs Bullivant who'd attended Nelly's mother. When I told Mum she'd died Mum sprang to Mrs Bullivant's defence.

'Yer carn't blame the midwife fer that. Any'ow yow ain't gooin' ter die, yer too young an' 'ealthy, an' another thing, she's brought 'undreds o' babbies inter the world. It ain't 'er fault if any died,' she concluded. She convinced me and I ceased worrying and set to to knit the little garments the baby would need. With Mum's help I washed and ironed the nappies, nightgowns and 'belly binders' that would be needed.

When my labour pains started Mum came at once while Charlie ran for the midwife. Mum was right. I had a trouble-free confinement and on 7 October 1921 my first child, a boy, was born. He was a fine, healthy baby weighing in at 6 lbs 12 oz. It was the custom then to bind babies and after he'd been washed Mum fastened his belly binder round him before she put on his nappy and wrapped him in his nightgown. Then she held him close.

'My little gran'son,' she whispered, and as she put him on my breast there was a tear in her eye. She bent over and kissed me too. At that moment I felt the happiest woman in the world; I had my son, my husband, my dad and, finally, my mum.

Charlie and I had our son christened Charles Samuel, after his father and grandfather, at St Paul's Church when he was a month old. By then I was back at work, doing press-work, with Mum looking after little Charles, but I had to pay her five shillings a week for his milk and rusks. My husband was now on short time and we were very hard up. Between us we were earning two pounds ten shillings a week which had to cover rent, food, coal, lighting and the boy's food, as well as 'club money' for sheets and blankets which I was buying on hire purchase, the 'never-never'. I'd scarcely stopped breast-feeding and my milk had only just dried up when I found I was pregnant again. Mrs Larkins found out from the neighbours' gossip and she told us we would have to look for other rooms.

Mum had angry words with her but Mrs Larkins was adamant. So Mum said I'd better get my few 'traps', as she called our belongings, and move in with her and Dad until Charlie found a better job. Dad agreed with this but it was the last place I wanted to live. Liza was the only one still living at home and Mum said she could sleep in their room and we could have the attic. When Charlie returned footsore from looking for a place we discussed Mum's offer and reluctantly decided to accept the room, at least for the time being. When he heard, Dad said that we should have all our belongings in our room to avoid any arguments with Mum. I was happier living up there, out of Mum's way, but first I had to scrub and disinfect the room which was filthy. I paid Mum eight and sixpence a week for that small room, plus the coal which she rationed out and the washing.

I worked until a week before the baby was due and my second son was born eleven months to the day after my first, on 7

September 1922. He was christened John Ernest after my eldest brother and my husband's brother. Charlie was out of work altogether by now and we were in terrible straits with two small babies to look after. With no money coming in I had to go back to work a few weeks after my baby was born and leave my two sons with Mum. How hard I persevered to get us away from that hovel no one knows; I even went office cleaning after I'd finished my press-work at the factory and had fed and put the boys to bed. I literally worked all hours God made to earn a little extra to take care of their needs, but as hard as I worked we seemed to be no better off; it was like treading water to stay afloat, we were always short of money. We tried to find our own place but that was just as hopeless; nobody wanted two small children.

Charlie tramped the streets day after day looking for a job but to no avail. Finally in desperation he decided to go to the timber mills and buy bags of sawdust to sell to pubs and butchers' shops. This he did, but it was an ill-fated venture because he made very little profit from it, only managing to give me two shillings or half a crown a day. And, more important in the long run, he started drinking heavily. I suppose visiting all those public houses to sell sawdust presented too much temptation and he would have a drink in each; by the time he rolled home he was very much the worse for drink. This went on for two years, during which time things went from bad to worse. It was more than anybody could stand; our situation never seemed to improve, and we seemed destined to a life of grinding poverty – what would be called 'deprivation' today. For me and those who lived through similar experiences it was just plain misery.

Dad was out of work as well. He was ill and at home with asthma, the legacy of his years in the casting shop, and Mum was at her wits' end. In the end there was no alternative: she went on the parish again and when the visitor came to inspect the house we had to hide because Mum had told them that she and Dad were living alone. She got away with this subterfuge and no one in the yard split; how could they when they were in the same boat themselves? I was utterly exhausted each night after leaving my second job and I would crawl into bed with the babies and pray to the Lord to get us away from all that poverty. I cried all the time. I suppose in retrospect that I was emotionally as well as physically drained.

Dad was not one to give up, though. He bought himself a last and mended the boots of everyone who could afford to pay, even some of the firemen at the Albion Street Fire Station. This helped us for a while, but soon Dad became too ill even to do this. Then to cap it all I became pregnant again and had to give up my job and fall on the parish. Needless to say when they found out that Charlie was selling sawdust I was refused help. This time I had a daughter, christened Kathleen like me, born on 13 March 1925.

It was during this period that I had two lady visitors from the welfare call with clothes for the children and blankets and sheets for the bed. Later we became entitled to Salvation Army soup and bread, sometimes a meat dinner, but you had to be in the queue early or the food would be cold. To me at that time all this seemed like history repeating itself, and I could see no way that I could do what I wanted most which was to ensure a better future for my children. Charlie had lost his spirit and seemed content making the sawdust rounds for a few coppers a day, most of which went to finance his heavier and heavier drinking. It was enough to break your heart. We quarrelled often but the rows did no good and only increased the bad feeling. I threatened to leave him but then what would become of my babies? Charlie himself stayed out more and more and we seldom saw him, and then rarely sober. There was only one alternative for me. I would have to go back to work and hope that the children would be all right without me.

One day not long after Kathleen was born I was taking the children for a walk when I happened to spot what I'd been hoping for: a notice in a window that read, 'EXPERIENCED ENAMELLER WANTED, YOUNG AND MUST BE USED TO BADGES AND MOTOR-PLATES'. I could hardly believe it: it was just up my street. I left the two boys sucking a toffee apple on the step and, carrying the baby in my arms, I went in. The boss, a Mr Butler, looked me up and down and asked me how old I was. I told him twenty-three, though I was a year younger than that. He asked what experience I'd had and I told him that I'd worked at Joseph Fray's Tenby Street North, but I didn't tell him about all the other jobs I'd had. He seemed satisfied with this and fetched out a motor-plate and asked me how I would enamel it. I showed him, and with that he said I could start the following Monday morning at thirty shillings per week. I couldn't get home quick enough to tell Mum the good news, and later that week I pawned my wedding ring and with the money I bought coal and extra food. Mum too was glad of the money I gave her for looking after the children while I was working, and Mr Butler was pleased with my workmanship and I received two increases in wages in consequence. I was able to save, after all was paid for, about five shillings a week, but I should have known that this was too good to last.

When I found out I was pregnant with Jeanette I was afraid to tell Charlie and I certainly didn't want any more babies. I couldn't adequately feed and clothe the children we had already, and in the absence of child benefit and family income supplement and the other support that the Welfare State provides, another child was simply another mouth to feed, reducing a family's ability to care for the children it had already. I was so desperate that many times I made up my mind to ask one of the neighbours to abort me, but fear rather than conscience prevented me – fear of what would become of little Charles, John and Kathleen if I should die. I knew of many young women who had died through trusting the ignorant old women of the neighbourhood to terminate their pregnancies.

Abortion was also a crime, and prosecution would surely follow if you were found out.

The reason why Charlie and I hadn't taken precautions to prevent another pregnancy is simple: I had no idea that contraception existed, nor did I until after my fifth child was born. To young women such as I was then the subject of sex was completely surrounded by ignorance, myth and misunderstanding throughout the working-class community. I cannot speak for those who were better off and better educated, but in our neighbourhood these things were never spoken of.

Despite the poverty-stricken circumstances of my early married life there were some happier moments. I remember Dad and Charlie spending many happy hours with the children when I was at work and Mum was too lazy to see to them. They organised games for the kids in our yard like 'kick the can' and 'tip cat' and if the weather was fine and windy Dad would make a kite from newspapers and take them all to the recreation ground in Goodman Street where they would take turns in flying it. I also remember young Charlie worrying us because he'd not got a ball to play with like the other boys at his school; he must have been five then, and he couldn't understand that we couldn't afford to buy him one. So one day his dad brought him home a golf ball he'd found or been given. My son treasured that little white ball, even putting it under his pillow at night. Then one day the inevitable happened and it was kicked through the window of a nearby shop and we had to pay the proprietor half a crown we could ill afford. A crying match followed and eventually Charlie promised to get him a ball that would do no damage. How he managed this shows the lengths parents had to go to then to provide even the simplest toys for their children. One of Charlie's customers on his sawdust round was Knight's, the pork butcher, on the corner of Great Hampton Row and Tower Street, Hockley, and he asked the butcher there for a pig's bladder. What fun we had trying to inflate it! In the end we succeeded and Dad, Charlie and my two sons had many happy hours playing football with it in the yard.

Those were the good times, when I or one of the neighbours was able to play with Kathleen and the other little girls in the yard. We would hold the skipping rope for them or they would play at marbles or with their spinning-tops or else draw a grid with chalk on the bricks and play hopscotch, games that children of this present generation seem to have forgotten. The pig's bladder football was not to Mum's liking though. When she first saw young Charlie bring it indoors she exclaimed, 'I ain't 'avin' that stinkin', greasy thing in my 'ouse an' if I see it about it'll goo on the fire.' So to avoid his grandmother's wrath Charlie dropped it down the cellar grating at night before coming in to bed and then retrieved it to play with the next day. Until one afternoon when he returned from school and went down the cellar to fetch it and found it had gone: the rats had eaten it. There was another tearful scene before his dad brought home another one. To avoid a similar fate Charlie hung this one high up on a nail outside the attic window where it was safe from the rats' gnawing teeth.

My fourth child, Jeanette Elizabeth, was born on 3 September 1927 after I'd been rushed by ambulance to Dudley Road Hospital. There I experienced a proper childbirth with real medical attention and I was well looked after, even being given a bottle of stout every evening. This would give me strength while I was breast-feeding I was told. While I was there I was very concerned about my other children and received a reprimand from the matron for worrying. 'You'll lose your milk,' she warned me. She was right because when I returned home I found that the neighbours had each taken it in turns to look after them. We were all in the same boat and there was always help at hand if needed.

I was shocked to discover that Dad had been taken into the poorhouse on Western Road while I'd been away. As soon as I could I went there to see him. The workhouse was a forbidding-looking building and I shuddered as I walked through the heavy wrought-iron gates and across the cobbled yard. I was standing not knowing where to go when an old man in grey corduroy trousers and heavy boots approached me and asked who I was looking for. When I told him he led me into the building and up several flights of steep stone steps to the second floor. When I entered the ward and looked around I saw that it was filled with men of all ages lying on their beds in an eerie silence. They stared at me and looked so dispirited that I felt like bursting into tears. I searched down the ward for my dad but couldn't see him. Then a male nurse came up and showed me which bed he was in. When I reached his bedside I couldn't believe my eyes; he'd changed so much in the ten days since I had seen him last. He looked old and drawn and had a faraway look in his eyes, as if he was looking at something a long way away. I just broke down and wept; I was so shocked to see him like this. I took his hand which seemed pitifully thin and wasted in my own and kissed him.

'Dad,' I managed to say, 'it's me, Katie, I brought you some oranges and some twist.' He didn't answer or move at all but continued to stare into space as if I wasn't there. The male nurse, seeing my distress, told me that he'd had a stroke, and as he led me away, still crying, I wondered if Dad knew what a terrible place he had come to.

I couldn't believe that my father would end his days in the poorhouse when he'd been good, honest and kind and had always worked hard when there were jobs to be had. I visited him several times but his condition didn't change. I have often wondered since if he was conscious of what was happening but had simply suffered a temporary paralysis. Either way, his suffering, if suffering it was, didn't last long and a few days later a policeman called at my mother's house with the news that Dad was dead. My mother began to wail and cry when she heard this, and soon a crowd of our neighbours had gathered round to offer their sympathies, but to me these were only crocodile tears and I couldn't believe she would mourn his loss long. Dad had always been my favourite. I loved him and came to rely on his kindness and sound advice and I never forgave my mum all the pain and suffering she'd caused him over the years. After Dad's death she took to drinking more heavily, which she was able to do because she was receiving ten shillings a week widow's pension. As we laid Dad to rest I reflected on my own life: twenty-four years old, I'd seen nothing of life, only poverty and hardship, and it seemed to me then that I'd been born simply to breed. Yet I couldn't afford the luxury of self-pity for long; life had to continue and my four little ones had to be cared for.

By now both Charles and John were at school. I'd refused to send them to St Paul's School in Camden Drive, the school I'd gone to myself, but had insisted instead that they go to Nelson Street, off the Sandpits, where the school had a better reputation and I hoped they might get a better start in life than I had had. While I was at work and the boys at school, Mrs Taylor, my long-time friend, looked after the girls and we were able to cope sufficiently for me to cast aside the *Daily Mail* boots that were always blistering the children's feet and buy them ones that fitted properly. Again things were looking up for us – if only I didn't become pregnant again.

Each Saturday evening Mrs Taylor would look in – Mum was hardly ever at home any more – and when I'd put the children to bed she would keep an eye on them so that Charlie and I could go out together.

'If yer want me ter mind 'em, it's no trouble, as long as yer bring me back twopenn'orth o' snuff,' she would say.

I always cherished these Saturday nights when Charlie would embrace me and say, 'Get yer togs on, I'll tek yer out.' I knew well enough where we would be going. We would take a penny ride on the tram to the terminus at the top of Snow Hill, outside the railway station. Our first stop would be to buy a tuppenny bag of baked potatoes or roast chestnuts, then off we'd stroll, arm in arm, to the Bull Ring markets where we would haggle with the barrow boys for our fruit and vegetables or whatever we needed. Then when we had made our purchases we'd call in at the Nelson where Charlie would have a pint of bitter and I would have a stout, sometimes two if we had the money to spare.

We had the house to ourselves more now as well, including the room downstairs. Mum was often away. She took trips to Gloucester, she said to visit relatives, but I knew of no relations there. However, I did not ask questions, being only too glad she was out of our way. I'd lost whatever interest I had had in her, and despised her for the drunkard she was turning into. When she'd collected her pension and our rent money she would disappear for days at a time. Things went more smoothly then. I even managed to save a few pounds without Charlie knowing. This was for a 'rainy day' or, perhaps, my dream – to get away from this bug-infested hovel I'd lived in all my life. I imagined being able to bring my children up properly, without their arses hanging out of their trousers and in a clean, tidy house in a pleasant district. But this was just not to be.

The next blow came just as things were beginning to look up for us. One Monday afternoon there was a knock at the door and there stood a policeman. He had come to break the news of my son Charles's death. Even now, nearly sixty years later, I cannot describe how I felt and feel about the loss of my eldest child. He'd been knocked down by a butcher's delivery van on his way home from school at lunchtime, and I never forgave myself for the foolishness of insisting on his going to that school in the Sandpits rather than the close, safe school at the top of the Drive.

I was out of my mind with grief and guilt and although people were kind in their sympathy, nothing seemed to help. I kept breaking down and crying, and I suppose I had what today would be classed as a nervous breakdown but then was not understood as other than a mother's natural grief. People came from all over the district to his funeral but this simply made me worse. I couldn't face them without breaking down and I isolated myself from contact with people. I experienced frightening nightmares and refused to allow my children out of my sight lest something should happen to one of them too. I suppose I was trying to give them the protection that I felt in my misguided way I hadn't been able to give Charles.

Looked at rationally I had nothing to reproach myself for, but logic is not what guides one's actions or thoughts in the state of shock following bereavement. Eventually, I had to send John back to school because the man from the school board threatened us with a summons if I didn't. Still I hid indoors with the girls, more mad than sane. Each time I looked out of the attic window and saw the old pig's bladder hanging there it started me off. Then one day it was no longer there. I asked Charlie what he'd done with it and he said he'd buried it next to our son's grave in Warstone Lane cemetery. Strangely enough, that act was like laying a ghost, because although I still grieved, after that I began to pull myself together. I realised that I was making Charlie suffer, and the children whom I was neglecting, to indulge my own feelings. I still had a heavy heart but I determined to get on with life which did, after all, have to go on. I went back to work and resumed my role as the main support for my family.

Charlie was still out of work. He did have a few odd jobs but nothing permanent, and he continued with his sawdust round. In truth his health was not good. The doctor had warned him, but every penny he could lay his hands on he drank. He had spells when he drank less but often he came home raving and would fall asleep at the foot of the bed. I think he was probably just as upset about little Charlie as I was and his drinking was a form of escape for him.

This was how the first few years of married life went for me, hardly fulfilling the childish fantasies of a bright prosperous future that I'd cherished when Charlie and I had met that Christmas only a few short years before. Since then it had been a seemingly inevitable cycle of pregnancy, hard work, poverty and grief, but although life for me was rough, it was no rougher than it was for thousands of other people like us in Birmingham in the 1920s.

Chapter 21

My World Collapses

After my son's death I returned to work. I couldn't return to Butler's because my timekeeping was not up to standard, so I applied for a part-time job with a Mr Brain in Tenby Street North. He took me on at once and I joined his workforce, which consisted of his two elderly daughters. His workshop was an old converted redbrick house, and his business was enamelling the round, metal Union Jack badges for Standard cars.

After working there about a week I confided in one of the sisters that the job was getting me down because I had to rush home to breast-feed baby Jean. She must have mentioned it to her father because Mr Brain told me that if I still wanted the job I could bring the baby along and feed her during my working hours. Crêches were then unheard of, but this arrangement suited me perfectly; John was at school, so Mum had only Katie to take care of.

I borrowed a pram from a neighbour and was then able to push Jean to work and leave her in the pram in the entry beside the workshop. I could work and listen for Jean's cries to tell me she was ready for her feed. The sisters were kindness itself to me. Each day they would bring a little something in the grocery line for me to take home for the other children. Often they would change Jean for me if she was wet. And thus by such little kindnesses they made working life bearable and at the same time I was able to provide food and clothing for my family. I was even able to supplement my earnings by making toffee apples and selling them to the children as they came out of school. I sold them two a penny and every penny I earned I had to spend. It was useless trying to save anything now. Charlie was drinking more heavily and contributing next to nothing to the family income. Mum was boozing more too and causing more quarrels as a result. I survived by closing my eyes and ears to what was happening and concentrating all my attention on the children and their needs.

It was too good to last, I knew, and sure enough one morning I arrived at work to find Mr Brain alone, packing his tools into a tea chest. I was too horrified to speak when in response to my shocked inquiry as to what he was doing he told me he was being forced to close because of lack of orders. I stayed to help him pack his things away. Then he handed me my insurance card and three days' pay that was owing. He did say that if he should start up in business again I would be the first to know, but this was scant consolation to me now that I was out of a job and penury was staring us in the face. There was no alternative: I would have to apply for relief again. Mum suggested we take in washing and ironing and I agreed since there was no other way of earning money. This arrangement was doomed, of course. After two weeks she demanded a larger share of what little we were able to earn and we quarrelled.

'Well, they're my tubs an' mangle, an' coal, yower usin',' she insisted.

After that the situation quickly deteriorated. Her constant nagging got on my nerves and the strain began to tell. One night it finally became too much for me to cope with any longer and I almost did a terrible thing. I washed the children as usual and put them to bed. Katie and Johnny slept between Charlie and me. I could not bear him near when he was drunk, which he was every night now, and we had not made love for nearly a year. Jean's bed was a makeshift one in the wardrobe drawer. This particular night she wouldn't stop crying for me to feed her, but my milk was drying up and she got little satisfaction from my breast. Then as I was putting her back in her drawer cot, Mum began banging on the ceiling with a broom.

'Stop that babby cryin'. I want ter get some sleep!' she bawled.

'I'm doin' me best,' I shouted back from the top of the stairs.

'About time yow got 'er a dummy,' came the reply.

I'd never used a dummy because I'd seen too many little children drop them in the filth and then pick them up and put them back into their mouths. It was no wonder to me that so many children died of gastric diseases, diphtheria and the like. I returned to try to comfort Jeannie without resorting to a dummy but then the broom banged again. At that moment something snapped inside me. I flung my baby into the drawer and kicked it shut before collapsing on the bed exhausted. It must have been several minutes before I'd calmed down sufficiently to realise what I'd done. I jumped up and pulled the drawer out. It was just in time; another few minutes and she would have suffocated. I took her in my arms and wept. I could have fallen asleep and let her die. I might have been hung for murder, I thought, and thanked the Lord that I'd come to my senses.

I tried one more trick to quieten my wailing baby. I smeared condensed milk thickly over my nipple and gave her that, and for a wonder it worked. She lay contentedly sucking the empty breast.

The next morning I went to see the doctor, Doctor Mackenzie, who had a front-room surgery in Arthur Place. His manner was abrupt but he could be kind and he listened sympathetically while I told him what had happened.

'How old are you?' he asked when I had finished.

'Twenty-four,' I told him.

'And how many children have you got?' he asked.

'Three now, doctor,'

'Any miscarriages?'

'Two.' Both had been brought on by doing heavy press-work.

After asking several more questions he gave me a bottle of 'Parrish's Food' and told me to take two teaspoonfuls at night and to return to see him in a week's time. I found that his prescription seemed to do me good and that I experienced a good night's sleep for a change. I must confess that I also put a teaspoonful in Jeannie's milk bottle and she seemed to thrive on it; so did Katie and Johnny. But instead of the medicine lasting a week it was gone in two days. It was like a drug: I wanted more. So I went back to the doctor and lied.

'You again,' he snapped when I entered the surgery. 'I said a week's time.'

'I'm sorry, doctor. I had an accident and the bottle broke.'

'Very well, try not to break this one.' He handed me another bottle.

I went easier with that bottle and when I visited him again he gave me a panel note. This meant that I could draw sick pay, which wasn't much but enabled us to manage better with the little my husband was bringing in. It might be enough to tide me over until I was strong enough to work again. The rules about entitlement to sick pay were strict. You had to be indoors when the visitor called, otherwise your benefit would be stopped. You could only draw sick pay for six week; after that you had to submit to a means test and see the doctor again. When he re-examined me the doctor wrote out a letter.

'I want you to take this letter to 161 Corporation Street and have your chest X-rayed,' he told me as he wrote. This alarmed me.

'What's the matter with me chest?' I asked tentatively. 'Have I got consumption?'

'Nothing to be scared about. This is only routine and in the meantime I want you to take this medicine.'

I was hoping for some more Parrish's Food but no such luck. I took the other stuff as directed, but two days later I developed a cough so decided to do as I had been instructed and go to be X-rayed. It was a bitterly cold morning as I readied myself to make the journey into the city centre. Mum and Charlie were out and I was glad I didn't have to tell them where I was going. Mrs Taylor agreed to look after Katie and Johnny and I wrapped Jeannie in my threadbare shawl and hugged her to me; then off I went on the two-mile walk into town. When I arrived at Corporation Street I was exhausted and I flopped down on the dirty wooden stairs to catch my breath. As I sat there Jeannie began to cry and I wished that I had brought some condensed milk with me. There was only one thing for me to do to quieten her cries. I unbuttoned my blouse and took out my breast, praying that she would find enough milk there to satisfy her. She tried her best, dear little thing. Then I happened to look up and found a small, well-dressed man gazing down at me. I felt a rush of embarrassment and fumbled to cover my nakedness but he put his hand gently on my shoulder.

'Don't cover yourself, mother. You both make a lovely picture.' And with that he pressed a ten-shilling note into my hand before he walked past me up the staircase. I could scarcely believe my good fortune; that money was a godsend. All thought of the X-ray vanished and I set off for home to buy some food. I made my first mistake by telling Mrs Taylor of my luck.

'That's all right, dearie, yow goo an' get yerselves summat ter eat an' collect yer kids when yer get back.' I thanked her and asked if I could get her anything for looking after the children. 'Yer can get me twopenn'orth o' snuff,' was the predictable reply.

I bought sugar, tea, bacon, lard, bread, some stewing steak and milk for the baby. I still had change and I slipped it into my purse, which I carried between my breasts. I returned and spread my purchases out on the table, then I put Jeannie in her makeshift bed and went for Katie and Johnny. I went into the yard to find Mrs Taylor gossiping with some other old women. I ignored them and gave Mrs Taylor her snuff, and as I did so I noticed the others looking down their noses at me. I had nothing to be ashamed of although I could imagine how they would be speculating about how I got my ten shillings. I left Katie and Johnny with the other kids playing in the yard and went in to prepare a meal. I was so happy that afternoon that I even sang a tune as I waited for the kettle to boil. Just then Mum came bustling in. She looked in amazement at the food laid out on the table.

'Where yer got all this grub from?' she asked and I gladly told her.

'Yer a liar,' she exclaimed before I had hardly finished.

'It's the truth, Mum,' I protested.

'Men don't give yer ten bob fer just lookin' at yer breast,' she sneered. 'Yer sure yer dain't let 'im feel yer up a bit?' she asked slyly. That did it. I flared up in a fury at her suggestion.

'Yer disgustin'! Men don't bother me that way. I've got enough with Charlie. I ain't Liza yer know,' I yelled at her.

'Yow leave Liza outta this!' she bawled at the top of her voice. 'An' close that bloody dower. I don't want all the neighbours ter 'ear!' I had touched a sensitive nerve because Liza had always been her favourite; in all the years I'd lived under her domination I'd never found the courage to retaliate until that moment. I had bottled my resentment up but now I let the cork out and my temper with it. Funnily enough, now that I had plucked up courage to speak my mind I felt no inhibitions whatsoever.

'No! I won't shut "the bloody dower" as you call it. Let the neighbours 'ear a few home truths for a change!' I had my dander up now all right.

Suddenly she lurched at me as if to strike me.

'Yow dare!' I screamed, grabbing the iron saucepan from the table. 'I'll bash yer brains out with this!' She could see that I meant it so she walked deliberately round the table and kicked the door to.

'Nosy lotta bastards!' she yelled through the closed door.

'One o' these days yer'll get summonsed fer yer language,' I told her.

' 'Ave yer finished?' She spoke more softly, sitting down on a chair.

'No! You've never loved me. Even before I was born yer never wanted me.' I was going to speak my mind now I'd started.

'Yer don't know what yo'er talkin' about,' she said, poking the fire with her back to me.

'I've bottled up all yer secrets fer years because I didn't want ter 'urt Dad while 'e was alive but now I'm goin' ter tell yer this. I know all about the 'ot baths you had an' the pikey pills and penny-royal you took ter get rid of me.'

'That's a lie!' She shifted round to face me. 'Yer don't know nuthin',' she screamed.

'They're not lies. Mary told me when I was first married. You tried ter get rid of me an' you gave Mary the money ter give ter Mrs Taylor to get you all sorts of concoctions. My sister was only nine years old then an' she 'ad ter look after Jack an' Charlie an' the twins that died. Mary told me the whole thing. I know Dad came home and found you in the bath with Mrs Taylor helping, and when he started to knock you about Mrs Taylor went for the police. He ran off an' didn't come back for a week.'

'Yer sister's got a lot ter answer for when I see 'er agen,' she yelled. Then, just as she started up from the chair, Charlie walked in.

' 'Ave yer finished, you two?' he asked irritably.

'It's 'er,' Mum exclaimed.

'It's not all 'er, Ma, I've 'eard every word,' he told her.

I started crying while he was speaking. I was drained by the effort of all this arguing.

'Wipe yer eyes, luv, an' collect up that food. We'll cook ours upstairs. I'll fetch the kids.'

As I pottered about in the attic it occurred to me how like Mum I'd sounded when I lost my temper and I shuddered to think that I might become even more like her as I grew older. I just sat down and wept until I heard the children on the stairs. Then I pulled myself together and wiped my eyes. While I busied myself laying the table, Charlie lit the fire. As I waited for the kettle to boil I watched Charlie playing with the children on the floor. Katie had my old straw-filled golliwog, Topsey, that was made for me by Granny when I was a child. As she was doing so Charlie spoke to her.

'Katie, Daddy's goin' ter buy yer a real dolly one o' these days an' some lead soldiers for Johnny.'

I couldn't believe his thoughtlessness. 'There yow go again!' I flared up. 'Promising them things yow can't afford.'

'But we will when I start work tomorra,' he said, smiling. I could hardly believe my ears as he added, 'I start at a factory an' there's a regular job if I keep good time. An' believe me, Katie, I'll keep it this time.'

I threw myself round his neck and as I kissed him I realised that it had been so long since I had done this that I'd almost forgotten how to do it. I couldn't remember being so happy as I was that teatime with a full table, my children, my husband and the prospect of a brighter tomorrow. Then when I'd put the children to bed and tucked Jeannie up in her drawer I sat down next to Charlie by the fire. He asked what we'd been quarrelling about and I told him about the ten-bob note.

'I already 'eard that,' he spoke softly.

'But you don't think I'd let a man do that to me, do yer?' I asked.

'No, luv, but if it'd been Liza I would 'ave.' He chuckled. I had to stick up for my sister though, despite the fact that we didn't get on.

I was that pleased Charlie had a job and things seemed suddenly much brighter, like a black cloud had lifted. I turned down the lamp, undressed and lay in my place at the foot of the bed. Charlie lay down beside me and took me in his arms and we made love, the first time we had for a year.

Mum and I seldom spoke in the months after our showdown, but I didn't mind. I was happy being a housewife, looking after my husband and children. I no longer had to go and humiliate myself before pompous relief officers. With Charlie earning full wages I could pick and choose when I went to the shops. I bought second-hand woollens, unravelled them and knitted them up into clothes for the kids. They looked like Joseph's many-coloured coat. John was attending St Paul's School at the top of Legge Lane where I had gone myself. Katie went to Nelson Street School and I had more time to myself, and for a few brief months everything seemed rosy. I breathed a sigh of relief and thanked God for my blessings. Life, however, had taught me that it was just when things were going well that disaster struck. Existence was at the best of times precarious, and people like us never crossed our bridges before we came to them.

I was not so much surprised as resigned when Charlie was put on short time. I knew what I had to do. The two eldest were at school and Charlie could look after Jeannie while I went out to work. It had to be a part-time job that fitted in with my husband's hours, but luckily I found one at Canning's jam factory. My job was topping and tailing gooseberries, and sometimes sorting out the over-ripe strawberries. Unfortunately the job lasted no more than a month. I was sacked for helping myself to the fruit. I suppose I should have expected this, but the kids loved them.

Troubles do not come singly and no sooner had I lost my job than Charlie, whose health had never been good, was brought home from work ill. Then I thought the bottom had fallen out of my world. I helped him up to bed and sent for the doctor. He took one look at Charlie and ordered him to go to Dudley Road Hospital. Charlie wouldn't hear of this and he prevailed upon the doctor to give him some medicine. He got his medicine but the doctor warned him that if he became worse he must send for him immediately.

The few shillings of savings we had soon dwindled away, but I refused to go on relief again and concentrated on nursing Charlie back to health. My efforts were rewarded. After a month he recovered sufficiently to return to work. He couldn't keep good time though, and soon he was given the sack. He went downhill after that. His spirit was being sapped away. He was irritable with the children and snapped at me. I used to take them on long walks and often visited my brother Frankie and his wife, Nellie, who were very kind to me. They had their own problems though, and I didn't like imposing on their generosity. I dreaded returning home, knowing that I would find Charlie raving drunk or snoring on the bed.

I now had to turn my hand to anything to earn a few shillings to pay my mother rent and to buy food. One Saturday night my eldest sister Mary, who was now a part-time barmaid at the Vine Tavern a few yards from where she lived in Carver Street, came to see me.

'Kate, would yer like to earn ten shillin'?' she said.

'Ten shillin'? Are yer kiddin'?' I exclaimed.

'No, I ain't kiddin',' she replied, and began to smile.

When I asked what I had to do she said, 'There's an old couple comin' to the Vine tonight to celebrate their golden weddin', and the missus at the pub asked me if I knew anybody who could sing a few old songs for them and—'

'Why ask me?' I asked before she had time to finish.

'Well, the woman she engaged 'as let 'er down, and I mentioned you.'

'But Mary, I've never sung in a pub before, only when I was about ten years old when me dad sat me on the counter and I sang for his beer money. Any'ow, Charlie would kill me if I went an' he found out.'

'Charlie won't find out unless yer tell 'im, an' I know you ain't that daft! Any'ow, you'll only be away about an hour, you'll be back home in plenty of time before he returns. Knowin' 'im, he won't be back till they throw him out!'

'I'll think about it, Mary.'

'I must have me answer now, or she might get somebody else.'

'But I ain't even got a decent frock to wear!'

'That's no trouble, you can wear my blue taffeta one. It's too tight for me now, I know it will fit yer. So if you'll say you'll come, I'll give it yer.'

I always envied her that dress and ten shillings seemed a fortune to me in those days so, knowing I would be the owner of the blue taffeta dress, I agreed to go.

First I tiptoed up the attic stairs and, seeing that my children were fast asleep, tiptoed down again.

Mary had already got the curling irons in the fire for my hair, and after she had brought in the dress and I slipped it on she put a little powder on my face and neck. As she made my lips up with her lipstick, she said, 'Now look at yerself in the mirror.'

I couldn't believe my eyes – how different I looked, and what an improvement on my old blouse and skirt that I had to wear all the time and wash weekly to try to make myself look presentable wherever I went!

As I stood admiring myself, Mary said, 'Why, yer look ten years younger. If yer stand admiring yerself much longer you'll crack the mirror.' Then we both laughed.

Before we left the house I listened once again at the bottom of the attic stairs, satisfied that all was quiet. We made our way towards the Vine. I was still very timid, but my sister put her arm in mine and said I would be OK once I got inside the smoke room. I felt as if everyone's eyes were on me as I looked around. In the far corner was a long table with all kinds of eats laid out, and bunches of flowers. I was told later that evening that kind neighbours had had a door-to-door collection for Mr and Mrs Wright's anniversary. In another corner of the room was an upright piano – its lid was open and as I looked at it I thought: I hope it plays better than the one I tried to practise on when I was a young girl.

Flo, as everyone called the missus of the pub, was no stranger to me; often she used to serve me in the bottle and jug department when I fetched my dad's beer. She was a small dumpy woman with black frizzy hair which came down to her shoulders. To me she always seemed overdressed, and that night she wore a long flowing red velvet dress, long red dangling earrings, several rows of different-coloured beads and several rings on her fingers.

She put her arm round my shoulders and said, 'I'm glad you could come, my dear, your sister has told me all about you. So sit down, and don't look so nervous.'

'She won't afta stop long, Flo,' Mary said. 'As soon as she's sung a couple of numbers I'll 'ave to go 'ome with 'er before 'er 'usband comes back.'

'Very well,' replied Flo as she turned to me again. 'Now, sit yourself down. We're not ready to begin yet, so would you like a drink? Whisky or gin, or—'

'Oh, no, no, thank you,' I answered quickly. 'But I would like a glass of stout.'

The old barman brought over the glass of stout and a gin for Mary, who was to accompany me at the piano.

While I was waiting to be announced, I still felt nervous, for I'd never sung in front of a lot of people before. But after another couple of stouts and a sip of Mary's gin I had plenty of Dutch courage to sing my numbers.

I knew I had a good singing voice. When I followed my sister towards the piano and she started to play, everybody in the room applauded. Then, it was my turn to sing. I sang my favourite, 'Home Sweet Home', which was a song I'd learned at school. Everybody applauded and I felt then that I could have gone on singing all night. An old white-haired gentleman came towards me and asked if I would sing again.

'That was lovely, me wench, but could you please sing "When Your Hair Has Turned to Silver" for me an' me wife?' he asked. I stood beside the piano again and as Mary struck the first notes, I began to sing:

> *'When your hair has turned to silver,*
> *I will love you just the same.*
> *I will always call you sweetheart,*
> *That will always be your name.*
> *Through a garden filled with roses,*
> *Down a sunset trail we'll stray.*
> *When your hair has turned to silver,*
> *I will love you as today.'*

I don't know how I sounded, for all the time I was singing tears filled my eyes as I saw the white-haired old couple kiss and embrace like a pair of young lovers. The applause was deafening – not only for me but for the old couple, who were still hugging each other.

'Mary,' I managed to whisper, 'it's getting late, I'll have to go.'

'Can't you stop an' do another number?' she asked.

'No! Yer know I've got ter get back 'ome, I've stayed too long as it is.' I didn't stay even for a sandwich.

'Oh, all right. I'll go over an' speak to Flo.'

But the missus was already walking towards me with a large bunch of flowers and the ten-shilling note. As she gave them to me she asked if I would come again.

'I'll 'ave to think about it,' I replied. 'But I'll let my sister know.'

She thanked me again and as Mary and I walked out into the street I put the ten-shilling note down inside my frock and, hugging those lovely flowers to me, I said, 'Mary, I think you better have these flowers, or me 'usband or me mum will start askin' questions an' I wouldn't know what to say. Any'ow,' I added, 'I've got what I want and the money will come in useful.'

But while we were laughing and saying what a wonderful night we'd had, I happened to glance across the street. I saw my husband standing beneath the light of the street-lamp watching me.

'Kate,' I heard my sister say, 'don't be scared. I'll come 'ome with yer an' explain.'

But there was no time. Before we got a few steps further he suddenly dashed across the road. The next thing I knew, he snatched the flowers out of my arms and threw them across the street, then as he struck me across my face I saw stars, then as he tore the frock almost from my back I called out for my sister, but she had already fled. Crowds were now gathering around, and as he turned to answer some of the women who were yelling at him I saw my chance and ran home.

But there was Mum, sitting by the fire ready to greet me. 'Serves you bloody well right, an' I 'ope 'e gives yer some mower!' she cried out when she saw my eyes swollen and my lovely frock all torn.

'But I've done no 'arm,' I began to whimper. 'I was only singin' an' I needed the money.'

'But yer know 'e's ferbid yer gooin' in a pub!'

I knew it was useless to try to explain to her, or to expect any help. So I went upstairs, and as I sat on the foot of the bed weeping, I heard Charlie come up. I was now scared stiff, expecting him to give me a belting. But when he pulled me up off the bed and saw what he had done, he just said he was sorry and walked back down the stairs. I didn't see him until the early hours of the next morning. Then he took me in his arms and said again how sorry he was for what he'd done.

I had no choice. I had to get a job if Charlie could not or would not. I was fortunate I suppose. At least I was skilled enough to find work; there were plenty who were not. I was taken on at B. H. Collins in Frederick Street and I was happy there, enamelling metal badges of all kinds. We were able to survive and if I didn't see much of my family at least I was able to put food on the table.

Each Friday night after we'd been paid for the week the girls I worked with went for a drink in the Rose Villa, a local pub. They were forever urging me to join them and couldn't understand why I always refused. I was tempted but I couldn't spare the money I would spend on drink. Then one Friday Harry from the toolshop repeated the offer.

'Why don't yer stay an' 'ave one? It'll doo yer no 'arm,' he said, laughing.

'It's not the drink I'm worried about, 'Arry,' I told him. 'It's my 'usband. If my 'usband comes home drunk and finds I'm not there, I don't know what will 'appen. Anyway,' I added, 'I have three children to see to.'

'Just 'ave the one then, it'll do yer good,' he persisted.

And I relented: where was the harm in just one drink? I thought. I joined them that payday and had a glass of stout before leaving. My mistake was making a habit of it. I went regularly and never thought that it was close enough to home for Charlie to get wind of it. He did and the next Friday night was waiting for me.

'So it's drinkin' in the Rose Villa now, is it? And with a married man as well!' He shouted so all the neighbours would hear. I tried to explain but he began raving, saying I'd been whoring, and he hit me several times. I don't know what he would have done if Mrs Taylor hadn't come running up the stairs to rescue me. When she appeared Charlie stamped off, still ranting.

I gave the job up. I was too ashamed to go back with my face bruised and my eyes blacked. Charlie was sorry when he'd sobered up; he promised to give up the drink, and he did for a time. He did his best to make it up to me and was kindness itself. I softened and forgave him that and other things.

I found another job the following week but this time it was not so pleasant. I was swinging a heavy press and it was dirty work, but the money was twice as good as I'd been getting. Now Charlie came to meet me from work and we walked home with the children. He was no healthier, however, and often complained about stomach pains. The doctor gave him tablets and they seemed to ease his pain for a while.

It was during this time that I noticed an advertisement in a shop window for a 'strong man to mend packing cases' at Gaunt & Sons, Warstone Parade. I was on my way to Frankie and Nellie's with the children and I hurried on my way. I was determined to get that job for Charlie, even if I had to beg. Strong man or not he needed a job and I had worked for this firm myself when I was sixteen. I left the children with their aunt and uncle and went along to inquire about the job and go down on my knees if necessary. I arrived breathless and pressed the bell, hoping that the job hadn't already been taken. I didn't have to wait long. The forewoman I had known years before appeared. She recognised me at once.

'I seem to remember you, don't I? Didn't you work here before?'

'Yes, years ago. I'm married now, with a family,' I replied.

'Yes, I remember you. Your name was Katie Greenhill, wasn't it?' Nothing had ever escaped her beady eye. 'Well, if it's a job you've come for I'd be glad ter start yer,' she began, but I interrupted her.

'I'm sorry, Mrs Lane, it's not for me; I've come about the job for my husband,' I said in a rush. She looked surprised. 'Carn't 'e come 'imself?' she asked suspiciously, but I assured her.

'No, he's not at home at the moment.' I nearly said he wasn't well, which would have lost him any chance of the job.

'Very well, you wait here an' I'll 'ave a word with Mr Booth. I'll do me best but remember, Katie, if you ever want a job yourself come an' see me.' With that she went away and I prayed she would succeed on her errand.

A minute or two later Mr Booth the manager appeared and asked how old my husband was and if he was strong.

'Oh yes, he's very strong,' I replied eagerly. I had to lie if he was to get the job.

'Very well, tell 'im to come and see me straight away, before five o'clock, and I'll see if he's suitable.' And with that he turned and went back into the workshop. I didn't wait around but made haste home, without collecting the children, I was so eager for Charlie to get that job. I fell into the kitchen and found Charlie talking to Mum.

'Charlie, I got you a job at Gaunt's, in the packing shop. You've got ter go an' see Mr Booth at once,' I told him, full of excitement. He didn't believe me at first until I'd spelled out the details. 'Now hurry yerself, before he changes his mind!' I was frantic at his apparent lack of concern. However, he had a quick shave and made himself presentable and went off without so much as a 'thank you' or a kiss. 'Come straight back an' let me know 'ow you get on,' I shouted as he rushed out.

I returned for the children and after putting them to bed waited hours for Charlie to return with the news. I imagined all sorts of things had happened to him as it got later and later and still no sign of him. It was eleven o'clock when he eventually rolled in, drunk as a lord.

'I gotta start in the mornin',' he managed to say before I exploded with anger.

'An' a nice state you'll be in in the mornin'! An' where did yer get the money from for the drink?'

'I borrad it from me brother an' we've bin 'avin' a little celebration,' he mumbled.

'It's a pity 'e can't lend yer some food instead o' that lunatic soup you've bin drinkin'.' I turned away in disgust as he fumbled to undress himself. Then he tried to put his arms round me and I pushed him away in a fury: I was not having him mauling me.

'Stay there yer drunken beast!' I screamed, pushing him over on to the foot of the bed where he collapsed in a heap and started snoring.

I stood watching him sinking into his stupor. I was so bitter. He had to be up at seven o'clock in the morning and he had just selfishly gone out drinking with money he had yet to earn instead of thinking of me and the kids. Where would all this end, I thought, as I stripped off his shirt. I washed it and hung it over the chair to dry, then I undressed myself and lay down at the opposite end of the bed and hugged Katie and Johnny until I fell into a fitful sleep.

The next morning I was afraid to look at the foot of the bed in case he was still there but he must have got up early and left without disturbing us. He did keep the job for a few weeks too, and even brought part of his wages home to me but the rest he spent on drink. We quarrelled often. Nevertheless we were both working now and I was able to put a little aside each week for the inevitable rainy day. And there were happier times. If Charlie was off the drink he could be very good company and although the first flush of love had passed long since we would go out together some Saturday nights visiting our old haunts around the Bull Ring markets. Mum even brightened up now she was receiving more rent money.

Then a few months later I discovered that I was pregnant again and I was horrified. I didn't want another baby just as we were beginning to get on our feet. We still had no real home and were sleeping five in a bed. It was too much. I prayed to God for a miscarriage: an abortion was out of the question. I had to carry on for the children's sakes and couldn't risk anything that drastic. I continued working as long as I could but I knew that after the baby was born we would be back to square one and probably end up on parish relief again. I was more determined than ever that I would have no more children after this and that I would work as hard as I could to get us a place of our own, although I knew how difficult this would be when no landlord wanted to rent rooms to a couple with so many children.

Then one afternoon in April 1931 I became ill at work and two of the girls had to bring me home. We arrived to see Charlie being laid on a stretcher and rushed off to hospital. He'd been under the doctor and taking pills he had been prescribed for about two weeks, but apparently one of the ignorant neighbours had tried an old wives' treatment on him that day and now he was unconscious. With that I fainted and the next thing I remember was coming round to find that my labour had started. I could hear the children downstairs crying for their daddy and I felt totally lost.

Then a friend of mum's called Gert Wilcox stepped into the breach. She said she would take the children for a few days and come back later to see how I was. So she took them off to play with her kids and left Mum to look after me. I shall never forget that woman's kindness to me in that time of need. She lived nearby in Pope Street and her husband Harry, who was an old friend of Dad's, was a barman at the George and Dragon. She was 'a busy little body', always bustling about, cleaning and tidying. She always wore a starched white apron and although she was not a qualified midwife she was the next best thing.

She had telephoned the Hallam Street Hospital in West Bromwich where Charlie had been taken and they had told her he was comfortable. This eased my worries a bit but I was still in labour and experiencing very painful contractions. I didn't want this baby and that made it worse. Without doubt this was the most difficult birth I had ever undergone. I thought at one stage I was going to die and have never been so frightened in my whole life as I was then. I prayed that the child would be stillborn and that my mother or Gert would take it away and bury it somewhere, but that changed when it had been born and I'd seen Gert hold it up by the feet and slap it into life.

'You've got a luvly baby daughter, Katie, and sure enough she's got a good pair of lungs,' she said, smiling. She was as exhausted as I was and Mum had to do the tidying up. Gert washed the baby and put her on my breast. Then I knew she was here to stay. She was such a pretty little thing, with a mop of black hair, and as she sucked my breast I hugged her to me and thought how proud Charlie would have been to see her. But he never did see his daughter: three days later the news came that Charlie had passed away. That was 25 April 1931, our tenth wedding anniversary.

Chapter 22

I Give Up My Children

Thus, at the age of twenty-eight, I was left a widow with four young children to bring up now that Mary, two months premature, had arrived. I prayed for the Lord's guidance before and after Charlie's funeral. I had absolutely no idea how I would cope now. I wouldn't have had enough money for the funeral without my maternity money and the collection that the kind neighbours took up for me. I was too weak physically and emotionally to work. I applied for a widow's pension but was turned down because Charlie hadn't had enough insurance stamps for me to be eligible.

It seemed and still seems very cruel to me that I was forced back on the parish. There was, it goes without saying, no child allowance or supplementary benefit in those days. The good old days they may have been for some, but for me and plenty like me they were not good. It was pitiful to see the men and boys of all ages walking the streets looking for work or hanging around the yards idling away their time. Mum had had only her pension since Dad died and most of that went on drink. Now she said, 'If they won't pay yer a pension then the parish'll 'ave ter keep us.' So I went along to the Gospel Hall in Hockley Street where I had to queue outside for over an hour before being called in to state my case. I shall not forget easily the two stern-faced women who sat behind the table looking down their noses at everyone. I thought of the time I had considered gassing myself and the children but had had no money for the meter. I was sure that if I was refused help again I would start stealing or do something desperate. Then my name was called and I had to make myself humble. While I explained our plight to one of the women the other one shuffled through files.

'So you've had another child since you were here last?' She spoke coldly.

'Yes,' I replied, 'an' I've lost my husband too.'

'Have you applied for a pension?' she asked.

'I have but my application was turned down.'

'Turned down?' she asked in obvious disbelief. Then fixing me with her cold, emotionless eye she continued, 'But you say you were married or weren't you?'

'Of course I was,' I snapped. I explained the situation about the lack of insurance stamps and she wrote it all down.

'I see. So, you have four children and you are living with your mother? I see she is on our files too.'

'I 'aven't come about me mother,' I said, becoming angry. 'I've come for food for me children.' My impatience was showing now.

'I don't want any insolence. You sit over there and wait. I'll call you when we're ready.' She indicated a seat next to an old woman.

I gazed blankly round the room at the drabs, old and young alike, resignedly waiting for their handouts. Then I silently said a prayer that if God gave me my strength back I would do something better for my children than sitting here being humiliated. Then I was called back to the table to be told they were sending a visitor to conduct a means test.

'But I'm desperate now! I want food for my children,' I insisted.

'You heard what she said,' the other woman chimed in. 'We can't give you anything until the visitor has called.' Then as I stood there dumbfounded, the other woman whispered, 'Some of these women shouldn't have children.'

The visitor didn't call for two weeks, which I suppose was their way of punishing me. In the meantime I'd pawned everything I had left of any value to buy food. Then when that was gone I went back to the relief office and threatened to leave my kids there with them if they didn't help me. There was a man there that time and he was more sympathetic. He asked me to sit quietly and he said he would try to help. Down came the files and we went through the same rigmarole again. It was all I could do to manage the children while I waited. Then he called me into an office. There he asked me about all the details of where Charlie had worked and about his illnesses and after he'd written every little detail down he eventually gave me a ration card to take to Baker's, the grocers. I thanked him. I was so happy to be getting anything. He told me to call once a week for food vouchers and in the meantime he said he would see about my pension although he couldn't promise anything. I thanked him again and told him I had every intention of starting back to work as soon as I was well enough. I might have saved my gratitude because when I found out what my ration was I discovered that it didn't amount to enough to feed me, let alone the children.

I wouldn't have survived at all if I hadn't taken the risk of trying to earn a few extra pennies doing odd jobs. I went into business making ginger pop for the kids. I worked with a neighbour, but after all the washing of bottles it was hardly worth it. So when I heard about a job cleaning at Cullis's pawnshop I decided to investigate it.

I put the two youngest into a borrowed pram and set off. I went to the rear entrance and gave a girl who was hanging about a penny to look after the babies. I saw Mr Cullis in the back room where he lived and slept. It was filthy but I couldn't afford to turn my nose up at the money. It took me over an hour to scrub clean those bare old boards. When I told him the job was done he said I could clean the shop window. Before starting I popped out to see if the children were all right and found them fast asleep. Relieved, I fetched a bucket of soapy water and wet and dry rags and set to work. When I'd finished to my satisfaction I asked Mr Cullis when he wanted me again.

'Ye've done a very good job but I won't want it done agen for a long time now, so I'll let yer know.' And with that he handed me two shillings. I was livid and threw the bucket, dirty water and all, across the counter.

When I got back to the yard I couldn't find Johnny anywhere. I was beginning to become worried when I spotted a policeman bringing him down the yard.

'What's 'e bin up to now?' I asked, half scared and half angry.

'I found 'im beggin' outside the factory gates an' I'm warnin' yoo now, if this 'appens again I'll 'ave ter take 'im ter the station.'

I was desperate, friendless and almost at my wits' end. In the weeks that followed I tried my best to make ends meet and even asked my sister Mary if she would take one of the children until I could get back on my feet. But she'd hardened since her second marriage.

'Sorry Kate, but I've got me own three. Anyway, me and Bill are thinking of selling up and going to try our luck in America.' That was that. It was a similar story when I went to Jack.

'Rosie's mother's livin' with us now an' we ain't got the room,' he said.

'But it's only for a few weeks while I get a job,' I pleaded but to no effect. I got nothing from him but a promise to try to help later; I saw neither hide nor hair of him for years after that.

Suicide was not far from my thoughts during that period, and I also considered becoming a prostitute. But I was too shy to talk to a stranger let alone lift up my frock for one. After all, I'd never undressed in front of Charlie even. I'd always insisted on blowing the candle out before going to bed. Charlie used to laugh at me but I didn't change my ways.

Then I was lucky enough to get a job cleaning at the George and

Dragon. I had to start at six o'clock in the morning and work an hour lighting fires and scrubbing the bar. The ten bob the publican paid for this was very useful and the time was perfect for me. I could creep out before the children were awake and be back to get them off to school. I tried to keep this job quiet and told no one at all about it. The publican was well pleased with my work and gave me a cup of tea as well as bread and cheese and a bottle of stout to take home. It made me sad when I scrubbed that step. It was the same step I had sat on with my bum freezing while I waited for Dad to call for me to sing for the customers.

I might have realised that luck like this could not last. One morning when I'd finished the landlord called me into the smoke room. 'Mrs Flood, I've bin told you're on parish relief. Is this true?'

'Yes,' I admitted. It was no good lying.

'You should 'ave told me. I'm sorry, but I'll 'ave ter let yer go. We'll both be in serious trouble if they find out. But if you sign off, I'll take yer on again with pleasure.'

'I carn't do that,' I answered tearfully. 'What little they give and what I earn 'ere is the least we need. I'll 'ave ter find something else.'

I tidied away the brooms and brushes and was about to leave when he appeared with a parcel of bread and cheese and a bottle of stout as usual. I almost refused to take them but I thought twice. I could not afford pride in those days if it meant cutting off my nose to spite my face. I took the gifts and thanked him and he slipped a pound note in my apron pocket.

I realised that it was pointless trying to get a job on the quiet; there were plenty of wagging tongues to give the game away. However, I decided to try anyway. What could I do? With four young children and no husband I couldn't have held down a full-time job. So it was back to chopping and selling firewood, and I found myself plodding round the streets till late at night touting my wares for a few pence.

I would dearly have loved to leave the hovel we shared with

Mum but there was no point simply moving to a similar house, and the idea of living in a better house in a pleasant district was a pipedream. I wanted above all to give the children a decent upbringing away from all the bad influences around them. They were always in and out of the neighbours' houses and came home repeating the bad language they'd heard. I hated having to correct them and it was a vain task trying to counter the combined force of the circumstances of our lives. Some children had been taken into homes and I came to believe that this was the best thing for them. Many times I'd considered allowing my own children to go into a home but I lacked the courage to go through with it, and as long as I could continue selling firewood we existed. I still hadn't notified the parish about this sideline but each week as I collected our ration I became more nervous.

Eventually the day of reckoning arrived. The visitor called one morning and told me I had to go to the office at once. I was terrified of what they would do to me but I had to go; if I didn't they would send someone to fetch me. When I arrived at the church hall I found there were several others there with equally worried expressions on their faces. I waited to be called to stand in front of the long wooden table behind which the inquisitors were seated. Finally my name was called and my heart sank to my boots.

'Come along, we have something to ask you.' The harsh voice echoed in the large hall and I crept slowly towards the speaker who sat there, hard faced and threatening. I have never felt so utterly humiliated and ashamed and defeated.

'It has come to our notice that you have been selling firewood,' the woman said loudly so that all could hear, and she wagged her finger at me so there could be no doubt to whom she was addressing her remarks.

'Yes,' I almost whispered, too scared to lie.

'And you haven't declared your earnings, have you?' She did not look at me but glared round the room at the others. 'You know we can prosecute you for this deception, don't you?'

Then something inside me snapped and I forgot my fear in my frustration and anger. 'Earnings? You call it earnings! Sellin' a few sticks of firewood! What you lot dish out 'ere isn't enough to keep a sparra alive!' I shrieked at her.

'Stand back there, we'll deal with you later,' she said, reddening, indicating with an irritated gesture that I was to move to the back of the queue. But I was not budging. I was determined to say my piece now I'd summoned up the courage.

'You stand back there an' beg for crumbs an' see 'ow yow feel! Anybody'd think it was your money that paid for our chickenfeed! We're entitled to it an' a good deal more!' By now all eyes were on me and you could have heard a pin drop when I stopped, breathless.

'You'd better leave now,' she hissed, suppressing her obvious fury, 'or I'll call the police.' But she could not outface me that easily.

'Yow can send for the whole bleedin' police force, yer bloody ol' cow!' There were murmurs of agreement from amongst the audience.

Then a young man left his place in the queue and, taking my arm, led me outside. 'I'm glad you spoke up for all of us. I'd have liked to back you up but I've got my own family ter think about an' I can't afford to offend them,' he said gently.

'Neither can I but I'm glad now I've got that off me chest,' I replied.

Then I turned and walked slowly away from that miserable place. It was only when I had calmed down that I realised what I'd said and done, and when I returned home I sat on the sofa and wept bitterly. And it was then that I decided to send the children to the only place where they would be well fed and cared for. I would put them into a home before they were taken from me, which they would be if I was sent to prison. I fretted and tossed sleeplessly all that night and the next morning made my final decision. I went down to Mum's bedroom to tell her of my intentions, but her bed was unslept in so after I'd sent John and Kathleen to school, I called on Mrs Taylor to keep an eye on Jean and Mary.

'Mary, Mother of God!' she gasped, when I told her where I was going. 'Whatever's goin' ter become of us all?' she wailed. I left her in this state to look after the children and went to get it over with.

It was a cold, wet morning and although I had pieces of cardboard in my shoes my feet were still frozen. I pulled my coat closer round me and made my way to the tram stop. I walked along in a trance, still not finally decided. In my heart of hearts I knew there was no other course for me. I was in a corner from which there was no escape. We would get no more parish relief, I couldn't take a job without neglecting the children and I couldn't earn enough from the firewood to feed and clothe them. I knew where to go, and without being really conscious of how I got there I found myself outside the gates of the Dr Barnardo's home in Moseley Village, which was almost in the country then but has now been swallowed up by Birmingham.

Nervously I knocked at the door, which was opened at once by a middle-aged, kindly-looking woman who had on a long grey dress covered by a white starched apron and with a matching bonnet on her head.

I was too choked with emotion to speak but she put me at my ease and said she was the matron as she showed me into a large room and indicated that I could warm myself by the fire. There were four leather chairs and a large oak table laden with cakes, jam, bread and butter. In a corner stood a bookcase with books and ledgers. The floor was bare but brightly polished and above the fireplace was a large portrait of an elderly gentleman who I guessed was Dr Barnardo. As I looked up at this picture the matron spoke.

'Would you like a cup of tea, my dear?'

'Yes please,' I murmured. She offered me a cake but although I was hungry I couldn't have eaten a thing. I was overwhelmed by emotion and on the verge of tears. I perched on the edge of a chair and tried to explain why I'd come. After I'd completed my tale of woe I could see by the look on her face that it wasn't going to be plain sailing.

'I don't know whether we can help you. This is only a home for orphans,' she said quietly.

'But I must find somewhere for them, matron. It's only for a short time, till I get work an' find a proper home.'

'Well, perhaps if you tell me all about yourself we can do something to help.'

So saying, she reached for a large sheet of paper and began to note down everything I told her about myself from the time of my marriage. After this she offered me another cup of tea and told me she would send two visitors round the next day. As I was about to leave she asked if I'd walked from Birmingham and when I told her I had walked part of the way she pressed a half-crown into my hand.

'I shouldn't do this,' she said, 'but maybe it will help.' I would have kissed that matron if I'd dared. I thanked her profusely as she showed me to the door. As I walked down the gravel path I could hear the sound of children's laughter.

I boarded the tram, tired and hungry, and as soon as I alighted I headed for the first butcher's shop where I bought sixpenn'orth of stewing steak. I spent the rest of the money on vegetables, bread, margarine, tea, sugar, jam, a tin of Nestlé's milk and a few rusks for Mary instead of her usual sop. I busied myself preparing the meal until the children came home from school. I had to keep active to take my mind off my troubles. That day we had a meat dinner for a change and Mrs Taylor joined us. After the children had returned to school I put Mary to sleep on the sofa, and while Jeannie played in the yard Mrs Taylor and I set to work to scrub and clean the attic ready for the visitors' inspection the following day. I was glad Mum wasn't about because it would have been 'Don't move that', 'Leave that there', and 'I want my things where I can lay me 'ands on 'em'. When we'd finished, Mrs Taylor left.

A little later there was a loud knock on the door and when I peered through the curtain I saw a tall man and a woman standing there. My first thought was that it was the police come for me. I didn't know whether to hide or not, so I called out that Mum was out.

'We haven't come to see your mother. We've come to see you, Mrs Flood. We're from Dr Barnardo's,' the man's voice replied. I opened the door slowly to let them in and as I glanced round the yard I noticed the neighbours' nosy faces peering out of their windows.

'The matron said I wouldn't have any visitors till tomorrow.'

'Yes, but the matron thought we had better call as soon as possible. May we look around and see the children?' the woman answered my question.

I picked Mary up off the sofa and hugged her to me and managed to say, choked with emotion, 'This is my baby; Jeannie is playing in the yard, and John and Kathleen haven't come home from school yet.' They inspected my two youngest and then went up to inspect the attic. Then they asked me all the same questions that I had already answered for the matron. Finally the woman asked if I really wanted to let the children go into the home.

'No, of course I don't, but there's no alternative for me, is there? We're living 'ere with my mother who don't really want us, we've no money for food, an' all I've got is what I earn sellin' firewood,' I answered in exasperation.

'Are you sure you can't get help from the parish?' the man asked again.

'Not now. They're goin' to prosecute me for not tellin' them I'd bin sellin' firewood,' I explained patiently. 'An' now if you refuse ter 'elp us I might end up doin' something desperate.'

'I'm sorry to have upset you, Mrs Flood. If you bring the children to the home tomorrow we can talk some more and make the necessary arrangements,' he said.

A weak 'thank you' was all I could say as I showed them out. Then as soon as they'd gone I collected all the children's clothes which, although well worn, I was determined would be clean.

I wondered when I would wash my children's clothes again. That night I gave the children a good wash ready for the morning.

'But Mum,' Johnny said when I fetched in the zinc bath, 'it ain't Friday night.'

'No, I know, but yer 'avin' a bath tonight anyway.'

'But why?' He was like all small boys, reluctant where washing was concerned.

'I'll tell yer in the mornin'.' I could hardly speak, I was on the verge of tears.

I helped him give himself a good scrub, then he took himself up to bed. Later when I went up to turn in, Jeannie was asleep but Katie and Johnny were sitting up waiting for me to read them the 'funnies' from the newspaper. I thought to myself, this is as good a time as any, so I steeled myself to get my secret off my chest. I settled down to explain where I was going to take them the next day. I didn't know where to begin until Johnny spoke.

'Mum, what yer tryin' ter tell us?'

'Well,' I began, 'you and Katie aren't goin' ter school tomorra, I'm takin' yer on a kind of holiday to a place where there's lots of trees and flowers and a big lawn ter play on with other little children. There's a kind lady there too who'll look after yer an' give you cakes and nice things to eat.' I struggled to make it sound inviting but I really had no idea what life in the Barnardo homes was like; all I had to go on was their reputation and the few brief impressions of my visit.

'Are yoo comin' too?' they chorused.

'Yes, I'm takin' yer in the mornin' but then I'll 'ave ter leave yer but I'll come an' visit yer and bring yer treats ter eat too.' I soothed them as well as I could. 'Now lie down an' I'll read the funnies.' But as I tried to read to them I had to turn my face away to hide my tears. Bless them, they didn't seem to notice or to question that they were going on holiday but simply accepted what I had told them and soon they were fast asleep. Then I kissed their cheeks and tucked them in. I busied myself putting the bath away and eventually went back upstairs, undressed and climbed into bed beside them and quietly cried myself to sleep.

The children were up bright and early next morning, excited at the unexpected prospect of going on a long tram ride and having a holiday from school. I dressed them in their clean rags and after a breakfast of porridge we started on our journey.

The trams in those days had two long wooden benches facing each other on which the passengers sat. When we got on, there were only three vacant seats so I had to sit down with Mary and Jeannie on my lap. The people on the opposite seat seemed to stare at us as if they knew where I was taking the children and I imagined they must be thinking what a heartless mother I was to be parting with my children in this way.

When we arrived at the home the matron was ready waiting for us with warm milk for the little ones and a cup of hot cocoa for me. Then she sent the children out to play while she talked to me. She said they'd decided to take the children into the protection of the home until such time as I was in better circumstances and was able to provide a better home for them. When I thought that this time had come I would be visited by their inspectors who would, if they saw fit, recommend that I could have my children back. I remember thanking the matron and promising that I would work night and day to get back on my feet, and I really meant it. But I had no idea then how long this would take or how difficult it would be.

When we had talked for a while the matron got up and showed me through a glass door which led on to a large lawn where I could see Johnny and Katie playing and laughing with the other children. They didn't notice me; they were too absorbed in their game to see me standing there, but as I watched them I began to feel easier in my mind, seeing them settled down so quickly to their new surroundings. I hoped then and later that they wouldn't feel that they'd been abandoned by their mother, and indeed I was determined to visit them every Saturday afternoon as the matron had informed me I could. She called the children over for us to say our 'goodbyes'. I was choked with emotion and sorrow when I kissed them but they didn't seem to notice and ran off, eager to rejoin their new chums.

I returned in a trance to my mother's house, overwhelmed by feelings of loss and loneliness. Just how much I'd given up I realised when I went into the kitchen, empty now with no grubby little faces to greet me and none to greet for I had no idea how many months or years. It was then that I knew how lonely and single-minded would be the furrow I must plough if I was to achieve my goal, a goal I was determined to reach at any sacrifice.

'Oh God, what 'ave I done ter deserve this?' I moaned self-pityingly, hunched in Dad's old armchair, but the mood passed and I pulled myself together. I must get away from this unlucky house and my mother as soon as possible, I thought. The warning from the parish inquisitors about setting the law on me was also in my mind. Suddenly I was galvanised into action. I crammed a few clothes into a shopping bag and went downstairs to leave, vowing that I would never return. I closed the door behind me and looked round the yard for what I thought was the last time.

These were the familiar sights and sounds of my entire lifetime, stretching back to before I could remember anything, but I was not sorry to be cutting myself off from them. All my troubles resulted from this poverty and degradation. Anything would be better than this. I saw the twin three-year-old daughters of a neighbour sitting on a cold, wet step, frocks up over their knees so you could see they had no underclothes on and sucking grubby dummies. There were other girls and boys fighting and swearing while their mothers gossiped, oblivious. I was sad but also angry to think that these young drabs were fellow creatures who'd been worn out by the struggle, day in, day out, year in, year out, simply to survive in the web of penury and squalor that had trapped them. As I struggled with my wordly possessions up the hill I was thankful that the Lord had given me the strength to go through with my resolve.

I might have known that I wouldn't escape so lightly. My mother must have heard on the grapevine about what I had done because as I neared the corner I heard her shout, 'Katie', in her too-familiar bray and I turned to see her and several neighbours bearing down on me.

'Yer oughta be ashamed o' yerself,' she started, 'tekin' me gran'chillun away. An' where d'yer think yer gooin' now?' She could see what I had in the bag.

'Away from this unlucky hole! An' yoo! An' I ain't ever comin' back either!' I yelled, near to tears.

'Yow'll be back, yow'll see,' she said triumphantly, looking around at her cronies for support. I didn't answer her. Instead I went on my way, but I could hear them muttering about how I was 'a terrible woman', 'the wust woman in the district', for putting my children into a home. It mattered not to them that I couldn't properly care for them. As far as they were concerned any kind of inadequate dragging up was better than allowing your children to be taken care of in an institution. I hurried away tearfully, cursing them for their ignorant prejudice and me for the terrible fortune fate had dealt me.

There was only one person in the whole world I could turn to now: my brother Frank. And, bless their memory, he and his wife Nellie welcomed me with open arms when I reached their door. I broke down and wept bitter tears as I tried to tell them what I'd done but they comforted me and told me I needn't explain to them. They understood, and in any case Mum had been there already. Nellie put her arm round me and sat me by the fire to warm up, and soon I had a cup of tea in my hand and we talked while she prepared the supper.

'Yoo know if yer'd asked Nellie an' me, we'd 'ave taken two of 'em until yer got back on yer feet,' Frankie said with regret in his voice.

'No, Frank, it wouldn't 'ave worked out. Yow an' Nellie 'ave enough on yer plate, what with two daughters an' another babby on the way. An' yoo on short time as well. No, I couldn't think of that.' I didn't want him to feel hurt that I hadn't turned to him in my hour of need.

Chapter 23

Struggling Alone

Next morning I came down to find Nellie, Frank and my two nieces sitting down to Sunday breakfast.

'We thought we'd let yer sleep in a bit longer, Kate,' Nellie greeted me.

'Thanks, Nellie.' The last few days had been exhausting and now the immediate pressure was off, fatigue had hit me. I pulled a chair up to the table and joined them. When I saw the delicious-smelling bacon, egg and tomatoes on the plate I realised how hungry I was as well, and I tucked in with a will. I hadn't eaten for nearly two days.

After breakfast was over and the breakfast crocks cleared away I gave Nellie a hand with the housework. While I was busy sweeping and dusting I found myself glancing up at my brother sitting in his armchair, smoking his pipe. It was then that it dawned on me how very like our father he was and tears welled up into my eyes.

A little later Frank asked me what I planned to do and where I was going to go.

'I'm gooin' ter look for a job first, Frank. Then I'll have ter look for lodgin's,' I replied.

'Well, yer welcome ter stay 'ere till yer find summat suitable,' Frank assured me.

When I thought it over I was grateful to stay where I was wanted although anxious to get away from the district with its myriad of mostly sad memories. I confided my plans to Nellie in case she thought I wasn't grateful for their help and she understood my feelings perfectly. So it was decided that my stay with them would be as short as possible.

Escaping completely from the Jewellery Quarter was of course impossible. I would keep clear of the Camden Street area but this was the only place I knew, and more important the only place I could find work as an enameller. I was soon out tramping about on the lookout for something. I could have returned to Collins's in Frederick Street but I was well known to all the girls there and I didn't want to have explain to them what I had done. They would have been sympathetic, of that I had no doubt, but it was sympathy I could do without: I wanted to put that behind me and square up to the task I'd set myself. In any case, it was too near the streets I wanted to avoid.

After I'd been walking for what seemed like hours, I spotted a notice in the window of Canning's for 'a young woman to work press', and I hurried in to inquire how long the notice had been there. The lad who was serving said it had just gone in, and hearing that I dashed to the address he'd given me as quickly as I could in case anybody had got there before me. When I arrived at the factory in Vittoria Street I spoke through the trap to the boss, a Mr Gibbons, who told me that the job was still vacant. He asked me my name and age and then, asking me to wait, went to fetch the foreman who turned out to be a pleasant little fellow named Bingham.

'Well,' he said, looking me up and down, 'you don't look strong enough to work a press.'

'Oh, but I am,' I told him eagerly, 'I've worked a hand press before.'

'All right, if yer like ter give it a try, the wages are two pounds ten shillings a week, eight o'clock till six, an' one o'clock Saturday. Bring yer unemployment card and yer insurance card an' yer can start on Monday.'

I ran nearly all the way to Frank's to tell them the good news. They were as pleased as I was, and had also found me lodgings with a middle-aged widow who lived in Warstone Lane. Frank told me her name was Knight and the rent was a pound a week for my bed, which turned out to be poor, and my food. I moved into Mrs Knight's as soon as I could and started work at the foundry. During this period I was able to begin to sort myself out. I saved some money and got myself some new second-hand clothes. I treated myself to a hairdo as well: a Marcel wave which was all the rage then. The hair was curled tightly to the head with heated irons which waved it like corrugated cardboard.

Despite my change of fortune the job on the press was getting me down: I still aspired to something better, and when I asked the boss for a change he put me on an even heavier job. On that I had to use both hands and duck each time I swung the press handle round, otherwise it would have laid me out. The grease and oil got in my hair and on my clothes and each night when I returned to my digs I had to have a thorough wash down. By the time I'd followed this with my supper I was too exhausted to do anything but drag myself off to bed.

Further up Vittoria Street, however, was an enamelling firm, T. A. Butler's, and when I saw they were advertising for learners and experienced girls I gave my notice at the brass foundry and went to work there. This time I was determined to learn everything there was to know about the business and complete my training. The job was a vast improvement on my previous one: it was clean work and so was the workshop, and after working there only a few days I went on to piecework and was able to earn four to five pounds a week with all the overtime I did. Naively I thought that if I could keep this up for a few weeks I would soon have saved enough to be able to afford to rent a house, buy some second-hand furniture and have the children back with me. At that stage I had still to discover how tenaciously Dr Barnardo's clung on to your children once they had their claws in them.

One night when I returned to my lodgings a man was already seated at the table eating his supper.

'This is Fred,' Mrs Knight introduced us, 'he's come fer a few weeks.'

'Good evening.' I greeted him formally and shook his hand. He turned out to be a rather nice-looking fellow, dressed in a dark suit, clean white shirt and dark blue tie. His dark, thick hair was brushed back from his open face and I noticed what a personable manner he had.

'So you're Katie. Very pleased ter meet you.' He spoke gently and all through supper I could hardly keep my eyes off him, but when he looked up and caught me looking at him I became embarrassed and, making excuses, left him talking to the landlady and went off to my bedroom to write a letter to the children.

A few days after this he asked me if he could take me to the pictures. 'Make a nice change for yer, Katie, instead of stayin' up in yer room each night,' he said persuasively, but I was too tired to go anywhere and refused his offer. 'Some other night then, Katie?' he replied, taking my refusal well. 'Perhaps I will, one night,' I assured him, and after thinking it over on the tram to visit the children I made up my mind to accept his offer.

We went to the cinema, and afterwards dropped in at the Vine in Carver Street for a drink. He was quite the gentleman and showed me the sort of consideration I had not experienced for years, and when we got to our digs he wished me 'good night' with not so much as an attempt to kiss me. Although he was kind, he was also persistent, and took it for granted that I would go out with him again. When I refused he told me he would like to be more than a friend. I knew what he meant but feigned obtuseness, but then he came out with it and asked me to marry him.

'I'm sorry, Fred,' I replied with difficulty, 'I like you very much but marriage no.'

'Well, at least say yer'll sleep on it an' think it over,' he insisted and held my hands tightly so that I couldn't turn away from him.

'I will, Fred, but now let go of my hands an' I'll give yer my answer in the mornin'. Good night,' I added as I made my way up to bed. But I had no intention of reconsidering: my mind was made up. I was glad the landlady was out when I came downstairs the following day. I could face him alone and give him my answer.

'Good mornin', Kate,' he said, advancing towards me eagerly. 'Have you considered my proposal, dear?'

'Yes, I have, Fred, and I'm afraid I don't want ter marry again. All I want ter do now is ter work 'ard an' get a home of me own.' I began to weep and although he tried to comfort me I pushed him gently away and told him as well as I could between sobs, 'No, Fred, that's my final answer.'

I was relieved when at that moment the landlady walked into the room and I was saved from further difficult explanations. She wanted to know why I was upset, of course, but I left Fred to tell her and sat down to recover myself.

'Well, Katie, yer could doo worse,' was her first reaction. This was more than I could stand and I went straight up to my room without saying a word and waited for him to go out. I kept out of their way until I returned from work the following evening to find Mrs Knight in tears. When I inquired what was wrong she turned on me.

'He's gone!' she yelled. ' 'E's taken 'is clothes an' left. I put 'is supper in the oven an' while I was out he must 'ave took 'is things an' gone,' she wailed, upset more about her reduced income than anything else as far as I could see.

I washed and changed and took a walk to visit Frank and Nellie.

I talked things over with them and Nellie advised, 'Yer know yer own mind best. Yer an attractive young woman but I know yer'll be careful.' I stayed a while with them, then wished them good night and returned to my lodgings. When I got to the step the door opened and Mrs Knight dragged me inside and slammed the door.

'That bugger was married! An' 'is wife's lookin' for 'im fer maintenance!' she gasped breathlessly.

'How do yer know?' I could not believe this.

'The police 'ave bin 'ere asking questions. I knew he sounded too good ter be true,' she said, as if she'd known all along that her lodger was a con man. To me it was a complete shock when I realised how close I had been to being duped.

'Come an' sit down, Kate, an' I'll get 'is supper outta the oven. It'll still be all right an' we can 'ave a double 'elpin'. Open that bottla stout an' we'll 'ave that an all. Yow was lucky to turn 'im down.'

'Yes, an' ter think I might 'ave weakened when you said, "yer could do worse",' I said, mimicking her, and we both burst out laughing and continued until our sides hurt. When we'd calmed down sufficiently she said she'd try to get a proper gentleman lodger next and at that point I decided that before that happened I too would leave for a quieter berth.

The same weekend I began answering adverts for rooms but they were all too expensive; some landladies wanted almost as much per week as I was earning. However, I was determined not to admit defeat but to keep on until I found some respectable digs in a better class of area than I was living in in the Jewellery Quarter.

Finally I found what I was looking for in the small-ads columns of the local evening paper, the *Evening Mail*. It was a notice for 'a young respectable woman' and the address was Soho Road, Handsworth. Handsworth was then a solidly middle-class district of quiet streets of large terraced houses. The houses had double bay windows and neat little gardens and it was a pleasure to walk along the streets. I found the house and from its size and appearance I anticipated another disappointment, but since I'd walked all the way there I decided to inquire anyway. I lifted the brass knocker and waited for my knocks to be answered.

I waited for several minutes but, becoming impatient, I eventually turned to walk away. It was then that I heard a woman's voice behind me say, 'Did you knock, dear?' When I turned round I found myself facing a neatly dressed middle-aged woman. She wore a white blouse, long black skirt and had pearl drop earrings in each ear, with a matching string of pearls around her neck. She had a pleasant smile on her face.

'I'm sorry, I must have come to the wrong house,' I apologised, but I noticed her eyes light on my newspaper.

'Have you come about the room?' she asked, and I had to admit that I had. 'But I'm afraid it'll be more than I can afford.' But she put me at ease immediately and brushed aside my protests. I followed her into a beautiful room she called 'the parlour'.

'Sit down by the fire, dear, and I'll put the kettle on. Then while we're having a cup of tea I'll tell you about the room and you can decide if you want to see it or not.'

When she'd gone to the kitchen I looked at the wonderful things the room contained. Against one wall stood a large oak dresser with several shelves full of china dishes and plates and glassware of every description. There was a highly polished leather couch which matched four high-backed chairs. Around the fireplace were a low brass fireguard, brass fender, brass fire irons and a small bellows, all of which shone as if they'd just been polished. On the mantel stood silver-framed photographs. The whole room was spotlessly clean. I was still trying to take it all in when the lady of the house returned with the tea and in answer to her question I told the lady my name was Mrs Flood.

'Oh,' she said, 'but I didn't see you wearing a wedding ring. I thought you were single.'

'I'm a widow,' I replied.

'Do you have any children?' was her next question.

I hesitated before answering, but I could see no harm in telling her, particularly since I wouldn't be taking the room in any case. She looked disappointed when I told her I had four children and said she was sorry that she had no room for them.

I made to get up, tears welling into my eyes. 'I only wanted the room for myself until I can get a home of my own and have them with me,' I blurted out.

'I'm sorry, I didn't mean to upset you, dear. Now sit down and have another cup of tea.' And while I drank my second cup I told her a bit of my story. Then I noticed the time and made my excuses and made to leave.

'But you haven't seen the room,' she said. 'Would you like to?'

I followed her up the red-carpeted stairs and into a well-furnished bedroom off a small landing. I was amazed at how sumptuous it was, right down to the rose-patterned bedspread. There was a bedside electric lamp that could be switched on and off. It was simply luxurious and I was glad to have seen it because it gave me ideas about what I wanted to do when I could afford a house of my own.

'Well,' she said finally, 'do you like it, my dear?'

'It's lovely, but I couldn't afford to rent a room like this. But I would like to know how much it is. Just for curiosity's sake,' I replied.

'It's twenty-five shillings a week all found,' she told me to my amazement. There must be a catch somewhere, I thought.

'Did I 'ear you right?' I asked.

'Yes, Mrs Flood. You see, it's not the money I need. It's someone to keep me company, to talk to. I'm afraid I get very lonely by myself at night and I've got this spare room, so rather than keeping it empty I thought I'd let it. I've had several young women call to see it but I'm going to let you have it, if you wish.' She said she'd taken to me at once and said I had an honest face and that I could move in as soon as I wished. I told her about Mrs Knight's and why I had to find new lodgings.

'I understand your reasons,' she said kindly. 'But you're an attractive young woman. Do you think you'll ever marry again?' she asked.

'No. All I want is to work hard and save enough to rent a house with a garden and get my children back.'

'Well, I wish you good luck in your ambition. In the meantime I'll do my best to help, but be on your guard in case any more Freds come along.' She smiled and we shook hands and it was arranged that I should move in on Monday evening. As I walked back down Soho Road I seemed to be floating on air. I thanked my lucky stars I'd found such a delightful berth and such a sympathetic confidante.

I went to see Nellie and Frank straight away. They were pleased to hear I had better digs. Then as I was telling them about the house, Frank interrupted to tell me Mum had been by and left a letter, which he handed to me.

'But it's bin opened,' I said at once.

'Yes, she said she opened it, thinking it was summat important,' he replied.

'But she can't read.'

'She probably got one of the neighbours ter read it,' said Frank.

'Bloody cheek. She thought there was money in it.' I was furious. I saw that it was a week old and had come from Barnardo's. I was to call to see the matron as soon as possible to discuss my children's welfare. This was worrying and my anger at Mum's lack of concern for the urgency of the matter increased. I decided that I must go first thing in the morning. It was Saturday, the day of my weekly visit anyway.

I stayed with Frank and Nellie and joined them in a bite of supper. I was famished for I'd not eaten all day, and after the meal, over a glass of stout, we chatted and Frankie told me Mum had reapplied for relief now I'd left her.

'But I thought she had a couple living with her.' I didn't see that it was my fault.

'She did, but they left after a row last week, so I was told. So the visitor asked her how many sons she had working and now Jack, Charlie and me have ter allow her two an' six each per week to 'elp maintain her,' Frankie continued.

This was typical of the meanness of the parish officers, but as Nellie pointed out it was better than having her there to live with them.

'She's got money hid away, if I know my mother.' I knew she wouldn't go short if she could help it. But by this time it was late and I had to face Mrs Knight and tell her I was leaving.

As I walked up the gravel path to the front door of Barnardo's next day I was surprised that it was so quiet. There were no children's voices screeching in the background. I assumed they had been taken out for walks and thought no more of it as I lifted the knocker. Then, almost at once, it opened and I was confronted by a tall, elderly, stern-faced woman, dressed in the same uniform as matron.

'Well?' she asked sharply. 'What do you want?' I was very nervous but managed to stutter that I had come to see matron.

'Matron is not here any more but you may leave a message,' she informed me snootily.

'But I've come ter visit me children,' I blurted out.

'Oh, I see. Matron and all the children have been transferred to the homes at Barkingside. Weren't you notified? This is only a receiving home for a few weeks.'

'But why wasn't I told? An' when will they be back?' I asked, unable to grasp the situation until she told me where Barkingside was. Barkingside, Ilford, Essex meant nothing to me until she explained. Then I was shattered. I couldn't understand why they'd taken the children away without my consent and I received little in the way of explanation from this cold-faced woman. Soon I found myself facing a closed door and all I could do was turn and retrace my steps down the gravel path to the street. I was broken-hearted. I imagined I would never see them again.

I had only a few shillings in the world, but the next day I boarded a train bound for Essex. When I got off the train I found a policeman and asked directions to the home, then after jumping on and off several buses I found myself outside an imposing institutional building that made me feel scared. But I'd come this far and was determined to see my children. I'd walked only a few steps towards the house when I was stopped by one of the 'mothers', as the women in charge were called, who asked me who I was looking for. I told her I had come from Birmingham to visit my children, and I was surprised that this seemed to displease her. She told me that all the children had gone to church, it being Sunday of course, and that I couldn't see them anyway without a pass, and then only once a month on Saturday afternoons. This was too much for me and I collapsed in tears.

'Please let me wait an' see them. I've come such a long way,' I pleaded.

All she said was, 'Wait here,' before turning on her heel and disappearing into the house. While I waited I kept a lookout, hoping to catch sight of the children but all I saw were a few older girls. They were dressed in uniform grey, with white, lace-trimmed pinafores. Just then the house mother reappeared and beckoned for me to follow her and we made our way to an almost bare office where without another word she handed me a pass with the rules and regulations. I handed over the basket of fruit and sweets I had brought and read the paper through my tears. I pleaded with that woman to let me see the children but I could see that there was no melting her hard heart, and eventually I left. But I hung around for a long time in the hope of catching a glimpse of them until I was spotted and ordered off the premises with a warning not to return.

I know if I'd seen them that day I would have run off with them. Anything to get them away from the prison I had inadvertently handed them over to.

I was only just in time to catch the late train for Birmingham. I flopped into a seat and took a closer look at the pass and saw that it was only three weeks until the next visiting day, and that cheered me slightly. During that three weeks I had to work very hard to save the extra for the fare and the basket of treats. It was years later that I found out that my children received none of the presents I had taken for them. Whether the staff had them or they were added to the general food supply I do not know: all I know is that it was very cruel to leave my children thinking that their heartless mother never took them even the smallest gift. I suppose that to the people at Barnardo's I was an inadequate mother who was incapable of looking after her children. My efforts to improve my life were not regarded with much interest by Barnardo's, because in the eight years the children were with them they sent somebody to visit me only once.

Those three weeks seemed like years and when the time eventually came the train seemed to crawl. But at last I arrived outside the main gate. I was led into an office where a stern-faced 'mother' faced me from behind a large oak desk strewn with files. She asked me whom I had come to visit and when I gave my children's names she reached for a handbell and rang it loudly. In no time at all a young girl aged, I would think, about twelve, appeared at the door. The child was thin and pale and dressed in the uniform grey and white pinafore of Barnardo's. She had thick stockings and heavy boots and her hair was cropped as if someone had put a basin over her head and cut round the edge. She bowed to the mother and stood waiting for her orders.

'Bring in the Flood children,' she snapped at the timid-looking girl.

I didn't have long to wait when Kate and Jean appeared, curtsied as well and stood there awaiting their instructions. They too were clad in grey and had the same prison-cut hairstyle. I went towards them and as I bent down to kiss them they forgot their drill and threw their arms round me and we embraced. I asked where my son John was and I was told he'd been transferred to the boys' home in Kingston-upon-Thames. I visited him there later. He was there for nine months until he was eleven years of age, when he was sent to Watts Naval Training School at Elmham, Norfolk. Mary was only a babe in arms and too young to understand, and when I held her to me she seemed unused to affection and didn't respond. Soon we were all in tears, but this only provoked the mother to reprimand me for this show of emotion. But I kissed and hugged them and told them that they would only be there a few weeks while I got a home for them.

After a few minutes they were led away and I was informed in cold tones that if I upset them again I would have my pass revoked and would be prevented from seeing them. I had no idea that it would take me eight years before I had them back with me. Today this kind of institution would be exposed publicly in the media but before the war nobody thought that the parents of Barnardo's children had any more rights than the poor children did themselves.

While I was visiting the children regularly all my money was going on travel and I was unable to save enough to have any realistic hope of ever getting my own home. I used to lay awake nights thinking about the children and wishing I had Mary with me at least. Then one day on my way to the station I bumped into Liza who offered to go with me. I agreed; I could do with the company, I thought.

'I'd like ter see 'em too,' I remember her saying and when I told her I was going to try to take Mary back she replied, 'The best thing yow can do anyway. If they were my kids bloody 'ell an' 'igh water wouldn't stop me from takin' them away from this cold-lookin' prison,' Liza exclaimed angrily when we arrived. 'You leave this ter me.'

We didn't have long to wait. We spotted one of the housemaids coming across the yard with my daughter in her arms. Liza went over to her casually and engaged her in conversation, then I grabbed my baby and made for the gate. But Mary didn't know what it was all about and she began to scream. Before I realised what was happening she was roughly snatched back from me by one of the staff whose attention had been attracted by the screaming and I was caught. I tried to explain but it was no good. I was desperate and hadn't stopped to think of the consequences. Now it was too late. We were ordered off the premises and were warned that if we were seen around the grounds again we would be dealt with severely. We left crestfallen and later that week I received the inevitable letter informing me that I would not be able to visit my children until further notice and should I attempt to contact them I would be dealt with by the law. My sister and I quarrelled before we parted that day and I didn't see her for many years after that.

Chapter 24

Some Dreams Come True

After my ill-fated attempt to snatch Mary away from Barnardo's I could do nothing except wait for replies to my letters and work at my one aim of saving as much money as I could, living in hope of my dreams being realised one day. However, I seemed to be dogged by bad luck: often I was unwell and had to have time off work, and after three warnings I was given my cards and left Butler's. Then I had to take a job on a power press at Joseph Lucas's in Great King Street. I had had plenty of experience on a hand press but none on a power press, so when I applied I lied. The money was attractive so I had to try. The following Monday morning I received my brown overall and cap and, nervous as a kitten, made my way to the block where the power presses were. Then as luck would have it a young woman spoke to me.

'Don't be nervous,' she said, 'I'll show yer the ropes.' She was a real chatterbox and a jolly girl. I soon found out her name was Ada.

'I've only worked a 'and press before, Ada. I shouldn't 'ave started really, but I need the money.'

'Don't we all?' she smiled. 'But there's nothin' ter be afraid of. The noise from the presses gets on yer nerves but yer'll get used to it in time.'

Then the hooter sounded for everyone to get to their places. I took a three-legged stool like the other women and sat in front of the machine. When the motor started I nearly jumped out of my skin. Ada pushed me down on to the stool and showed me how the press was operated before the foreman had time to come down the block. Fortunately, I picked the job up quickly.

'Yer OK now, Katie?' Ada shouted above the din. I stuck my thumb up and nodded. Ada was cutting out blanks which were passed to me to have holes pierced through them by the press. Then they were sent to the assembly shop where wires were threaded through them before they were sent to car plants to be fitted to dashboards. Ada and I could talk only in the canteen during breaks because talking was forbidden while the presses were in operation to cut the risk of accidents. She told me she'd only been there a month and I was sorry to hear that she was leaving soon to join a friend who was learning to be a dressmaker.

'Don't yer like it here, then?' I asked.

'Well, the money's good, but the bloody job's too dirty and greasy for my liking,' she replied and I had to agree. We chatted like this whenever we had the chance and became quite friendly.

The following week everyone on the power presses had to go over to piecework. The rate fixers came with their stop-watches and stood over us. Every job was timed according to the Beddow system, the name of the organisation expert who dreamed the method up. This system was not devised for the benefit of the workers. It was real sweated labour and there was scarcely time to go to the lavatory. There was great pressure to cut corners to make sufficient money and one day my friend Ada did a very foolish thing. She tied back the safety guard to work more quickly. Suddenly I was startled by a scream which pierced the hubbub of the workshop. It came from the direction of Ada's machine and I went over immediately to see what had happened. I bent over Ada who was on the floor and blood spurted over me. I'm afraid I fainted at the sight of blood and when I came round I found myself lying beside my friend in an ambulance. She was unconscious and when I looked I saw she had lost several fingers; I vomited and passed out again.

The next thing I recall is coming round in bed in a hospital ward. I'd been washed and was lying between clean sheets. I enjoyed being waited on but I couldn't see why I had been kept in. I inquired of one of the nurses but all she could tell me was that I would have to wait until the doctor had seen me the following day. I didn't think there was anything wrong with me but I was enjoying the service, particularly when a boiled chicken dinner arrived followed by a mug of Ovaltine for supper. Later, in the middle of the night, I got up to use the toilet. I tiptoed down the ward to the lavatory but before I could switch on the light I felt something squelch under my bare foot. I was horrified when I flicked the switch and looked at the floor. There were dozens of cockroaches scuttling for the skirting. I screamed and fled back to my bed. This awakened some of the patients and brought the nurse running. She smiled when I told her what had happened and explained that although they 'tried to keep them down, the building was old'. I still wanted to go to the toilet though so I asked the nurse for a bedpan.

'You are a nuisance, aren't you?' she replied. 'You'll have to wait. Didn't you go when you went to the bathroom?'

'No. Not with them things running around me feet. An' I'm cold now,' I added.

She went away and returned in a few minutes with a hot-water bottle and a warm bedpan. Such kindness, despite my troublesomeness, was more than I had experienced for some time and I revelled in it. When the doctor examined me all over he gave it as his opinion that there was nothing wrong with me, simply that I was undernourished. I was told I was to be discharged the next morning and to call at the dispensary where I received tablets and Parrish's Food.

I returned to Lucas's the following afternoon and gave in my notice, having decided to have another try at enamelling. I was determined to leave the heavy factory work alone; indeed, just the mention of a power press made me nervous. I often thought about Ada and wondered how she was. She would never be a dressmaker after her accident. I wished many times I had taken her address so I could have kept in touch.

My next job was in a small shop; 'Hart's, enamellers to the trade' it said above the door. There were ten other women beside myself, one of whom, a young woman called Rose, was in charge. She was a bit of a snob and very stern. She wasn't liked because she lorded it when the boss was not around. Sometimes he would be away for days 'on business', that is to say at the races. We could tell when he'd lost and then we dared not say a word, but when he'd been lucky he would bring in cakes.

One day Mr Hart gave me a special job. I had to enamel a little white dog on a brooch. This was to be the sample for an order. I tried hard to get it right and the boss was pleased, as was the customer. It was to be a big order which would last for weeks, but when Rose found out I was in Mr Hart's good books she became very jealous. This was compounded when Mr Hart commented that I was turning out more than she was. Inevitably she had to have her revenge.

A few days later I found I was having difficulty with the white enamel, which kept bubbling up. I kept swilling the colour and used a clean cloth, but to no effect. Then Mr Hart saw what was happening. It must have been one of the losing days because he flared up a temper and started to rave. Then I noticed the smirk on Rose's face and realised something was wrong. So did he; he sat down and examined the frit.

Then he exclaimed: 'I knew as much! There's salt in here.'

He sent for Rose in the little back room he called his 'office' and after a few minutes she emerged in tears. She'd been given the sack on the spot. This I thought a bit unfair, but later the girls explained that this had happened before when she'd taken a dislike to somebody. I felt a little less guilty when I heard them say 'good riddance'.

After this Mr Hart joined us in the work for a bit until a couple of weeks after Rose's departure he called me into his office and asked me to take charge and inspect the finished work. Then he went out 'on business'.

I was able to get to know much more about the business side of the trade in my new position: the prices of every kind of enamel badge, invoicing and accounts. I was now chargehand enameller, viewer and office worker all rolled into one. I was not complaining; I knew the trade inside out and I was getting top wages with a promise of a bonus on our turnover. Some of the girls worked faster than others so we worked as a team and got on well, especially when Mr Hart was out. However, his unpredictable moods could be extremely trying, and in the end too much.

Late one afternoon he came bounding in, picked up a handful of badges, glanced at one and then threw them on to the floor in a temper. 'These are the wrong colour!' he bawled.

'But that's the colour we always do them,' I replied.

'You should have asked for the sample,' he yelled at me and before I could reply he'd disappeared into the office. When he came back he almost threw the badge at me. 'Now that's the one! Pick it up, I want you in the office!'

This was the final straw for me: I couldn't tolerate his tantrums any longer. 'Pick it up yourself. You should be 'ere to run yer own business instead of 'avin' it out of me when yer lose on the 'orses!' The girls stared at me, mouths open. So did he when I added, 'See if yer can get somebody else ter do the work I do. I'm leaving right now!' And with that I put my coat and hat on and left.

On the following Friday I had to fetch my pay and my unemployment card. Hoping he was not at a race meeting, I rang the bell and waited. I was ready with an answer if he started on me again.

Almost at once the door opened and he asked me in. It must have been one of his good days.

'I've come for the few days' pay that's due to me and me cards,' I said before he could say anything.

'Won't you think it over and come back?' he asked very pleasantly.

'No, Mr Hart, I've got my old job back,' I told him.

'Enamelling?'

'Yes, just enamelling and more money.'

'Well, I can give you a rise.'

'No, I've made up my mind.' And so I had.

'Well, if you should change yer mind, you've only to ask,' he said. Never, I thought. As he handed over what was due to me he said how sorry he was to lose me. I nearly told him he should have thought of that before now, but I buttoned my lip, seeing no further point in arguing with him.

I started back at T. A. Butler's the following Monday morning. I didn't intend to let the grass grow under my feet now I was saving hard and fast. I was still lodging with Mrs Green in Soho Road and enjoying being there. Each night we would chat about our respective days and we were on Christian-name terms.

Then one day the tide turned for me. My opportunity arrived at last. It happened that Mr Butler – Tom, we all called him – had a large order for different kinds of badges and motor plates but he couldn't employ enough experienced workers to cope. So one night I asked Nell, my landlady, if she would rent me her small empty back room to do some work at home. She agreed willingly and offered to help, to learn herself.

It was easy to talk to Tom; he was like one of the workers, who would always find time for a friendly chat with his employees. My chance came to raise the subject with him and I offered to do some of the filing, a process prior to firing, at home. He agreed at once and let me take some Castrol badges and return them the next day. I laid the enamel on during the day and took three or four gross of the red and green badges home in the evening. Nell and I would sit up in her little back room after supper singing to the gramophone as we filed the badges with carborundum stones.

For me this extra work was worthwhile because I wanted to earn more and more and one day start my own business. You had to work much harder then than today. There were no paid holidays except for Bank Holidays, and normal working hours were long – 8 a.m. to 6 p.m. – and included Saturday mornings as a rule. In the two years after I started doing home-work I worked through, only taking off Christmas Day, Boxing Day and Good Friday. The only recreation I had was when Nell and her friend George took me for a drink on Saturday nights or occasionally to the pictures. During those two long years I managed to save over a hundred pounds which in the 1930s was a considerable sum of money. However, it still was not sufficient to buy or rent a house and obtain furniture and all the things I needed for the children. I thought about what I was to do and decided to ask Tom Butler if he would supply out-work if I could find suitable premises and, bless him, he agreed.

After that I kept my eyes peeled for a workshop and it was on Good Friday 1937 that I happened to be walking along Spencer Street and saw a notice which read, 'Top Floor Shop to Let. Apply Within'. Everything was closed for the Easter holiday so it was the following Tuesday when, hair newly Marcel-waved, in my Sunday-best hat, coat and gloves, I went to try my luck. The name of the principal occupier of the premises was 'F. Marson, makers of diamond rings, 90 Spencer Street'. I was interviewed by Mr Marson himself. His questions concerning my age, marital status and so on made me nervous, but I told him what I wanted the rooms for, who I worked for and what my boss's name was; but Mr Marson still said he needed references. I told him that Mr Butler would vouch for me and he said he would ring him and that I should hear from him in a few days.

Later in the week Tom Butler called me into his office to tell me he had given me a good reference, and I thanked him sincerely. He told me to let him know when everything was fixed, and when I was ready to start he would send his errand boy round with badges and motor plates.

That weekend I was so excited I couldn't sleep in anticipation of going round the following Monday to see the rooms. Mr Marson took me up to the top floor and when I looked round I could see that it hadn't been used for years. There was rubbish everywhere and it was thick with dust, but I didn't mind the filth. That could soon be cleaned away and I was eager to start. Against one wall there was an old roll-top desk and some machinery including a rusty old motor which was nevertheless in working order. In the corner was a cupboard that was supposed to be an office. All in all it was scarcely believable that such a place could exist, but when Mr Marson told me the rent was twelve shillings and sixpence a week I could have jumped for joy. I sealed the bargain by giving him a month's rent in advance and said I would be cleaning it out that week. He gave me the key and we shook hands.

When I got back I told Nell all about it. It had been a glue factory at one point, but with a little elbow grease would be just right. We set to and used just that. Frankie and a mate of his whitewashed it for me the following weekend. Then I went to the bank and withdrew fifty pounds to buy materials. I purchased enamel from Hutton's in Great Hampton Row, carborundum files and wire panning from Harry Smith's, Key Hill, and several second-hand three-legged stools and tables as well as pestles and mortars.

When everything was cleaned and scrubbed I put a notice for experienced enamellers and learners on the wall outside and I was in business. During the next month I employed four experienced women and two learners. Later I took more girls on and a mixed bunch they were, but I worked beside them and we were quite a happy family. I was always first to arrive at seven thirty in the morning and last to leave after seven o'clock most nights. I'd always been a jack of all trades but now I had my own business and I was independent for the first time in my life.

I was still at Nell's in 1937, and at weekends would sit with her and George who was very interested in what I was doing. It was during one of these evenings that they told me that they were getting married in a few months and that they would sell up and go abroad. I was not surprised: I knew they slept together at weekends. I didn't comment: they'd been good to me and it was none of my business what they did. I would have loved that house and the furniture it contained but I couldn't afford to buy it, so I had to start looking for a house to rent.

I was extremely busy now. After paying the girls and taking care of all the overheads I was able to bank money each week. I was now able to visit the children. Kathleen was still at Barkingside but Mary and Jean were fostered out to two maiden ladies they called 'aunties'. When Nell and George had sold up I rented a house in Albert Road near Handsworth Park. I was in seventh heaven furnishing the front room, sitting room, the kitchen and the three bedrooms. What was best was the large garden at the rear where the children could play.

As soon as everything was ready I wrote to the Barnado's offices at Ilford and told them about my business and the house and that I was now in a position to have my children back with me. Two weeks later I received a letter informing me they would be sending a visitor to inspect my business premises and my house as soon as they could. In the meantime the work from Butler's went slack and I had to look round for other customers. First of all I took down the sign outside and replaced it with one which read, 'K. FLOOD, ART ENAMELLER TO THE TRADE, TOP FLOOR'. My first customer, the next day, was R. Gomm. He gave me a good price for the work I did and he supplied me with orders for years, and after I had retired I continued to do outwork for him.

I obtained work from Munster's in Hockley Street as well. Often Mr Munster himself would bring the work. He was a well-dressed, elderly gentleman and rather thickset. He had silver-grey hair and I thought him very distinguished-looking. He was German but spoke very good English. He was quite the gentleman and had beautiful manners. So one day when he invited me out to lunch, I accepted even though he was old enough to be my father.

I had some happy times with him; he was wonderful company, very considerate and not an emotionally demanding man: each time we parted he would just kiss me on the cheek and say, good night. Then one night after dining out he took me in his arms gently and asked me to marry him. This was both flattering and upsetting because I had to tell him that I could not marry him, not until I had my children with me. He knew about them and how they came to be at Barnardo's. He was obviously disappointed but said if I changed my mind he would take me to Germany and make a future for the children there. In the meantime he was going abroad on business. But, he said, he hoped I would say yes when he returned. Next day I saw him off on the train and when we embraced and kissed he said, 'Goodbye my dear, don't forget your promise.' However, I never saw Mr Munster again. I heard some years later that he'd been interned for the duration of the war. If I had not had the children to think about and the business to pursue I believe I might have married him. I might have married several times in those years before the war; I had several proposals, but when I told them I had four children their ardour seemed to subside.

During these years I lost touch with most of my family – Frank and Nellie excepted, of course. Then one day when I was picking up some work from a customer in Albion Street I saw my brother, Jack. I tried to avoid him but he spotted me and approached.

"Ello Kate,' he called out. 'I dain't know yer in yer smart get-up. An' 'ow's the kids?' he inquired cheerfully.

'No thanks ter you that they're all right!' I snapped, and made to walk away. But he grabbed me by the arm.

'Don't yer wanta know 'ow yer mum is?' he asked.

'No! Nor yow! An' yer know why.' I'm afraid I was still very bitter about how they had failed to help me when I needed them. Then he changed the subject.

'Yer know Mary's back from America, don't yer?' And I was willing to listen to what he had to say about my older sister who I hadn't seen for years.

'No, I didn't,' I answered more calmly. 'Where's she living now?'

'She's livin' in the Drive, in the top yard for the time bein'.'

'Oh, my God!' I exclaimed. 'What a comedown for her. If you see her will you tell her I'll come an' see her in a day or two. Thanks for telling me, I've got to be off now.'

As I turned away he said, 'I'm just goin' in the George an' Dragon to 'ave a drink. I'll buy yer one . . .'

'Don't bother, I don't drink!' I snapped in bitterness at him.

I decided I would look Mary up, and a few days later I was on my way there when by coincidence I bumped into Mrs Taylor's twin boys. They were in their mid-twenties now but unmistakable as the little tots I used to drag along in my go-cart to Titty-Bottle Park all those years before. Joey was still bandy and Harry hadn't lost his squint. I still had a soft spot for them. Joey was pushing a basket carriage full of firewood and Harry was walking beside him. I tapped Joey on the shoulder.

'Don't yer know me, Joey?' I inquired jokingly.

' 'Ello Tatie,' they both replied in unison: they always called me 'Tatie'. 'Where'd yer spring from? An' where're yer gooin'?'

'To see my sister Mary, but I'm glad I've seen yer both. An' what are you two up to these days?'

Then they both looked sheepish and Harry replied, 'I 'ope yer don't mind but when yer went away an' yer told ower mum yer wasn't comin' back, we thought we'd take over yer customers, an' now we've got a good little business goin'. One day we 'ope ter buy an 'orse an' cart, don't we Joey?' he added and gave a broad grin.

'Of course I don't mind, Harry. I'm glad yer both doing well, but don't trust anybody on the slate.'

'No fear. We only sell for cash an' we put money in the post office every week.'

'Harry, will yer do me a favour?' I asked.

'Yes Tatie, anything fer yoo,' came the prompt reply.

'Would you go down the Drive an' see if my mother is about? I don't want ter see 'er if I can 'elp it.'

'Don't worry. I'll go. You mind the basket, 'arry,' said Joey before running off in the direction of the Drive. While he was gone I asked Harry how his mother was.

'She died a few weeks after yow left,' he answered sadly.

'Oh, I am sorry to hear that,' I replied, shocked. 'I loved your mum, she was good to me.'

'Yes, she always said 'ow kind you were to 'er an' us when we were little lads,' he said with a tear in his eye.

Joey came hurrying back, all smiles. 'Yow don't 'ave ter worry, Tatie. The ol' battleaxe 'as gone away agen an' the door's locked.' He grinned. 'Yer know,' he added, 'when yer left she took in a coupla lodgers who 'ad a little lad. Poor little bugger was all skin an' bone. 'Is dad was always beatin' 'im with 'is belt an' one night ower mum 'eard 'im cryin' down the cellar among the bleedin' rats. Well, she sent for the cruelty man an' when 'e see the bleedin' red weals on 'is arse 'e tuk 'im away. Then when yer Mum found out, she threw 'em out with all their things in the yard.'

'An' yer know summat else,' put in Harry. 'We admired what yer did.'

'Well, the children should be coming home soon an' when they do I'll bring 'em down ter see you.' I was pleased that I was not universally condemned for sending the children into a home. 'An' now

I'll 'ave ter be on me way.' And I turned to go. Then Joey spoke shyly.

'Doo yer mind, Tatie, if we give yer a kiss?' he asked.

'No, course not. But hurry up; I don't want the people round 'ere to get the wrong idea.' And they each pecked my cheek and blushed. Then they hurried off.

I continued towards my sister's yard where I asked a small girl which house Mrs White lived in.

'In that one,' she told me, pointing to the fourth house. As I approached it I saw a tray of steaming doughnuts on the windowsill which made my mouth water. The door stood wide open. My sister was nowhere to be seen and when I looked round the place, I was surprised to see it was almost bare. It was clean enough, apart from flour all over the floor, but the only furniture was two wooden chairs and a deal table. There was a fire in the grate and on the green mottled gas stove stood a bubbling pan of fat. As I stood taking this in my sister came bounding down the stairs with a large bag of flour in her arms. I could hardly believe my eyes; she'd put on so much weight. Round her ample waist she wore a hessian apron and she had men's boots on her feet and was covered from head to toe with flour. She gave an exclamation of surprise, dropped the bag on the table and flung her arms round me. We kissed and wept as you might imagine after such a long break.

'Oh Mary, I can't believe you've come down 'ere to live.' I was genuinely shocked because as the reader will remember Mary was always so disdainful of the yards. 'What a hole!'

'Oh, don't let that worry yer; this is only temporary,' she assured me.

'But I thought you were doing well in America,' I said.

'I was, at least at first, but the Americans don't live like we do an' ower money didn't last. But when I was there I did learn to make doughnuts an' now I've got a little business selling to neighbours an' supplying the shops. Carn't make 'em quick enough in fact.' She sounded cheerful enough.

We sat talking for a long time and I told her about my business and the house in Albert Road. She made tea and I sampled her doughnuts, which were delicious, and I bought two dozen for my workers. Like me, Mary wanted to better herself and neither of us had any reason to be ashamed of wanting to join the ranks of the employers. We'd been downtrodden, starving even, ourselves, and there was little chance that we would forget that in our dealings with our people. There were plenty of Brummies, born in poverty, who pulled themselves up by their own bootstraps. One, now a scrap-metal millionaire, had been sweet on Mary in the old days. Perhaps she should have encouraged him. There was Joe Lucas, who founded the famous engineering firm, who still lived in Carver Street in those days and who my dad could remember selling tin bowls and kettles from a wheelbarrow. There were plenty more like these. I knew many like them. We didn't have parents who could give us a start in life, nor government grants, nor even social security when we were at rock bottom; just hard work and sink or swim. Unfortunately, Mary never really made it but it was not for want of trying. I haven't got any answers, but the grinding poverty of the old slums did breed some very determined people.

I was doing well enough now to think about getting a small car. Then as luck would have it I bumped into Freddy Jones, an old mate of Frank's, and he happened to mention he had an Austin Seven he wanted to sell.

'Why ask me?' I asked, my suspicions roused.

'Yower Frank ses yer might be interested. It's me own car, an' paid for,' he added in his salesman's patter.

'How much do yer want fer it?' I asked him, still not convinced by a long way.

'Well, I 'ave bin askin' thirty poun' but I'll let yow 'ave it for twenty-five.'

'Why do yer want to get rid of it?' I thought it sounded too cheap to be any good.

'It's like this, yer see. I've bin put on the labour an' the kids ain't got any boots on their feet,' he explained.

'All right. When can I see it?' I asked, my doubts answered to some extent.

'I'll bring it round,' he said eagerly. As good as his word, five minutes later he appeared in a black Austin Seven. It was mud-splattered and full of junk but when Freddy saw the look on my face he cried out cheerfully, 'It only wants a good clean out an' it runs like a bird. Jump in an' I'll show yer 'ow ter drive it.'

There was no harm in having a demonstration drive, I thought, and if Frank had recommended him he must be all right. I climbed into the driver's seat full of trepidation. I listened carefully to the instructions and amazingly I set off successfully and did three circuits of the block. When I arrived at the starting point, excited after my first drive, I stopped to exchange a word and then made to set off again.

''Old on! Yow'll be usin' all me petrol an' yoo 'aven't said if yer'll 'ave it yet,' Freddy exclaimed.

'Right. Bring it round to 90 Spencer Street – you'll see my name on the door – an' I'll give you the money.' I had decided to take this opportunity to become mobile and I must admit that the thought of driving about in my own car had me in quite a state of anticipation.

'Thanks, Mrs Flood. I'll get the missus ter gi' it a good clean out,' Freddy shouted as he drove off.

That night when I got home I wondered if I'd done the right thing. It was a battered old banger and I knew nothing at all about motorcars. But it was too late to change my mind now I'd accepted his price, so I put any lingering doubts out of my mind. Freddy kept his promise and arrived with the car the following afternoon and when I went downstairs, there it was, shining black and well cleaned inside and out.

'I've filled 'er up with petrol, Mrs Flood,' he assured me as I climbed into the driver's seat and clutched the wheel again to savour that feeling of being a car owner.

'Yoo are gooin' ter 'ave it, ain't yer?' he asked.

'Yes, Fred. Stay 'ere while I slip up an' get yer the money,' I said finally.

I didn't have enough cash on hand so I wrote out a cheque to bearer. However, when Fred saw this he wasn't pleased.

'I carn't tek that. I'll 'ave ter tek the car back if yow ain't got cash.' He sounded annoyed. He needn't have done though, because I'd fallen in love with the car.

'Jump in then,' I smiled, 'an' I'll draw some out of the bank.' We drove round to my branch and I took out twenty-seven pounds and I gave him a pound extra for the petrol and a pound for his wife for cleaning it up for me. He was pleased as punch with this and thanked me. He wanted a lift home so we set off, me needing no excuse to experience the thrill of being behind the steering wheel.

I went everywhere in that old banger. You didn't need a licence to drive in those days so I never passed a test. I could drive quite well considering. However, I made one mistake. I could drive straight and change gears correctly when turning corners but I couldn't reverse for the life of me. One Friday afternoon I went to draw the workers' wages and came out of the bank to discover that there was a dustcart in front and a motor behind so that I could only get out by reversing first. I sat there for nearly two hours and I dozed off. The next thing I knew I felt a hand on my shoulder and when I opened my eyes I saw a policeman standing by the open car door.

'You all right, Miss?' he inquired in a fatherly tone of voice.

'Y-yes, why?' I managed to say.

'I've been round the block a couple of times and seein' you still here outside the bank, I wondered . . .' His voice trailed off.

'I'm all right, thanks, Constable.' Now I could see the road was clear I was anxious to be off. He smiled when I added why I'd been parked for so long. No doubt a policeman today wouldn't have seen the joke.

Chapter 25

My Children Come Home

It was during 1938, while I was waiting for Barnardo's to make up their minds to give me my children back that the fears about war were growing. These were fuelled after Hitler invaded the Sudetenland, and nobody was fooled by Mr Chamberlain when he returned with his scrap of paper and promises of 'peace in our time'. Everybody made jokes about Hitler and Chamberlain's paper but the reality of the situation made itself felt when we saw the young lads joining up and the Territorials parading the streets and strutting about pretending to be grown-ups in their ill-fitting uniforms. The sight of them made me feel sick and I became depressed thinking about life in wartime without my children by me. Then came the ultimatum and we were really at war with Germany.

My old banger eventually gave up the ghost in the spring of 1939 and I had to leave it by the side of the road and catch a bus. It was some time since I'd had to use one and I'd forgotten what it was like to travel home on a bus loaded with workers. The conversation was about air-raid shelters and ration books. One old woman was very agitated.

'Gawd 'elp us all. I remember the larst lot. Me 'usband was gassed.'

'Don't worry, ma,' an elderly man reassured her, 'it won't larst long this time. It'll be over by Chris'mas, yow'll see.'

'It's the bloody gover'ment wot causes all these bleedin' wars!' exclaimed another old codger. 'But I don't see any of 'em goin' out ter fight. No! That lot live in the lap o' luxury while the young 'uns get theea 'eads blown away. I done me bit in the last bleedin' lot but they ain't gettin' me this time for the King's bloody shillin' an' two bob a day!'

'I was a conchie in the last war an' I 'ad an 'ell of a time with the neighbours. Called me a traitor they did,' ventured another, more forthright than prudent. 'But thank Gawd, I'm 'ere ter tell the tale now,' he continued.

At this a big burly fellow jumped up from his seat and made for the last speaker.

'Tell wot tales?' he yelled down at the unrepentant conscientious objector. 'It was yower bleedin' sort that stayed at um, werkin' an' gettin' rich while others 'ad ter goo ter the Front an' fight fer the likes o' yow.' He was getting red in the face.

'Somebody 'ad ter go ter the munitions,' the other said timidly.

'Yus! Young girls an' women who 'ad ter leave young babbies. Werked all hours they did, an' my mother was one of 'em,' put in a third.

I believe that they would have come to blows if the conductor hadn't appeared and pushed them back into their seats. This was typical of the sort of talk there was in the final months of 1939.

Production was going over to war work and I had to let some of my girls go because my work went slack as the demand for the luxury enamelled brooches I was making declined. Soon I had too little work to keep going and I had to look for some kind of war work myself. I was fortunate in spotting an advertisement for a contractor to enamel officers' pips. I had a regular order making these for years, as well as other orders for enamelling Auxiliary Fire Service badges, WVS badges and other enamelled items. I had to take on more workers and things were looking up, at least financially; but I was still depressed about the children. It seemed Barnardo's was determined to prevent me ever seeing them again.

Then one day in November 1939 I arrived home to find a letter marked 'Urgent'. I picked it up and tore it open. It was to inform me that I was to meet the midday train from London the next day and that my children would then be handed over to me. I was so excited I couldn't eat or sleep that night. I kept looking at the clock, imagining that it was going slow and thinking that day would never break. Eventually it was time to get up and I went along to the shop, then when the girls arrived I told them I was giving them the day off and why. I locked up the premises and hurried home to light a fire, warm the beds and tidy everything before going to meet the train.

It had been eight long, worrying years since I'd kissed the children goodbye at Dr Barnardo's in Moseley and the Second World War had just begun, not the most auspicious moment to resume a settled family life. In retrospect it seems likely that Hitler had as much to do with Barnardo's deciding I was a fit person to care for my children as anything else. However, I was not thinking about why they were returning that morning as I nervously prepared the house to receive them. I was more anxious about whether they actually remembered me still. Kathleen was now fourteen years old, Jean was twelve and Mary nearly nine. I knew Mary wouldn't know me because she'd been a mere babe in arms when she left, and she showed no signs of recognition on the few occasions I'd seen her since. She'd been fostered out with Jean for about eight years and we'd had no real contact in the interim. I had seen Kathleen more; she'd been there at the homes when I had visited, but these visits had been few in the last years while I had been so busy building up the business.

So midday found me waiting on the windy platform, stamping my feet to keep warm and scanning every train that arrived in case

I should miss them. The porters got fed up with me inquiring which was the London train only to receive the same reply: 'It'll be 'ere at two.' Then finally it drew into the station, all steam and swirls of smoke. I surveyed the passengers disgorging from the carriages and for a terrible moment doubted whether they were on the train, but then I saw Kathleen step down from an open carriage door and as I ran along the platform towards her I saw two women, holding Jean and Mary by the hand, follow her out of the carriage.

'Hello, Mum,' Kathleen called out as soon as she'd spotted me. I threw my arms round her and we hugged each other. When they saw this the two stern-faced elderly women came towards us.

'Are you Mrs Flood?' one of them inquired.

'Yes,' I replied.

'Sign here,' the other said curtly, handing me a document. I'd been caught by Barnardo's getting me to sign things before and I wasn't going to put my name to this without reading it carefully. I then asked her about my son, John. She said her instructions were only to deliver my daughters safely. But before she boarded the train again she wrote down the address of Watts Naval Training School, where John had been sent when he was eleven, and said I should inquire about him there. Then without another word the women returned to their carriage, leaving me alone with the somewhat bewildered children.

Jeannie wasn't sure who I was, and Mary had no idea: that was clear from the puzzled expressions on their faces and their silence. Then Kathleen told them and I kissed each in turn and we made our way back along the platform to the gates. They were famished, not having had anything to eat since they had left, so I took them into a nearby café where they ate ravenously. They were excited and apprehensive and it wasn't until I got them home that they began to settle down.

I stoked the fire and took their coats and berets and while they sat round the fire, taking in their new home, I laid the table with cakes and other goodies I'd bought specially for them. When they'd eaten their fill I took them upstairs to show them their bedrooms and I was relieved to see they were pleased with what they saw.

That night, after tucking the girls up in their beds, I wrote a letter to Watts, asking why my son hadn't been returned to me. A few days later I received a reply saying that he was now serving on one of His Majesty's ships. While still only eleven, John had been put on HMS *Ganges* at Shotley, where he was trained for warships and practised with live explosives and firearms and did bayonet practice. It is horrifying to think that Barnardo's had the right to force the youngsters in their care into the armed forces at such a tender age. Needless to say the life at HMS *Ganges* was even more strictly disciplined than in the homes and the men who were in charge were all hardened naval men. It seems clear to me that the Navy used Barnardo's to ensure a supply of young recruits who had no choice at all about whether they were pressed into service or not. When John was barely fifteen he was put aboard the HMS *Hood*, a battle-cruiser. When I found out I wrote to the Admiralty and to his captain explaining that I was a widow and that he was too young for active service, but they brushed my protests aside because he had signed on for the duration of the war. After that my letters went unacknowledged and I became very bitter. If I had had the right contacts I could have got him out but what could a poor widow like me accomplish when it came to the Navy's need for cannon fodder?

After he joined the *Hood* all I could do was pray that the Lord would watch over him and keep him safe from harm. He broke his arm while doing PT, however, and was given leave while his arm healed. It was during that period, in 1941, that the unfortunate ship was sunk with all bar two or three hands, so I suppose my prayers were answered. John was next sent to the HMS *Dorsetshire* where he was the youngest leading seaman as well as a torpedo man. He was aboard during the engagement with the *Bismarck* as well as seeing service against the Vichy French fleet off West Africa. The *Dorsetshire* engaged the battleship *Richelieu* which was fortunately out of ammunition. Later John saw service in the HMS *King George V* on Russian convoys before being based at Simonstown, South Africa, where his ship engaged in escort duties. Those war years were the most worrying of all my life.

The girls and I had lots to talk about after such a long time: they about their 'aunties' and me about the firm. When Kathleen heard about this she was excited about starting there herself and this is what she did. I taught her the skills involved, how to check the work for quality, how to make out orders, invoices and statements of accounts. She received a wage and was very happy. This suited me because now I had only to attend to the workshop in the mornings and had the afternoons free to be with the younger children.

Taking care of Jean and Mary was harder than I had imagined it would be. They seemed restless and couldn't settle down in their new surroundings. I suppose, looking back, that I was a stranger to them; they had been young when they'd left and although they had been well cared for by their 'aunties', they'd been deprived of a mother's affection. It must have seemed as if I had abandoned them to the not-so-tender mercies of the 'mothers' at Barnardo's; they were too small to grasp the situation and probably wouldn't have understood even if they could. Then, out of the blue, they were brought back and here was I lavishing all the care and attention on them I could, trying to make up for the years we'd been apart. Yes, it must have been extraordinarily difficult for them to adjust, especially for Mary, to whom I was literally a complete stranger. I was trying to buy their love and affection and I realised later that I rushed them in my eagerness to develop a maternal relationship with them. I gave them too much, too soon: that was my big mistake and they saw only the gifts and treats, not the love that prompted the giving of them. In short, I spoiled them.

We moved from the rented house into one I had bought in Waverhill Road, and it was just as well we did because the house in Albert Road was bombed not long afterwards. We fell into a routine of having tea, closing the blackout curtains, then listening to Radio Luxemburg before heading for the shelter to sleep. The problem was that Mary could not settle to life in a city, having been used only to the countryside, and when she came home one day in tears because she was not being evacuated like the other children in her class I relented and agreed to let her go. I was very upset because I was only just beginning to know her and it hurt that she was so keen to leave me, but she was more affected by the Blitz which was then at its height in Birmingham and I decided reluctantly that it would be for the best if she went. During the time she was evacuated I took Jean and Kathleen to see her and I could see that she was happier living in the country than she had been in bombed-out Birmingham.

But troubles with the girls were not over. Jean began to rebel. One night I heard her crying in bed and when I went to see what was the matter with her she turned on me.

'I hate you! I hate you!' she screamed at me as I stood helpless beside her bed. In truth I had missed out on a lot of motherhood and I didn't really understand the children. All I could do was to ask limply, 'Why?'

'I don't like this town, nor the bombing. I want to go back to my aunty's in the country,' she wailed.

'But Jean,' I answered, 'I wanted you home here because I thought we could start a new life and be happy together.'

'No! I don't like it here and one day I'm going to run away!' She spurned my attempts to break down the wall of resentment that she'd built between us. I attempted to reason with her and I even promised that I would buy a cottage in the country when the war was over, but she just pulled the bedclothes over her head.

I was getting nowhere so I returned downstairs to make a cup of tea and think. I wondered if I'd done the right thing to bring them away from the country where they'd been happy with the two maiden sisters for eight years. Perhaps my ambitions for them were simply a reflection of my own selfish desire to have them with me. With the war at its height and Jean such an obviously self-willed child I was concerned lest she should take it into her head to run off one day while I was at the workshop. I didn't know what to do for the best so I decided to talk it over with Kathleen, who was now sixteen. She had a bright idea that I hadn't thought of: why not let Jean come to work with us where an eye could be kept on her? I put this to Jean and she jumped at the chance. I paid her a wage and she settled down there and really enjoyed it. Now she was happy I began to relax too.

One cold day in February 1941, I happened to be standing in the queue outside the greengrocer's in Icknield Street. It was my birthday, and I was trying to buy some extra fruit to give my daughters a treat when they came home from work. I felt someone tap me on the shoulder, and turning around I was very surprised to see my eldest sister, Mary. We threw our arms around each other.

'I'm so happy to see you, Kate,' she cried out tearfully.

'Me too, Mary,' I managed to say as we hugged and kissed each other.

'How long has it been since I saw you last, Kate?'

'The last time was over three years ago. You were making doughnuts.'

We both began to laugh. 'You don't know how glad I am to see you again, Kate,' she said.

'Where are you living now?' she asked.

'Still in Handsworth, Mary, you'll have to come and visit me some time. I'm sure the girls would love to meet you.'

'I'll try, but Kate, don't you think you should go and see Mum? I think she'd like to see you after all these years. How long is it since you saw each other?' she asked.

'It's been over ten years now. But I don't want to see her. I can't ever forgive her the way she treated me and my children all those years ago,' I replied bitterly.

'Don't be too hard on her, Kate. You'll find she's changed a lot lately. Wouldn't you like to come with me some time and talk to her?'

'No, Mary, I won't. If you can forgive her, I can't. Ever since I was a child, as far back as I can remember, she was cruel and unkind. Maybe, Mary, she never led you the life she led me.'

'Don't be too sure about that, Kate. It wasn't all honey for me. I'd like to tell you about my life as far back as I can remember, when I was only a small child, and when you've heard it, Kate, you may understand why our parents were like they were.'

Mary went on to tell me a lot about the family in the days before I was born: about a brief period of prosperity, when Dad had a good job and he was able to rent a nice house, and how they lost all that and had to return to the slums; and about the little brothers and sisters who had died, especially her beloved brother Sammy, who died of consumption. Through what she said I did come to have a better understanding of Mum and Dad, and why my family was as it was.

I still couldn't bring myself to go and see Mum, but when Mary told me how hard up she was I arranged to give my sister five shillings a week for her, on condition she didn't know where it came from.

Then, one afternoon while I was home, busy laying the table for my daughters' teas, I heard the front-door bell. When I opened the door, who should be standing on the step but my mother. I couldn't believe my eyes. She hadn't altered a bit.

'Well!' she exclaimed. 'Ain't yer gonna call me in then?'

'Yes, come in,' I replied.

As soon as she sat down I said, 'How did you find out where I lived?'

'Mary told me. An' thank yer fer the five bobs yer sent me,' she retorted sharply.

'Would you like a cup of tea, Mum? I'm just getting it ready for the girls when they come in.'

' 'Ow are me gran'children?' she asked.

'They're fine.'

'But why ain't yer bin ter see me? I suppose yer too stuck up now ter come ter see me.'

I didn't answer. I thought it was best not to reopen old sores.

'Will you stay and have a bit of tea?' I asked.

'No, not now. It's openin' time. But don't yow forget ter send me gran'children down ter see me, even if yow don't wanta come,' she added, slamming the door behind her.

When I told Mary about this visit she was glad some contact had been made. She also said she would talk to our mother and make arrangements for us to meet at her house. When the three of us met, later that week, I asked my mother if she would like to come and stay with me for a few days. She seemed all for it, and Mary too was pleased.

After that first visit Mum came to stay several times, but she always went back to her own house from Friday to Monday. I tried my best to make her feel wanted, but always towards the weekend I could see she was restless to be gone again. I realised she was eager to be back where she could be drinking with her neighbours. At the back of my mind I knew I'd made a mistake in asking her to stay. She was very bombastic towards me and my teenage daughters, and they didn't like her ordering them about. It was very hard to keep peace in the home while she was there. And she was a great worry during air raids. She would never go down the shelter when the sirens sounded, she just went upstairs with her bottles of beer and stayed in bed. ' 'itler ain't got me name on one fer me,' she'd say.

We were spending every night down the shelters. These were actually the large cellars under the shops along Soho Road which had been converted from storerooms. During the war anything of use was conscripted into the war effort and these makeshift shelters were second home to us. Some people were Air Raid Wardens but there was a need for more to volunteer their services; I dearly wanted to do so, but what with my business and the children I couldn't find time to do a regular duty. However, I did the next best thing. I called on all the women who were neighbours of ours, except those who had young babies, and organised them to knock on people's doors and help the old and infirm to the shelters at the first sound of the sirens. Several of us organised ourselves into a patrol and we brought back the news that everyone wanted to hear, namely that their houses were still standing. We were given whistles to blow if we were in trouble and out we went amidst the falling incendiaries to keep watch.

One of my companions was a young woman named Phoebe. She was Black Country born and bred, a rough-and-ready sort who swore like a trooper. She had a heart of gold though and we became friends. Many's the time we patrolled the streets together and it was during these walks that we exchanged stories: she had had as rough a time as I had. One night as we walked along the darkened street we paused to light fags and she said, 'I wundeer wheea my olt mon is ternight?'

'Why don't 'e come down the shelter, Phoebe?' I asked.

'Not 'im!' she replied with a laugh. ' 'E's too busy knockin' it off with some tart. 'E's an 'orny olt bleeda.'

I cannot say I was shocked exactly; such carryings-on were all too common in my experience but I was curious as to why such a spirited lass as this should put up with that kind of treatment.

'If 'e's like that why don't you leave 'im?' I asked.

'Well, Kate, 'e brings 'is money um, that's one good fault 'e's got. But I wouldn't care if 'e dain't drink sa much,' she replied.

'Does he drink a lot then?'

'Drink a lot?' she repeated with a laugh. ''E soaks 'is bloody bread in it!'

As I began to laugh she nudged me and said, 'Yo' ain't 'eard nothin' yet. One night I was in bed when 'e cum um drunk, it musta bin about two in the mornin' an' as soon as 'e got in bed – just in 'is shirt – 'e lit a fag an' fell asleep. It warnt lung afore I smelt summat bernin'. It was the flock bed smoulderin'. With thet I kickt 'im outta bed an' ran fer a bucket o' wata. Well, when I come back 'e was standin' in 'is short shirt with 'is cock in 'is 'and, pissin' over the bed.' At this we both burst into fits of laughter before I recovered enough to ask, 'What 'appened then?'

' 'E 'ad the bleedin' sauce ter arsk me ter get back in bed with 'im. "Cum on," 'e said, "it's wet but warm."'

'And did yer?'

'I 'ad ter, there wus nowhere else ter goo, but I did manage ter turn the mattress over an' sleep at the foot.' When I continued to laugh she said in mock seriousness, 'Yo'll larf yer bleedin' 'ead off one day when I got time ter tell yer some of 'is antics!'

Phoebe was a great tonic to me on those blacked-out nights and in later years we remained great friends and neighbours. She was dragged up, one of sixteen children, and her father a miner. In turn I told about my own childhood, little better than hers, about the theft of the pig when we went hop-picking, and about Granny. We amused each other for hours with tales about 'the old days'.

There was a spirit of camaraderie in the shelters; we had sing-songs to raise our hearts. There was a young woman named Rose Smith; her father owned the cut-glassware shop above, and each night she and her young man would play banjo and concertina while we sang our hearts out to drown out the sound of the bombing. They were a great bunch of characters; often they would slip across to the Freighted Horse for a nip and return tiddly, but who could blame them for trying to remain merry? None of us knew if we would see tomorrow.

While we were out on patrol one night, Phoebe and I called in to my house to fill flasks with cocoa to take back for the children.

Suddenly a series of incendiaries rained down nearby. We dashed out to see what damage had been done but in the confusion I lost sight of my friend. I blew my whistle and a second or two later she appeared, tearing down the street carrying two dustbin lids.

'Put this on yer bleedin' 'ead,' she cried out to me over the din, 'while I get a bucket o' sand.' Being unofficial we had no tin hats like the regular Wardens. We looked like a couple of coolies that night, rushing about with buckets of sand, trying to quench the flames. It was real panic stations and no mistake.

I always left my door open, day and night. You could trust everybody in those days. I would leave a big kettle of boiling water on the stove and several cups, milk, tea and sugar on the table for the Wardens to go in and make themselves a cup of tea. There was also a drop of the hard stuff should any of them prefer that to the weaker brew. On quiet nights when there were no raids I would invite the neighbours in for a sing-song. Somebody would play the piano and I would start the ball rolling with one of my jolly songs or a story and soon I had the nickname 'The Merry Widow'.

During April 1941 we had the worst raids. They lasted from dusk to dawn and although we women did our best, the Wardens almost pushed us down the shelters, saying that it was not fit for us to be out. Then the shelters were really crowded with people from all over. Children would be crying and women weeping and all were praying to the Lord to bring us safely through the night. We sang 'The White Cliffs of Dover' and 'Pack up Your Troubles' to keep up our spirits until the morning when the 'All Clear' sounded and we emerged, blinking, into the cold grey light of dawn to survey the night's destruction. Several of our neighbours had been killed in their cellars. This was the nearest the reality of death had come to us so far but I was soon to discover to my shock the personal horror of the Blitz. A Warden came running up, breathless, and asked for me by name. When I told him who I was he informed me that Camden Drive had been bombed and that my sister Mary and Mum had both been killed.

The cold, damp walk to the Drive sticks clear in my memory even now. I prayed that the Warden had been mistaken or that it had been another house that had been hit. Although we'd never seen eye-to-eye, blood is thicker than water after all. I stumbled over bricks and rubble where bombs and incendiaries had destroyed buildings in the streets leading to the Drive. Then I came to the top of the hill and could see at once that my worst fears had been realised. There were dozens of people standing about looking dazed; some were weeping quietly. Parties of rescue workers were digging into the rubble for the bodies of victims. I pushed through the crowd until I found myself prevented from going further by an Air Raid Precaution Warden and a fireman. It was only after I'd explained why I was there that they let me through. When I got to the heap of bricks that had been my childhood home I found that Jack, Frank, Charlie and Liza were already there. Frank said there was nothing we could do, which was true, and Jack went on to say that no one had had a chance because the bombs fell before the warning had sounded. A few survivors had been dug out but many had suffered the same fate as Mum and Mary.

I was angry that they'd died like rats without a chance. They were like plenty of others who struggled along for years through the Depression in the hope of a better tomorrow and this was it. They'd had a brief glimpse of prosperity when the war industries had taken on labour, and the same war had snuffed them out as if they had never been.

I shall never forget the day of the funerals. There wasn't a dry eye in the Lane, and as we entered the cemetery I saw men and women alike still digging to make room for those communal graves.

As I stood there and wept, with my brothers and sister Liza, I thought only of the harsh words my mother and I had often exchanged. And the saddest thing of all: it's too late to withdraw them – but they still live in my memory.

If only my mother had come to live with me when I pleaded with her to leave Camden Drive! She wouldn't have been lying there in that communal grave with my sister Mary and their many neighbours.

Phoebe, too, was at that same graveside weeping with many other people who had lost loved ones, for she had lost a young brother and her dad, whilst fire-watching.

After that terrible night of bombing in April 1941 there was a lull, and I saw less and less of Phoebe. The only times she came was when she wanted to borrow.

As everything was now on ration it was hard for everyone to manage. Queuing up for hours outside different shops, you would be lucky if you got three sausages. Other times, after waiting, when it was at last your turn, as soon as you got to the door, you'd see the butcher put a notice in the window: 'Sorry. Try again tomorrow.'

It was on a morning like this that I saw Phoebe at the end of the queue.

'He's sold out, Phoebe, let's try some of the other shops – we might be lucky for a few scrag ends,' I said.

' 'E ain't sold out! I know 'im, the crafty ol' bleeda! 'E keeps 'is best pieces under the counter, ter sell on the black market. Somebody oughta shop 'im!' Phoebe shouted for all to hear.

'Why don't *you* shop 'im?' cried one of our neighbours, who already had her three sausages.

'You shut yer gob, you ol' bag!' yelled Phoebe. 'I see you've got yower three sausages, an' it's not only sausages 'e lets yer 'ave. It's p'raps a feel of '*is* sausage, if I know 'im.'

Everybody began to laugh, and the neighbour, Mrs Reeves, suddenly screeched, 'I'll wrap these bleedin' sausages around yer bleedin' ear'ole, yer saucy bleeda!'

'Goo on then!' Phoebe shouted back. 'I could do with a feed.'

As Mrs Reeves was about to dash across the way, she stopped and seemed to have second thoughts, for she knew Phoebe was a tough customer. As Phoebe stood waiting for her next move, crowds of bystanders were listening, expecting to see a rough-and-tumble.

'Come on, Phoebe,' I said, pulling her coat sleeve. 'Let's go before the coppers come.'

'All right, all right!' she replied angrily. 'But I'll see that butcher closes down. Anyway,' she added, 'I know where I can get a piece of meat, without any trouble.'

'But where?' I asked.

'There's a bloke I know who's got a butcher's shop.'

'Where?' I asked again.

'It's in Aston, near the House that Jack Built.'

'But I can't go now, Phoebe, I've already spent three wasted hours trying to get three sausages I dain't get, and my daughters will be waiting for their tea.'

'Got summat nice, then?' she asked.

'Well, no, we got to make do with yesterday's left-over mutton, tough as an old horse,' I added.

'I 'ad some 'orseflesh last week off Alf, an' it was better than a piece of steak,' she replied.

'Who's Alf?' I asked.

''E's this friend of mine who's the butcher – now are yer cummin' or not?' she cried impatiently.

'All right, but I'll have to leave a note where I'm going.'

'Whatever yer do, Kate, don't tell 'em where we're gooin', I'm supposed to keep quiet about him.'

'All right, I'll just say "I won't be long".'

Off we hurried. But as soon as the butcher saw me, he asked, 'Who's 'er?'

'She's me friend,' replied Phoebe.

'Is she all right?' I heard him whisper.

'Yes, she won't say anything.'

'All right, me old cock, but where yer bin 'idin' yerself these days?'

'I'll explain later, but can yer manage to let me 'ave a bit of liver an' a few chops?'

'Anything for you, me darling,' I heard him whisper. I saw him pinch her bottom and put his hand up her skirt. She burst out laughing.

I blushed all over, and wished I hadn't come. I was beginning to feel embarrassed.

As soon as he had given her a parcel and we were outside, I said, 'Why did yer let him do that?'

'Do what?' she asked.

'Pinch yer bottom,' I replied. 'And let him put his hand up yer skirt, and what was yer whispering about?' I added.

'Oh, nothing that would be of any interest to you, Kate. Any'ow, there's no 'arm done, 'e's only me cousin.'

I'd heard that one before, and I wasn't as green as she thought I was. But I was grateful for the liver, and next day we sat down and enjoyed our fried liver and onions, and no questions asked. Later, Phoebe came to say Alf had had to go in the army. As everything was rationed, it was hard to manage.

I hadn't seen Phoebe for a couple of weeks, then one day I was surprised to hear her knock on my door.

'Can I cum in?' she called through the letter-box. As soon as she came into the front room, I saw that her eyes were all black and blue.

When I asked her how they got that way, she replied, 'It's a long story. I ain't got time ter tell yer now, but could yer let me 'ave a bit of sugar?'

As I didn't take sugar myself, I gave her what was left in the basin. She said she'd return it later, but she never did. Another day it was a bit of lard, or margarine, then I never saw her again until a week later. And as I opened the door to let her in, she flopped down on the chair. I noticed that her eyes were still discoloured. All at once she asked if I could let her have a bit of tea.

'I'm sorry, Phoebe,' I replied, 'but I only have my two ounces a week and you know how far that goes; you'll have to stew the leaves up.'

'I've got no leaves ter stew up now. Arthur teks 'is two ounce an' shares it with 'is mates at work, an' sometimes I can't even find me ration books, 'e even teks the coupons out and changes 'em for Player's Weights, *an'* some of me clothes coupons,' she added.

'But can't you hide the books?' I replied.

''E'd find 'em any'ow, an' if I don't give 'em to 'im, 'e starts beatin' me. But as soon as this bleedin' war is over, I'm goin' ter leave the drunken bastard, an' the kids.'

As soon as I saw the tears, I felt sorry for her.

'Here you are then, yer better have half of what I've got. But that'll have to be the last.' I gave her half what was in the caddy, and as she went to go out she said, 'Kate, could yer lend me ten shillin'?'

'No, I can't! What yer want ten shillings for anyway?'

'Well, I can get a bit of black market off that bloke in Graham Street.'

'I'm sorry, Phoebe, but I can't.' At that she left, but I remember I was glad of a bit of black market when my daughter Kathleen got married later.

Mrs Hitchman, who had a fruit and vegetable shop in Hockley Street, supplied everybody, as long as she could see their money. I knew it was wrong, but it was a temptation – you could get a fine or imprisonment or both. Many times I was worried in case I was found out. But many of us didn't care, for we never knew if we would be alive from one day to the next.

Yet often, if I got an orange or a couple of bananas, I'd give them to a neighbour for her hungry baby. And they never asked how I came by them. No doubt they guessed. Once I gave Phoebe some tomatoes. When she asked me where they came from I replied, 'It's very hush-hush.' She was the last person to tell, otherwise I could see her going to that shop and making a nuisance of herself.

The next time she called she walked in and as she sat down on the settee, she asked at once, 'Kate, I ain't cum ter borra any of yer rations, but I was wonderin' if yer could lend me yer fox-fur stole? Yer see, I've bin invited to this birthday party.'

'What party's this?' I asked.

'It's a young woman I used ter work with – lives in Nursery Road,' she added.

I'd always had a soft spot for her, for she hadn't many clothes and often I gave her what I could spare and liked to see her wearing them. I hadn't worn my furs for a couple of years. I'd never liked them anyway, they were still in the wardrobe.

As soon as I brought them down and handed them to her, she cried at once, 'They're lovely, Kate. Wanta sell 'em to me?'

'No, Phoebe, but see as you bring them back – remember, I'm only lending them to yer.'

I would willingly have given them to her, but I could see now I was only encouraging her to come borrowing.

Three weeks later I was still waiting. I decided this was the last time I would believe or trust her and I made up my mind to call at her home and fetch them back.

I had never been inside her house, but as I stood outside I noticed that the place didn't look very wholesome. As I stepped over rubbish, broken bricks and slates, and broken windows, some still holding together with sticking plaster from previous bombings, I wondered if anyone still lived there. As soon as I knocked on the door it suddenly flew open wide, and there stood Phoebe's husband, a tall, thin, sallow-faced man. I noticed several days' growth of grey stubbly hair sprouting from his chin and upper lip, where hung a half-broken fag. The sleeves of his grubby shirt were rolled up to his elbows, his arms were covered in blue and red tattoos. His trousers were greasy and tied round his waist with his braces. And as he stood there in his stockinged feet, staring at me, he shouted, 'Wot do you want? If yer cum ter see Pheeb, she ain't 'ere!'

'But can I come in and wait?' I asked.

'Yo'll 'ave a lung bleedin' wait then! She's left me, an' me kids!' he bawled.

Then I saw two grubby little girls, about three or four years old, staring at me as they came and stood beside him.

'Lizzie!' he bawled. 'Cum and fetch these kids in!' But they seemed scared and ran into the room.

'I'm sorry,' I replied. 'I'll call again.'

I was about to go, when he yelled, 'Wot yer cum for any'ow?'

'Could you tell me if she's left my furs here? If so I would like them back,' I replied.

'No, 'er ain't!' he snapped. ' 'Er's p'raps took 'em with 'er, ration books an' all!' he added. ''An' if yer *do* see 'er, yer can tell 'er from me, I ain't ever 'avin' 'er back!' As I turned to go he slammed the door in my face. I didn't bother about the furs now; all I kept thinking about was those two unwashed, neglected children.

A few days later I was surprised by a loud knock on the door. When I opened it, a young woman stood on the step. I noticed she was overdressed, with well-rouged cheeks and painted lips; also her eyebrows had been shaved and pencilled over. I could see she had attempted to dye her hair blonde; the black roots were showing. She wore long dangling red earrings, a long green dress and a short rabbit-skin fur coat (we used to call them bum-freezers).

As soon as I asked who she was, she replied, 'I'm Pheeb's sister, an' I've brought yer furs back.'

I couldn't believe she was Phoebe's sister, she hadn't even mentioned she had one. She wasn't anything like her. As she handed the parcel to me she cried as she looked across the yard, 'I see yer got plenty of nosy neighbours.' I saw Mrs Carter turn her nose up at her as she passed.

'But why couldn't she come herself?' I asked.

'That's 'er bloody business!' she snapped. 'Any'ow,' she added, 'I'm only 'ere ter look after Arthur's kids!'

I took the furs and as I said 'thank you' I closed the door. As soon as she'd gone I peeped through the curtain to see several women across the street whispering together.

She didn't look the type of person to care for children. Yet, I thought, if she *was* telling the truth, then it was none of my business. Later that same evening I was to find out from neighbours. She was the barmaid from the Globe Tavern, and was also Arthur's fancy woman.

A couple of days later, when I opened up the parcel, I found that one of the tails was missing. I took the furs upstairs, pushed them into the wardrobe, and forgot about them – until I decided to have a clear-out. I saw that moths had decided to have a loan of them, and threw them away.

Chapter 26

Life in Wartime

Each night, when the All Clear sounded and we came up from the shelters, none of us knew what changes we would find to our homes. Many times I wondered, too, if my small workshop would be intact after the raids.

That terrible morning after Camden Drive was bombed, I arrived at my workshop to see several firemen still putting out fires at the buildings across the street. I was scared to think what I would find as I climbed up those two steep flights of stairs, but when I entered the room, everything seemed to be in order. The girls were all busy doing their work, and listening to Tommy Handley on the wireless. Happening to go to the other end of the shop, I looked up and saw a gaping hole in the roof. At first I thought it must have been made by a piece of shrapnel, but then I saw another hole in a bench. When I peered down I saw an incendiary bomb resting on a ledge beneath the bench. I screamed out, 'Leave everything, girls! And hurry down into the street!' We were all down those stairs like a flash. Then before I could stop her, one of the girls suddenly rushed back up the stairs again. She cried out, 'I'm goin' back fer me tin 'at an' gas mask.' A few seconds later she was back with them in her hand. But she was lucky, and so were we all, that the bomb turned out to be a dud. Often, later, we teased Lily about her attachment to her tin hat and her gas mask. But she never even smiled.

For most of the war my enamelling business was run by me and my daughters and ten young women. At one time my workers had to clock in before starting work. But when the war started in earnest I said they could forget it, I didn't mind how late they arrived for work; I quite understood their worries and sleepless nights. Some of the workers brought sandwiches to eat at dinner times. But during the cold weather some of us would pool our rations. One would supply a few carrots, another a couple of onions, someone else some carrots or split peas, and whenever I could I brought a piece of meat. While the girls were working, and listening to *Music While You Work* on the wireless, I'd prepare our dinner, put everything in the pot on the gas ring and let it stew away until it was time for us all to have a small basin full, with a piece of dry bread to mop it up.

When we had an occasional rest from the bombing, usually all we wanted to do was catch up on our sleep. But one night during a lull, for a special treat, I took my daughters and two of their friends to see a show in town. It was late when the show was over, and we'd missed the last tram home, so we had to walk.

It was a lovely moonlit night, but the roads were icy. By the time we got as far as Hockley Brook we all wanted to pee. Looking around we couldn't see anywhere we could go. We were afraid to stoop down in the gutter, in case someone came along and saw us. But when we'd walked a little further, we noticed a low wall jutting out on the pavement. Dropping our knickers down over our ankles, we sat down on it. As we were giggling and peeing, from out of nowhere a policeman came towards us. We were all scared to move now we could only sit there with our bare bums freezing and the steady stream trickling down the pavement for anyone to see. He said, 'You young ladies should be indoors at this time in the morning.' When I tried to explain we'd missed the last tram, he replied, 'Come along, then, I'll see you home.'

'Thank you, officer,' I answered quickly. 'I'm their mother, and we've only a few yards to go.'

I noticed he was smiling as he replied, 'Very well, mother, you'd better hurry along before you all freeze sitting there.'

As soon as we saw him stroll away, we quickly pulled up our wet knickers, but as we slid down from the wall we saw he was waiting and looking at us from the corner of the street. You couldn't see us for dust as we fled up the Soho Hill. As soon as we got indoors we kicked off our wet knickers and made a mad dash towards the fire to thaw out our bums.

We laughed, later. But we suspected that policeman was probably laughing too!

One cold November day my brother Jack came to see me, and said if I'd lend him my old Austin Seven he'd give me some petrol coupons. He wanted to go to Henley-in-Arden market where there were some live chickens for sale. I said he could take the car providing that I could go with him.

The old jalopy spluttered and rattled all the way, but eventually it got us there. Jack bought four hens and a cockerel, and on his recommendation I bought a turkey to fatten up for our Christmas dinner. I didn't know where I was going to keep the turkey. But when Jack suggested he'd take it home with him and bring it back on Christmas Eve, ready for the oven, I didn't trust him. I hadn't forgotten the pig he'd stolen when we went hop-picking when we were young, and I didn't think he had changed much meantime. So I refused. I decided that the only place I could keep the turkey was in the coal-house outside. I moved what little coal I had, and set the turkey on some straw. My daughters named her Gertie, and grew very fond of her.

One bitterly cold night Jack borrowed the old car again and brought me back a sack of coke, which I mixed with the coal I had to make a roaring fire in the scullery grate. When I went to feed Gertie, I suddenly noticed that the brick wall between the back of the fireplace and the coal-house was red-hot. Quickly I dragged poor Gertie into the kitchen, where she had to sleep that night, for otherwise she might have been cooked alive.

We were unable to risk lighting a fire in the scullery after that. A few nights later it was again freezing hard. So I put extra coal and coke on the living-room fire and, as my daughters sat around warming themselves, I held a piece of newspaper up to the fire to help it along. Suddenly it was sucked alight by the draught and blown up the chimney. In no time at all, the chimney was on fire. Soot covered us like black snowflakes. We panicked and rushed outside. But the firemen arrived even before we had time to call the fire brigade; they had seen the flames and sparks shooting out of the chimney-pot. The fire was so fierce, they had to go into the back bedroom and knock a hole in the chimneybreast before they could put it out.

What a mess, and what a crowd of people we had outside looking in! And then, no sooner had the firemen done their job and left, when in walked a policeman. I recognised him at once. He was the same tall, handsome young man who had seen us sitting on the wall, with our bums freezing. I felt so embarrassed. My only hope was that although I knew who *he* was, he might have forgotten us.

As he took out his note pad and pencil, he asked, 'When did you last have your chimney swept?'

'I never used this fireplace till tonight,' I replied.

While he was writing down all my answers to his questions, I saw him look up and smile at my daughters. Suddenly he asked, 'Do I remember seeing you from somewhere?'

'No, I don't think so,' I answered quickly.

But he looked across at my daughters again, and he smiled more broadly as he said, 'Ah, I remember now. You were all sitting on the wall at the bottom of Soho Hill, late one night.'

The girls almost knocked one another over as they dashed back into the kitchen. And there they stayed until he had gone. I felt more embarrassed than ever now, and I was eager for him to go, before he asked any more questions. I was relieved when I saw him tear up his notes as he went down the path, thinking all the time we'd been talking about how he knew what we had been doing that night as we sat on that wall, with our bare bums freezing as we giggled and piddled.

It was a few days before Christmas and snowflakes were falling fast when my brother came to see me again. As soon as he got indoors and took his wet overcoat off I said, 'Jack, I'm worried about Gertie.'

'Why, what's the matter with 'er?' he asked.

'I don't know, she hasn't eaten her food these last few days, and she sits in her corner all broody and looking so pitiful, as though she knows what's going to happen to her, and the children are upset too about having her killed.'

'Well, she's old, Kate, an' if I don't do it soon she'll probably die on yer later, then she'll be no good to eat, an' she'll 'ave ter be buried somewhere.'

'Oh, well, you'd better start to do it now, before the children come home,' I said.

'I can't do it now, Kate,' he replied.

'Well, what have you come for?' I asked angrily.

'I was goin' ter ask yer ter lend me the car again.'

'Sorry, Jack,' I said, 'I've taken it to be overhauled and it won't be ready till after Christmas. If then.'

'Pity,' he replied sullenly. 'I could 'ave done yer a good turn.'

'What! Like the turkey you said was a good buy?' I said angrily.

'Sorry about that, Kate. Anyway, I'll come Christmas Eve morning and fix 'er fer yer,' he said, as he walked out of the house.

The next few days Kathleen, Jean and Mary (who was home for Christmas) tried their utmost to make Gertie eat. They even talked to her like you would to a child. But she just sat in her corner of the coal-house, looking broody and all forlorn, as though she knew what was going to happen to her.

It was still snowing when my brother came on Christmas Eve. While he sat in front of the fire smoking his pipe, the girls came in. As soon as they saw their uncle, Jean ran up to him and asked, 'Have you really come to kill Gertie, Uncle Jack?'

'Yes, luv,' he said. 'She's old and she'll die if I don't do it now. Anyway,' he added, 'it'll be a nice change fer you all ter sit down ter turkey instead of a couple of sausages.'

At once there was a crying match. But my brother explained to them why it had to be done, and I thought they understood. Still, I didn't want them to be anywhere near the house to witness the killing, so I gave them some money and sent them off to the pictures. While I worked in the kitchen, busily washing up and preparing the vegetables for the next day, Jack went into the coalhouse and did what had to be done. Then I plucked the bird and began to clean it. When I put my hand inside it I pulled out one large egg in its shell, another almost ready, three yolks, and dozens of small eggs the size of peas. I put them into a basin to be made into custard, for pouring over the Christmas pudding. When I'd finished cleaning the turkey, I hid it in the larder where the girls wouldn't see it, until the next day when it would be cooked.

I was determined to make this a happy Christmas, for in those days no one knew whether we would ever see another one. On Christmas morning, while the girls were still asleep, I slipped up to the bakehouse in Soho Road with the turkey and paid a shilling for it to be cooked. When I got back I set the table with all my best china and glasses, and added Christmas crackers and four paper hats I'd bought at a garden fête. Also a few goodies I'd collected over the past weeks, and a bottle of port wine my brother Jack had given me for the loan of my car. I took up the girls' breakfast and their small presents, and I said they should stay upstairs until I called them down. When I had fetched the turkey from the bake-house, I drained off the fat into a basin, put the bird in a dish, and put it in the oven to warm. Then, as soon as all the vegetables were ready, I called the girls.

I was pleased as they sat at the table drinking their port, laughing and smiling. But as soon as I put Gertie on the table and began to carve, there was another crying match. 'We don't want any!' they cried out, and sprang up from the table.

I did my utmost to persuade them to eat, but it was a waste of time even to try. I did manage to get them back to the table again to eat their Christmas pudding, which I could see they relished. But if they'd known the custard had been made with Gertie's eggs, they wouldn't have eaten that either.

After they went out to see their friends, I began to weep. What a waste of time and energy and money, I said to myself. I was too upset now to eat any of Gertie, either. So I wrapped it up and gave it to one of my neighbours who I knew had a lot of mouths to feed. When they asked why, and I tried to explain, the old grandad said, 'The ungrateful little buggers, kids are terday. They'll be glad to eat 'orse-flesh before they're much older.' (Little did we know, we already had.)

When I got back home I sat down again and wept, and after clearing the things away I thought to myself, if only my brother Jack or Charlie had come that Christmas morning they might have persuaded the girls to eat some of it. But I felt alone now, and it was Christmas Day. Suddenly I couldn't think of anything else, only to put the crackers and the paper hats on the fire and take the rest of the port and a glass of whisky up to bed. It was night-time when I awoke, with a fearful headache. I hurried downstairs and just as I was making myself a cup of tea, my daughters came in. When they said they were hungry, I snapped, 'You can be bloody hungry! You can have some bread an' drippin', but you can get it yerselves!' Little did they know it was Gertie's dripping they were spreading on their bread.

Later in the spring Jack brought a dozen little chicks for the girls. They were so delighted they kept them in a basket while it was cold. But one morning when we came downstairs they all lay dead on the hearth. After that I said, 'No more livestock in this house,' and if they wanted a chicken or a turkey it would have to be a dead one from the butcher's.

But I understood really how my daughters must have felt that Christmas Day. I'd have felt the same when I was a girl – though I wouldn't have dared refuse anything I was offered.

I managed to stick to the 'no livestock' rule for a while, but it wasn't easy. Often my daughter Jean would bring home some stray cat or dog, then I'd have to sort out who owned it.

One night the girls were in bed and I was sitting reading the newspaper, when all at once I heard a sound like a baby crying in one of the bedrooms. I opened Jean's bedroom door, and knew it was coming from there. When I turned the bedclothes back, I saw a black kitten lying in Jean's arms, mewing for all it was worth. As I picked it up and put it on the floor, Jean woke up.

'What have I told you!' I cried out at once. 'No more livestock!'

'He followed me, Mum,' she protested as she sat up in bed.

'I've heard that before! Like the other cats and dogs you tell me follow you!'

'But it's the truth, Mum, I tried to shoo him away but he wouldn't go. I thought if I gave him a drop of milk he'd go away.'

I knew then we'd never be rid of it.

'Now, I want the truth,' I said. 'How long have you had it in bed with you?'

'Only a few nights, Mum. Please let me keep him,' she pleaded, as the kitten jumped up on the bed. As soon as I saw her tears flow, I began to weaken.

'I'll think about it. But you can't have it sleeping with you in bed, it's unhealthy. It can sleep in the kitchen tonight, then I'll decide what you can do with it in the morning. Now, lie down and go to sleep.'

I picked up the black kitten and took him downstairs, where I gave him a drink of milk. Then I put him outside to do his business. At the back of my mind I hoped he'd go back to where he came from but after a while he began to meow louder than ever outside the kitchen door, so I let him in. I found a discarded old woollen jersey, and as soon as I picked him up and laid him down on it he snuggled up and went to sleep.

Next morning I told my daughter she had to try to find out who owned the kitten, but if no one came forward she could keep him. I warned her it was her responsibility to teach him to be clean. The next day I bought him a basket to sleep in. And Jean gave him the name of Sooty.

As Sooty grew older, he began to stay out late. By then I was as silly as Jean, and I wouldn't go to bed until he was indoors. One night he didn't come home until one o'clock. I scolded him for keeping me up late. But he just purred and rubbed against me.

The following night he stayed out again. I waited for a while and called him, but no Sooty came. 'Very well,' I said aloud, 'you can stop out,' and I locked the door.

It was early in the morning when I heard him meowing outside the back door. I couldn't sleep now, knowing he'd be almost frozen out there, so I went down and let him in. But I was still angry with him for disturbing my sleep.

This went on for a couple of nights more. Then one night there was a caterwauling session of toms and she-cats under our windows, and the neighbours'.

I couldn't sleep, and nor could the neighbours. I heard windows being pushed open and all kinds of oddments being thrown at the cats, and I heard somebody say, 'Bleedin' cats, I'll drown the bleedin' lot on yer if yer don't get away from under my winda.'

After a while it went quieter, but I still couldn't sleep until I knew Sooty was back. As soon as I heard his cry I went down and opened the door. There he sat, looking so pitiful, and soaking wet.

'It's yer own fault,' I said as I dried him before I went back to bed.

I knew it was Sooty's nature to go out courting, but I had to do something about him staying out late. So I decided to leave my kitchen window a little way open for him to come and go as he pleased, so that I could get some sleep. This worked until one late night I heard a great din coming from the kitchen, and I went down to find Sooty and his girl-friend, a ginger she-cat from down the road, making love. I got the broom and swiped at them, and they both fled through the window.

'That's the last time I leave my window open, or let you in again when you stop out,' I said to myself. There was only one answer to the night prowling, I would have to have him castrated.

The following day I put him in his basket, and while my daughters were out I took him to the People's Dispensary for Sick Animals in Soho Hill. As I sat waiting my turn with other people with their pets, I began to weep. How could I do this to Sooty? I was just about to take him home again when the vet called me in.

When, a little while later, the vet laid the unconscious Sooty in my arms, he said to keep him warm and watch for him to wake up, and then to give him a drink. I put Sooty gently in his basket and carried him home. When I laid him down on the rug in front of the fire I began to weep again. He lay there so still, I thought he was going to die. I thought, what was I going to say to my daughters? I couldn't tell them the truth; things like this were never discussed in front of children in those days. I sat and waited, hoping he would come round before the girls saw him. And a few minutes later, I was pleased to see him come to. Soon he was on his feet and walking, and he seemed to be his usual self as he looked up at me and drank his milk. But as the weeks went by, and I noticed he wasn't so frisky as he used to be, I began to be sorry again that I'd taken his little pleasures from him.

Then one day Jean walked in with a little all-black kitten in her arms. I was furious, and shouted, 'You're not bringing any more cats in here!'

'I'm not, Mum,' she protested. 'I've only brought him to show you.'

'Well! You can take it right back again to where you've had it from.'

'Mrs Wilks says her cat's got four, and three of them are just like our Sooty.'

'I don't care if they're like King Kong!' I replied angrily. 'Take it back at once. And if you're not satisfied with Sooty, I'll give him away.'

'I still love Sooty, Mum. But he isn't playful any more.'

'Well, he's growing older now, you can't expect him to play like he did when he was a kitten. Anyway, love, I can't put up with any more cats. I must have my rest. What with the air raids and getting up half the night, and one thing or another, I don't get much sleep. You can have anything else, but definitely no cats.'

Tears began to fall, but she didn't miss her chance. 'Can I have a dog, then, Mum?'

'I'll have to think about it. Now, do as yer told and take the kitten back.'

A few weeks after, I heard that Mrs Wilks had given the kittens away, but kept her ginger female. Later, after her house was bombed, she went to live with her sister in another district, but she didn't take her cat with her and left it to roam the streets. Day and night that cat would whine outside our back door. I couldn't see her hungry, so I used to feed her out in the yard. Then one night it poured in torrents, and Jean began to plead for me to take her in.

When I dried her with a piece of cloth, she nestled up to me. After that I couldn't let her go out in the rain again. So I gave her a home, and we called her Sandy.

Sandy too had to go to the vet's, for I made sure I wouldn't have any more kittens in the house. And from then on Sooty and Sandy were content to sleep side by side, without any sign of lovemaking. They grew old together, and when they died I buried them beneath my kitchen window. Eventually Jean got her dog, but that was years later.

During May 1945 the war was nearing its end and there was less bombing, if any at all, over Birmingham. During these times we could go to our beds and try to catch up on the many hours of sleep we had lost during the heavy raids. We were still living in Waverhill Road, but I had every intention of leaving for a better house in a much quieter district as soon as the war was over.

I remember that my kitchen was very small and the door opened inwards, so it always banged against the wall. I thought if I could get someone to rehang it so that it opened outwards, that would give me a bit more room in the kitchen.

A friend of mine said he could do the job for me, but that I would have to have another door as the old one was warped. He also said he could get an old door from a bomb site. After he had planed it down it fitted, and after a lot of hard work and strong language he managed to make it swing outwards, and I had a bit more room. We didn't realise it was now going to be a tight squeeze to get outside between the door and the wall in the entry, yet my two daughters and I managed somehow.

A few weeks later, I was surprised to see my brother-in-law, Bill. He worked for a butcher in Handsworth, fetching and carrying meat from the markets in his van.

'Hello, stranger!' I cried as I opened the front door and saw his meat van outside. 'Come in.'

'I can't stop long, Kate,' he replied. 'But I happened to be passing, so I thought I'd call and see if yer wanted a bit of lamb.'

'Thank yer, Bill, but I ain't got any coupons to spare,' I said.

'That's OK. I've got some to spare if yer want the meat.'

'All right, bring it in then,' I answered eagerly.

'I ain't got any with me now, but I'll drop yer some in in a day or two. So long, I've gotta 'urry now,' he added as he went out.

A couple of weeks went by. No Bill came with any lamb, so I forgot about it. I was glad really, I knew it was on the black market, and I made up my mind that if he did come now I wouldn't accept it, for I was scared I would be found out.

A few nights later I was awakened by noises which sounded like bombs being dropped, a long way off. Half asleep, I waited for the sirens to wail. I heard a loud thud, then another, and another, which seemed to sound much nearer. I sat up in bed now, wide awake, but there was no more noise, so I lay down and tried to go back to sleep. But I was too restless. It was almost dawn when I decided to go downstairs. As I slipped my dressing-gown on and lit the gas stove to make myself a cup of tea, I looked up at the clock. It was five thirty.

It was very stuffy and warm as I stood waiting for the kettle to boil. I thought I'd unbolt the back door and let in some air, but when I tried to push it outwards it wouldn't budge. I knew then that something was blocking it. Suddenly I became scared in case it was a delayed bomb, but I had to get outside to see. I went out through the front door and round the back towards the passage-way, hoping and praying that someone would be walking along the street, and would come with me to see who or what was lying there. But there wasn't a soul in sight; everywhere seemed deadly quiet.

Warily I crept up to the back of my house, and when I got almost to the kitchen door I couldn't believe my eyes. Wedged between my kitchen door and the wall were three whole lambs. I had to step on them and push them against the wall before I could get the door open.

I was relieved to see that none of my neighbours was about, but had to hide those lambs somewhere. I managed to drag each one into the kitchen, and after closing the door I sat down exhausted. I had to get them into the cellar somehow and hide them from my daughters. After drinking my welcome cup of tea, I found an odd piece of rope. I tied it round each lamb's neck and dragged them towards the cellar steps. As soon as I reached the edge of the steps I unfastened the rope and pushed them down.

I had expected that Bill would show himself with a few chops, or a half a leg, not *three whole bloody lambs*! Whatever was I going to do with them? I was more scared now than if they had been a dud bomb.

As luck would have it, half an hour later my brother Jack called. When I told him about my brother-in-law and what he'd left me with, he began to laugh.

'It's no bloody laughin' matter, Jack!' I yelled. 'What am I goin' ter do with 'em?'

'Well,' he replied, still grinning all over his face, 'I'll tek 'em away, I'll soon get rid of 'em.'

I didn't care what he did with them as long as they were out of the house. So it was arranged that the three lambs would stay where I had pushed them until after dark, when Jack would take them away in his car. When he came later that night, he said he had room for only two and he'd call later to pick up the other one.

Soon after he left, my brother-in-law called. As soon as I opened the door I yelled, 'Yer better come in and explain yerself!'

He looked around and asked, 'Wot yer done with 'em?'

'What yer think I've done with em!' I replied angrily. 'I had to throw 'em down the cellar.'

Smiling, he said, 'Well, I'll tek the two and leave yer the other one.'

'I don't want it! And if yer think yer can use me or my house for any of yer dirty deals, you've got another think coming!'

His smile changed when I told him my brother had taken two of them away and was coming back later for the other one.

''E won't, yer know! Not if I can 'elp it. I'll tek the one 'e's left fer now, an' I'll see *'im* later!'

He was fuming as he made his way down into the cellar.

I shouted, 'This is the first an' last time yer try ter use me for your black-market deals!'

Later my brother came, expecting to take the other lamb away, but when I told him what had happened he replied, ''E won't bother me, Kate, 'e knows we're in the same boat. But,' he added, 'if yer want a few chops, I'll . . .'

'Yer know what yer can do with yer chops! You and 'im! Keep away from my house. I never wanta see you nor 'im again!' I bawled as I slammed the door behind him.

My three teenage daughters were now growing up fast in mind and body. I knew I couldn't keep them under my wing all the time, but whenever possible I always took them out and about with me. I used to worry when they went out by themselves. There were lots of American troops in the district, and many young girls (and married women too) found them hard to resist, with their gifts of chocolates, cigarettes, silk stockings, and other scarce luxuries. Many a young girl was left holding a baby. I remember one of my neighbour's daughters had fallen this way, and I often think of how she said once about her daughters, 'They make your arms ache when they're young, but they make your heart ache when they're older.'

One day I received a letter from my son, John, who was still serving in the Navy, to tell me that while he was on leave in Scotland he'd met a young Scots girl whom he wished to marry. I was very upset. I'd had other plans for John. I'd been hoping that as soon as the war ended he'd take over my business, so that I could care for the girls and the home. I wrote at once asking him to wait until the war was over, as they were both too young to think about marriage. But John wrote back to say that the banns had already been read. I went up to Scotland with my daughters, still intending to talk him out of marrying if I could, but when I got there I found I couldn't say anything disapproving. They looked so happy, and so much in love. After the wedding John had to go back to his ship. His wife stayed with her parents until he came out of the Navy when the war ended.

During 1944 my daughter Kathleen was married. I planned to give her a wonderful wedding, a better day than I had had. My one trouble was the food rationing. But again my brother Jack came to the rescue.

'If yer can lend me the old car again, I'll see what I can do,' he said.

So I lent him the old jalopy. He said he'd be back in an hour. I waited all that morning, getting more and more worried. All kinds of thoughts entered my head. Then about two o'clock in the afternoon he came in with another chap, both drunk, and laden with parcels of food.

Although I was pleased to see him, I was also angry. 'Where've you bin till now, our Jack?' I cried out. 'I've been worried stiff.'

As they dropped the parcels on the table, he managed to say, 'It's all right, sis, but I got some bad news ter tell yer.'

'Well, sit down and tell me, before you fall down!' I replied crossly.

'When I drove back 'ere, the bottom of the old jalopy fell out and the grub fell inter the road. This chap 'ere,' he said, waving his hand towards him, ' 'elped me ter pick it up and bring it 'ere.'

'Where's the car now?' I asked.

'We dragged it on some waste ground an' 'ad ter leave it.'

'Oh, well,' I replied, 'I knew it would happen one day. As long as you're all right, that's all that matters.' I thanked the young chap for his help and asked him if he'd like a cup of tea, but he said he was in a hurry to get back to work. When he called again a few days later, I invited him to the wedding, which was to be in two months' time.

My next worry was we couldn't hire a hall for the wedding reception: every possible room seemed to be booked for ARP (Air Raid Precautions) meetings. But a friend of mine who was a builder talked me into having the wall between the front room and the dining room knocked down and made into one large room. I later called it the lounge. And in the end everyone seemed to have a jolly time at the wedding. Piano-playing and singing went on far into the night, well after my daughter and her husband had left to start their honeymoon.

Later Kathleen and her husband, Jim, went to live in Scotland. After a while she wrote to say she wasn't very happy where she was living. I replied that I was thinking of leaving the old house and buying another, and if she was still not settled they could come and take over the house in Waverhill Road. And when I bought my house in Landgate Road, and Jean and Mary and I moved there, Kathleen and Jim moved into Waverhill Road. A little later Kathleen came to work with me again. Then when Jim lost his job he came to work along with us. He didn't know the trade, but he was happy to do all kinds of jobs, and worked very hard.

It was of course a great pleasure to me that Kathleen and Jim had settled down so near. But many were the times I'd lie awake at nights thinking about my son John, on the high seas and perhaps in battle, and pray to the Good Lord above to keep him safe. There were now only my two younger daughters, Jean and Mary, at home with me. I dreaded the thought that some day soon they too would fall in love and leave me to be married. I knew I'd miss their love, excitement and laughter when I was left in this house alone.

I had had many offers of marriage over the years, but I hadn't been interested. All I had wanted was the love and affection and comfort of my children around me. But how foolish I was to think I could keep them by my side for ever.

My youngest daughter, Mary, was restless, always trying one job after another. One of her jobs was serving in the fruit and vegetable shop owned by a Mr and Mrs Hitchman in Hockley Street. Mrs Hitchman was kind to anyone really in need, but she was a very domineering woman, and very large, and I often felt sorry for her husband, Fred. He was so different, a weedy, hen-pecked little man.

Mrs Hitchman was sweet on my brother Jack, who was very plausible. And many times Jack would take her in her car to markets. She'd get all dolled up when she was going to see him. I used to hear customers whisper, 'Silly old cow! 'Er's old enough ter be 'is mother.' One day I told my brother how people were talking. But he said it was none of my business, or other people's. 'Let 'em talk,' he said. 'That's the only time I can get any black market off 'er, when I give 'er what she wants.' I was furious at his attitude, and we quarrelled. I didn't see him again for a few weeks after that, but I knew really that, as he said, it was none of my business. So when I did see him again I thought it best not to mention it. Then one day Jack's wife heard about their affair, and threatened to leave him. He never went near the shop again, nor was he ever seen taking Mrs Hitchman about. Whether he met her secretly I couldn't say. But he always had plenty of black-market food.

During that period my daughter Mary came home one afternoon and said she'd seen a notice in Mrs Hitchman's shop window for a young girl to serve behind the counter. I knew if I refused to let her go she would go anyway, for she was very self-willed. So, to save any arguments, I let her have her fad out. I went to see Mrs Hitchman and we agreed on the wage, and that Mary would have her meals free. As food was still on rations, it was a help for me to save the coupons. But she had only been there about three weeks, when she came home one day crying.

When I asked her what was wrong, she said she wasn't having enough to eat, and that she'd been helping herself to bananas and couldn't find anywhere to hide the skins. When I asked why she hadn't told me before, she said, 'I was too scared, Mum.'

'Well, what *did* you do with the skins?' I asked.

'There's a big vase on the top shelf and when I thought she wasn't looking I threw them inside the vase. But it's getting full, and I was scared, and when she asked me to go up the ladder and reach down the vase, I panicked.'

'What happened then?' I asked, as the tears flowed.

'I ran up the stairs. As soon as I heard her talking to a customer I crept quietly down, but halfway down I met Mr Hitchman coming up and . . . er . . .'

'Go on, and what?'

'He pinned me against the wall. I knew what he was after. So I punched his face and pushed him down the stairs, and ran away.'

'But why didn't you tell me about this before? And why didn't you tell her you had the bananas because you were hungry?'

'I was afraid, Mum, because she'd know I'd stole them.'

'Oh. You knew you were stealing, then?' I snapped.

'Yes, Mum,' she whimpered.

'Very well, dry your eyes, and any time you get into any scrapes in future, come and tell me at once.'

'Yes, Mum,' she replied, as she dried her eyes.

Next day I called to give Fred Hitchman a piece of my mind. But he was nowhere to be found, and after that he always avoided me when he saw me. In the end I thought it would be better to leave things unsaid, to save any trouble which it would cause between him and his wife.

After Mary left the fruit shop she went to train as a nurse at the

TB Hospital in Selly Oak. She got along fine there, until she became tired of working all hours and left to try her hand at a hairdressing salon. Soon after Mary left the hospital the matron came to see me. She spoke very highly of Mary, and asked if I could persuade her to come back again. I said I'd do my best. But no matter how I tried for her to see reason, it was hopeless.

When she got dissatisfied with hairdressing, she tried being a conductress on the buses. Later she joined the forces, and she met and married her husband in Singapore. After the war, she and her husband made their home in Scotland. Later I had a letter from her to say they were going to live in America. Now Mary has four sons: two I have never seen. And I have only seen my daughter twice in twenty-seven years. For years I never heard from her, although I knew she received my letters. And I felt very hurt. But recently she has telephoned me a couple of times, which has been a great joy.

Over the years I have often asked myself if Mary still hasn't forgiven me for parting with her, when I left her at Dr Barnardo's.

Chapter 27

My Second Marriage

My daughter Jean stayed at home longest, but I knew I would lose her too some day. And when she began courting I was often very lonely. I really felt I needed a companion and friend, someone to talk to of an evening. One night, as I was reading the *Evening Mail*, a knock came. When I answered I was surprised to see standing on the doorstep my brother Jack. I hadn't seen him for several months.

'Hello, stranger!' I said, sarcastically.

'Anythin' troublin' yer, Kate?' he asked.

'No, I just feel a bit under the weather,' I replied.

'Yer know what's wrong with yer, Kate, yer want to get out more and find yerself a man friend. 'Ow old are yer now, forty?'

'Forty-two. Maybe I will, one day,' I said.

'Yer know, sis, yer a good-looking chick and yer dress smart and—'

'Oh, go on, flatterer,' I interrupted, smiling up at him, as he stood with his back towards the fire.

He said, 'Well, there's many a decent chap who'd be proud ter be seen walkin' out with yer. So take my advice an' don't leave it too late.'

'I won't,' I replied. 'Anyhow, what's brought you here? I haven't seen you for months.'

'I've bought a second-hand car and I thought you might like to accompany me and the missus on a ride out in the country, ter-morra afternoon.'

'Thanks, Jack,' I replied, eager for the treat. 'I'll be ready when you call.'

It was a beautiful run, and I enjoyed the company – until we called in a pub to have a drink. The smoke room was crowded, it being market day. And when my brother kept showing me off in front of everyone, I felt embarrassed. I was glad when we left. As soon as we got outside to the car I lost my temper and stormed at him.

'If I want a fellow I don't need *you* to find one for me. I'll find my own! Thank you very much.'

I was still angry when he dropped me outside my house. 'Next time you try pairing me up, Jack, don't! I can do my own pairing up, thank you!' I snapped. Then I went in and slammed the door.

The car had just driven away, when Mrs Morgan, my next-door neighbour, called with a message. 'Come in while I put the kettle on,' I called out to her. She was a kindly person and she had been very helpful when I first came to live next door. I liked her, and I was glad of her company when I was alone. But she had one fault, she was an awful gossip, and knew everybody's business. When I had given her a cup of tea, I asked her what the message was.

'Oh, yes,' she said. 'I almost forgot. A young man called about an hour ago, an Air Force sergeant, said his name was Joe, and he knew you years ago. I asked him to come into my place and wait for you, but he said he had somewhere else to call, and he'd be back in an hour. Do you know who he is? He was a handsome fellow,' she added.

'I'm not certain who he could be, Mrs Morgan, but thank you for telling me.'

'Would you like me to wait with you till he comes?'

'No, thank you, dear,' I replied. 'I think I'd better see him alone. But thank you all the same for coming to tell me.'

'Well, don't forget to give me a knock on the wall if you need me,' she said as she went out.

As I tidied myself up, I wondered who this handsome fellow could be. I was soon to find out. A few moments later the bell rang, and when I opened the door there he stood.

'Hello, Kate,' he said, as he put his hand out for me to shake. But I didn't take it, I was too surprised he even knew my name.

'Sorry,' I said, 'I don't believe I know you. Anyhow, you'd better come inside.' (I was thinking of my nosy little neighbour, watching.)

He came inside and took off his Air Force cap, and I told him to sit down. 'Would you like a cup of tea? I've just made one. Then maybe you can enlighten me as to who you are,' I said.

He drank some of the tea, then he said, 'You sure you don't remember me?'

'I'm sorry, I don't,' I replied, still wondering.

'Well, we only met a couple of times. It was before you were married.'

Suddenly I remembered my first boy-friend, that I'd had such trouble with. He had been called Joe. Could this be him? But the stranger went on, 'You were about seventeen, and I asked your dad if I could take you to the Albion Picture Palace. And do you remember, you let me put my arm around you, but when I tried to kiss you, you slapped my face and ran out. I never saw you after that.'

Then I remembered. I began to smile, and he asked me what I was smiling about. I asked him, 'What became of the box of chocolates I threw at you when you tried to kiss me?'

'Oh, them? I gave them to the usherette.'

We chatted for a bit, and I found that Joe had met my brother Jack, and that was how he knew where I was living. After a while he got up to leave. He took my hand. 'Kate,' he said, 'I hope you don't mind my asking, but could I call and take you out one evening?'

'I'd like that very much, Joe,' I said.

'What about next weekend?'

I'd been hoping he'd say the next day. But I tried not to be too eager to see him again. 'Yes, Joe, that will suit me nicely.'

Then he said, 'Would you mind, Kate, if I kissed you – just once, before I go?'

I didn't answer, but as I put my face close to his he kissed me and squeezed my hand. That was the first thrill I'd had in years, and I hoped then that it wouldn't be the last, and that this would be the beginning of a long friendship. I wasn't the teenager he'd known any longer, I was a grown-up woman with a family. But I needed a man's love and companionship.

As he walked down the front path and waved to me, I felt sorry to see him go. He closed the gate and waved again, and I saw Mrs Morgan coming down her path. I knew she wanted to find out who he was, but I didn't feel inclined to gossip. I went inside and closed the door. I needed to be alone and sit down to think things over. I wanted to see him again. But I couldn't help wondering if he was married. I should have asked him straight out, but I'd been afraid the answer would be yes. Anyway, even if it was, I thought, we could still be friends.

As I sat there thinking, I said to myself, if he was a married man, what if my daughters should find out? Whichever way it was, I would have to come to that decision later. I climbed the stairs and got into bed that night with a feeling that my life now was going to change for the better.

For several weeks after that Joe and I kept company, going to the pictures or to the theatre to see a show. But each time he kissed me goodnight before leaving me I wondered if he had a wife. I was still afraid to ask him, but I couldn't go on like this without knowing. So one night when he brought me home, I asked him to come in for a while and have a cup of coffee. He sat down and I handed him his cup, then I picked up courage to ask him – dreading the answer.

'Joe, I, er – wanted to ask you – er – are you – married?'

'I'm glad now you've asked me, dear. I should have told you that first day we met, but I didn't think it mattered then. But now it does, darling, because I've fallen in love with you.'

Now I knew the truth, I began to weep, and as he handed me his handkerchief I managed to say, 'I'm in love with you, too, but we mustn't see each other again after tonight, Joe.'

'Listen, Kate love, wipe your eyes, and try to listen to what I have to say. My wife and I have been at loggerheads ever since I came back from India. We're divorced now. Your brother Jack knows all about it. I'm only waiting for the divorce to be made absolute, and then I want to marry you.'

'Are you still living with her?' I asked.

'No. I'm living with my dad and my sister. *Will* you marry me, Kate?'

'I can't give you my answer now, Joe. Let me have a few days to think it over.'

'Very well,' he replied. 'But I hope you'll say yes, because I do love you, truly I do.'

'Joe,' I answered, 'give me a few days to think it over, then I'll give you my answer, one way or another. You'll have to go now before Jean comes home.'

'Good night, then, Kate darling. But don't forget, I'll be coming for my answer. And whatever you may decide, I'll try and understand.'

I kept my tears back as he took me in his arms and kissed me several times. But as soon as I heard the door close behind him, I broke down and sobbed.

I don't know how I got through the next few days, as I went about my daily routine. I was missing Joe's fondness for me, and his company, and the things he used to say to make me laugh. I knew

I was in love. But how could I tell my daughters that I was in love with a married man? Yet I knew I had to tell them sooner or later.

My brother Jack called to see me, and he asked why I was looking so worried. As soon as I tried to explain, I began to weep.

'Yer old enough to make up yer own mind, Kate, and now's yer chance to make something o' yer life. When Jean's married yer'll be left all alone. So think it over carefully. They're not children any more.'

'But, Jack, I'm worried about what the girls will say when I tell them I'm in love with a married man.'

' 'E won't be married when 'is divorce papers come through. Now, listen to me,' he replied sternly, 'yer never 'ad a 'appy life with yer 'usband befower 'e died. So now's yer chance. 'E's a good bloke, sis, so make up yer mind before it's too late. An' if yer want me to talk to the girls and explain, yer've only ter say.'

'Thanks, Jack, but I think it would be best coming from me,' I said.

'Well, remember, Kate, yer've put them first in everythin' fer years, and now yer've the chance to be 'appy with someone who really loves yer. Make up yer mind before it's too late.'

After he left I began to think over what he had said, and I decided that as soon as Jean came home from work I would try and explain to her what I intended to do. But when she came home I was still on tenterhooks how to begin. After she'd had her tea, we both sat by the fire.

Before I could begin, she said, 'Mum, do you mind if Sam calls for me tonight? He wants to take me to the pictures.'

'But, Jean, I wanted to talk to you about something that I've been trying to tell you for some time.'

I was taken aback when she answered at once, 'Is it about you and Joe? Because if it is, I know what you're going to tell me.'

'Very well,' I replied. 'If you know, I'd better tell you what my intentions are. Joe has asked me to marry him.'

'Are you going to marry him, Mum?'

'Yes, as soon as his divorce papers come through.'

'I already knew he was married,' she replied.

'How did you know?'

'I met Uncle Jack the other day, and he told me everything. But why do you want to marry him, Mum?' she asked.

'I've thought all this over carefully. When you and Sam are married I shall be left on my own, and I couldn't face that again.'

'But we'll come to visit you, Mum.'

'That's not the same. When you are older and have a family you will understand what I mean. Now there's no more to be said. So you better get yourself ready if you're going to meet Sam.'

As she went upstairs to the bathroom, I began to feel sorry I had spoken so sharply. But soon the doorbell rang. It was Joe. I was just letting him in when Jean came down the stairs. When he began to wish her good evening, she didn't answer, but pushed past him and walked out. I felt very angry with her.

That same night I told Joe I would marry him. But no matter how we both talked to Jean and tried to make her understand, we had many quarrels. A few days later she came home to tell me she was going to live with her sister. And as she was packing her belongings, I said, 'Very well, Jean, if that's what you want. But remember, if you wish to change your mind your home is always here – and remember,' I added, 'whatever happens, I shall always love you.'

A few weeks later, in February 1947, Joe and I were married at the registry office in Edmond Street.

During the war, as a sergeant in the Air Force, Joe had been stationed in India and South Africa. Often he used to show me his album and tell me about some of the places he visited. He said that one day he would save enough money to take me to South Africa, but he never got round to it.

When he came back to Birmingham, he could never settle down to work inside a factory. He loved giving orders, but couldn't take them. He had several outdoor jobs, where he could earn himself a bit of extra money on the side, for he loved handling money. At one period he worked on a milk cart delivering milk. When he wasn't able to straighten the books, he told the manager money was still owing from bad payers. Later he was sacked. The next job was hulking hundredweights of coal around the streets from a horse and cart. That job didn't last long either. His other job was at Perry Barr Dog Tracks exercising the dogs. One day he brought home Hopwas Reward, one of the greyhounds, to show me. It was his favourite, but when I saw its ribs showing through its skin I asked, 'What do yer feed 'em on to win a race? Starve 'em?'

'No, they have to be on a special diet.'

'I don't know about callin' 'im Hopwas Reward. The name would suit him would be Tin Ribs,' I replied.

Often Joe would leave the dog with me for a couple of hours while he went to see his dad and brother-in-law to give them a tip-off. While he was out I felt so sorry for that animal sitting in front of the fire shivering, I gave him a roll of pig's pudding. He was ravenous – another day I gave him lumps of cheese and buttered toast and meat gravy soaked in bread. Each time Hopwas was left with me I would feed him up.

The trainer saw he was putting on weight, but he couldn't understand why. Hopwas was never entered in another race. A few weeks later, I was told he had died. I was glad Joe never found out that in my ignorance I had overfed him with the wrong kind of food.

While my husband was still working at the dog track, he came in contact with one of the bookmakers, Jimmy Budd. Jimmy asked Joe if he would like a part-time job collecting a few bets. As Joe loved the feel of money, this job went well for a while. On bad nights when betting was slack, Jimmy didn't want to pay much. They argued, and when Joe helped himself to his wages, that was the end of that job.

One night as we were on the way to the picture house, Joe slipped into the betting shop owned by Jim and Joe Smith, to have a bet. As soon as he came out we walked towards the Elite in Soho Road. He said, 'Kate, I've had a word with Jim and Joe. They've asked me if I'd like a job collecting bets on our street corner.' As this was illegal, I was worried. 'But what if the police catch yer?' I said.

'That'll all be arranged. They'll put another dummy runner in my place, while I'm hurrying away to take in the bets. Anyway,' he added, 'I'll be workin' on commission.'

'Please yerself, if that's what yer want to do, but don't come to me to bail yer out if yer get caught!' I said.

'Come on,' he replied, 'or we'll be late for the pictures.'

Joe and I loved to see a cowboy film, but as we fumbled in the dark to find two seats, we discovered the programme had been changed. They were showing Gracie Fields in *Queen of Hearts*.

We watched it for about ten minutes until all of a sudden Joe said loudly, 'Kate, come on! I ain't watchin' no mower of this bleedin' rubbish!'

I felt so embarrassed as I got up and followed him out. On the way home we had our usual quarrel, yet our arguments never lasted long. Often Joe would change the subject and make me smile with his sense of humour.

A few days later, Joe Smith called at our house to make all the necessary arrangements. Soon he had punters come from all districts, for my husband was well known and well liked, especially amongst the women. He would often be seen with his hands in his pockets whistling some kind of ditty while waiting for bets on the street corner. He was also known as 'The Bookie's Runner'. Often he would have pieces of toffee or a penny ready to give to some little urchin to keep a watchful eye out and warn him when he saw a bobby coming.

He'd be seen standing beside a low wall, laughing and joking to some of the people who handed him the bets. Yet he was always on the alert to scale the wall and hide in someone's back entry or in their attic. When the All Clear came, women would hand over their threepenny and sixpenny each-way bets, and when anyone asked him to tip them a horse or a dog, he used to say, 'Do yer think I'd be standin' 'ere if I knew any certainties? Yer betta try stickin' a pin in, yer might be lucky.'

Often the police disguised themselves in slouched trilbys and long shabby raincoats, but Joe was no fool – he knew them all and was over that wall and out of sight before they ever caught him.

One morning as I walked down the street I saw Mrs Jenks, one of our neighbours, having an argument with my husband. When she saw me she came towards me. I asked her what the trouble was, and she said, 'Yer know, Mrs Dayus, I like yower Joe, until he tries ter pay me out short. I know I can't read but I know 'ow ter reckon up to a farthin'.'

'Oh well, Mrs Jenks,' I replied pleasantly, 'we all make mistakes,' and I walked away.

During the winter months we'd sit beside a roaring fire and play cards or dominoes. He taught me all kinds of games, but he was a poor loser and often grumbled when I beat him. 'Beginner's luck,' he used to say, and he said red cards were unlucky for him. When he had another-coloured pack he'd say, 'Let's have a shilling on who wins.' But when I won he wanted to double up. I knew he'd win in the end, so I gave up and put my winnings in my pocket.

Some nights he would read to me from one of his cowboy books, and, if I felt tired and closed my eyes, he'd ask me if I'd been listening.

'Yes,' I'd reply. 'I'm only restin' my eyes.'

But when he asked me what the last chapter was about and I

couldn't tell him, he'd say, 'Never mind, I'll continue tomorrow night', and put the book away.

For most of our married life, Joe worked as a bookmaker's clerk. After taking bets on street corners for a while he got a job in a Conservative Club of which he was a member. Off-course cash betting was illegal then, but luckily for Joe he was never caught. Still, I was always on edge until he came home.

Working on commission, he did very well. On the days of big races, such as the Derby, or the Oaks, or the Grand National, he'd earn twice as much as if he'd been working in a factory (which he couldn't have stood, anyway – he never liked people giving him orders). Sometimes his commission at the end of the week would be over £100 (that was very good money in the forties and fifties). I didn't ask him for much, because I still had my small enamelling business. But he never hesitated to buy me something he thought I wanted. He was always kind and generous. Unfortunately, though, he was a habitual gambler himself. I used to get very worried when he lost heavily on the horses or the dogs, but he always seemed to come out on top in the following weeks. When I tried to tell him that he should be more careful, his job wouldn't last for ever, he would reply, 'You won't go short. And as long as I've got me fags, and a few shillings in me pocket, and you, I'm happy.' But I didn't know what he had in his pocket. I knew he wouldn't tell me even if I asked.

One day he brought home a television set he'd bought so that he could watch the horses running on Derby Day. By the time of the big race he was very excited. He'd already won over £30 on the first two races, and he'd put it all on a horse called Devon Loch to win the Derby. As soon as the horses started he got down on his knees and pulled the screen nearer to get a better view. Devon Loch was winning easily. 'Come on, you little beauty!' Joe kept yelling at the screen. When the horse was nearly at the post, its legs splayed out and it dropped dead. Joe went berserk. He picked up the television and slung it across the room. I knew then it was time for me to vanish. I didn't come home till late that night, and by that time he'd cooled down. But he never stopped talking about that Derby horse. He always swore it had been doped.

Every Friday morning Joe would do his Littlewoods football pools coupon and post it on the way to his club, and on Saturday nights he'd light up his fags and watch the results on television. Once he won a fourth dividend, but he knew it wouldn't be much because there were such a lot of draws. The following Wednesday the letter came and when he opened it out fell a postal order for 2s 6d. He looked disappointed. As he went to sling it into the fire I took it from him and put it in the desk. A couple of weeks later he had got up early to light the fire and bring me up my usual cup of tea, when I heard him call up from the bottom of the stairs, 'Kate, what did you do with that postal order?'

'It's somewhere in the desk. Why?' I called down.

'Where's the key?' he asked.

'In my bag. I'll be down in a minute,' I replied.

As I opened the desk and gave it to him, I said, 'Surely you're not that hard up!'

'Of course I'm not. I thought of using it on the last coupon of the season.'

He didn't even study it, just filled in eight draws and went out and posted it.

As a matter of fact we both forgot all about it, and we didn't even watch the television that Saturday night. The following Wednesday we had a letter, and a cheque for £1,400. As soon as I saw it, I took hold of it.

'You're not having this to gamble with,' I cried out. 'If you do, I'm leaving you – and I mean it.'

He stared at me hard. But I was absolutely determined. I knew

I'd given him something to think about. 'Very well, then, I'll put it in the bank,' he said.

But I still couldn't trust him. So I replied, 'It's not going into your bank. It's going into mine.'

It didn't stay there long. Soon after, Joe had a windfall on the horses, and won over £200. With that plus the pools money and the money we got for our house in Uplands Road, we were able to buy a new house in Rookery Row. And we still had enough left over for a fishing holiday in Ireland.

Chapter 28

Life With Joe

Joe and I had many happy years together. We had our disagreements (no one is perfect); but he was kind and considerate, and I loved him.

Some funny things happened as well. I remember one very bright moonlit night when we were first married and still living in Landgate Road. Something, perhaps the light, woke me, and I got out of bed to open the window wide to let in some air. As soon as I got back into bed I must have dozed off to sleep. But it wasn't long before I was woken again, by a kind of cooing sound. The light from the moon flooded the bedroom, so I didn't have to switch on the light. I was sitting up to see where the sound was coming from, when all at once I saw two large, bright eyes staring at me through the open window. Terrified, I slid down the bed beneath the bed-clothes, and I pinched Joe's leg.

'Joe,' I managed to say, 'wake up! There's somebody staring through the window!'

Quickly he sprang out of bed, and as I held on to the tail of his shirt and followed him towards the window, we saw a large owl sitting on the window-ledge, gazing at its own reflection in the glass. After Joe shooed him off and closed the window, we lay back in bed and laughed. My husband said that the owl, seeing its reflection in the glass, must have thought it'd found a mate.

But soon after that I got really scared. Ever since I'd come to the house, I'd been bothered by creaking noises in the bedroom at night. When I tried to explain to Joe he just laughed at me, saying I was imagining it.

'But, Joe,' I said to him one night, 'I can't sleep sometimes. It seems that there's someone in the room.'

'Yes,' he said, trying to put me off. 'It's us two.'

Then, one day while Joe was out, Mrs Morgan called to say the postman had left a parcel for me. I asked her in to have a chat and a cup of tea. As soon as we settled down together I began to tell her about the weird sounds I heard at night.

She just said, 'I'm surprised you've stayed here this long.'

'Why? What do you mean? I've only been here twelve months.'

'Well, didn't you know the house was haunted?'

'No, I didn't. But how do you mean, haunted?'

She asked me what bedroom we slept in, and when I told her the back bedroom, she said, 'Well, that's the room where a young woman murdered herself.'

'You mean she killed herself?'

'Yes, in that very room. And three families have lived there before you came.'

'And you told them what you've told me?'

'I didn't have to, they found out for themselves.'

Now I was more nervous than ever. I found it hard to sleep at night, and when I did drop off I awoke imagining all kinds of weird sounds. Joe said I was being foolish and superstitious, and we quarrelled. But I was now determined to look for another house. I walked for hours until I saw one I liked that was for sale. I went at once to get the keys from the agent.

The house, which was in Uplands Road, was older than the one we were living in, but it was in good condition, and newly painted and decorated. It also had a long, well-kept back garden, where my husband could build a loft for his pigeons. Pigeon-racing was one of Joe's favourite hobbies. After I had looked over the house, I asked the woman next door if she could tell me why the last people had left. She said they had been a very nice couple who had lived there for nearly thirty years, and had now gone to live in Canada with their son. I felt satisfied, so I went back to the agent, paid a deposit, and said I would call and make the necessary arrangements in a few days.

I hurried home, happy to think I would soon be leaving that house and those weird sounds behind me. But when I told my husband what I'd done, he flared up at me.

'The least you could have done was to tell me you intended to leave here. I like it here, and so would you if you hadn't listened to that bleedin' old busybody next door.'

One word brought up another. But I was adamant. We hardly spoke to each other for days, and when we did, we snapped. I knew that I really should have discussed it with him, but I was desperate to move. The following week I made a start packing china and glass and other articles, which kept me busy during the day, but when night-time came, no matter how much Joe tried to convince me I was imagining things, I still couldn't sleep. Then something else happened. I had been awake for most of the night, as usual, but finally I dozed off. Soon after, we both woke with a start, to find that the wardrobe door was wide open. Joe jumped out of bed and looked inside. He found that our savings had been stolen during the night. His wrist-watch had gone from the bedside table too. There didn't seem to be anything else missing. We pulled on some clothes and Joe went downstairs to phone the police, with me following very close behind him.

'I can't understand it,' he said. 'I always make doubly sure that the doors and windows are locked before we go to bed.'

'I told you the house was haunted,' I cried out at once.

'Don't be foolish, Kate. Why would a ghost want a watch? And it couldn't spend money. It must have been somebody already in the house when I locked up.'

The police searched the house, but they found no clues to the intruder's identity. They left saying they would send someone to take fingerprints later.

As soon as it was daylight Joe went out into the back garden to feed his pigeons and I went with him. But there another shock awaited us. Many of Joe's beloved birds lay dead on the lawn, and their eggs were strewn all over the path. Joe just went back into the house and wept. I too began to weep. Neither of us could understand why anybody would do such a cruel thing.

At least after this Joe too was pleased to get out of that house, and move to the villa in Uplands Road. But it took me a long time to get over my nervousness.

I'll never forget the first night we went to bed in our new home. We were both very tired after arranging the furniture, and we fell asleep as soon as we went to bed. But during the night I woke up with a fright. 'Joe! Joe!' I screamed out. 'There's a tall man standing beside the bed!' He sprang out of bed and switched on the light. I covered my head over with the bedclothes, scared to look.

'Where? There's nobody here,' he exclaimed.

When I pointed to the bedroom door he became angry.

'What have I told you about imagining things! What you saw was my dressing gown hanging on the back of the door. Now, let's get some sleep.'

After he got back into bed, we began to laugh at my foolish fancy, and cuddled up together and slept.

I realised that my husband was often mean, and at times he was not very easy to get along with. Yet despite his meanness he had a sense of humour, which was one of the things I liked about him.

There was one thing I was grateful for: he didn't drink beer, or any kind of alcohol. Tea was his favourite drink. We had our differences of opinion, as many couples do, but when he was in one of his *good* moods I only had to ask and he'd give me the money to buy whatever I needed. But taking bets and staying at his club late at night to pay money out to punters was not my idea of life. It meant I had to be left alone in that house until he came home.

Sitting alone, waiting, I was always nervous, wondering if this old house was haunted, like the previous one. Sometimes I was scared of my own shadow. I'd switch on all the lights, but as soon as I heard him coming down the path I ran and switched them all off.

We had a front room, a dining-room, a small kitchen, and three bedrooms. This house was not centrally heated – our hot water came from the boiler at the back of the fire grate, which supplied us only with hot water from the tap in the kitchen sink.

I was always active, and I seldom felt the cold weather, but my Joe was forever complaining about his cold feet. One week we had rain, snow and ice continually, non-stop. Joe decided to buy himself a rubber hot-water bottle. As soon as I saw it I cried, 'Thinkin' of yerself agen – why couldn't yer buy me one?'

'Yer tell me yer never feel the cold,' he replied, smiling across at me.

'Well, I do! When yer come up to bed late and put yer freezin' legs an' feet against me.'

'No need now, I've got me bottle,' he answered, grinning. I knew it was a waste of time to argue.

Every night he was last to come up to bed. Then one night, when I thought he was asleep, I pushed my feet down the bed. I grasped the bottle between my feet and smiled to myself as I kicked it over to my side. But I felt his hand slide down the bed and fail to find the bottle, then sliding up my bare thigh.

I shot up and shouted at him, 'No yer don't! If yer too mean to buy *me* one, you ain't goin' to use me to get warm!'

'All right, I'll sleep downstairs,' he replied.

It was no use arguing any more. But he didn't stay long – back he came with a hot refill. I thought: one of these days he'll get that water too hot and the bottle will burst. Sure enough, I woke up one day to find the foot of the bed wet – the bottle was leaking.

I screamed at him and threw the bottle on to the floor. 'Now look what's 'appened!'

'Oh, shut up!' he yelled back. ' 'Tain't my fault the bottle's leaked.'

'Is that all you can say? Well, this is the last time you 'ave a bottle in my bed,' I yelled. I picked up the dripping bottle and, opening the window, I threw it out into the yard below, and went downstairs.

The following night he was very late. I looked at the bedside clock – it was nearly one thirty and he still hadn't come up to bed. Surely, I thought, he can't still be sulking! I crept downstairs, but he wasn't in his chair or sitting on the couch. I began to get worried. I went into the kitchen, and there I saw him trying to fix a piece of sticking plaster on that bottle.

'How mean can you get!' I cried as I snatched it from him. 'This time it's goin' into the ashbin and if yer want ter get warm I'm going to buy an electric blanket.'

'What for? They're dangerous! You can get electrocuted with one of them!'

'Not if you switch 'em off!' I replied.

'Well *I* ain't buyin' one, I'm quite satisfied with a bottle and if you aren't I'll buy *you* one too.'

'If you do, I'll sleep in the spare room, where I can get a proper night's sleep.'

'You wouldn't, would yer, Kate?' he grinned. 'You always say you're scared to sleep on yer own.'

'What do you care?' I replied angrily. 'Yer come up late and wake me up, trying to lift me nightie, so yer can put yer cold feet on me belly. Even when I turn over yer try pushing 'em up me back. So now I'm going up ter bed an' I'm goin' ter sleep in the spare room, so good night!' I replied angrily.

I snatched up a couple of blankets and left.

As I tried to settle down to sleep, I heard him creep into the room.

'Are you awake, love?' I heard him whisper.

'Yes! Go away and leave me alone!'

'I've brought you up a nice hot cup of tea.'

'I don't want it!'

'Well, come back in the other bed where we can cuddle up an' keep warm.'

'No! I know your cuddle-ups.'

'If you'll come back, I'll even do without me water bottle. I *promise*. I only want for us to cuddle up together. I'm cold.'

I suddenly began to feel guilty at the way I had behaved. I drank the tea and followed him back to bed. As we cuddled up close, he broke his promise and we made love.

Next day he gave me the money to buy a blanket. I called at Lewis's Stores in town and bought a full-sized one, before I changed my mind. On the way home with my purchase, I began to smile to myself, thinking how possessive he'd been with his water bottle. But there won't be any more squabbles about whose side *this* would be on, I said to myself.

I called the blanket 'Sheila', a name I gave to most things I possessed. Joe often used to laugh at me, saying I was crazy.

The first night I put it in the bed, I was pleased he took to it straight away. I could have said 'I told you so.' But I thought: let sleeping dogs lie. The trouble was, it was a hard job to wake him up in the mornings. He was always first to bed and last out.

One night a few weeks later, we had a terrific storm. It was lightning, thundering and raining all through the night. For once Joe was already fast asleep when I went upstairs, and the last thing I did after getting undressed and into my nightdress was to take out my teeth, put them in a pint jug of water with a pinch of salt and leave them on the bathroom shelf. Joe knew I had false teeth, but I never let him see me take them out – I would have felt embarrassed.

As soon as I got into bed I heard him snoring like a contented pig. After a few digs and a couple of grunts, he turned on to his side and went quiet. I picked up my book and tried to finish reading it, but after a while I lost interest. I switched off the bedside lamp, and it wasn't long before I fell asleep.

I don't know how long I'd slept, when a loud clash of thunder woke me up. I shot up in bed and switched on the light. I felt so hot I thought I was suffocating, and as I slung back the bedclothes, a waft of smoke hit me.

Suddenly I flew out of bed. 'Joe, Joe!' I screamed as I shook him. 'Wake up, wake up!'

'What the bloody hell's the matter with yer now?' he cried, glaring up at me. 'Seen a few mower ghosts?'

'No, Joe, look!' I shouted, pointing to the foot of the bed. 'The bed's smoulderin'.'

Now he too flew out of bed. 'I told yer what would 'appen as soon as yer bought that bloody "Sheila", as yer call it! Yer run downstairs and bring some water up, while I try to smother it afore it gets alight.'

When I came back with a bowl of water, I could see he had already opened the window and thrown the feather bed into the yard below – 'Sheila' too.

After a few sharp words, we went to sleep in the spare bed.

Early next morning, when I awoke, it was still dark and still raining heavily. I decided to leave Joe asleep and go downstairs to make myself a cup of tea. I went into the bathroom to put in my teeth. As soon as I looked inside the jug, I saw there was no water – nor my teeth. I was certain I remembered putting them there. I began to think: had somebody or something come in the night and stolen them? I suddenly became frightened. I began to panic, and as my tears fell I ran back into the bedroom and tried to yell through my toothless gums,

'Joe, Joe! Me teef 'ave gone! Somebody's took me teef!'

'What yer mumblin' about now?'

'Me teef, me teef, they've gone!'

'What yer mean, yer teef 'ave gone!' he mimicked. 'You ain't swallowed 'em, 'ave yer? Anyway, where did yer put 'em?'

'In a jug a water in the baffwoom,' I managed to say.

Suddenly he burst out laughing. 'Then they must be still in amongst the feathers when I used that water for the bed.'

I fled downstairs, hoping and praying they hadn't melted. It was still raining when I bent down, put my hand in and felt among the wet feathers. I couldn't feel them anywhere, then suddenly I gave a sigh of relief – I saw my teeth clinging to 'Sheila'. Apart from a few wet feathers sticking to them, I was pleased to see that my teeth were intact.

It was still thundering and lightning in the distance as I hurried back upstairs. Shivering and sneezing, I managed to brush the wet feathers off my teeth and put them in a fresh jug of water. After changing my wet nightie for a dry one, I decided we had to sleep in the other room. Joe already had a cup of hot cocoa waiting for me. 'Come on, love, drink this and get into bed before yer catch yer death of cold.'

After drinking the cocoa I got into bed beside him. He put his arms round me, and as we cuddled up close to get warm, he whispered in my ear, 'You and yer teef!' We both saw the funny side and burst out laughing.

Next morning, when I went into our bedroom to clean up the mess, I knew at once: it wasn't 'Sheila's' fault the bed nearly caught fire. I realised I must have forgotten to switch it off before falling asleep.

When I told Joe, he surprised me by saying, 'Never mind, love,

I've remembered it's your birthday tomorra. I'll give yer the money to buy another one. But,' he added, 'I'll have the switch my side, then I'll be sure to take the plug out. But first, you'll have to buy another feather bed.'

The bed would cost *me* several times more than a blanket would cost *him* – I thought how mean he was.

But I didn't argue, in case he changed his mind.

Chapter 29

Winnie

It was during 1955 – I remember it well. One lovely sunny afternoon, I went to Handsworth Park for a bowling match, but as I was too early I sat down on the bench outside the pavilion and waited for the other members.

As I sat on that bench, wiping my woods and getting ready to give my partner a game, I happened to glance across the green and noticed a poorly clad elderly woman sitting on the far side. I saw that she kept staring across at me. Playing beside her were two ragged children, a boy and a girl, about four years old, pushing an empty dilapidated pram.

Just as Annie, my opponent, and I began to start our match, the children ran across the bowling green. Suddenly we saw the boy pull out his little willie, and as the little girl scratched her head and watched, he began to piddle.

Annie cried out, 'Yer dirty little bugger! Sod off!'

Quickly the little boy fumbled to push his willie back. As the remains of the piddle ran down his legs, he began to cry. This held up our game as the other players began to laugh, and we were getting annoyed.

'Look at 'er, their grandmother!' Annie cried out. 'She ain't even botherin' about 'em, an' if they don't clear off, I'll goo over meself an' clout their ear'oles!'

'No need for that, Annie,' I replied. 'I'll take 'em over to their gran.'

Annie still stood there fuming as I held their grubby little hands. When I asked their names, the little boy replied 'Georgie'. 'An' my name's Jenny,' the little girl whispered.

As soon as I reached the woman, I asked, 'Are you their mum?'

'No,' she replied. 'I'm their grandmother.'

'Well, will you please keep the children off the green?'

As I began to walk away I heard her call out, 'Don't yer know me, Kate?'

'I'm sorry, I'm afraid I don't,' I replied. 'But if you're still here when the match is finished, I'll come back to yer.'

I heard Annie yell out, 'Cum on! Yer 'oldin' up the bloody game!'

'All right! All right!' I yelled back. 'I'm coming!'

All through our game I kept wondering who the woman was, and why she said I should remember her, which made me lose my concentration. I lost my game, twenty-one nil. That was the first time I ever lost with such a score, and I never lived it down. But I was pleased to know that the team had won.

I was still thinking and wondering who she was as I made my way with the players for tea, and as I looked through the window I could still see her beside the pram. I took my cakes and some tea on a tray to give them. As the children stuffed the cakes into their mouths, their granny said, 'Where's yer manners?'

'Thank yer, Miss,' they managed to reply.

As soon as she had drunk the cup of tea, she said, 'Yer sure yer don't know me, Kate?'

'No, but if you'll tell me yer name, I might.'

'I'm Winnie Nash. We grew up together in Camden Drive.'

Suddenly I remembered. I couldn't believe my eyes. Although I remembered that she was my age, she looked old and worn. Her

face was well lined and her once beautiful red hair was now turning grey. I flung my arms around her and kissed her. All in one
breath I cried out, 'Oh Winnie, Winnie, I'm ever so happy to see
you again after all these years. Where are you living now?'

'I live in one of the side streets in the All Saints district near the
coal wharf.'

'Why haven't yer tried to get in touch before?'

'I didn't know where yer was livin' and it was only by talkin' ter
one of me neighbours about yer, that she told me yer was playin'
'ere.'

'Well, I'm glad you found me, anyway. Come home with me
and we can talk about old times,' I said.

'I'd like that, Kate, but I've gotta get back 'ome. George will be
waitin' for 'is tea.'

'Who's George, yer husband?' I asked.

'No, 'e's the children's father,' she replied.

'Well, do you mind if I come home with you? I don't want to lose
you again.'

'Yes, I'd like that, Kate, that's if yer don't mind the place we're
livin'.'

'I ain't coming to see yer place, only you. Now stay there while I
fetch me coat.'

As soon as I took the empty tray back to the clubhouse, everyone asked who she was.

'A long-lost school friend I haven't seen for years,' I replied as I
put on my coat and left.

Winnie had already put the twins in the pram and was wheeling
it towards the park gates when I caught up with her. It was almost
twenty minutes before we reached her home. This place was no
better than the bug-infested hovels where we lived and played
when we were children, many long years ago.

These back-to-back slums were a reminder of those forgotten
years, with damp green slime clinging to the outside brickwork.

There was still the familiar cry from the rag-and-bone man, and smells of urine drifting into the air from the gutters, and all kinds of rubbish littered those pavements. I'm no snob, for hadn't I too been dragged up in bug- and rat-infested slums? Yet as I looked around these godforsaken places these people called their homes, I felt I didn't want to be reminded of the past, or to go inside. But I couldn't hurt her feelings by making some excuse.

As Winnie pushed the old pram up a side entry, the children climbed out and joined their playmates in the yard. When we entered the living-room, I saw a thickset man in his none too clean shirtsleeves. His square chin sprouted grey stubble. When he stared at me as he sat up to the table, I noticed he had a flat nose and a cauliflower ear. I thought he must have been a prizefighter. I could see he'd had plenty to drink, for as he got up from the table he stumbled and just glared at me.

'I've brought me friend 'ome with me, George,' Winnie said.

As he made his way towards the stairs, the children ran in.

'Daddy,' the little boy cried out, 'can I cum up an' watch yer fly the pigeons?'

'Very well,' he mumbled, 'but watch yer sister don't fall down the loft this time.'

After they had gone up to the attic, Winnie closed the door.

'Is that yer daughter's husband, Winnie?' I asked.

When she nodded, I couldn't help but say, 'Whatever could she see in him – he must be old enough to be her father?' And so ugly, I thought.

'Yes,' replied Winnie. 'He was forty an' Alice was only sixteen when they got married. She 'ad ter get wed, she was four months in the family way. But 'e was good an' kind ter me an' Alice. He ain't always bin like this, an' 'e was a good-lookin' bloke until 'e went in the war, an' when 'e cum back from the army 'e looked different. It's shrapnel,' she added. 'But me daughter couldn't bear the sight of him near 'er. She used to go off with other men and leave the twins for hours, and when George found out, 'e used ter belt 'er. I tried talkin' some sense into them both and things seemed a bit better for a while – until George got a job on nights, then she'd go out an' never cum back until the early hours. Then one mornin' as I was givin' the twins their porridge, she told me she was packin' 'er things an' leavin' in a few days' time.'

'What happened about the twins – did she say she was taking them with her?' I asked.

'No, Kate, she asked me if I'd take care of them until she got settled elsewhere. I was afraid to tell George she was leadin' a bad life an' was thinkin' of leavin' us. I couldn't stand any more fights and rows. So, as long as there was peace, I kept my mouth shut. I prayed often she would cum to 'er senses. Then, to make matters worse, she told me she'd tried to 'ave an abortion, an' when I asked why, she said she didn't want another babby, because it wasn't George's. When I asked 'ow she knew it wasn't, she replied, "Well, we ain't slept together or med luv for six months an' I'm over three months now." That same night she packed 'er bags and left.'

'Where is she now?' I asked.

'I don't know, Kate, and I don't think I care any more, an' I don't believe George cares, either. He gives me wot 'e can ter look after the twins, but 'e ain't over-generous.'

'But how do you manage?'

'Well, I used ter mek peg rugs like me mum an' dad showed me. But there ain't much call for 'em today. I almost 'ave ter give 'em away.'

'But why don't you try and move away from here?'

''Ow can I? This is my 'ome. Anyway, I can't leave me gran' children to the mercy of 'im. 'E's all right till 'e gets the booze down 'im, then I puts on their 'ats an' scarves an' we leave 'im to it. That's why I came to find you at the park.'

'I'm glad you did, Winnie. But ain't their dad got any sisters or relations that can take *their* share?'

'They don't want ter know us, but I've got plenty of kind neighbours.'

'Well, Winnie, I'll have to be going now or my Joe will be wondering where I am. But will you promise to come next Tuesday when my husband has gone to the races and we'll have a good old natter about when we were kids?'

'I'd love that, Kate.'

'Very well, you know where I live – Uplands Road. Now promise me you'll come. Don't forget, next Tuesday.'

'I won't forget,' she replied, smiling.

As she stood on the step, several neighbours eyed me up and down, wondering who I was, but I left Winnie to explain. As I flung my arms around her again and kissed her, I said, 'Don't forget!'

When I got home I felt very sad to think that Winnie hadn't tried to make something better of her life.

The following Tuesday, I made a large cake and laid the table with bread and jam and beef sandwiches. What they couldn't eat, I would wrap up for them to take home. About three o'clock there was a knock on the door. As soon as I opened it I asked Winnie where the twins were. She said one of her kind neighbours was looking after them.

'It don't do for 'em to 'ear too much these days,' she added.

As she came into the room I could almost see what she was thinking. As she glanced around she exclaimed, 'Wot a nice place you 'ave, Kate!'

'Never mind the place, you come and sit down and have something to eat with me.' I wasn't going to show her around the house – not because I didn't want to, but I had so much more than she had, I didn't want her to feel out of place. But all the while we were having our tea I could see her eyes wandering around everything in the room, taking everything in.

To distract her mind from her surroundings, I said, 'You're very quiet, Winnie.'

'I was thinking what I could do if I 'ad a place like this.'

'Well, it's not too late, maybe some day you will, but first you have to get out of that rut you're in.'

'How can I, with me gran'children needin' me?'

'But Winnie, you've got to think of yourself as well, and try and make a new life for yourself. Did you ever get married?' I added.

'No, Kate, I did go with a young chap but when he found out I'd had a love child, I never saw him again.'

'I'm sure you'll meet the right man one day.'

'Yes, the neighbours are always telling me that. But 'ow can I leave the twins? I luv 'em like they was me own, an' if I left 'em, who's goin' ter look after 'em?'

I knew now how she felt. I still remember it was a bitter blow for me, when I had to part with my four young children – but under very different circumstances. That was in 1931, during the Depression.

To cheer her up, I thought it best to change the subject. 'Winnie, do you remember how hungry we was when we were kids, and I raided my mum's cupboard and stole a piece of fat bacon? And as we sat on the step I told you to suck it slowly to make it last?'

'Yes, I remember. It slid down our throats before we could even chew it, an' we nearly choked.'

As soon as I saw her smile, I said, 'And do you remember when I told you about my brother Jack, stealing the pig from the farm where I went hop-picking, and how the court case ended?'

'Yes, Kate, but did 'e really steal it? It wasn't proved,' she replied.

'Yes, Winnie, he did steal it, but I don't believe he took it back to the farm; for the next few weeks we ate nothing but pork, pork and more pork. Mum even boiled the pig's trotters with all the leftover bones. We ate that much pork, we began to feel like pigs.'

She began to look more cheerful, and I carried on talking.

'Winnie,' I began again, 'do you remember when all the kids and us two had whooping cough and our mums dosed us with castor oil, and Mrs Turner said the only thing to cure us was fumes from hot tar, and while the navvies was laying the wooden blocks between the tramlines, we were all marched down the Parade, where we had to bend over that cauldron and inhale the fumes?'

'Yes, Kate, an' we nearly choked, but we still 'ad to 'ave our dose of castor oil.'

'And still have our chests rubbed with hot tallow candles,' I replied.

'An' don't forget the old socks, Kate, soaked in camphorated oil an' fastened round our necks, when we caught mumps off the other kids in the yard.'

I felt then that I didn't want to talk about our sad experiences, but over another cup of tea Winnie began to remind me of the one night I wanted to forget.

'You remember that night, Kate,' she began, 'when we 'ad that foursome, when we was fifteen?'

'Yes,' I replied. 'But let's talk about something else.'

But she was persistent in reminding me.

'But I must tell yer, Kate, I 'aven't seen yer since that day me mum beat me an' turned me out, when I was in the family way. It took a lot of years ter forget 'Arry, but time 'eals wounds.'

'We were two silly foolish girls then, Winnie. I'd almost forgotten that night,' I replied.

'Not me, I 'ad something to remind *me*.'

'How long has it been, then?' I asked.

'Well, Alice would now be twenty, so it's gotta be over twenty years when I fell for 'er.'

As soon as I saw her tears, I quickly changed the subject: 'You'd never believe the struggle I had with that other chap, that same night. I can smile now, when I think back, but not then. He pushed me in a doorway, and when I felt his John Thomas come out I got a fright and pulled it for all I was worth, and when he screamed and rolled into the gutter I ran for my life. I thought I'd killed him. Next day I kept buying newspapers to see.'

'Did yer see 'im after?' she asked.

'Yes. But he said how sorry he was, and when he had his call-up papers, he asked me if I'd wait for him. I said I would. Some time later he sent me a birthday card with lovey-dovey words written on the back, but I never heard or saw him again.'

When it was time for Winnie to leave, I made her promise to come again and meet Joe. She said she would. But she never kept that promise. I wondered why. I went to her home a few days later, but as soon as she saw me she said she wished I hadn't come.

'But why?' I asked.

'Well, Kate, I feel ashamed of this place for yer ter see.'

'That's nonsense, Winnie. If you'll come and see me next week, I'll see what I can do to help you.'

I waited two whole weeks before I called again, hoping to give her some good advice. But it was too late. I found the house empty, and neighbours said they'd done a moonlight flit.

Sad to say, I never saw Winnie again. Yet my childhood memories of her still live with me, and I pray and hope that one day I shall meet her.

Chapter 30

Goodbye, Joe

In 1963, when I was sixty, I decided to sell my business and retire so that I could stay at home and have more time with my husband. I put the money in the bank, and for a while we lived comfortably on the commission Joe earned from taking bets. But a few months later his employer sent for him to say that now off-course betting had been legalised she was going to open up a betting office where the punters could go and put on their bets and hear the results, so she wouldn't be needing his services in the club any more. She offered him a job working behind the counter, but he said he wouldn't work inside for no gaffer. Although I did my best to persuade him, he was adamant.

'I'll find something,' was all he said, when I asked him what he was going to do.

But when he came home late one night and said he'd got a job at Perry Bar Stadium, cleaning and feeding the dogs and taking them out for exercise, we began to quarrel.

'Can't you find a better job than that?' I snapped.

'Well, I ain't working in a factory, if that's what you mean!' he replied angrily.

Then one night he persuaded me to go and see the racing. I saw enough that night to know I didn't want to see any more. One young chap had put all his money on a certainty (so he was told). It came in last. I saw him kneel on the ground and punch it several times, shouting out, 'It was doped! The bloody dog was doped!' People crowded around him, asking if he'd had a fit. I never went to the dog track again.

Each night Joe came home late we quarrelled. He'd got in with a gambling crowd and lost more than he earned. Foolishly I helped him out and paid some of his debts, but he just went on gambling. Until at last I made up my mind to do something about it.

During my retirement, several of my old customers had come to see me and asked if I would help out by doing some enamelling at home. It seemed to me that if I could persuade Joe to work with me it might keep him away from the gambling crowd. I put it to him.

'It's up to you, Kate, if that's what you want,' he said.

'It's not only up to me,' I replied. 'I'm asking you! Would you help? And if we don't agree, we'll have to think of something else. But I'm telling you one thing now, Joe, you're to give up gambling or I'm selling up and leaving you.'

'Very well,' he said. 'I'll try.'

We built a workshop in the garden and had the gas and electric put in, and then we started to work together on the enamelling. Joe gave up going out gambling. I didn't mind him having a small bet once a week on the phone – I realised how miserable he would be if he couldn't have one little squander – but I knew and he knew how far he could go. We worked together happily each morning. In the afternoon, we went to Summerfield Park, where he taught me how to bowl. During the months that followed I won many trophies in prize money and we joined Handsworth Victoria bowling club, where later I was made Captain of the Women's Team. Later still I became Captain of the Warwickshire Ladies' Team.

These were happy years. Until I began to worry about Joe's cough. I knew he was almost chain-smoking, but each time I asked him to cut down, he became very irritable and bad-tempered. One day he complained about a pain in his chest and while he lay in bed I rang for the doctor. When he came he had Joe taken into hospital straight away. He'd had a heart attack.

I visited him in St Chad's Hospital the following day. But the next day while I was getting ready to visit him, he walked into the house, saying, 'If I'm going to die I'll die at home.'

I was too shocked and upset even to answer him. After that he smoked more than ever. And one morning he collapsed on the floor. The doctor and the ambulance came at once, and Joe was taken to Dudley Road Hospital. When he began to improve, he phoned me each night, telling me he was now getting better and that I was to bring him some fags. I refused. But someone must have taken him some when they visited, and when the sister found out she warned him of the danger.

Late one night Joe phoned me, sounding very upset. When I asked him what was worrying him, he said, 'Kate, you'd better bring my clothes.'

'Whatever for?' I asked.

'Never mind what for. Bring me my clothes. I want to get out of here!' he snapped. Then he added, 'What chance have I got when yer doctor drops dead in the ward?'

I rang the sister at once, but could get no reply. Next morning, after a sleepless night, I went to the hospital to visit him, and when he had calmed down he told me what had happened. Apparently the doctor had indeed had a heart attack and died while he was doing a ward round. Other patients too said the ward was all topsy-turvy when they took their doctor out on a stretcher.

Towards the end of the week Joe was discharged. He had been given some heart tablets to take, and I was pleased to see he was making an improvement. But he still smoked heavily. I knew it was useless now to try and persuade him to give up. A few weeks later I had to captain the bowling team in Manchester. When I asked him if he was coming with us, he replied, 'Not today, Kate, some of the chaps at the club have asked me to make up the team to bowl away. But I'll have yer tea ready by the time you come back home, love, and don't forget,' he added, 'I want to hear all about yer bowling.'

Then we kissed each other and waved goodbye. Those words were the last he ever said to me. That same evening when I arrived home from Manchester I was told that he had died while playing on the bowling green at Dudley.

I wish he were still here today. I still miss him. More so than ever now. Many times during the bowling season I watch the couples playing and think to myself how lucky they are that they still have each other, that they are able to talk to each other and share their worries and troubles. During many cold winter evenings I sit alone and think of those days and nights when we would pull up our armchairs close to the coal fire and make toast on the end of the fork. Sometimes later we would sit and play cards or dominoes, or do a crossword together until it was time for bed. Or he would pick up a detective story and read to me.

It all seems so sad, when you lose someone you love.

But I hope and pray, when the Good Lord opens up His book, and calls out my name, maybe I shall meet all my loved ones again.

Who knows?

Epilogue

Memories and Tomorrows

There are many reasons why I like to stroll down Memory Lane: hoping to see some of the old haunts I used to visit, hoping also that I might meet some of the people I grew up with who still remember those days and the streets where we used to linger, thinking about our tomorrows and what they might bring.

But as for me, I can never forget those bug-infested back-to-back hovels where I was born in 1903 and lived twenty-nine years in poverty and hardship, until I made heart-breaking decisions to leave all this behind me and to begin a new life for the better, for myself and my young family.

Often today, in my late years, I still find myself wandering around these old haunts, around the Jewellery Quarter, and recalling those once cobbled horse-roads and back alleyways, where I used to run to school with bare feet, in rags, with many other poor half-starved kids, begging for food outside factory gates. Many parents had no time to give us love or affection, which we needed, only strong discipline with the bamboo cane at the ready. Many times, too, old Vicar Smith would chase us with his walking-stick if he caught us playing in the churchyard of St Paul's Church, or Titty-Bottle Park as we called it.

And as I stroll along today, in 1991, I notice how bright and clean this church and the surrounding district are. There are no more of those dilapidated back-to-back hovels where, I remember, people often begged and scratched for a crust of bread. Today you can see lovely flats and restaurants, where people live and dine in comfort, yet many of these surrounding buildings have only had a facelift. Many famous landmarks have gone now to make way for progress – but let us not forget our history, and who we are.

Yet as I stroll around St Paul's Square and down George Street, I notice that the King Edward pub is still there, reminding me of the time I used to follow the hurdy-gurdy man around the square and along the Parade. Many of us kids, when we came out of school, would hide up an entry and dance to the tunes he played, with our ragged frocks well above our knees. Newhall Street had many little shops then. There was one shop I still remember well, where I used to fetch Mum's faggots and peas and dip my finger in, but not enough for Mum to notice. Newhall Street was famous for cheap food. The shops sold almost everything: cow heels, tripe, chitterlings, pigs' trotters – you name them, they sold them, all piping hot.

Leaving the shops behind, I walk along Legge Lane, where I come to the old Camden Drive school, which I attended with my brother and sisters eighty-three years ago. I was then five years old. Yet many of these old buildings have now been renovated and turned into offices and workshops.

I recall the stories my granny used to tell me: how this district was always called the Jewellery Quarter. Many people with large families – like my mother and father, and their families – who once lived in these hovels had no prospects, just living from hand to mouth, and many who could not afford their rent let off their living-room to people who wanted to start a small business. They themselves moved to the upper floor to live. But Granny said as soon as the landlords or the agents found out, they raised the rent to a level they knew the tenants couldn't afford. So they were either turned out into the street or sent into the workhouse. This left entire old houses to be let or sold to people who wanted to start up making jewellery. From then on, it grew to be what is still called the Jewellery Quarter today. There are many more alterations to be done to these buildings, yet many have only had a fresh coat of paint. There are still the back yards, brew-houses, and even old brick sheds where people used to keep pigeons, and did their washing ready for the pawnshops, yet people still ply their trades there.

As I walk on down the cobbled alleyway, Camden Drive, where I was born, I am surprised to see the school wall and its playground, still just as Hitler's bombs left it. That was in the heavy raids on Birmingham in April 1941. Alongside the school wall, also, are to be seen the ruins of the iron foundry where my two eldest brothers once worked.

A lump comes to my throat as I think how sad and neglected and forgotten this place is today – just as we people were, who lived down that narrow cobbled alley many, many years ago.

It was a sad time for all of us that night the bombs came without warning. Many of us lost loved ones, some to be buried in a communal grave in Warstone Lane Cemetery, just a few yards from where we once lived. This cemetery is neglected too, and I hope that one day it will have a facelift, to remind us not to forget our loved ones.

Just a few more yards I walk, and I come to the junction of Warstone Lane, Vyse Street and Frederick Street, where one of our famous landmarks, 'Joseph Chamberlain's Clock', stood with its ironwork painted dark green and gold, all faded and rusty. It has now been removed to be repaired and have a facelift too, but I'm told it will soon be restored to its original place. As I stand on the corner and look at that empty space, I remember the day my mother told me that when I was twelve months old she carried me to see that clock – which was erected in 1903, the year I was born – and to hear its chimes. Also, I think of the times when many of us kids leaving school at twelve midday would take it in turns to play around that monument, and look out for the Lodge Road tram making its way up to Warstone Lane, past the cemetery, round the clock, down Frederick Street, down Newhall Hill, and to the town terminus, and back again. That ride cost one penny. But today there are no trams, only buses, and you wouldn't get that same ride for less than £1.

Many years ago, I asked my teacher why the trams had holes in their slatted seats. She said they were for bugs, fleas and lice to drop through off dirty people.

As I stroll towards the city centre, near the Council House in Colmore Row, I notice that the statue of Queen Victoria is still there. Yet I can't understand why her son's statue is no longer standing beside her. I ask several people what has become of King Edward's statue – or Nelson's Column, which once stood in the Bull Ring, and many more famous statues – yet no one seems to know, or isn't interested any more.

Yet the fountain is still in the same place. That too has had a facelift, and as I stand and gaze up at it I think of the happy times we children had, dabbling our dirty sore feet in that cool, clear water. We weren't fussy, either, about having a drink afterwards. But we kept our eyes peeled for the bobby coming along.

Often we had to make our own fun and games, which cost nothing, for our parents couldn't afford to buy us toys; we gave them every farthing or penny that was given to us or begged for. But we had many happy times sharing what other bits and pieces we had given us.

There was the loan of a whip and top; we'd spin it with one of Dad's borrowed leather bootlaces from his hobnail boots, or a skipping rope made from a discarded old clothes line. Sometimes if neighbours were in a good mood they'd skip with us. We also played hopscotch, making the beds from pieces of slate that fell off the roof, or we drew with a piece of chalk if we were lucky enough to take a piece from the blackboard while teacher wasn't looking. And we girls made up many, many more games.

The boys would never be seen playing with the girls – they'd be called sissies, which often ended up in a fight. The boys found other games to play – sometimes they'd sort the ashcans over to find a Nestlé's milk tin, knock some holes in the side and tie a piece of string round it. When washdays came round they'd hide up the entry, then as soon as they saw a neighbour leave the brewhouse quickly they'd dash in, poke a few hot embers into the tin, then run off swinging it round and round their heads to keep warm.

Another game I remember them playing was football, but as they couldn't afford to buy a ball they would sneak into the dry closets, tear the newspaper (we called it bum paper) off the backs of the doors, soak it well, and when it was rolled into a hard ball tied with string, this was their football. It cost us kids nothing to keep happy in those days. Yet I believe we were happier than kids today, who only have to ask and get everything: too much, too soon.

During the hot summer days we would dig up hot pitch beneath the cobblestones or the wooden blocks between the tramlines, roll it into balls and play fivestones (jackstones they were often called). Some of the worst times were our punishments with the cane, but we were used to the cane and expected it. But we never learned our lesson; we were as bad as ever when the pitch wore off our hands.

One hot summer's day, during my travels down Memory Lane, I found myself in Great Hampton Street, and as I came to Snape's the chemist's (that was) I stood looking up at the old sign hanging from its rusty hinges. I remembered that when I was about fifteen, and thinking of the boys I used to flirt with, I often used to call in and ask Mr Snape for a penny box of carmine, a tuppenny box of

Phul-Nana or Shem-el-Nisim face powder, and a threepenny tablet of Erasmic soap. And for each sixpence you spent he would give you a scented card. This was to push down between your breasts to make you smell nice. But I had only small titties then, if any at all, so I used to tear the scented card into two pieces and slip them down each leg of my drawers – or passion-killers, the boys used to call them, because they had elastic round the bottoms.

Many a time, when I couldn't afford to buy these so-called luxuries, I used to lift one of Mum's pictures from the wall, spit on my fingers and rub one of the red roses from the wallpaper into my cheeks and lips.

As I walked along, I came to Hockley Street. I was now very thirsty. I knew there used to be a little café once, but it was no longer there. I looked around for somewhere to have a cup of tea, then I decided to go into the Jeweller's Arms pub and a have a shandy. This pub is still there today, on the corner of Hockley Street and Spencer Street, facing the small factory where I first started my enamelling business in 1931. It was crowded with young men and women factory workers having their lunch break.

As I ordered my pint of shandy I saw two elderly men staring across at me. I heard one of them call above the noise, 'You go over an' ask her, Harry.'

My first thoughts were: did they think I was a pick-up? Surely not – I was far too old; but you never know in this day and age! I didn't wait to find out. I drank the rest of my shandy and left hurriedly.

I got only halfway down the street when I noticed they were close behind me. Quickly I turned round and asked why they were following me.

'We're sorry to have upset you, dear, but we want to know if your name is Mrs Flood, that used to live down Camden Drive.'

'Yes,' I replied. 'I'm the same woman that lived there, but who are you?'

'Don't you remember us? When we lived in the end house in your same yard?' the taller one said. 'We're Harry and Joe Taylor, the twins you used to look after for me mum, when we all went hop-picking.'

'Well, well, I would never have known you. You're both grown-up, and handsome too. The last time I saw you, you were trying to sell fish-boxes for firewood in a basket carriage. That must have been before the war.'

'We done better than that, Kate . . . er, Mrs Flood . . .'

'You can call me Kate,' I replied, smiling up at him. 'Wonderful to meet you, and how you been doing?' I asked.

'We saved every farthin' we earned and later we bought an old horse and cart off Kinver. You remember old Skinflint Kinver, Kate, the one who kept the old stinking stables at the end of Camden Street?'

'That must be the one who lent my granny the nag and cart when she left our house,' I said.

'Kate,' Harry said, 'come and have a drink with us. We've only half an hour to spare and there's lots we'd like to talk about.'

How very happy I felt that day when we sat together in that smoke room!

'What do you do, if you don't mind me asking?' I said.

'We travel the markets, Kate, going from town to town, and we're doing well. But we're honest,' they both replied, grinning at me. 'We saved our little nest egg an' put it in the post office savings bank, and left it there when we went into the Army. So when we was demobbed we had a few quid to start us off.'

'I'm so happy for you both,' I replied. 'But may I give you both a word of advice? Never be ashamed of your past, or who you are, or where you come from,' I added.

'We'll *never* be that, Kate,' Harry said, then added, 'What brings you around this district, Kate?'

'I like to take a stroll around these old places where we were dragged up and to reminisce, hoping to find some of the people I used to know around this district. I've written three books about the story of my life, and about the people who tried to exist in those days. Now I'm giving talks to schoolchildren and elderly people in homes and community centres.'

'Have you mentioned *us* in your books, Kate?' they asked, like a couple of excited kids.

'I sure have, there's pages of you and all the people who lived in that bughole Camden Drive. *And* when we all went hop-picking – you were both only about three or four years old then – and at my sister's wedding, you got lost and we found you in the brewhouse copper, draining the empty whisky bottles.'

They burst out laughing. 'We don't remember that. Was we drunk?'

'You was too tiddly to be lifted out, until I called me dad.'

'But we do remember, don't we, Joe,' Harry said, 'when our mum told us that your brother Jack stole a pig from the hop field and how your mum won her black eye.'

'Is that in the books, too?' Joe asked.

'Yes, Joe,' I replied. 'It's all there in black and white. There's photos, too, of the families and where we lived, and all the kids in the back yards.'

I felt rather sad having to say goodbye to them for I felt I would never see them again, but they both promised to write. I hoped they wouldn't forget. We walked outside the Jeweller's Arms and Joe said, 'Do yer mind, Kate, if we kiss yer?'

I held up my face and they hugged and kissed me. 'The last time we kissed you, Kate, was when we was trying to sell the smelly herring-boxes for a living.'

How well I recalled those sad times, many years ago!

As I waved them both goodbye, my tears began to flow. They were the first two people I had met on my walks, only now to lose them again so soon. Yet I hoped they would keep their promise and that one day soon I would hear from them both, or meet them again.

There is little left to tell of my story. You could say that all in all, despite some sticky patches, I've had a successful life. I have twelve grandchildren and ten great-grandchildren. My one regret is that I missed out on Kathleen, John, Jean and Mary's childhood but I can do nothing about that now. I have got lots to be pleased about. I have many dear friends and to cap it all I am an author whose work, I am told, has been enjoyed by many people. My original ambition, that my people should not be forgotten, has been achieved and now I have only that one nagging regret: the loss of those years half a century ago when my children needed a mother's care and love so much.

THE HOUSE IN SOUTH ROAD

Joyce Storey

The House in South Road is destined to join the ranks of Laurie Lee's, Helen Forrester's and William Woodruff's autobiographical classics of the twentieth century. Born near Bristol in 1917, Joyce began her autobiography at the age of sixty-six.

The House in South Road follows her pre-war life in Bristol, an era of corset and chocolate factories, of 'service' and glamorous silent movies. With a brilliant eye for the comic in the tragic, Joyce unfolds her experiences at school, her first job, her first love and a mismatched marriage and motherhood. During the war, like countless other women with an RAF husband rarely on leave, she fights on the home front: air-raids, in-laws, machine work and poverty. Then, after the war, Joyce begins to enjoy the luxury of a prefab house, first holidays, the growing independence of her four children, but suffers a breakdown in her marriage and her husband's final illness.

With humour and intelligence Joyce Storey charts the ordinary story of an extraordinary working-class woman's life.

WEST WITH THE NIGHT

Beryl Markham

West with the Night was first published in 1942 and became an instant bestseller. It is still a wholly compelling and wonderful insight into the mind of one of the most extraordinary women of the twentieth century.

Beryl Markham moved to Kenya with her father at the age of four and stayed until her death in 1986. Her incredible autobiography describes the Africa she learnt to love: her childhood surrounded by the tribal people, her tangles – often nearly fatal – with its wild animals and her passions for racehorses and aeroplanes.

Markham achieved notoriety and success as a horse trainer when one of her horses won the most prestigious race in Kenya. She turned her hand to aeroplanes with Denys Finch Hatton, the lover of Karen Blixen, as a teacher and became the first woman in Kenya to receive a commercial pilot's licence. Her adventures and courageous career as a bush pilot are recounted in vivid detail here, along with the richness and fascination of life in Kenya in the twenties and thirties.

'She can write rings around all of us . . . it is really a wonderful book' Ernest Hemingway

PARIS WAS YESTERDAY

Janet Flanner

In 1925 Janet Flanner began dispatching her famous *New Yorker* 'Letter from Paris', from which most of the pieces in this collection are drawn. Together, they give an incomparable view of French political, social and cultural life in the years between the electrifying debut of Josephine Baker and the evacuation of Paris at the outbreak of war.

In a sequence of dazzling vignettes and essays, Paris is captured in its golden hour.

'Cafe Society described from the best table in the place, by a writer with rare and vivid gifts. Make yourself comfortable – and order up a dry martini' Robert Lacey

LOVE LESSONS

Joan Wyndham

August 1939. As a teenage Catholic virgin, Joan Wyndham spent her days in London's bohemian Chelsea trying to remain pure and unsullied and her nights trying to stay alive. Huddled in the air-raid shelter, she wrote secretly and obsessively in her diary about the strange yet exhilarating times she was living through, sure that this was 'the happiest time of my life'.

Monday, 13th May 1940 – After Jo had gone I looked at my flushed face in the glass and tidied my hair, thinking what an awful tart I am. There was a terrible love-bite on my cheek, so I got a pin and made a few scratches across it, and told Mummy a cat scratched me, but I don't think she believed me. Later we listened to a very stirring speech by Churchill about 'blood, sweat and tears'.

'A latter-day Pepys in camiknickers' *Scotland on Sunday*

www.virago.co.uk

Virago

To find out more about Kathleen Dayus and
other Virago authors, visit:
www.virago.co.uk

Visit the Virago website for:

- Exclusive features and interviews with authors,
  including Margaret Atwood, Maya Angelou, Sarah
  Waters and Nina Bawden

- News of author events and forthcoming titles

- Competitions

- Exclusive signed copies

- Discounts on new publications

- Book-group guides

- Free extracts from a wide range of titles

PLUS: subscribe to our free monthly newsletter